The Kamakura Bakufu

A STUDY IN DOCUMENTS

JEFFREY P. MASS

The Kamakura Bakufu

A STUDY IN DOCUMENTS

Foreword by Takeuchi Rizō

Stanford University Press, Stanford, California   1976

Stanford University Press, Stanford, California
© 1976 by the Board of Trustees of the
Leland Stanford Junior University
Printed in the United States of America
ISBN 0-8047-0907-6   LC 75-39335

Publication of this book was assisted by
a grant from the Japan Foundation

Map of the Japanese provinces reprinted
by courtesy of Yale University Press from
John W. Hall and Jeffrey P. Mass, eds.,
Medieval Japan: Essays in Institutional History

To John Whitney Hall and Seno Seiichirō
My Teachers in America and Japan

FOREWORD

Professor Asakawa Kan'ichi, while at Yale University, was the first scholar in America to show that Japanese and European feudalism, despite their many common characteristics, also had major differences. His monumental work, *The Documents of Iriki* (1929), not only helped shape the thinking of Westerners about Japan's medieval age, but served as well to alert Japanese scholars to the value of this great collection for the study of feudalism.

At present, almost 50 years after the appearance of Asakawa's work, the subject of feudalism remains one of the central themes of scholarly inquiry in Japan. Fundamental to this effort has been research on the power structure of the Kamakura Bakufu, Japan's first warrior government. The basic sources for this subject have traditionally been the chronicle *Azuma kagami* and the Bakufu's own Jōei Law Code. In recent years, however, it has been amply shown that the former, as a later compilation, contains many errors, whereas the latter is no more than a legal treatise. For a detailed understanding of the Bakufu and of early feudalism it has been necessary to turn instead to the numerous old documents that remain extant.

While this development was occurring in Japan, there was no parallel advance in America in the vital area of document research. The major reason for this was undoubtedly the extensive training required to learn to read and interpret medieval records. Under these circumstances, it was hardly surprising that no successor emerged to continue the pioneering work of Asakawa. Now, however, through the efforts of Jeffrey Mass, the way to progress in the document field has once again been opened. Unlike Asakawa, whose studies were mostly limited to the Iriki collection and the archives of the Daigoji in Kyoto, Professor Mass has consulted the full range of published document volumes, amounting to several hundred. From these, he has selected 177 old records to illustrate the various aspects of Kamakura rule. This direct use of documents is certainly the most reliable way for the historian to approach major problems; and Mass's handling of his materials is most admirable. The Glossary appended to Part I, similarly a pioneering effort, will be of additional help to scholars who wish to begin the serious study of medieval records.

The annotated Bibliography forming Part II is another major contribution. Presenting more than 550 works that contain documentary sources, it is a listing for which there is nothing comparable even in Japanese. Since its coverage is the entire pre-Tokugawa epoch, it will undoubtedly become the essential guide for anyone undertaking the study of medieval Japan through primary materials.

Takeuchi Rizō

PREFACE

Japan's medieval age has long been neglected by Western historians. Until recently we had virtually no monographs, and source translations were limited mostly to war tales and a few chronicles. The medieval era's most important source type, the official document, was overlooked entirely. It was this condition that prompted the compilation of the present work.

The two parts of this book might well have been published separately. Part I contains 177 Kamakura-period land records in translation, whereas Part II presents a comprehensive annotated bibliography of published pre-1600 documents. The decision to combine these two sections derives essentially from my belief that sources and source books are both important. A knowledge of where to find materials is prerequisite to using them. This is the more so since no similar listing exists even in Japanese. As for the documents themselves, their intrinsic worth seemed justification enough.

I was assisted in this project by several of Japan's most eminent medieval scholars. Seno Seiichirō of Tokyo University's Historiographical Institute not only introduced me to the world of documents at an earlier stage in my work, but also acted as principal advisor for the translation portion of this book. During the summer of 1974 he took time out from a busy schedule in order to do battle with passages that had continued to resist my best efforts. For the Bibliography, my greatest debt is to

Professor Kawazoe Shōji of Kyushu University, who corrected numerous errors in my readings of Japanese personal and place names and introduced me to a host of new titles, especially those relating to Kyushu. Professor Toyoda Takeshi of Tōhoku University was another source of great encouragement, offering the use of his extensive private library and calling to my attention several books that I had overlooked. Finally, Professor Takeuchi Rizō of Waseda University went over the entire Bibliography and invited me to hunt through the piles of books that fill most of his house in an effort to identify still more titles. Like a living organism, the Bibliography has grown in size at each step of the way.

In the United States, I wish to thank Frank Shulman, who first suggested a combined document and bibliography volume; William McCullough of Berkeley, who read the entire manuscript and made many valuable suggestions; and James Trosper, my editor at Stanford Press, who has helped in more ways than I can enumerate. The Center for East Asian Studies at Stanford provided generous financial support.

J.P.M.

CONTENTS

PART TWO: BIBLIOGRAPHY

PART ONE

Documents

THE PROVINCES OF MEDIEVAL JAPAN

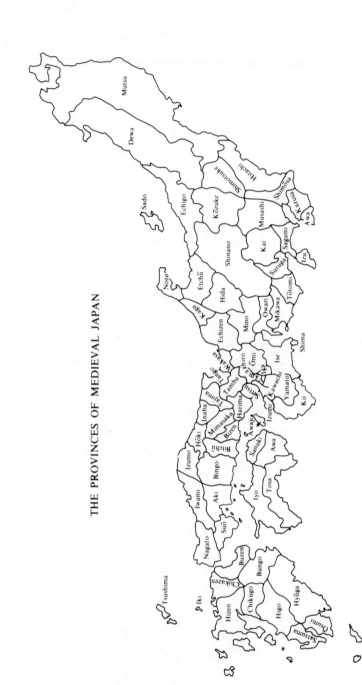

INTRODUCTION

The Kamakura age in Japanese history stands midway between the centralized rule of Nara and Heian times and the localism of the Muromachi era. In an earlier work, I attempted to describe this transition, focusing on the establishment of warrior government (*bakufu*) in the 1180's, the nature of the new civil-military dyarchy, and the activities of the thirteenth century's most important local officials, the *shugo* and *jitō*.* In the present work, I hope to offer through documents a more direct representation of the institutions of this emerging medieval society.

Before turning to the records themselves, however, and to a survey of Japanese diplomatics in general, it will be useful to summarize the major historical developments that formed the background for the materials I present. The Kamakura regime was established several hundred years after the rise of a distinct warrior class in Japan. During the eleventh and twelfth centuries, warriors played an important role in governing the estates and provinces; but they never advanced beyond the general status of an administrative police, acting within hierarchies that were controlled from the court in Kyoto. This meant that throughout the Heian age authority continued to issue from a single source: the capital city and its institutions.

* Jeffrey P. Mass, *Warrior Government in Early Medieval Japan: A Study of the Kamakura Bakufu, Shugo, and Jitō* (New Haven: Yale University Press, 1974).

The first crack in this edifice came in 1180, when Minamoto Yoritomo, exiled leader of one of the country's two great military clans, determined to challenge the dominance of Kyoto. The problem for Yoritomo was that his rival, Taira Kiyomori, was firmly in command of the imperial capital and bureaucracy. In this circumstance, the only hope was to devise a program that promised fresh goals and rewards to prospective supporters. The plan Yoritomo hit upon was to disengage the eastern provinces and to create over them a new government controlled by warriors. It is interesting, however, that the primacy of imperial authority was still accepted by most potential rebels. For this reason, Yoritomo's declaration of independence was proclaimed as a throwing off of the Taira yoke.

The ensuing conflict (1180–85) is known as the Gempei War, after the clan names Genji (Minamoto) and Heishi (Taira); but the warriors who fought were aware from the beginning that a great deal more was potentially at stake than Minamoto or Taira honor. By submitting to Yoritomo's lordship, fighting men now stood to receive land titles and offices that simply bypassed the old lines of authority. With this as background, absentee ownership of estates was soon being called into question, and the "independence" movement, strictly eastern in origin, began to spread countrywide. By the middle of 1183, the Gempei conflict had fanned into a national civil war.

Such rapid growth posed dangers to Yoritomo's fledgling regime in the east. Like Kyoto, it was now in danger of being buried by the new wave of unrest and anarchy. The Taira had already shown themselves incapable of containing the local excesses of warriors and adventurers; thus it fell to the Minamoto, who had made peace with the court in mid-1183, to restore stability. For the warrior regime, this was to some extent a turning against its own class. Still, by issuing orders against lawlessness and land-grabbing in the provinces, it was slowly extending its influence—especially since warriors who submitted to Yoritomo and pledged to remain peaceful continued to be promised land confirmations or new grants. In this manner both aristocrats of the capital and fighting men from the provinces fell equally into Kamakura's debt.

The final downfall of the Taira generals came early in 1185, but society's larger war had not yet begun to dissipate. From 1184 on, refractory warriors began to assert local proprietorships under the title of *jitō*, and a year later Yoritomo decided to convert this office into a perquisite of his immediate followers. The objective here was twofold: to establish a uniform system of rewards for vassals, and to end the wartime proliferation of local authority without accountability. There thus appeared a network of elite officers whose responsibility was estate management but whose authority derived from outside the estate system. Absentee proprietorship had been given a reprieve, but Kamakura's backing would hereafter be needed to maintain it. The *jitō* lay outside the domain (*shōen*) owner's direct control.

In the 1190's Kamakura took another step toward institutionalizing its power. Partly to control the *jitō* and partly to secure a permanent share of the national policing authority, it began appointing provincial constabulary officials called *shugo*. Before long, the Bakufu could boast of parallel officer networks expanding throughout the land. To be sure, *jitō* were never appointed to more than a minority of land units, and *shugo* duties remained quite limited. In this sense, the older hierarchies had not been eliminated, merely added to. But there was little question that *jitō* and *shugo* represented something revolutionary on the land. By virtue of their immunity and their special status as Kamakura vassals, they became the period-defining figures of their age.

To Kamakura fell the task of balancing the new, double structure of authority. Yoritomo not only had to maintain control of his own vassals, but also had to ensure that the court and the traditional order would act as forces for peace. In practice, this was not easy. Estate proprietors were not always responsible men, and in 1221 the court itself unleashed another warrior bloodletting. The aim of this effort, the Jōkyū War, was to destroy the Bakufu and reestablish Kyoto's hegemony, but its effect was to destabilize society once again and make Kamakura's presence even more necessary. Nevertheless, even now the Bakufu's leaders understood their own limits and saw the threat of delegating new freedoms to warriors. And thus a pattern was set. Kamakura would judge suits affecting the interests of its men, but would eschew, where feasible, involvement in matters for which it could not guarantee compliance. This also had the effect of shoring up traditional authority by reaffirming that Japan had two legitimate governments.

In the end, of course, the forces of localism that had been unleashed in the 1180's and strengthened in 1221 were to prove irresistible. The local power of warriors could not be checked indefinitely, and military men, especially the *jitō*, began to step up their efforts to seize practical control of *shōen*. The owners of these estates had few options. They could continue to depend on Bakufu justice, though sanctions against warriors were becoming harder to impose. Or they could attempt to deal directly with the *jitō* and try to find areas of compromise. In both instances, however, the prestige of superior authority was wearing thin. There was little to prevent a warrior from ignoring a Bakufu mandate, or for that matter his own pledge. And thus by the end of the thirteenth century the Kamakura regime was itself becoming an anachronism. Regional power and local hierarchies, not a single vassalage stretched countrywide, were the clear wave of the future. In 1333, the Bakufu was overthrown, and a major restraint on military men everywhere was removed.

When one turns to the study of old documents, it is manifest that a true diplomatics field for Japan hardly exists in the West. Indeed, for the pre-Tokugawa age there are only a handful of works that present old records, and Asakawa's two volumes, especially *The Documents of Iriki*, continue to dominate.* The other major work in the genre, which bears some resemblance to the present effort, is a 1950 work by Jouon des Longrais.† This volume offers numerous Kamakura-age documents in French translation, providing a wealth of valuable background data. Nevertheless, the basic purpose of the work is to offer representative document types rather than to reveal institutions through documents. It is essentially a diplomatics handbook for the Kamakura period, and only secondarily a collection of historical sources.

The scant attention paid by Westerners to medieval Japanese documents is not easily explained. Clearly, the problem is not simply linguistic, since we now have translations of many of the basic chronicles, diaries, and war tales. Japanese historians themselves have long considered documents the most reliable source type; and European medievalists tend to think so highly of their own records that the materials constantly appear packaged as student "readers." Nor is the problem in Japan one of scarcity or inaccessibility. There are literally hundreds of Japanese books, containing many thousands of transcribed documents, and in terms of volume the historian of Japan may have more to work with than the historian of France or England. Yet the exploration of these abundant sources has barely begun. With few exceptions, the doc-

---

* Kan'ichi Asakawa, *The Documents of Iriki* (New Haven: Yale University Press, 1929), and *Land and Society in Medieval Japan* (New Haven: Yale University Press, 1965). *Iriki*, though presenting some 83 Kamakura documents, deals exclusively with a remote corner of southern Kyushu. *Land and Society*, a posthumous collection of essays and translations, presents sources that predate 1185; there are no Kamakura-age translations.

† F. Jouon des Longrais, *Age de Kamakura: Sources* (Paris, 1950). It is most unfortunate that this work, perhaps because it is in French, has stirred little interest in the United States. It deserves a much wider audience.

uments have been largely ignored, and new approaches to individual problems have come only slowly. Worst of all, many unsubstantiated ideas have continued to be accepted in the West as doctrine.

A few examples of the last problem will demonstrate what I mean. Literary embellishment is the root cause of a common misunderstanding concerning the brief period of Taira ascendancy. The greatest of the war tales, the *Heike monogatari*, depicts the Taira chieftain Kiyomori as an unprincipled autocrat who ruled over the capital for nearly a generation. This has gone unquestioned in Western history books. But a study of the documents from that age tells a much different story. The Taira ascendancy began slowly, with Kiyomori deferring to his patron, the retired emperor Go-Shirakawa, in most aspects of governance. This continued into the 1170's. At the same time, Kiyomori's control over the countryside, once generally assumed by historians, is barely in evidence until the end of that decade. We now discover, in other words, that the Taira's vast assemblage of governorships, *shōen* proprietorships, and high ministerial posts came not in the early 1160's but rather in a rush at the beginning of the 1180's. The *Heike monogatari* and all other later narrative accounts have simply read back Kiyomori's dictatorship to the start of his ascendancy.*

Let us look at another example. The standard account of the Gempei War's outbreak is in the chronicle *Azuma kagami*. We read of an anti-Taira call to arms, issued by a prince left out of the imperial succession. No mention is made of conditions before 1180, and we are left with the impression that loyalty to the throne, in the form of an anti-Taira sentiment, was what lay behind the Minamoto actions. But such an explanation, however appealing emotionally, badly distorts the motivations that were actually at work. Had this been a holy crusade, the Minamoto would certainly have gone in search of their enemy. Instead, as we know, they remained in the east and set about fashioning a new warrior government. As the documents clearly reveal, the origins of the rebellion lay not in some outmoded service ethic on behalf of the court, but in something quite the opposite: a desire to end, finally, the central authority's dominance over the provinces.†

A third example deals with the *Azuma kagami*'s handling of the origins of the *shugo*. In late 1185, we are told, this office was established by a court edict. Clearly, a directive *was* issued at this time to authorize the Bakufu's monopoly control of the provincial *jitō*. But it is equally clear that the post of *shugo* did not exist until the 1190's. The explanation for

* See Mass, *Warrior Government*, chap. 1.
† *Ibid.*, chaps 2–3.

this discrepancy suggests the tendency of later narratives to distort chronology. In this instance, *shugo* and *jitō* were to become the Bakufu's two main officer types; hence the easy logic of according them a simultaneous origin.*

Having stressed the value of original documents, I should add that these records, too, are not problem-free. For example, forgeries exist, especially for critical periods like the 1180's. This is not the real obstacle, however, since forgeries, once identified, can simply be avoided. A more fundamental lapse has been the general reluctance of scholars in Japan to subject this "last line of defense" to the critical analysis usually accorded to more narrative sources. Indeed, there seems to be a widespread feeling that to question the historicity of documents, especially for key periods, is to make the writing of history nearly impossible. As a result, the great compendia of records—*Heian ibun, Kamakura ibun, Dai Nihon komonjo,* and *Dai Nihon shiryō*—label only the most obvious of forgeries.

Even counterfeits should not be dismissed as entirely valueless, since the writer of a false document must have had some purpose in mind. By assembling and analyzing "categories" of such records, we are able to detect certain patterns. One of the most obvious is the clear importance attaching to records supposedly authored by Yoritomo. The possession of a Yoritomo confirmation, for example, was one of the most secure of all guarantees for a private landholding. Fortunately, the techniques for detecting spurious documents are quite standardized, including examination of the paper, script, seal, language, and content. Since the last two points are often sufficient in themselves, identifications can sometimes be made from the printed page.

A second deficiency of documents stems from their promulgation pattern and subject matter. We have no guarantee that what a single document says is either true or complete. For example, documents dealing with administrative or legal matters commonly ran in a sequence, and the affected agencies or authority levels might each have contributed a directive, endorsement, or acknowledgment, with information added, subtracted, or modified along the way. The problem is that few complete sequences have come down to us intact. If we choose to use an extant record, we may be basing our story on incomplete information.†

Related to this difficulty is the self-serving purpose to which docu-

---

* *Ibid.*, chap. 4.

† The difficulties of reconstructing a sequence of events are evident in the present work. See, for example, Documents 57–60, 100–106, 131–34, and 152–55.

ments were often put. In lawsuits, for instance, oral and written evidence was taken in advance of a judgment, and part of the Bakufu's responsibility was to weigh all testimony carefully. Documents that were false or fraudulent had to be identified and so labeled. But what if the settlement edict, which records such findings, is no longer extant? We may inadvertently be using a deposition that gives a one-sided impression. The problem is really one of observing proper caution, since documents need not be truthful representations of the past to be of help to the historian.*

Thus far I have not taken up the more technical problem of document parameters. What is it that distinguishes "documents" from other sources, and how embracing is the term as an overall classification? It is easiest to compare documents with chronicles and diaries, both of which treat long periods and divide material by calendar entries. Documents, by contrast, deal with specific subjects (or groups of subjects) and are authored on single occasions. It is interesting, moreover, that documents often appear within diaries or chronicles;† conversely, diaries and chronicles, owing to a shortage of paper, were sometimes written on the blank reverse sides of documents. Documents, in fact, need not be written on paper at all, and they sometimes appear as engravings on wood or metal, or letters written on fabric. Recent Japanese studies have even begun to include in document volumes messages engraved on tombstones. By contrast, Buddhist and Shinto liturgies and prayers, philosophical narratives, and essays or treatises are never so included, though private letters almost always are. It is clear, at any rate, that the document classification is still somewhat ambiguous. Perhaps the idea of "conveyance" comes closest to being a defining feature.

For the Kamakura period, about 30,000 documents remain extant, most dealing with land. It is significant that the great majority of these— upwards of 75 percent—are entirely unrelated to the Kamakura regime. This fact, so surprising at first glance, does not mean of course that the Bakufu and its officers were somehow outside the mainstream of thirteenth-century history. It suggests, rather, that countless estates simply

---

* If I have here exaggerated the pitfalls of using documents, I have done so largely as a self-reminder. Documents, like any source, are after all a means, not an end. But the special advantages of documents over other materials are their contemporaneity, their clear importance to the society that used them, and the fact that a researcher can usually prove his case through multiple examples.

† That is to say, copies of documents. For example, the *Kamakura ibun* series includes documents appearing in the *Azuma kagami* and other chronicles and diaries.

experienced no dramatic change between the Heian and Kamakura periods. *Jitō* were not appointed everywhere, and *shugo* did not dominate provincial governance. The Bakufu's authority, then, was far from comprehensive. Most Kamakura documents deal instead with the mundane matters of *shōen* administration—local appointments, tax collection, and the improvement of agriculture.*

In the matter of documents' survival, this has normally been in inverse proportion to age: there are far fewer records from the first third of the Kamakura era than from the last third.† Issuance patterns, by contrast, exhibit a somewhat different concentration. It is clear, for example, that political or military crises, which invariably produced rapid shifts in landholding, tended to prompt sudden upsurges in document writing. The Gempei, Jōkyū, and Mongol war years all have greater inventories of extant records than comparable periods of time in between.

In the matter of document categories, the standard criteria for classification are the identity of author and audience, the intent of an individual record, and the expected term of validity. Reflecting the hierarchical nature of society, the grammatical patterns and formats of documents were keyed to the identities of the persons (or agencies) involved. Relative status and whether or not the principals were part of the same authority system would dictate an appropriate style. Similarly, the basic content of a document—i.e., whether it registered a complaint, appointed a local officer, or treated any other of a myriad of possible activities—would greatly affect appearance and form.‡ Finally, whether the document was a momentary directive or a permanent decree (perhaps affecting land rights) would also influence its character.

When the Bakufu came on the scene in the 1180's there were innumerable document styles in existence. Some of these could trace origins back to the eighth century, but others were the product of middle or late Heian times. These last had appeared as private agencies became more central to government than actual public offices. The Bakufu, forced to decide which document formats to use, adopted two types and largely invented a third. The adopted patterns were the *kudashibumi,* which

---

* Of the records that relate to the Bakufu, by far the largest number deal in some manner with the *shugo* and *jitō,* and especially with the latter. The selection of documents offered here reflects this concentration.

† Yet we know a great deal more about the early Kamakura period, mostly because Japanese scholars have given relatively little attention to the Bakufu in its decline.

‡ See my Document Originals, pp. 14–23, for photographs of representative document types and detailed explanation of their formats.

was a permanent edict used mainly for appointments and confirmations, and the *migyōsho*, which was a communication vehicle and a device for admonishing vassals and some others. The invented style, *gechijō*, reflected the Bakufu's growing role as the country's leading judicial agency. This was a permanent edict used especially to settle land disputes.

In addition to these three basic document types, a number of other forms were important during the Kamakura age. These included: *kishinjō*, which were normally pledges commending land rights to a temple or shrine; *wayojō*, which recorded compromises between absentee and resident interests in land; *yuzurijō*, which were testamentary records; and *saribumi*, which were acknowledgments of some release (through sale, etc.) of land rights. But this is only a small sampling. At the same time, there are the many thousands of documents that fall into the category of *an*, that is, copies of originals. Historians consider these nearly as important as the originals themselves. *An*, in fact, were not working drafts, but rather copies to be disseminated. They were identical to the originals save for the absence of the issuing authority's formal monogram (*kaō*), and they were indispensable to the workings of government and society. In the case of legislative enactments, copies would be sent to the appropriate offices for distribution; or, as part of the judicial process, copies of original records were exchanged among litigants and even submitted in evidence.* Copies were also used in inheritance matters when only a portion of a family's legacy was being passed on. In these and other ways, document copies crisscrossed the country, moving from one house or agency to another. Originals were usually kept at home and regarded as among the most valuable of a family's treasures.

Turning to the documents contained in this book, my basic purpose has been to illustrate, through original records, the institutions of the Kamakura Bakufu.† It should be realized, however, that historical materials are not always as incisive or clear as we might wish. Portions of some records may be brilliantly illuminating, whereas other passages

---

* To be sure, document copies were carefully scrutinized for irregularities, and it was common for their accuracy to be questioned (see Document 71). Originals sometimes had to be produced.

† By no means all the institutions, however. For example, topics such as inheritance practices, litigation stages, and *shimpo jitō* (see Glossary) will be dealt with in a study I am now preparing, which will include many documents relating to these matters. The Mongol invasions and the Bakufu's decline are topics for future study.

are simply obscure. Notwithstanding this difficulty, I have thought it best in most instances to present whole documents. Only in cases of corruptions in the text, unusual length, or extensive repetition have I abridged my translations.

The reader will immediately discover that the most interesting of the Kamakura records are the judicial settlement edicts (*saikyojō*) of the eastern regime. This is because we are brought into direct contact with the desires and emotions of real people. In one document we may encounter a *jitō* attempting to justify or disguise lawless excesses. In another, we meet a self-righteous estate deputy deploring the plight of local peasants when his actual concern is their ability to pay taxes. Or a petition may originate with the cultivators themselves, inarticulate and defenseless, pleading for relief. It was the practice of the time for Kamakura to include in its settlement edicts quotations from documents submitted in evidence, as well as summaries of oral testimony. As with the transcripts of any modern-day court trial, the readability of these sources is not great. But there is little doubt that these records of the Bakufu tell us more about thirteenth-century warrior society and its tensions than any other source type.

A few technical points should be added. First, I have not sought to identify most of the personal names appearing in documents. Only prominent individuals have been so noted, and then usually only once. Similarly, I have not bothered to translate the office titles that dominate most signature space; these only infrequently connoted actual duties, and there seemed little reason to clutter the translations with meaningless and awkward-sounding English renderings. Third, the document citations follow accepted formats, though there are no absolute rules here. In all cases I have felt free to retitle a document when the original editor's title has seemed irregular. In the matter of citing document volumes, I have tried to note the book that is most closely identified with the particular collection involved.* This is followed by a reference to one of the standard compendia, in which the document also appears. As will be obvious, individual documents—indeed, whole collections—are often contained in more than one book.†

The Glossary at the end of the Documents section explains many of

* By "collection," I mean the records associated with (or kept by) a particular family, temple, or shrine. For example, the citation "Kasuga jinja monjo" refers to the documents (*monjo*) of Kasuga Shrine.

† The Bibliography that forms Part II of this book will amply show this. Documents may appear in a general compendium, a volume devoted to a particular religious institution or family, a city history, or a prefectural history.

the important terms found in the records of the Kamakura age. (To aid the reader terms included in the Glossary have been noted * when they appear at intervals in the documents.) This list is merely introductory, though it might be noted that even in Japanese there is no comprehensive catalog of difficult document terms.* A major reason for this is that the documentary vocabulary reflects the minute gradations of medieval authority and privilege: there are land and tax terms that simply cannot be understood today. The list I present, then, is necessarily selective. It excludes expressions still in use (e.g. *mura*), along with character compounds that are "coined" words and patterns that are more grammatical than terminological. But its coverage goes beyond the 177 documents offered in this book. In essence it is a beginning lexicon, which, along with the translations and the Bibliography, will hopefully expedite research in a difficult but challenging field.

---

* Partial lists appear in Ijichi Tetsuo, *Nihon komonjogaku teiyō* (Tokyo, 1969), II, 1071–1107; and in Nagahara Keiji et al., *Chūseishi handobukku* (Tokyo, 1973), pp. 180–91. See also the general index in Satō Shin'ichi, *Komonjogaku nyūmon* (Tokyo, 1971), and in Aida Nirō, *Nihon no komonjo* (Tokyo, 1968), Vol. II.

DOCUMENT ORIGINALS

Although the documents appearing in this book have all been translated from printed sources, some comment on manuscript originals seems in order. The documents of medieval Japan are scattered countrywide among museums, temples and shrines, universities, and private collections. Because of this, and because access to originals is often highly restricted, a few major research centers have sought to collect photographs of originals, and even to produce handwritten facsimiles. At the Historiographical Institute of Tokyo University, which is the country's leading research center, some hundreds of thousands of old records are now available for study as originals, photographs, or copies in ink. These last, it should be noted, are so finely produced that except for the paper they are all but indistinguishable from originals. A handful of skilled, modern-day scribes are at work transcribing these materials, even to the point of duplicating ink splotches, cracks, and other blemishes.

Although the Institute's resources are the largest in Japan, they are, unfortunately, far from complete. Professional jealousies and secrecy have worked to impede the free flow of information in this area, with the result that the Institute's published series especially have rather uneven coverage. A flagrant example is the great document collection associated with Tōji Temple: some thousands of old records are simply unavailable in any published or unpublished form. The upshot of this is that we must wait until the guardians of that portion of the larger Tōji collection decide either to allow photocopies to be made or to promote publication themselves. In many instances locally sponsored source volumes of this type are the only means of gaining access to specific records. This has meant that probably no scholar of early and medieval Japan is able to work exclusively from manuscripts.

On the question of how document originals differ from printed transcriptions, we may cite the following. First of all, most works appearing since the war have used modern characters. Also, commas are generally inserted by compilers to designate clause and sentence breaks; original *kambun* documents are entirely without punctuation. But that is essentially all. The various parts of transcribed records are positioned on the printed page in rough correspondence to originals, and few document books (unlike other published sources) bother with intrusive syntax marks (*kaeriten*). Moreover, when paper deterioration has obliterated characters, as often happens, empty boxes are placed in the appropriate spaces. Or again, identifying phrases or dates on the reverse sides of old records are generally included in special brackets. With the emphasis so clearly on reproducing originals, there are even some volumes that have added facsimiles of monograms.

Still, photoreproductions of documents remain the surest means of conveying what these materials were "really" like. The texture of the language seems somehow more vivid and our intimacy with the past more immediate when we are looking at actual originals. For this reason, I have prepared the brief section that follows. All photographs appear by courtesy of the Historiographical Institute, which owns the Shimazu collection, one of Japan's most famous.

Figure 1 (Document 137 in text). A Bakufu chancellery edict: 1197/12/3 *saki no utaishō ke mandokoro kudashibumi*.

The top characters of the right-hand line designate the issuing agency, in this case Minamoto Yoritomo's chancellery. Yoritomo himself is referred to as the former *utaishō*, a post he received from the court in late 1190 and immediately resigned. The *utaishō ke mandokoro* form was used by Kamakura during 1191–92 and then again after 1195. In between, Yoritomo used a *shōgun ke mandokoro* style. It is presumed that he resigned the shogunal title in 1195. The word "orders" (*kudasu*), diagnostic for *kudashibumi*, appears using the familiar character.

The bottom of the first line on the right designates the recipient: *sa hyōe no jō* Koremune Tadahisa, better known as Shimazu Tadahisa, the first scion of the great Shimazu house. In other *kudashibumi*, especially *shiki* investitures, the addressee was normally the affected area or its "residents" (*jūnin*). This is because appointment decrees to "public" offices were traditionally to be "announced" to those concerned. By the beginning of the Kamakura period, however, this practice was already a formality, since the person benefiting from the investiture was the recipient of the actual appointment edict. And by late Kamakura times, even the formality was disappearing: *kudashibumi* were most often addressed directly to the appointee.

The second line from the right summarizes the contents of the decree. Most public orders—and virtually all Bakufu edicts—used this device. At the top of the third line is the character for the number one (*ichi*), commonly used to designate a separate "item" or matter to be treated. This particular document has three items.

On the left side of the document are the final injunctions to the recipient. They conclude with the diagnostic phrase, "Wherefore, this order" (*motte kudasu*); thus most *kudashibumi* contain the word *kudasu* in two places. It should be noted, however, that various hybrid forms exist; and scholars often label as *kudashibumi* records that in fact do not use the word at all.

Next to the left is the date (the line just to the right of the large monogram) and blended with it the name of the official chancellery scribe (the break between date and name is barely distinguishable, a common practice; look for the characters after "3d day").

Next to the left, top and bottom, are the remaining signatures of chancellery members, along with two formal monograms. The signatures appearing on top always take precedence, with the first two (from right to left) normally signifying the ranking members. In this case, the name in between the two that have monograms is that of the chancellery chief, the famous Ōe Hiromoto. The presence of the monograms means that the document is an original. However, it is not necessary for all signatures to have monograms.

The document itself is a famous one, owing to the light it throws on the emergence of the *shugo* institution. Stylistically, it is a typical chancellery edict of the Kamakura Bakufu.

Figure 2 (Document 43 in text). A Bakufu directive: 1192/10/22 *Kantō migyōsho an.*

This document is a "communique" or "instruction" in the *migyōsho* pattern. It is also a "copy" (*an*), since there are no monograms.

The slanted characters in the upper right corner are representative of what I have called half-sized characters throughout the translations. Here, as usually, they are a kind of parenthetical clause or marginal note.

The two large characters to the bottom right of the slanted ones translate as "additional order" or "prescript." The next two lines are the body of the addendum.

Next comes the body of the document itself, in six lines, concluded by the standard closing phrase for a *migyōsho,* "It is so conveyed" (*shittatsu kudan no gotoshi*). This phrase literally identifies the document as a *migyōsho.*

The next line over is the date, with one of the two signatures at the bottom. The slanted words "ari han," which I have translated as "seal," appear just below each signature.

At the extreme left is the name of the addressee, in this case the same Shimazu Tadahisa referred to in the 1197 *kudashibumi* of Figure 1. It should be pointed out that *migyōsho,* being less formal and more "immediate" than *kudashibumi* (or *gechijō*), typically include the addressee's name at the end of the document, in the upper left (another diagnostic feature). *Kudashibumi,* by contrast, are assumed to have had permanent application and therefore do not reveal such "extraneous" particularization. Instead, a recipient's name will appear at the *front* of a *kudashibumi*—that is, *within* the text—where the emphasis is on "substance."

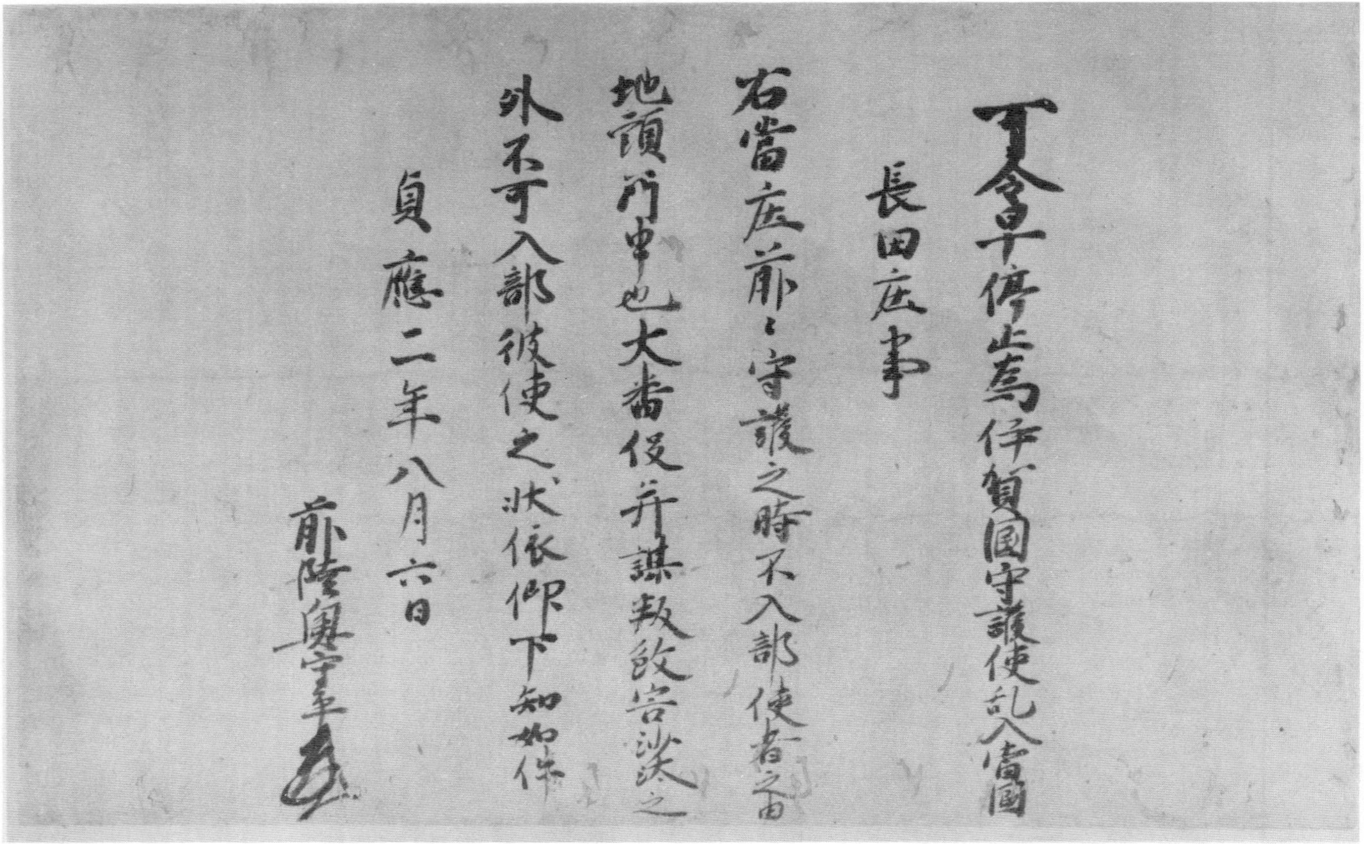

Figure 3 (Document 145 in text). A Bakufu order: 1223/8/6 *Kantō gechijō*.

This document is an order from Kamakura in the standard *gechijō* format. It deals with the limits of *shugo* authority. The two lines at the right are a diagnostic summary of the document's contents, posed as an admonishment. The body of the order follows in three lines, concluding with the standard phrase, "By this command, it is so decreed" (*ōse ni yori, gechi kudan no gotoshi*—the last six characters, third line). The appearance of the word *gechi* (order) is diagnostic for *gechijō*, though documents without the term are sometimes labeled *gechijō* by scholars.

Of special interest in this particular document is the phrase "by *this* command." In 1223 the Bakufu was without a formal leader: Minamoto Sanetomo had died in 1219, and the next *shōgun* was not formally installed until 1226. In normal times *gechijō* were always issued "by command of the Kamakura lord." In the absence of a lord it was the regent, Hōjō Yoshitoki, who filled in directly. To the left

of the dateline is Yoshitoki's formal title at this time: *saki no Mutsu no kami* (the former governor of Mutsu) followed by "Taira (monogram)." The Hōjō's position as regent (*shikken*) is never cited in documents. The Hōjō, of course, were of the Taira clan.

It might also be remarked that this particular example seems very close in substance to a *migyōsho*. Indeed, it could well have been issued as such. This reveals a puzzling aspect of Kamakura's use of documents: the absence of any clearcut divisions between the three basic document types. It is commonly assumed, for example, that settlement edicts were "always" issued as *gechijō*. In fact, however, there are some *migyōsho* that appear suspiciously similar, as well as some *kudashibumi*. (See Document 93, which is a *gechijō* in purpose and effect but uses a *kudashibumi* format.) The Bakufu was constantly experimenting with and adjusting its documentary forms, but the mixing of styles remains hard to explain at times.

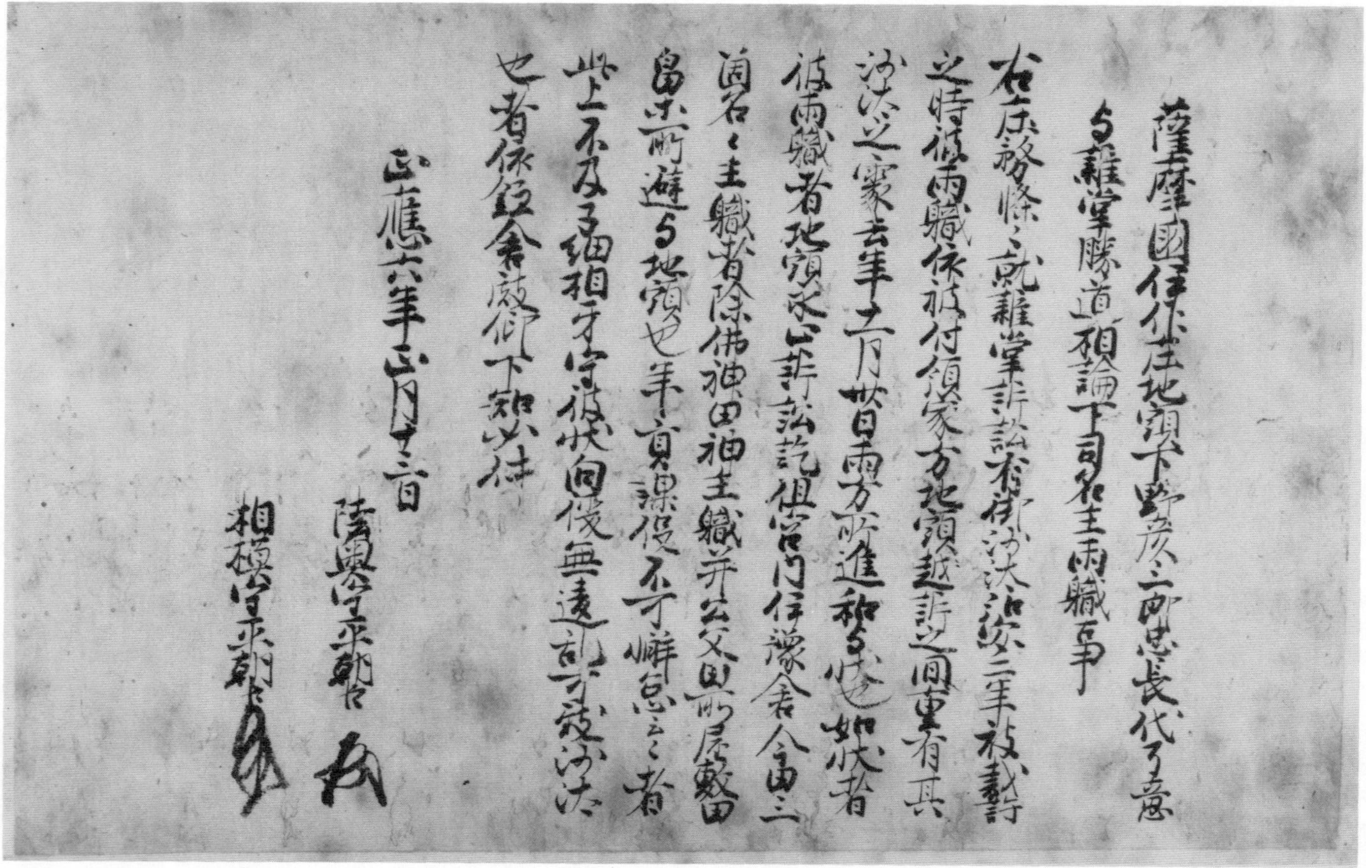

Figure 4 (Document 78 in text). A Kamakura judgment edict: 1293/1/13 *Kantō gechijō*.

This document is a Bakufu settlement decree (*saikyojō*) in the standard *gechijō* form. The two lines at the right identify the disputants and what in general the squabble is all about. This style is diagnostic from the late 1220's on. Another common feature is the appearance of the word *sōron*—the medieval term for dispute—toward the middle of the second line. However, the introductory summary in such a form, as well as the term *sōron*, could well be absent. Sometimes the reference is merely to a complaint's having been lodged, and on other occasions the introductory phrase specifically highlights a suit's outcome. An offending *jitō*, for example, might be admonished to cease his reported lawlessness.

The body of the document here is somewhat shorter than usual. The suit was at the appeal level (*osso*) and obliged the Bakufu merely to approve a compromise (*wayo*) worked out between the disputants themselves. The document ends with the standard phrase, "By command of the Kamakura lord, it is so decreed" (beginning with the third character of the last line).

The two signatures, to the left below the dateline, are those of the Hōjō "regent" and "cosigner." This was the standard form for almost all judicial settlement decrees. Monograms appear under each signature.

ABBREVIATIONS

The following abbreviations have been used for document source volumes frequently cited in the notes to Part I translations. Bracketed numbers indicate the source's position in the Part II Bibliography listing (pp. 217–324), where full publishing information and commentary are given.

AK   Azuma kagami [149]
DNK   Dai Nihon komonjo [6]
DNS   Dai Nihon shiryō [4]
HI   Heian ibun [2]
KBSS   Kamakura Bakufu saikyojō shū [8]
KI   Kamakura ibun [3]

THE WESTWARD EXPANSION OF KAMAKURA INTERESTS

DOCUMENT 1

Minamoto Yoritomo Prohibits Warriors' Outrages and Confirms a Traditional Proprietorship, 1184

One of the greatest problems arising from the Gempei War was the illegitimate seizure of land by local military strongmen. Here was the essence of the Gempei conflict: the beginning of an attack on the concept of absentee proprietorship. In the case described here, the seizure of an estate by an outlaw led to an appeal to the only force in the country capable of suppressing such banditry—the emerging Kamakura government.

(Yoritomo's monogram)[1]

ORDERED: to the Kamino-Makuni Estates, Kii Province.
That forthwith management and possession [of these estates] shall be exercised, as of old, by the *saishō chūjō* house.[2]

The aforesaid domains are the hereditary private holdings of this house. However, during the countryside disturbance of recent years,[3] Nyūya Hachirō Mitsuharu, under some pretext and without any specific proof,[4] has reportedly been looting [*ōbō**].[5] If he had held some historical claim [*yuisho**], he should have petitioned through the retired emperor;[6] instead, there are reports of his willful plunderings [*ranbō**]. Worst of all, this Mitsuharu, of no particular loyalty or merit, has covertly imposed his private power. Such acts are most unseemly. Furthermore, these estates have been commended to Takaozan.[7] Forthwith, his plunderings are to cease, and possession is to be as before. It is commanded thus. Wherefore, this order.

1st year of Genryaku [1184], 6th month,   day.[8]

SOURCE: *Jingoji monjo*, 1184/6 Minamoto Yoritomo kudashibumi *HI*, 8: 3139–40, doc. 4,182.

1. The presence of a monogram (*kaō*＊) signifies that the document is an original rather than a copy (*an*＊).

2. Evidently, this house possessed the estates at the custodial-managerial level. Jingoji Temple was the proprietor. The title *saishō chūjō* is an imperial guards' captaincy, but this tells us little about the family being referred to. It is for this reason that I have elected not to translate such honorary titles.

3. That is, the Gempei War.

4. "Proof" here may be taken to mean "sanction."

5. Terms marked ＊ appear in the Glossary, pp. 193–213. A variety of terms suggesting undifferentiated horrors committed by warriors appear in these documents. Often the terms are interchangeable, but at times their meanings are quite specific. In general, the translator is at a loss. The references usually imply foraging and plundering of one kind or another, but beyond that one cannot be certain. The most common terms are *ōbō*, *ōryō*, *ranbō*, *ransui*, *rangyō*, and *rōzeki*.

6. The "retired emperor" (*in*) was the dominant figure in Kyoto during most of the twelfth century. The person referred to here is Go-Shirakawa, who reigned as emperor from 1155 to 1158 and ruled as ex-emperor until 1192. The Taira were fully dominant in the capital only during 1179–83. See Mass, *Warrior Government*, chap. 1, for details.

7. The Jingoji Temple. Commendation by the *saishō chūjō* house occurred in 1182. See *Jingoji monjo*, 1182/7/8 sakon gon no chūjō kishinjō, *HI*, 8: 3067, doc. 4,036. For the term "commendation," see Glossary under *kishinjō*; cf. *azukari dokoro* and *ryōke*.

8. There is an empty space in the text here to denote the missing day. This is a common practice in documents.

DOCUMENT 2

Kamakura Grants a War-Levy Exemption to a Buddhist Temple, 1184

During the course of the Gempei fighting many temples tried to gain the support of the new regime in Kamakura. In this decree by Minamoto Yoshitsune (brother of Yoritomo and the first Kamakura deputy in Kyoto), an estate holding of Kōya Denpōin Temple was confirmed in an exemption from all war-related levies. Plundering by warriors on the pretext of collecting emergency war imposts was a major abuse during this period.¹

Nanaka Estate in Kii Province is a Kōya Denpōin land. The mustering [there] of local troops [*hyōji**], commissariat rice [*hyōrō**], and other [levies] shall forthwith be ended. There have been reports that a recent order [to this effect] is not being obeyed. This is most unseemly. Persons failing to abide by this prohibition shall be recorded in a name register [*kyōmyō**], which shall be reported. It is commanded thus.²

    1st year of Genryaku [1184], 5th month, 24th day.

Minamoto seal³

SOURCE: *Negoro yōsho*, 1184/5/24 Minamoto Yoshitsune kudashibumi an, *HI*, 8: 3137, doc. 4,174.

    1. The original exemption dated from late 1180, just after the Gempei War's outbreak; cf. the reference in *Negoro yōsho*, 1184/2 Denpōin shoshi ge an, *HI*, 8: 3118–19, doc. 4,141. At that stage, of course, the immunity must have been agreed to by the Taira, who were actively recruiting in central Japan.

    2. The problems of Denpōin Temple, however, did not end with Yoshitsune's decree. See Documents 131–34.

    3. This document is a copy because there is no formal monogram. Instead, the words *ari han* (seal) appear in half-sized characters. Throughout these documents I have indicated the presence of an actual monogram by parentheses.

DOCUMENT 3

Kamakura Admonishes Its Vassals to Cease Their Lawlessness and Pursue the Enemy, 1185

Warriors accepted as Kamakura followers commonly abused their new, elite status. Here, on the eve of the final Taira defeat, the Kamakura lord, through his agent, sought to redirect his vassals' energies from personal aggrandizement to the more immediate task at hand.

Minamoto ason seal

ORDERED: to the priests' office of Amano Temple.¹
    That upland game hunting and the cutting and removal of timber within temple [precincts] be prohibited forthwith.

Regarding the aforementioned matters, it is reported that men claiming to be *goke'nin*² have each day come from all directions to hunt deer.

If this is true, it shall forthwith be prohibited. Moreover, should this prohibition not be honored, name lists [of the guilty] shall be forwarded. It is also reported that upland timber is being felled and carried off. This, too, is prohibited. Now is the time for pursuing [enemies] and for prayer. In accordance with precedent, prohibitions should be laid down. If this decree is disobeyed, name lists of the persons who commit despoilments [*rōzeki**] should be reported. It is commanded thus.

        2d year of Genryaku [1185], 3d month, 13th day.

san-i, Miyoshi[3] seal

SOURCE: *Kongōji monjo,* 1185/3/13 Minamoto Yoritomo kudashibumi an, *DNK, iewake* 7 (Kongōji monjo), pp. 52–53, doc. 27 (also in *HI,* 8: 3169, doc. 4,238).
   1. In Kawachi Province.
   2. Vassals of Kamakura; see Glossary.
   3. Miyoshi Yasunobu, a court noble who had entered service with the Kamakura regime.

DOCUMENT 4

Kamakura Prohibits the Incursions of Vassals on an Estate in Central Japan, 1185

The Gempei War ended two months before this decree was issued, though the violence provoked by that conflict had clearly not yet begun to decline. A major problem was that many of the new Kamakura regime's leading officers in the field were themselves responsible for various illegalities. Here Kajiwara Kagetoki, one of Yoritomo's most trusted confidants, is admonished by the Bakufu's two deputies in Kyoto to cease his lawlessness against a Yamashiro Province estate. Two points are noteworthy: the equal prominence given to the retired emperor and the Kamakura lord; and the obvious importance of possessing documents.

The special agents of the Kamakura lord order: to the officials of the Izumi-Kotsu Estate,[1] Yamashiro Province.
      That in accordance with a directive of the retired emperor [*inzen**] and an order of the Kamakura lord [*ongechi*], the warrior Kajiwara Heizō shall immediately cease his despoilments [*ranbō*].

The aforesaid estate is a holding of the Fujiwara senior branch [*denka goryō**]. Notwithstanding, there has been a complaint that Kajiwara Heizō Kagetoki, who possesses no special warrant from the retired emperor or [the Fujiwara] chieftain, and no edict of the Kamakura lord, has been willfully plundering [ōryō*]. Such acts are most unseemly. His despoilments are hereby to cease, and [the estate] shall be subject to the patron's authority² [honke* no goshinshi]. It is decreed thus. Wherefore, this order.

2d year of Genryaku [1185], 5th month, 1st day.

Fujiwara (monogram)
Nakahara (monogram)

SOURCE: *Tanimori monjo*, 1185/5/1 Kantō gechijō, *HI*, 8: 3175, doc. 4,245.
1. In other documents the reference is to Kotsu Estate only; cf. *ibid.*, docs. 4,247–51. Perhaps this was a double estate, as in Document 1 above.
2. I.e. the Fujiwara chieftain's.

DOCUMENT 5

Kamakura Prohibits Lawlessness in Ōmi Province, 1185

No link can be established between the Bakufu and the outlaw referred to in this decree. Beginning early in 1184, Kamakura had assumed a countrywide policing authority, and was actively encouraged in this undertaking by estate holders who sought protection from the local ravages of warriors. As in Document 4, the retired emperor and the Kamakura lord are given equal prominence.

[ORDERED:]¹ to the officials of Konzeji, Ōmi Province.
    That in accordance with a directive of the retired emperor and an order of the Kamakura lord, the kurōdo* Murakami's unscrupulous plunderings are to cease.

The aforesaid temple, a branch [betsu-in*] of the Kōfukuji,² has been free of imposition, except temple services [jiyaku*].³ There is now a complaint, however, that kurōdo Murakami, in possession of no directive from the retired emperor, and granted no order from the Kamakura lord, has willfully committed encroachments. Such acts are most unseemly. His plunderings are to cease forthwith. By virtue of a directive of the retired emperor and a command of the Kamakura lord, it is so decreed.

2d year of Genryaku [1185], 5th month, 6th day.

Taira Yoshikane⁴ (monogram)
Minamoto Yoshimoto⁴ (monogram)

SOURCE: *Konzeji monjo,* 1185/5/6 Minamoto Yoshimoto–Taira Yoshikane rensho gechijō, *HI,* 8: 3175, doc. 4,246.

1. Character missing, but interpolated by the *HI* editors.
2. The Kōfukuji, located in Nara, was the patron temple of the Fujiwara of Kyoto.
3. I.e., services owed to the main temple, Kōfukuji.
4. The identity of these two signatories is unknown, but they were probably functionaries of Kamakura's special Kyoto headquarters. That office had issued Yoritomo's original command several days earlier. See *Konzeji monjo,* 1185/4/24 Kantō gechijō an, *HI,* 8: 3173–74, doc. 4,242.

THE WARTIME EMERGENCE OF
THE JITŌ SHIKI

DOCUMENT 6

Kamakura Prohibits Warriors' Usurpation of Jitō
Titles and Authority, 1184

The *jitō* title attained national importance in 1185 by becoming the official reward for favored Kamakura retainers. The process by which an office that had been relatively obscure before 1180 managed to gain notoriety during the war, and to come subsequently under the purview of Kamakura, is graphically revealed in this document. Warriors who fraudulently styled themselves *jitō* could be controlled only by the new eastern military regime. Hence a beleaguered shrine's turning to Kamakura after failing to gain satisfaction from the court.

[Introductory portion lost]

Regarding the aforesaid, an order of the 29th day, 1st month, from the [retired emperor's] chancellery[1] and a shrine petition [*shake* gejō**] of the 16th day, 4th month, have arrived. According to the latter, "Pursuant to an order of the [retired emperor's] office, agents of the shrine were dispatched to the various estates held by that institution. However, men of a military bent had either usurped power over estate affairs [*shōmu**] or had styled themselves 'privately appointed' *jitō*. During these unrestrained abuses of power, shrine lands have fallen into ruin, and food offerings [to the shrine] have been wanting. How could the neglect of divine matters have gone so far? These despoilments must certainly end." In accordance with a directive of the retired emperor and a shrine petition, these outrages [rangyō*] shall cease, and pursuant to precedent, the shrine shall exercise management and possession. It is so commanded.

3d year of Juei² [1184], 5th month, 8th day.

saki no uhyōe no suke, Minamoto ason

SOURCE: Ōmori Kōta shi monjo, 1184/5/8 Minamoto Yoritomo kudashibumi an, HI, 8: 3129, doc. 4,156.

1. The words in-no-chō (retired emperor's chancellery) do not actually appear, merely chō. But the reference is evidently to the ex-emperor, as we see at the close of the document.

2. The year 1184 is represented as either the third year of the Juei period (1182–84) or the first year of Genryaku (1184–85). Often, however, we find an overlapping of dates (e.g. in Documents 7 and 8). This could result from the normal time lag in dispensing calendar information around the country, or it could be the product of a deliberate design. For example, the rebel Yoritomo refused to recognize the year change to Juei (in 1182) because it had come at the instigation of the Taira. See a Yoritomo decree of 1183 dated Jishō 7 (Kōmyōji monjo, 1183/5/3 Minamoto Yoritomo kudashibumi, HI, 8: 3029, doc. 3,977).

DOCUMENT 7

The Retired Emperor Condemns the Activities of a Spurious Jitō, 1184

For an understanding of the revolutionary qualities of the emerging jitō shiki, this recently discovered document has no peer. The shock expressed by an estate's officialdom on encountering a noncentrally appointed land manager is notable. But the record offers much more than this, from a description of the normal commendation-confirmation exchange to a vivid commentary on Kamakura's expansion of power beyond the Kantō.

The retired emperor's chancellery orders: to the resident public officials [zaichōkanjin*] of Echizen Province.

That the despoilments of the deputy jitō [jitōdai*] Priest Jōza shall forthwith cease, and that this province's Kawada Estate, a Hōkongō-in land, be held, by virtue of inheritance, by Lady [nyōbō] Mino-no-tsubone.

A letter of accusation [*sojō**] received from the officials of this estate says:

"This domain, a hereditary private holding [*shiryō**] of the forebears of Fujiwara Kaneko, mother of Lady Mino, the present estate custodian [*azukari dokoro**], was commended during the age of Taikenmon-in as a Hōkongō-in seigniory.¹ Time passed thereafter, but owing to the estate's service as an imperial worship area of the highest importance, and because it was a land with accumulated imperial exemptions, Omuro² exercised jurisdiction [*on-sata*] during these generations, altogether without difficulty [*rōrō**]. Moreover, a Taikenmon-in chancellery order stated that the *jitō–azukari dokoro shiki*³ was to be held and inherited by the descendents of Kaneko.

"However, during the course of the former Iyo governor's rebellion,⁴ despoilments began to occur. As a result, about the ninth month of last year a chancellery order of the retired emperor was again granted,⁵ to the effect that these plunderings should cease forthwith, and that by right of inheritance Mino-no-tsubone should exercise permanent authority over estate affairs.

"In the meantime, [moreover,] after the eastern Genji's [*tōgoku no Genji*]⁶ entrance into the capital on the twentieth day, first month, of this year, a directive from the retired emperor [*inzen*] commanded that outrages cease, and that the main temple's orders [*honji no gechi*]⁷ be obeyed as before. As a result, estate residents [*shōmin**] were made secure, and conditions became quiet. But from the fourth month on, a self-styled *jitō* named Jōza, continuing the pattern of despoilment set by the Iyo governor [Yoshinaka], and citing the orders of Tōnai, the Kamakura lord's special deputy [*kannōshi**], moved onto the estate, and in violation of repeated orders by the ex-emperor extended his grip over domain affairs.⁸ During the course of these unrestrained ravages, not only have the regular temple tributes been neglected, but Buddhist fields [*butsuji*] on the estate have become wasteland. Outrages such as this are intolerable, and the evil of these actions exceeds all limits. Moreover, this estate, for which the present custodian holds the original authorizing decree [*kugen**], has had a hereditary local lord [*jinushi**] for generations. Who is it who would dare call himself *jitō* or *gesu** without a proprietor's authorization [*gechi*]?⁹ This seems self-evident, and we beg your indulgence. We respectfully petition that a retired emperor's edict be handed down ordering wayward and independent *jitō* permanently proscribed, [ordering] an agent of the present custodian to discharge estate affairs, and [ordering] temple services to be fully carried out."

The aforesaid estate, in possession of a hereditary lineage [*yuisho**],
has experienced no change in occupancy. Forthwith, despoilments
[*ranbō*] by the Minamoto [Genke] and the ravagings [*rōzeki*] of Jōza
are to cease; and Mino-no-tsubone shall manage estate affairs. It is so
commanded.

1st year of Genryaku [1184], 5th month,　day.

(signatures)

SOURCE: *Ninnaji monjo*, 1184/5 Go-Shirakawa In-no-chō kudashibumi an, "Ninnaji monjo shūi," p. 75 (*HI*, 10: 3915–16, doc. 5,088).

1. This was during the 1130's. Taikenmon-in (d. 1145) was the consort of Emperor Toba.

2. Ninnaji Temple, closely associated with the imperial house since the reign of
Emperor Uda (887–97). See Note 7.

3. An alternative reading is "*jitō*-type *azukari dokoro* office." See Document 8,
Note 3. It is significant here that the original Taikenmon-in order makes no mention of *jitō*. The words *azukari dokoro* (estate custodian) stand alone (*Ninnaji
monjo*, 1134/interc. 12/15 Taikenmon-in-no-chō kudashibumi, *HI*, 5: 1956, doc.
2,310). The adding of the term *jitō* 50 years later was certainly deliberate. See
Note 8.

4. Minamoto Yoshinaka's revolt of late 1183 against his cousin Yoritomo.

5. See *Ninnaji monjo*, 1183/9/27 Go-Shirakawa In-no-chō kudashibumi, *HI*, 8:
3102, doc. 4,107. The word "again" refers to an earlier edict of the *in*, now being
violated.

6. I.e., the forces of Yoritomo. See *AK*, entry for 1184/1/20.

7. *Honji* (main temple) apparently refers to Ninnaji; cf. Note 5 above. Ninnaji
is never explicitly referred to as *honke* (patron), but this would seem to have been
the case.

8. We might wonder why Jōza is referred to here as a self-styled *jitō* but is called
a deputy *jitō* in the document's introductory paragraph. As we saw, one purpose of
the plaintiff's petition was to establish Mino-no-tsubone as both *jitō* and *azukari
dokoro*: thus Jōza could be no more than a deputy under her authority. See the
reference to an "agent of the present custodian" near the end of the document.

9. In *Warrior Government*, p. 113, I assumed that this statement had been made
by the *in*. In fact, it is contained within the plaintiff's petition.

DOCUMENT 8

Yoritomo Grants a Tax Exemption and Warns Against Jitō Interference, 1184

One interpretation of this document is that Sagami Province, where Kamakura was located, already had numerous *jitō* in 1184; the coupling with
myōshu, a common title, seems to indicate as much. Unfortunately, this is

the only document of its kind; a more cautious explanation may thus be in order. The *jitō* title's dominance over other local offices was still more than a year away. We should also note Yoritomo's usurpation of the public charge over Sagami. The granting of a tax exemption was traditionally the prerogative of a court-appointed governor.

(Yoritomo's monogram)

ORDERED: to Naka-Sakama Gō, Sagami Province.
  That forthwith the stipend paddy and upland [*kyūdenpata**], and the homestead area [*zaike**], of Shinzaburō Iezane, wrestler of the Lower Shrine [*wakamiyazumō*],[1] shall be tax-exempt:
  One *chō*[2] of paddy, one *chō* of upland, and one homestead area.

The aforesaid paddy, upland, and homestead area have been made tax-exempt. No *jitō* or *myōshu*[3] shall interfere with them. It is so commanded.
  3d year of Juei [1184], 6th month, 3d day

SOURCE: *Tsurugaoka Hachimangū monjo*, 1184/6/3 Minamoto Yoritomo kishinjō, *HI*, 8: 3129–30, doc. 4,157.
  1. The reference here is obscure. We know only that the sport of *sumō* was practiced at this time, and that it held a place in the ritual of Shinto.
  2. A *chō* at this time was 2.94 acres (1.19 hectares).
  3. It is possible that this phrase should read *jitō no myōshu*, that is, "*jito*-type *myōshu*." Professor Toyoda Takeshi of Tōhoku University suggests a separation.

DOCUMENT 9

Yoritomo Appoints One of the First Jitō, 1185

What is significant in this well-known document is the balancing of rights with obligations. This was to be a major component of the Kamakura *jitō* office. Also noteworthy is the emphasis on continuity: one warrior is simply being replaced by another. The difference is that the appointment is now being made by Kamakura, a noncentral power base.

(Yoritomo's monogram)

ORDERED: to Hade Tribute Estate [*mikuriya**], Ise Province.
  Concerning appointment of a *jitō shiki*:
  Sa hyōe no jō Koremune Tadahisa.[1]

The aforesaid place has been a holding of followers of the late Dewa governor, Taira Nobukane. However, because Nobukane instigated rebellion, he has been destroyed.² In order that public services be discharged pursuant to precedent, a *jitō* is therefore appointed. Forthwith, administration shall be exercised under this title. It is commanded thus. Wherefore, this order.

2d year of Genryaku [1185], 6th month, 15th day

SOURCE: *Shimazu ke monjo,* 1185/6/15 Minamoto Yoritomo kudashibumi, *DNK, iewake* 16 (Shimazu ke monjo), 1: 1–2, doc. 1 (in *HI,* 8: 3179, doc. 4,259).
    1. First scion of the great Shimazu family of southern Kyushu.
    2. For the wartime exploits of Nobukane and his band, see *AK,* 1181/1/21 and 1184/8/2,3,26.

DOCUMENT 10

Yoritomo Admonishes an Appointive Jitō, 1185

Shimokabe Masayoshi, a Kamakura vassal, is here accused of using his *jitō* title for personal aggrandizement. To gain sway over an entire region, he had inflated the powers attendant on his office and forced the local population to recognize his hegemony. The Bakufu issued this prohibitory order in response.

(Yoritomo's monogram)

ORDERED: to the Kashima Shrine officials and resident public officials [*zaichōkanjin*] of Hitachi Province.
    That the depredations of the *jitō* shall cease forthwith, and that the divine affairs [*shinji*] of Tachibana Gō¹ shall be discharged under authority of Nakatomi Chikahiro.

It has recently been ordered that in the aforesaid *gō,* pursuant to precedent, the *jitō*'s depredations are to cease, and divine affairs are to be conducted in full. However, Shimokabe Shirō Masayoshi, utilizing his appointment as *jitō* of the southern districts, has expanded his power, claiming [full authority] within those districts.² Without specific historical claim [*yuisho**], he has reportedly confined local peasants [*hyakushō³*] and their women and children, and has forced from them sworn pledges [*kishō**] of their subjection to *jitō* control. Acts of such rashness will bring divine retribution. Pursuant to precedent, depredations by the *jitō* are to cease forthwith, and divine affairs shall be conducted in full. It is commanded thus. Wherefore, this order.

2d year of Genryaku [1185], 8th month, 21st day

SOURCE: *Kashima jingū monjo*, 1185/8/21 Minamoto Yoritomo kudashibumi, *Ibaragi ken shiryō, chūsei hen* 1, p. 168, doc. 124. (Also in *HI*, 8: 3183, doc. 4,273, though missing several characters.)

1. A standard unit of local administration. Above the level of *gō* were the *gun* or *kōri* (district) and the *kuni* (province); below was a unit called *ho*.

2. Appointment as a *jitō* carried only limited rights and duties. See Document 17.

3. Since *hyakushō* were often men of some standing—indeed, even *shiki* holders—the term "peasant" might seem odd. Nonetheless, convention probably requires its use here. For a document formally investing such a "local person" with a *myō*-level *hyakushō shiki*, see *Minowa Tatsu shi shozō monjo*, 1317/8/21 hyakushō shiki bu'ninjō, *Gifu kenshi, shiryō hen, kodai-chūsei* 1, p. 489. The appointee is directed to pay the fixed annual tax and other fees.

APPOINTMENTS AND CONFIRMATIONS OF JITŌ

DOCUMENTS 11-13

The Bakufu Experiments With Investiture Patterns During the Age of Yoritomo, 1186, 1192, 1197

From 1186 on, the number of *jitō* appointments issuing from Kamakura increased dramatically. Vassals in many parts of the country, but especially those from the east, were granted land managerships under this new title. The documentary form for investiture, however, had not yet become fixed. In the documents presented here we see a shift away from personal appointment by the Kamakura lord himself, at first to a more formalized order from the shogunal chancellery, and then to a decree issued by the chancellery of a captain of the imperial palace guard [*utaishō*]. The process was one of institutionalization, influenced by Yoritomo's decision (1195) to abandon the relatively low-ranking title of "shogun."

11

(Yoritomo's monogram)

ORDERED: to Shiota Estate, Shinano Province.
    Concerning appointment to a *jitō shiki*:
    Sa hyōe no jō Koremune Tadahisa.

The aforesaid person, as *jitō*, is to administer estate affairs [*shōmu*].

Regarding the annual tax and other levies, he shall perform those duties in accordance with precedent. It is commanded thus. Wherefore, this order.

2d year of Bunji [1186], 1st month, 8th day

12

The chancellery of the shogun's house [*ke*] orders: to the officials of Okuyama Estate, Echigo Province.
Concerning appointment to a *jitō shiki*:
Taira Munezane.

The aforesaid person is appointed to this *shiki*. It is so commanded. Estate officials shall take note, and shall not be remiss. Wherefore, this order.

3d year of Kenkyū [1192], 10th month, 21st day

ryō, minbu no shōjō, Fujiwara   anzu, Fujii (monogram)
  (monogram)   chikeji, Nakahara (monogram)
bettō, saki no Inaba no kami,
  Nakahara ason (monogram)[1]

saki no Shimōsa no kami, Minamoto ason

13

The chancellery of the former right major captain's house [*saki no utaishō ke*] orders: to the residents[2] of Niho Estate and Tsunetomi Ho, Suō Province.
Concerning appointment to a *jitō shiki*:
Taira Shigetsune.

The aforesaid person is appointed to this *shiki*. It is so commanded. Residents shall take note, and shall not be remiss. Wherefore, this order.

8th year of Kenkyū [1197], 2d month, 24th day

ryō, ōkura no jō, Fujiwara seal   anzu, Kiyohara seal
bettō, hyōgo no kami,   chikeji, Nakahara
  Nakahara ason seal[1]
san-i, Fujiwara ason seal

SOURCES: Document 11: *Shimazu ke monjo*, 1186/1/8 Minamoto Yoritomo kudashibumi, DNK, *iewake* 16, 1: 3–4, no. 4 (also in KI, 1: 15, doc. 36). Document 12: *Nakajō ke monjo*, 1192/10/21 shōgun ke mandokoro kudashibumi, *Okuyama-no-shō shiryōshū*, p. 97 (also in KI, 2: 51, doc. 631). Document 13: *Miura ke monjo*, 1197/2/24 saki no utaishō ke mandokoro kudashibumi an, DNK, *iewake* 14, p. 283, doc. 1 (also in KI, 2: 214, doc. 897).

1. Ōe Hiromoto, ranking aide to Yoritomo and chief of his chancellery. The other names here are those of additional chancellery members.

2. *Jūnin*, implying residents of prominence.

DOCUMENT 14

Yoritomo Settles a Dispute Over the Possession of a Jitō Shiki, 1187

The Bakufu, having seized total jurisdiction over the *jitō* title, immediately found itself exercising judicial authority. The disputes it settled were usually between rival claimants to a *jitō* title, or between a *jitō* and an estate proprietor or his agent. The attraction of the *jitō* office was essentially twofold: its possession symbolized elite status as a Kamakura retainer; and its powers guaranteed immunity from direct discipline by the estate owner. In this document, Kamakura resolves a dispute between local rivals, at the same time warning both parties that the estate's affairs were still subject to direction by its absentee owners. Aware that they could not be dismissed directly by central proprietors, many *jitō* proved conveniently forgetful of this point.

seal[1]

ORDERED: to Taira Michitaka.

That the false claim of Bingo Provisional Governor [*gon no kami*] Takatsune is denied; and that the *jitō shiki* of Sonezaki[2] and Sakai Befu's Yukitake Myō,[3] within Kii District, Hizen Province, is confirmed.

Because of the dispute between Takatsune and Michitaka over the aforesaid places, the relative merits of the two parties have been investigated and judged, and Michitaka's case has been found justified. He shall forthwith be confirmed as *jitō*. However, as concerns the stipulated taxes [*shotō**] and the annual rice levy [*nengu**], [the *jitō's*] authority, following precedent, shall be subject to the orders of the proprietor [*honjo no gechi*]. It is recorded in Michitaka's documentary evidence [*shōmon**] that originally these places were Heike lands. Therefore, in the pattern of confiscated holdings [*mokkan*], management should proceed accordingly. It is commanded thus. Residents shall know this and abide by it. Wherefore, this order.

3d year of Bunji [1187], 5th month, 9th day

SOURCE: *Sonezaki monjo*, 1187/5/9 Minamoto Yoritomo kudashibumi an, *Ōita ken shiryō*, 9: 425–26, doc. 501 (also in *KI*, 1: 142, doc. 235).

1. If this document were an original, Yoritomo's monogram would appear here.
2. The type of land unit is not specified.
3. That is, Yukitake Myō, located within Sakai Befu. For the meaning of *befu* see Glossary and Document 63, Note 2.

DOCUMENT 15

Yoritomo Again Settles a Dispute Between Rival Claimants to a Jitō Shiki, 1186

For the nascent Bakufu, the matter of determining which of the local warriors in a distant region deserved to become *jitō* was not always simple. Whatever documentation existed had to be scrutinized—as did the political sympathies of individual claimants. In the following case a simple loyal/disloyal yardstick yielded a clear resolution. Note the reference to *kezan*, an audience with the lord reminiscent of European homage.

ORDERED: to the residents of paddy and upland areas in Ryūzōji Village, Ozu-Higashi Gō, Hizen Province.

That Fujiwara Sueie shall henceforth be *jitō*.

Concerning the aforesaid place, and owing to Fujiwara Sueie's hereditary claim, a Dazaifu[1] order [*fusen**] authorizing him to administer it was granted. However, a local chief of Kanzaki District, *ama rokudaibu* Shigezane, has reportedly been obstructive. Sueie did not join the Heike rebellion and served loyally, honoring imperial authority. [But] Shigezane plotted rebellion as a Heike partisan, in itself a great crime. Worst of all, his failure to submit formally [*kezan**] before the Kamakura lord is evidence of a continuing sympathy for the Heike rebels. The import of this is outrageous. Accordingly, Shigezane's disturbances are to cease permanently, and Sueie is to hold the *jitō shiki*. However, regarding the stipulated taxes and annual [rice] levy, the orders of the proprietor [*honjo** no gechi*] are to be obeyed, and duty discharged in accordance with precedent. It is commanded thus. Wherefore, this order.

2d year of Bunji [1186], 8th month, 9th day

seal[2]

SOURCE: *Isahaya kakei jiseki shū*, 1186/8/9 Minamoto Yoritomo kudashibumi an, *Dazaifu-Dazaifu Tenmangū shiryō*, 7: 179–80 (also in *KI*, 1: 97, doc. 155).

1. The imperial government-general for the island of Kyushu.
2. That is, Yoritomo's seal.

DOCUMENT 16

Kamakura Updates an Earlier Jitō Investiture, 1192

In this document a sense of continuity with the past is once again evident. The original warrior residents of a region in Suō Province had refused to submit to the Minamoto and had been replaced, after which the new *jitō* holder was expected to perform all the traditional services in managing the area. This decree updates an 1186 appointment, now using the new chancellery format.

The chancellery of the former *utaishō*[1] house orders: to the chief residents of [the?] three estates [*sanka shō*] and the public lands [*kōryō*][2] in Ōshima [District], Suō Province.

That the former governor of Inaba, Nakahara *ason* Hiromoto, shall forthwith be *jitō*.

Regarding the above, an order [*onkudashibumi*] of the 2d year of Bunji [1186], 10th month, 8th day, states: "During the noble Heishi Tomomori's rebellion[3] he constructed a fortress on the said island [Ōshima] and resided there. At this time the local chiefs Yashiro Genzō, Oda Saburō, and others of like mind helped from beginning to end with the construction of the fortress. The import of this act is outrageous. Forthwith, Hiromoto is appointed *jitō*, and in accordance with precedent he shall discharge the lord's services [*honke no shokayu*]."[4] Now, however, by virtue of a command to issue a chancellery order (*mandokoro kudashibumi*), it is hereby altered thus.[5] Wherefore, this order.

3d year of Kenkyū [1192], 6th month, 3d day

ryō, minbu no shōjō, Fujiwara seal   anzu, Fujii seal
bettō, saki no Inaba no kami,   chikeji, Nakahara
    Nakahara ason seal[6]
saki no Shimōsa no kami, Minamoto ason
san-i, Nakahara ason

SOURCE: *Seijun shiryō gaihen* (*Kushibe monjo*), 1192/6/3 saki no utaishō ke mandokoro kudashibumi an, *Shōen shiryō*, 2: 1996 (also in *KI*, 2: 18, doc. 594).

1. This was Yoritomo's usual title during 1191–92 and after 1195. During 1192–95 he was called shogun. See Documents 11–13.

2. Synonymous here with *kokugaryō*. See Glossary.

3. For Tomomori's activities during the Gempei War, see *AK*, 1180/5/26, 1180/12/1, 1181/2/12, and 1185/2/16.

4. Technically, *honke* meant "patron," and *ryōke* meant "proprietor." In this instance, there may have been no *ryōke*, or the *honke* may have been clearly dominant.

5. In effect, the form is being changed from a personal appointment by Yori-

tomo to a decree issued by the Kamakura lord's chancellery (*mandokoro*). See Documents 11–13. The original 1186 investiture is no longer extant.

6. Ōe Hiromoto, head of the chancellery. In effect, then, he was adding his seal to a document directly affecting his own interests. As a ranking official of the Bakufu, Hiromoto remained in Kamakura and delegated his *jitō* authority to a deputy.

DOCUMENT 17

The Bakufu Appoints a Jitō to Lands Within an Estate, 1193

A *jitō* did not necessarily hold full or uniform authority over an entire domain; and his powers might be limited in terms of function, geography, or both. In the present example a *jitō* is assigned to particular areas within a larger estate.[1]

The chancellery of the shogun's house orders: to the officers of Kōzuma Estate, Chikugo Province.

That forthwith Fujiwara Iemune shall hold *jitō shiki* over seven places within this estate: Imahiro, Mitsutomo, Chikushibe, Toyo-fuku, Takumanda, Kumeikitada, and Sakaida.

The aforesaid person is appointed to this *shiki*. It is commanded thus. Wherefore, this order.

4th year of Kenkyū [1193], 6th month, 19th day

ryō, ōkura no jō, Fujiwara seal	anzu, Kiyohara [seal][2]
bettō, saki no Inaba no kami,	chikeji, [Nakahara][2]
Nakahara ason seal	
san-i, Fujiwara ason seal	

SOURCE: *Kōzuma monjo*, 1193/6/19 shōgun ke mandokoro kudashibumi an, *Fukuoka kenshi shiryō*, 8: 63 (also in *KI*, 2: 74–75, doc. 673).

1. See also Document 14.
2. Characters missing but inserted.

DOCUMENT 18

Kamakura Upholds a Jitō Shiki, 1205

In this document we see a further illustration of continuity involving *jitō*: the Bakufu refuses to dismiss a *jitō* who had lawfully taken over from an earlier holder.

Two matters:[1]

Item: concerning Tsuda Island, Awa Province, a Kasuga Shrine land.

The aforesaid island is the legacy [*ato*] of the former *jitō, hyōe no jō* Chikaie. Pursuant to custom, Shiina Gorō *nyūdō* was then appointed *jitō*. In such circumstances it is difficult to make a sudden dismissal [*kaieki**] without some specific error [i.e. guilt]. Nevertheless, the *jitō* has been instructed not to be negligent regarding the fixed annual tax.

. . .

5th month, 19th day

Reply to the Kusuga kannushi dono[2]   Tōtomi no kami[3] seal

SOURCE: *Ōhigashi ke monjo*, [1205]/5/19 Hōjō Tokimasa shojō an, *Kasuga Jinja monjo*, 3: 210–11 (in *KI*, 3: 238, doc. 1,543).

1. The second matter discussed, involving unlawful entry by a *sōtsuibushi**, is omitted here. See Document 163 for a reference to this incident.

2. The administrator-priest of Kasuga Shrine.

3. Hōjō Tokimasa, father-in-law of Yoritomo and chief Bakufu administrator. The Hōjō emerged as the dominant family in Kamakura soon after Yoritomo's death in 1199. The house expanded its power by becoming "regents" (*shikken*) for shoguns and seizing control of the major Bakufu agencies. Ultimately, Kamakura edicts (especially judicial settlements) came to be issued by the Hōjō in their capacity as proxies for the titular Bakufu chieftain. (See Documents 20, 21, and 45, among numerous others.)

DOCUMENT 19

The Bakufu Uses a More Formalized Procedure to Resolve a Dispute Over a Jitō Shiki, 1196

By the mid-1190's Kamakura justice had come to require not only the presentation of evidence but also, in some cases, the physical presence of the litigants. In this document, we see that persons from remote Kyushu had been summoned to Kamakura for a hearing.

The chancellery of the former *utaishō* house orders: to the residents of Ojika Island, Uno Estate, Hizen Province.

Concerning appointment to a *jitō shiki*:

The priest Jinkaku.

The aforesaid place was disputed by Jinkaku and Matsuura Jūrō Ren. Upon summoning and judging the two sides, Jinkaku was found to be in the right.[1] Accordingly, he is hereby appointed to this *shiki*. Wherefore, this order.

7th year of Kenkyū [1196], 7th month, 12th day

ryō, ōkura no jō, Fujiwara seal   anzu, Kiyohara seal
bettō, hyōgo no kami, Nakahara seal   chikeji, Nakahara
san-i, Fujiwara ason seal

SOURCE: *Aokata monjo*, 1196/7/12 saki no utaishō ke mandokoro kudashibumi an, *Aokata monjo* (1975 ed.), 1: 1, doc. 1 (in *KI*, 2: 193, doc. 856).
1. This seems to be a reversal, since later evidence notes that Ren, not Jinkaku, was granted a Bakufu investiture in 1188. (Referred to in *Aokata monjo*, 1228/3/13 Kantō gechijō an, *Aokata monjo*, 1: 11–14, doc. 12 (in *KI*, 6: 74–77, doc. 3,732). See also Document 20.)

DOCUMENT 20

Kamakura Is Forced to Retry an Earlier Dispute, 1204

One of the difficulties confronted by the Bakufu was maintaining consistency in its judicial decisions. The dispute here is the one described in Document 19. In 1203 Kamakura had switched its support to Ren, the loser in the 1196 encounter. This obviously confused things and led to the present courtroom action. The Bakufu here upheld its 1196 decision, but the matter remained in litigation until 1228.

ORDERED: to the residents of Ojika Island, Uno Estate, Hizen Province.
  Concerning appointment to a *jitō shiki*:
  The priest Jinkaku.

The aforesaid place was disputed by Jinkaku and Matsuura Jūrō Ren. Upon summoning and judging the two sides, Jinkaku was found to be in the right, and was accordingly granted an *utaishō* chancellery order in the 7th year of Kenkyū [1196], 7th month, 12th day. Reportedly, his possession [*chigyō**] was undisturbed after that.[1] However, a complaint has now been lodged that during the past winter Ren violated this state of affairs, and that after being served with a letter of inquiry [*toijō**] he seized [Ojika Island] without justification. If this is true, the effect of such an act is most unsettling. Forthwith, Ren's outrages are to cease; and Jinkaku, in accordance with the deceased lord's order, is to hold this *shiki* as before. By command of the Kamakura lord, it is decreed thus.

1st year of Genkyū [1204], 8th month, 22d day

Tōtomi no kami seal

SOURCE: *Aokata monjo*, 1204/8/22 Kantō gechijō an, *Aokata monjo*, 1: 4–5, doc. 4 (in *KI*, 3: 186, doc. 1,473).
1. In fact, this is incorrect, as remarked in the Introduction to this document. At times the Bakufu, not sure of whom to support, simply reversed itself.

DOCUMENT 21

The Bakufu Confirms a Jitō Shiki, 1221

In order to maintain control of its widely scattered *jitō*, the Bakufu developed the practice of issuing periodic reconfirmations for that office. These generally came after an inheritance, but could also appear in the wake of a major political reorganization. The Jōkyū War of 1221 was ostensibly a struggle between the court and the Bakufu, though actually it pitted one segment of the country's warriors against another. At its conclusion, the victorious Bakufu confirmed many *goke'nin* in their *jitō shiki*.

Concerning Jibi Estate, Bingo Province. Although *jitō* Shigetoshi's son, Tarō, was killed [fighting] on the court side, Jirō[1] showed loyalty in battle on our side. Therefore, Shigetoshi's *jitō shiki* shall be confirmed without change.[2] Pursuant to this command, it is decreed thus.

3d year of Jōkyū [1221], 7th month, 26th day

Mutsu no kami, Taira[3] (monogram)

SOURCE: *Yamanouchi Sudō monjo*, 1221/7/26 Kantō gechijō, *DNK, iewake* 15, doc. 1, p. 1 (in *KI*, 5: 27, doc. 2,783).
1. The second son.
2. Shigetoshi's own posture in the War is not specified. Perhaps he remained at home and did not join in the fighting.
3. Hōjō Yoshitoki, chief officer of the Bakufu. See Glossary under *shikken*.

DOCUMENTS 22-23

A Traditional Public Agency Confirms Some Jitō Appointments Made by Kamakura, 1203, 1213

In the Kantō region and in much of Kyushu the Bakufu came to dominate the old imperial offices. In such cases a provincial governorship might become subject to control or direction from Kamakura. In the following examples the governorships of Ōsumi (Kyushu) and Musashi (Kantō) added another layer of legitimacy to the Bakufu's *jitō* appointments.

22

Governor's edict: to the provincial absentee office [*rusudokoro**].
Concerning appointment to the Nejime Minamimata District *jitō shiki*:
Shami Gyōsai [Seichō].

Regarding the aforesaid *shiki*, the former *saemon no kami dono*[1] has stated: "Shigenobu exercised possession, but his death is [now] reported. Therefore, Seichō *hosshi* is appointed. However, if a challenger should appear, both sides shall be summoned and questioned, and justice adhered to."[2] Accordingly, the resident provincial officials shall take note, and shall not be remiss. The decree is thus. Wherefore, this edict.

3d year of Kennin [1203], 8th month,   day

ōsuke, Fujiwara ason (monogram facsimile)[3]

23

The absentee office orders: to the officials [*shinkan*] and peasants [*hyakushō*][4] of the second shrine [*ninomiya*].[5]
That in accordance with a [Kantō] order Himatsuri Naotaka shall forthwith be *jitō* over this shrine.

Regarding the foregoing, a [Kantō] order of the first day of the 9th month arrived here on the 7th day. Full particulars accompanied it. In accordance with the [Kantō] order, the said Naotaka shall be *jitō*. The command is thus. Know this and abide by it. Wherefore, this order.

3d year of Kenryaku [1213], 9th month, 7th day

> san-i, Himatsuri sukune (monogram)
> san-i, Himatsuri sukune (monogram)
> san-i, Tachibana ason (monogram)
> mokudai,[6] Fujiwara (monogram)

SOURCES: Document 22: *Nejime monjo*, 1203/8 Ōsumi kokushi chōsen an, *Nejime monjo*, 1: 12, doc. 13 (in *KI*, 3: 101, doc. 1,375). Document 23: *Ogawa monjo*, 1213/9/7 Musashi no kuni rusudokoro kudashibumi, *Sappan kyūki zatsuroku*, 2: 24, doc. 123 (in *KI*, 4: 86, doc. 2,028).

1. Minamoto Yoriie, Yoritomo's successor as Bakufu chieftain.
2. The original of the quoted document appears in *Nejime monjo*, 1203/7/3 Kantō kudashibumi an, *Nejime monjo*, 1: 12, doc. 11 (in *KI*, 3: 94–95, doc. 1,367).
3. When such a facsimile (or outline form) was affixed, the document was considered a copy (*an*).
4. See Document 10, Note 3.

5. The second-ranking "public shrine" within a province. The major shrine was called *ichinomiya*.

6. Personal deputy of a governor.

DOCUMENT 24

The Bakufu Confirms a Woman as Jitō, 1215

During an age in which warfare was only irregular, there was little risk either for *jitō* families or for the Bakufu in having women inherit *jitō shiki*. Only later, when *jitō* patrimonies had become badly fragmented and local instability had increased, did inheritance practices change.

The chancellery of the shogun's house orders: to the residents of three *gō* within Nitta Estate, Kōzuke Province; Iwamatsu, Shimo Imai, Tanaka.

In accord with the last will [*yuzurijō**] of the husband, Yoshikane, his widow shall forthwith be *jitō*.

The aforesaid person, in accordance with the will, is appointed to this *shiki*. As to the fixed annual tax and other services, these shall be paid in accordance with precedent. It is commanded thus. Wherefore, this order.

3d year of Kempō [1215], 3d month, 22d day

ryō, zusho no jō, Kiyohara (monogram facsimile)	anzu, Sugano (monogram facsimile)
bettō, Sagami no kami, Taira ason (monogram facsimile)	chikeji, Koremune (monogram facsimile)

minbu gon no shōsuke ken Tōtomi no kami, Minamoto ason
Musashi no kami, Taira ason (monogram facsimile)
shohakase, Nakahara ason (monogram facsimile)
san-i, Fujiwara ason (monogram facsimile)

SOURCE: *Nitta Iwamatsu monjo*, 1215/3/22 shōgun ke mandokoro kudashibumi an, *Masaki komonjo*, p. 16 (in *KI*, 4: 155–56, doc. 2,150).

DOCUMENT 25

Kamakura Reconfirms a Jitō Shiki After the Theft of the Original Appointing Documents, 1220

The importance of written proof of an appointment is graphically revealed in this case.

Hikokuma, the granddaughter of Shindō... *hosshi*,[1] has petitioned concerning the loss of generations of [Kantō] orders and the sequence of testamentary documents [*tetsugi no yuzurijō*] relating to the *jitō shiki* of Seirinji within Oharihara Estate, Etchū Province, and of Otobe Gō within Otobe Estate, Ise Province. According to this petition: "On the night of the 3d day of this month when valuables were taken by a thief from our Kamakura residence, the aforesaid documents were stolen." From the time of the late *utaishō* lord, these two places have been held by right of inheritance without disturbance. Even though the documents have been lost, there is to be no change. By this command, it is so decreed.

2d year of Jōkyū [1220], 10th month, 14th day

Mutsu no kami, Taira (monogram)

SOURCE: *Shindō monjo*, 1220/10/14 Kantō gechijō, *KI*, 4: 398, doc. 2,657.
  1. Three characters in this person's name seem to be corrupt and have been omitted.

DOCUMENTS 26-28

Kamakura Appoints New Jitō After Political and Military Disturbances and as a Reward for Special Merit, 1213, 1220, 1221

In 1213, the powerful Wada clan of Sagami attempted to contest the Hōjō's increasing control of the Bakufu. The result was a brief skirmish and the dispossession of the Wada. New *jitō* were immediately placed in their vacated lands. In 1220, a pair of *jitō shiki* was granted as a reward for special diligence in tracking down thieves. In 1221, the Jōkyū War led to a widespread purging of warriors and a new wave of *jitō* appointments; in this instance, the appointees were virtually all vassals from the Kantō.

26

(Sanetomo's monogram)[1]

ORDERED: to the residents of Futokorojima Tonobara Gō, Sagami Province.

Concerning appointment of a *jitō shiki*:
Sa hyōe no jō Fujiwara Motoyuki.

The aforesaid person is appointed to this *shiki* as a reward for meritorious service. It is commanded thus.

3d year of Kenryaku [1213], 5th month, 9th day

27

That forthwith *saemon no jō** Minamoto Mitsuyuki is to be *jitō* over Sadakiyo Gō and Shigetsugu Gō within Katakata District, Mino Province.

The aforesaid person is appointed to the *jitō shiki* of these two *gō* as a reward for hunting down mountain robbers in the 10th month of this year. Authority is to be exercised in accordance with precedent. In pursuance of this command, it is decreed thus.

    2d year of Jōkyū [1220], 11th month, 17th day

Mutsu no kami, Taira (monogram)

28

Concerning the *jitō shiki* of Nukushina Village, Aki Province.

The aforesaid person[2] is appointed to this *shiki* as a reward for meritorious service. In pursuance of this command, it is decreed thus.

    3d year of Jōkyū [1221], 8th month, 27th day

Mutsu no kami, Taira seal

SOURCES: Document 26: *Nikaidō monjo*, 1213/5/9 Minamoto Sanetomo kudashi-bumi, *Kanagawa kenshi, shiryō hen*, 1: 549, doc. 278 (in *KI*, 4: 78, doc. 2,007). Document 27: *Toki monjo*, 1220/11/7 Kantō gechijō, *KI*, 4: 403, doc. 2,671. Document 28: *Mōri ke monjo*, 1221/8/27 Kantō gechijō utsushi, *DNK, iewake* 8 (*Mōri ke monjo*), 4: 395, doc. 1,493 (in *KI*, 5: 41, doc. 2,817).

    1. Minamoto Sanetomo, third chief of the Bakufu.

    2. Through an apparent oversight, the recipient's name is omitted in this copy.

POLICING AUTHORITY AND THE CANCELLATION OF JITŌ

The Bakufu Exercises a General Policing Authority, 1186

In the crisis atmosphere of the immediate post-Gempei period the Kamakura regime was the only political force capable of quieting the countryside. Warriors were on the move everywhere, disrupting agriculture and challenging the basic hierarchy of authority. To the Bakufu fell the task of healing a country torn by the very anarchy that Kamakura had initially promoted. Over the next several years the Bakufu's involvement in governments at all levels would be diffuse and largely based on need.

(Yoritomo's monogram)

ORDERED: to the residents of Takebe Estate, Ōmi Province.
That the outrages of warriors while stopping over [in Takebe] during their travels shall cease immediately.

The aforesaid place is recorded as a Hie Shrine land. Nevertheless, when warriors have stopped over while traveling, they have let loose their horses and have foraged in cultivated fields. Not only this, but there are reports that tribute rice [*onkumai*] has been seized as commissariat rice. In the future, these outrages are to cease. Should there be persons who disobey this order and commit violations, a name list shall certainly

be drawn up and reported. It is commanded thus. Wherefore, this order.
2d year of Bunji [1186], intercalary 7th month, 29th day

SOURCE: *Sonkeikaku bunko shozō monjo*, 1186/int.7/29 Minamoto Yoritomo kuda-shibumi, *KI*, 1: 93, doc. 146.

DOCUMENT 30

Kamakura Cancels a Jitō Shiki, 1186

A direct product of the lawlessness gripping the country during the middle 1180's was the Bakufu's decision to take punitive action against its own men. What is of interest in the present document is that Yoritomo's own brother-in-law, Hōjō Yoshitoki, was the *jitō* being dispossessed. This kind of willing-ness to take bold measures undoubtedly contributed to the Bakufu's growing importance.

(Yoritomo's monogram)

ORDERED: to Yura Estate, Tamba Province.
That forthwith Yoshitoki's possession [*chigyō*] shall be terminated, and shrine services shall be performed.

The aforesaid estate is a Kamowake Ikazuchi Shrine holding. Neverthe-less, a shrine petition has held that because of Yoshitoki's possession the regular shrine services have been neglected. In response, an order was issued by the retired emperor.[1] Forthwith, Yoshitoki's possession shall be terminated, and shrine services shall be performed. It is commanded thus. Wherefore, this order.
2d year of Bunji [1186], 9th month, 5th day

SOURCE: *Kamowake Ikazuchi Jinja monjo*, 1186/9/5 Minamoto Yoritomo kudashi-bumi, *KI*, 1: 107, doc. 170.
    1. In other words, the complaint had first been sent to the court, which had passed it on to Kamakura.

DOCUMENT 31

Kamakura Issues a Desist Order to a Favored Retainer and a Local Notable, 1186

The Bakufu did not always dismiss *jitō* who were found guilty of local offenses. Often, it went no further than issuing a warning. Three points are noteworthy in the Suō Province case offered here. First, the Kamakura vassal Doi Sanehira may already have developed some kind of superior/subordinate relationship with a local notable in the troubled region; Doi himself was an easterner and probably unfamiliar with conditions in distant Suō. Second, lenience in the present case did not preclude harsher justice elsewhere: Almost simultaneously, Doi was removed from another *jitō shiki* in Bingo Province's Ōta Estate.[1] Third, the Bakufu's removal of a *jitō* in one Kamowake Ikazuchi holding was not duplicated for other holdings of that shrine, even on the same day (see Document 30). Kamakura's freedom to dispose of *jitō*-related incidents was total.

(Yoritomo's monogram)

ORDERED: to the residents of Iho Estate, Kamadono-seki, Yajima, and Hashirajima,[2] of Suō Province.

That the violations of Doi Sanehira and the improprieties [*futō*] of local resident Ōno Shichirō Tōmasa shall cease forthwith, and that the authority of the proprietor [*ryōke no shinshi*] be obeyed.

The aforesaid estates are reported to be Kamowake Ikazuchi Shrine holdings. Nevertheless, an appeal by a shrine official has held that, in addition to Doi Sanehira's plundering [*oryō*] in recent days, the local notable Ōno Shichirō Tōmasa has been laying waste the interior of these estates. In response, an order was issued by the retired emperor. When summoned for questioning Sanehira stated that a commissariat rice exemption had [in fact] been in force, and moreover, that there had been no plundering.[3] Whose evil plot, then, can this be?[4] Also, Tōmasa's vandalizing of these estates is most unlawful. Henceforth, their outrages are to cease, and the shrine's authority shall be obeyed. It is commanded thus. Wherefore, this order.

2d year of Bunji [1186], 9th month, 5th day

SOURCE: *Kamowake Ikazuchi Jinja monjo*, 1186/9/5 Minamoto Yoritomo kudashibumi, *KI*, 1: 106, doc. 169.
1. Cf. *Kōyasan monjo*, 1186/7/24 Minamoto Yoritomo shojō, *KI*, 1: 37, doc. 131.
2. All four are place names.
3. Sanehira's remarks end here.
4. I.e., if not Sanehira, then who?

DOCUMENT 32

Kamakura Judges a Tax Case in Central Japan, 1188

During its early years the Bakufu often accepted appeals for justice on issues it would later eschew. In the incident described here Kajiwara Kagetoki, one of Yoritomo's favorites, endorses a temple's position on a tax exemption matter. It is not certain, but presumably the Settsu Province governor had reasserted his jurisdiction over the disputed land. Kamakura's action on behalf of the temple was a clear intrusion into a quarrel between rival proprietors.[1]

ORDERED: to the administrators [*satanin**] of Suita Estate.[2]

> That forthwith 1 *chō*, 1 *tan* [1.1 *chō*] of paddy land shall be exempt.

The aforesaid paddy land was reportedly commended in former years to Katsuozan[3] as *myōden** by Takiguchi *nyūdō*. Afterward, this authority apparently lapsed. But now a priest from this temple has come forward and requested that the [tax] exemption be as before. Therefore, by order of the Kamakura lord, the exemption is hereby authorized. The administrators of this estate shall take note, and shall not be remiss. Wherefore, this order.

> 4th year of Bunji [1188], 9th month, 6th day

> Heizō (monogram)

SOURCE: *Katsuodera monjo*, 1188/9/6 Kajiwara Kagetoki kudashibumi, *Katsuodera monjo*, p. 171, doc. 216 (in *KI*, 1: 196, doc. 343).
  1. With increasing frequency, Yoritomo would tend to refuse this kind of involvement. See, for example, *Hosaka Junji shi shozō monjo*, 1189/7/11 Minamoto Yoritomo shojō, *KI*, 1: 334, doc. 397. See also Documents 48–49 below.
  2. In Settsu Province.
  3. Katsuo Temple.

DOCUMENT 33

Kamakura Cancels the Shiki of a Guiltless Jitō, 1205

Hoping to inject a measure of uniformity into its *jitō* system, Kamakura was willing to listen to appeals for cancellation of an office because of "illegal" appointment. These were not always accepted, but in the present instance mistaken identity proved sufficient to justify the abolition of a *jitō* post. Evidently, the person originally dispossessed to make way for a *jitō* had not been the lawful manager of the estate in question.

ORDERED: to the residents of Ōhashi Estate, Ise Province.

> That the *uemon no suke's* possession of the *jitō shiki* shall forthwith be terminated.

Regarding the aforesaid: because it was reported that this estate (also known as Tanabashi) was a holding [*ryō**] of Yamabe, *uma no suke*,[1] a *jitō* was appointed. However, not only has the shrine [Ise shrine] appealed this, but the estate holder [*ryōshu**], *hokkyō* Keison, has claimed that it was not [Yamabe's] land.[2] In consequence, the *uemon no suke's* possession shall forthwith be terminated.[3] By command of the Kamakura lord, it is so decreed. Wherefore, this order.

2d year of Genkyū [1205], 3d month, 13th day

Tōtomi no kami, Taira[4] seal

SOURCE: *Daigoji monjo*, 1205/3/13 Kantō gechijō an, *DNK, iewake* 19 (Daigoji monjo), 1: 173, doc. 188 (in *KI*, 3: 232, doc. 1,527).

1. Probably a Heike follower.

2. For details of this claim see Keison's petition in *Daigoji monjo*, 1204/12 sō Keison mōshijō an, *KI*, 3: 220–22, doc. 1,513. Keison himself was a priest of Daigoji Temple. Evidently, Ise Shrine was patron (*honke*) for Ōhashi Estate.

3. On at least two subsequent occasions the Bakufu was called on to reaffirm Keison's authority over Ōhashi Estate. *Ibid.*, 1216/2/15 Kantō gechijō an, *KI*, 4: 202, doc. 2,210; *ibid.*, 1222/8/8 Kantō gechijō an, *KI*, 5: 122, doc. 2,989.

4. Hōjō Tokimasa.

DOCUMENT 34

Kamakura Cancels a Jitō Shiki and Restores an Original Officeholder, 1204

In some instances an appeal for a *jitō's* removal had little to recommend it beyond a local holder's traditional association with his homeland. Here an estate manager (*gesu**) had been dispossessed after 1185, and apparently a *jitō* had been appointed in his stead. Two decades later Kamakura acceded to a petition that the original holder be reinstated.

Concerning the *gesu shiki* of Tarumi [Estate], Settsu Province.

Regarding the above, the former *gesu* Shigetsune had his lands confiscated because of his Heike affiliation. However, the *uneme*[1] Izumo-no-tsubone has stated: "This estate is a land first opened by my ancestors, with a *gesu* [title] that is hereditary. Given this original-holder status, we request that [the *shiki*] be [re]conferred."[2] Since it is difficult to ignore a suit lodged by a *kunin*,[3] the [re]appointment will be made to this *shiki*. By command of the Kamakura lord it is decreed thus.

1st year of Genkyū [1204], 9th month, 6th day

Tōtomi no kami, Taira seal

SOURCE: *Tōji hyakugō monjo.* 1204/9/6 Kantō gechijō an, *KBSS*, 1: 6, doc. 7 (in *KI*, 3: 188, doc. 1,479).

1. A palace woman.

2. According to Seno Seiichirō, this appeal was made on behalf of former *gesu* Shigetsune. See *KBSS*, 1: 6. Ten years later, however, the *gesu's* name was Ieyuki, and he was a vassal of Kamakura (Documents 68 and 159). There are no intervening records to explain what had happened, though it is clear from Document 68 that the *gesu* authority had long been hereditary.

3. A court person or official. See Glossary.

DOCUMENT 35

Kamakura Cancels a Jitō Shiki in Deference to an Important Shrine, 1205

The identities—and precise authority—of the people referred to in this document are not always clear, but the travails of one estate over a 30-year period emerge in bold relief. Of special note is Kamakura's early effort to win the support of a major shrine, as well as a reference to the only known pre-1180 *jitō shiki* in the Kantō.[1]

ORDERED: to Tachibana Gō, Hitachi Province, a Kashima Shrine land.
That Kunii Hachirō Masakage's *jitō shiki* shall forthwith be abolished.

The aforesaid *gō* is a land commended to the Kashima Shrine in the 5th year of Jishō [1181], under the authority of the late *utaishō* lord. Following this, it was repeatedly ordered that the excesses of the *jitō* should cease,[2] and that shrine duties [*shingi**] be carried out under Nakatomi Chikahiro's exclusive authority. In fact, [Tachibana's] status as shrine land is not something new. A governor's edict was issued during the Angen period [1175–77] to the effect that the authority of Hiromiki, then *jitō*, be abolished, and that [Tachibana Gō] become Kashima Shrine land. During the time of the *saemon no kami*,[3] however, Masakage, under false pretenses, was appointed to the *jitō shiki* and [afterward] reportedly violated shrine expense funds [*yōto**]. In keeping with the status [of the *gō*] as shrine land, and according to the import of the documents [on hand], Masakage's *jitō shiki* is herewith terminated, and shrine duties are to be discharged under the sole authority of acting *negi** Masachika. It is so commanded.

2d year of Genkyū [1205], 8th month, 23d day

sa kon'oe chūjō, Minamoto ason[4] (monogram)

SOURCE: *Kashima Jingū monjo*, 1205/8/23 Minamoto Sanetomo kudashibumi, *Ibaragi ken shiryō, chūsei hen*, 1: 167, doc. 121 (in *KI*, 3: 250, doc. 1,574).

1. For corroboration of this reference see *Kashima Jingū monjo*, 1228/5/19

Kantō gechijō, *Ibaragi ken shiryō, chūsei hen*, 1: 220, doc. 317 (*KBSS*, 1: 40–43, doc. 47).

2. For these "repeated orders," see, e.g., *Kashima Jingū monjo*, 1184/12/25 Minamoto Yoritomo kudashibumi, *Ibaragi ken shiryō, chūsei hen*, 1: 219, doc. 312 (*HI*, 8: 3157, doc. 4,223), and Document 10 above.

3. Minamoto Yoriie, Yoritomo's successor as Bakufu chieftain (r. 1199–1203).

4. Minamoto Sanetomo, Yoriie's successor.

DOCUMENT 36

Kamakura Cancels a Jitō Shiki Instituted After the Jōkyū War, 1233

A harder line adopted by the Bakufu after 1206 virtually ended *jitō* cancellations until the Jōkyū War of 1221. New appointments made after this incident led to another round of *jitō* "adjustments." The present document is vivid on this point.

That the *jitō shiki* of Fushino Estate, Suō Province, a Tōdaiji Temple land, shall forthwith be terminated.

According to the temple's appeal: "The appointment of a *jitō* at the time of the Jōkyū treachery, in the absence of any specific guilt by this estate's residents, is something that is hard to endure. Ōgori and Kagawa Gō make up this estate. During the time of the *utaishō* house, in the 9th year of Kenkyū [1198], 4th month, Shiramatsu Tōji Suketsuna contrived to receive a *jitō shiki* here. By virtue of a temple petition, however, the appointment decree [*onkudashibumi*] was recalled in the 5th month and granted to the temple.[1] Handled by Moritoki."[2]

According to Tokihiro *hosshi*'s statement of refutation [*chinjō**], the [present] *jitō shiki* was granted in the 1st year of Jōō [1222].[3] However, [this document] does not clearly state the background details.[4] Hence the temple's argument does not lack justice. In accordance with precedent, the *jitō shiki* is herewith terminated. By command of the Kamakura lord, it is so decreed.

1st year of Tempuku [1233], 7th month, 9th day

Musashi no kami, Taira[5] seal
Sagami no kami, Taira[6] seal

SOURCE: *Tōdaiji yōroku*, 1233/7/9 Kantō gechijō an, *KBSS*, 1: 50, doc. 53 (in *KI*, 7: 56, doc. 4,538).

1. That is, the *jitō shiki* was canceled and full authority over the estate's management restored to Tōdaiji. The temple's appeal, of which the present paragraph is a summary, appears in *Tōdaiji monjo*, 1232/9 Tōdaiji mōshijō, *KI*, 6: 403, doc.

4,380. According to this document, the disallowed *jitō shiki* had been secured by a false claim to hereditary possession.

2. Characters only half-size. The reference is to Taira Moritoki, an important Bakufu official in the 1190's. Moritoki's signature, as was common for that period, had been affixed to the recall order cancelling the *jitō shiki*. See the document cited in Note 1.

3. Tokihiro *hosshi* was the new, post-Jōkyū *jitō*. He was arguing that the earlier return of authority to Tōdaiji had now been rendered void.

4. I.e., the circumstances behind the appointment. Evidently, Tokihiro was unable to produce an original investiture decree specifying details.

5. Hōjō Yasutoki.

6. Hōjō Tokifusa. Yasutoki and Tokifusa were, respectively, regent (*shikken*) and "cosigner" (*rensho*) for Kamakura, and thus the Bakufu's two leading administrative officers. It was the usual practice for judicial edicts to bear both their names.

DOCUMENT 37

A Jitō Shiki Is Canceled Because of Disobedience by a Vassal, 1192

We have looked at several examples of *jitō shiki* canceled after complaints or appeals by estate proprietors. But negligence as a vassal could also lead to dismissal. In the present instance a certain *jitō* in Kyushu had failed to appear as ordered for two military campaigns.

Yoritomo seal (monogram facsimile)

ORDERED: to the residents of Ikata Estate, Buzen Province.

Concerning appointment of a *jitō shiki*:

The former *tokoro no shū*[1] Nakahara Nobufusa.

The former *jitō* Sadatane did not cross over to Kigajima.[2] Moreover, at the time of the Northern [Ōshū] Campaign he did not appear. In consequence of this double negligence, his *shiki* will be terminated, and Nobufusa appointed. As for the stipulated [estate] services, they are to be discharged in accordance with precedent. It is commanded thus. Wherefore, this order.

3d year of Kenkyū [1192], 2d month, 28th day

SOURCE: *Sata monjo*, 1192/2/28 Minamoto Yoritomo kudashibumi utsushi, *Hennen Ōtomo shiryō*, 1: 213–14, doc. 220 (in *KI*, 2: 11, doc. 581).

1. A low-ranking title traditionally associated with the Board of Archivists (*kurōdo dokoro*).

2. Site of a minor punitive action conducted by Kyushu special deputy Amano Tōkage in 1187. For details, see *AK*, 1187/9/22.

BAKUFU CONSOLIDATION
IN NORTHERN JAPAN AND KYUSHU

Kamakura Issues Directives to Jitō in Northern Japan, 1212, 1220

In 1189 the Bakufu launched a military campaign in northern Japan that quickly succeeded in bringing the region under Kamakura control. This area was underdeveloped, however; hence the logic of orders like Document 38. Political domination, moreover, was no guarantee of smooth or efficient administration. Directives like that of 1220 were common not only in the North but also closer to home.

38

The villages held by the *jitō* in Nagayo Ho, Mutsu Province, together with any wastelands hereafter opened to cultivating, are to provide his allotted income [*tokubun**]. Existing fields are not to be laid waste under some pretext or other. By command of the Kamakura lord, it is so conveyed.

2d year of Kenryaku [1212], 12th month, 3d day

san-i, Nakahara seal

39

Concerning repairs to the two shrines of Dewa Province,[1] priest-administrator Hisanaga complained that the job had not been completed. In consequence, agent [*zōshiki**] Masaie was sent in the 6th year of Kempō [1218], 12th month, to expedite the matter. Owing to the momentous passing of the lord right minister [*udaijin dono*],[2] Masaie returned [to Kamakura] without accomplishing his task. But the necessary repairs must not be left unfinished. Therefore, to expedite [completion], agent Sanemitsu is being sent. This task should be completed without fail. Through the agency of the Mutsu governor,[3] [the order] is so conveyed.

2d year of Jōkyū [1220], 12th month, 3d day

[To] Kitame, jitō shin rusu dono   san-i, Fujiwara (monogram),
                                          sent respectfully
                                          san-i, Miyoshi (monogram)

SOURCES: Document 38: *Takasu monjo*, 1212/12/3 Kantō migyōsho an, *KI*, 4: 49, doc. 1,955. Document 39: *Ōmonoimi jinja monjo*, 1220/12/3 Kantō migyōsho, *KI*, 4: 406, doc. 2,681.

    1. Ōmonoimi Shrine and Komonoimi Shrine.
    2. Minamoto Sanetomo, assassinated on 1219/1/27.
    3. Hōjō Yoshitoki. In the absence of a formal lord, orders were given directly by the regent.

DOCUMENTS 40-41

Kamakura Issues Directives to a Sōjitō of Kyushu, 1189, ca. 1191

In Kyushu the Bakufu adopted the practice of placing eastern-born chief *jitō* (*sōjitō**) over indigenous sub-*jitō* (*shōjitō**), mostly because the region contained a great many estates with large bodies of armed warriors. Best known of the Kyushu *sōjitō* was Koremune (later Shimazu) Tadahisa, who was in charge of the great Shimazu Estate. In the first document Tadahisa is directed to gather armed men and bring them to Kamakura for the military campaign in the North (see Document 37). Later, he is ordered in another context to report the names of all who resisted his authority.

40

                           (Yoritomo's monogram)

ORDERED: to *jitō* Tadahisa of Shimazu Estate.

That estate officials [*shōkan**] shall forthwith be mustered.

Among these officials, those able to fight should bring their weapons and arrive in the Kantō before the 7th month, 10th day. To be received by the lord [*kezan**], each must demonstrate loyalty [*chūsetsu*]. It is so ordered.

5th year of Bunji [1189], 2d month, 9th day

41

Officials of Shimazu Estate have failed to obey the orders of *sōjitō* Tadahisa. Such action by estate functionaries is outrageous. Should there be any who remain defiant, let them be reported. The order of the former *utaishō* lord is thus. It is so conveyed.

7th month, 10th day[1]

[To] Mune, hyōe no jō dono[2]   Taira[3] (monogram)

SOURCES: Document 40: *Shimazu ke monjo,* 1189/2/9 Minamoto Yoritomo kudashibumi, *DNK, iewake* 16 (Shimazu ke monjo), 1: 7–8, doc. 9 (in *KI,* 1: 205, doc. 364). Document 41: *Shimazu ke monjo,* [1191?]/7/10 Kantō migyōsho, *DNK, iewake* 16, 1: 8, doc. 10 (in *Sappan kyūki zatsuroku, zempen,* 1: 100–101, doc. 67).
  1. It is tempting to try to connect these two documents, since both cite the date 7/10. Moreover, their adjacent placement in *DNK* and in *Sappan kyūki zatsuroku* seems to confirm this. However, the second 7/10 date cannot be the one referred to in the earlier document, for Yoritomo was not appointed *utaishō* until late 1190.
  2. Koremune Tadahisa.
  3. Taira Moritoki (cf. Document 36). Appearing in half-sized characters above the Taira name is the incorrect identification "Hōjō, Tōtomi no kami, Tokimasa." This was obviously added later in error; see the note in *Sappan kyūki zatsuroku,* 1: 100.

DOCUMENTS 42-43

Sōjitō Tadahisa Confirms a Kamakura Vassal's Holdings in the 1190's; A Bakufu Order Urges Other Such Confirmations, 1192

The native *jitō* within Shimazu Estate often worked through *sōjitō* Koremune Tadahisa in seeking confirmation of their holdings. In Document 42 Tadahisa recognizes such a claim, although it is clear that he is functioning merely as an agent of the Bakufu. In the second document Kamakura clarifies the status of a new sub-*jitō* in Shimazu. Note that the actual *jitō* appointments are not made by Tadahisa himself.

42

Samejima Muneie has stated: "By virtue of a long-standing right [*nenrai menkyo*], and in view of previous [Kantō] orders [*ongechi*], I hum-

bly request a new validation [*gedai**] of Ata [District's] *myō** boundaries, orchard areas, and upland fields."

Regarding the said orchard areas and other places in Ata District and
elsewhere, the miscellaneous obligations and tributes [*manzō kuji**] are
clear from previous [Kantō] edicts [*onkudashibumi*].[1] There shall be
no change. The order is thus.

[undated]

Tadahisa (monogram)

43

Additional order:

Among the following holdings, one place[2] shall be granted to the
priest Kakuben (however, certain other lands lying within this
grant are not included).[3]

Concerning these [former] holdings of the Satsuma Province notable
Ata Shirō Nobuzumi: Taniyama District; Southern Hioki Gō in Isaku
District; Northern [Hioki] Gō; and the *myō* fields of new *goryō*.[4] At the
time of the Heike rebellion this Nobuzumi was a ringleader. In consequence, the aforesaid *shiki* were terminated. Forthwith, this *jitō shiki*
shall be held [by Kakuben]. By command [of the Kamakura lord], it is
so conveyed.

3d year of Kenkyū [1192], 10th month, 22d day

[To] Mune, hyōe no jō dono   Taira seal
                                    minbu no jō seal

SOURCES: Document 42: *Sappan kyūki zatsuroku*, undated (1190's), Shimazu Tadahisa shojō, *Sappan kyūki zatsuroku, zempen*, 1: 114–15, doc. 79 (also in *Satsuma
no kuni Ata Gun shiryō*, p. 7, doc. 7); this document is in *kana* script. Document 43:
Shimazu ke monjo, 1192/10/22 Kantō migyōsho an, *ibid.*, p. 7, doc. 5 (in *KI*, 2:
51, doc. 632).

1. I.e., the amount and character of local economic obligations apart from the
rice tax (*nengu**) have been clearly stipulated.

2. The place referred to is the *gō* of Southern Hioki. See the transcription in
the main source (*Ata Gun shiryō*) just cited. Other texts of the document (e.g. those
in *KI* and in *DNK*) do not identify the exact holding granted to Kakuben.

3. This first sentence is the "additional order"—a sort of postscript added to each
of a series of identically worded documents to identify the particular grant in question. The phrase in parentheses appears in half-size characters as a qualifying addendum. Presumably, it was necessary to exclude various holdings *within* southern
Hioki Gō that had not been confiscated.

4. A term used to refer to lands held in full proprietorship by the Bakufu. But it
could also refer to the estates of any high-ranking institution or family. See Glossary.

DOCUMENT 44

Sōjitō Tadahisa Addresses a Deputy Jitō, 1218

So vast was Shimazu Estate, with its various *shōjitō* (and at least two *sōjitō*[1]), that Tadahisa evidently appointed more than one deputy *jitō* to help out. Unlike the *shōjitō*, who were vassals of Kamakura, the deputy addressed here was a vassal of Tadahisa himself. Also noteworthy is the confirmation of land rights within an individual village.

(Tadahisa's monogram)

Concerning the *myō* headmanship [*myōzu* shiki*] of Yamada Village, in Satsuma District, an appeal for confirmation [of the post] has been made on the basis of records [*shōmon*] held by a lady of the Ōkura family. In response, and by reason of the documents presented, a validation [*gedai*] is granted authorizing the possession [of that *shiki*]. Without interference, the Ōkura family is to be settled forthwith in this village. It is so commanded.

6th year of Kempō [1218], 11th month, 26th day

[To] the deputy jitō for Satsuma[2]　　　　nakatsukasa no jō Tadayoshi,
　　　　　　　　　　　　　　　　　　　　　　secretary

SOURCE: *Shimazu ke monjo*, 1218/11/26 Shimazu Tadahisa andojō, *DNK, iewake* 16, 1: 11–12, doc. 15 (in *KI*, 4: 300, doc. 2,411).
　　1. The Chiba family of Shimōsa held a *sōjitō shiki* over lands lying within Shimazu. See the reference in *Iriki monjo*, 1250/4/28 Kantō gechijō, *KBSS*, 1: 99–100, doc. 86.
　　2. The various holdings of Shimazu Estate occupied well over half the total land area of Satsuma, Hyūga, and Ōsumi provinces. Hence the reference here is to the Satsuma sector of Shimazu Estate.

DOCUMENT 45

The Bakufu Judges a Dispute Between Sōjitō and Shōjitō, 1248

This is the longest and most revealing of all Kamakura documents dealing with *sōjitō*. The document is unique for the light it casts on relationships over a long period; and the strengths and weaknesses of *sōjitō* and *shōjitō* emerge with unusual clarity. Also noteworthy is the reference to the *sōjitō* as a Kyushu institution.

The points of a dispute [*sōron**] between *jitō sakan no suke* Yasufusa, of Kanbara [and] Jirōmaru [Myō], Kōzuma Estate, Chikugo Province, and *myōshu* Yoshida Saburō Yoshishige *hosshi*, priestly name Sokua.

Item: Concerning the Kanbara [and] Jirōmaru *myōshu shiki*.
On the occasion of a trial confrontation [*taiketsu*],[1] Yasufusa stated: "These holdings were granted to me in the 2d year of Kangen [1244]. Nevertheless, Sokua has willfully seized authority [*shomu**] without any justification. It is apparent from a long series of the *sōjitō's* private orders [*watakushi no kudashibumi*] forwarded by Sokua that the *sōjitō* is to exercise jurisdiction [*shinshi**]. Thus, although [Sokua] has petitioned for a transfer of the *shiki*,[2] jurisdiction [*shintai**] should lie henceforth with the *sōjitō* in accordance with the import of these records [*shōmon*]."

According to Sokua's statement: "The *jitō shiki* of Kanbara [and] Jirōmaru were granted in the 2d year of Bunji [1186] during the time of the *utaishō* house to my grandfather, Iehide, and my father, Ieshiki. After that, although Tōnai *minbu daibu* Tōkage[3] and *kamon no kami* Chikayoshi *hosshi*[4] were appointed as [successive] *sōjitō*, there was no change in Ieshiki's *shōjitō shiki*. In this respect Ieshiki was granted a [Kantō] chancellery order in the 8th year of Kenkyū [1197]. However, after Suruga *zenji* Suetoki *hosshi*[5] became *sōjitō*, Ieshiki petitioned Suruga *zenji* in the 3d year of Kempō [1215] on the occasion of a dispute with Ieshiki's retainer [*rōjū**] Iemura over the *myōshu shiki*. The [original] order was enforced [by Suruga], who held: 'Regarding the aforesaid, the *utaishō* house edict is clear; hence Iemura's false claim is dismissed.' Since then, in accordance with the *utaishō* edict, our possession has been unchanged; and even though it was a *sōjitō* order that was obtained, this was understood to be a private confirmation of our position."[6]

Yasufusa stated: "The *utaishō* house *shōjitō* investiture of the 8th year of Kenkyū [1197] was an earlier award [*zempan*].[7] Likewise, during the terms of Chikayoshi, Suetoki, and *inyō no kami* Tadanao *ason* as *sōjitō*, *myōshu shiki* investitures were obtained by that same *shōjitō*. Even though confirmed as such, the *shōjitō* [later] claimed to be a local lord [*jinushi**] possessing original jurisdiction and refused to have dealings with the *sōjitō*. Because of this abuse of power the *sōjitō's* [authority] became only a title, not a fact."

Sokua stated: "The investiture of Kenkyū [1197] was issued after the *sōjitō* title had been granted to Chikayoshi. [Ours] was [thus] a *shō-*

jitō investiture. Also, [following] the western-province custom [*saigoku* no narai*]⁸ it is the practice for all *shōjitō* to be placed in areas where *sōjitō* have been appointed."

According to a [Kantō] order of the 2d year of Kangen [1244], 12th month, 22d day, submitted by Yasufusa, "Yasufusa is to hold the *jitō shiki* of Kanbara and Jirōmaru."

According to a similarly submitted letter of accusation [*sojō*] by a resident of Jirōmaru Myō, Tsunemura: "Concerning the Jirōmaru *myōshu shiki*, when this Tsunemura went to the Kantō and presented full details, an order was handed down that the matter need not be judged at the top but should be settled [*seibai*] by the *sōjitō*."⁹ Although [the letter] stated thus, the evidence is not conclusive, inasmuch as Tsunemura was a foe of Sokua.

According to the *utaishō* house investiture edict of the 2d year of Bunji [1186], 5th month, 6th day, as submitted by Sokua: "Ieshiki is to hold the *jitō shiki* of Kanbara and Jirōmaru."

According to a similarly submitted [*utaishō* house] investiture of the 8th year of Kenkyū [1197], 11th month, 7th day: "Regarding the Kanbara *jitō shiki*, Ieshiki is appointed to this post."

According to a similarly submitted investiture by Chikayoshi *hosshi* of the first year of Kennin [1201], 11th month, day: "Ieshiki is to be Kanbara and Jirōmaru deputy *jitō* [*jitōdai shiki*]."¹⁰

According to a similarly submitted investiture issued by Suetoki *hosshi*, of the 3d year of Kempō [1215], 4th month, 3d day: "Concerning the Jirōmaru *myōshu shiki*, the *utaishō* house investiture and the testamentary record [*yuzurijō*] of the father [of Ieshiki], Iehide, are clear. Iemura's authority is now terminated, and this authority shall be exercised by Ieshiki in accordance with precedent." It is evident from this that the [1197] *utaishō* house edict was in effect.

According to a similarly submitted investiture [by Suetoki] of the 1st year of Jōō [1222], 7th month, day: "Concerning the Jirōmaru *myōshu shiki*, by hereditary right Yoshiyasu (the lay name of Sokua) is to hold this post."

According to a similarly submitted investiture [by Suetoki] of the 3d year of Karoku [1227], 6th month, day: "Yoshiyasu is to be Kanbara and Jirōmaru deputy *jitō*."

According to a similarly submitted investiture by Tadanao *ason* of the 2d year of Ninji [1241], 8th month: "Sokua is to be Kanbara and Jirōmaru *myōshu shiki*."

Yasufusa claims that according to these various documents the *myō-*

shu shiki are titles under the *sōjitō's* jurisdiction; also that the *utaishō* house *jitō* investitures of Bunji and Kenkyū [1186 and 1197] were superseded. However, since Ieshiki was clearly granted these decrees, there is no lack of reason in Sokua's claim that the *shōjitō* title went unchallenged for generations, despite the appointment of a *sōjitō*. Moreover, during the age of the *utaishō* house it was the practice in Chinzei [Kyushu] that persons who had been granted *jitō* investitures would have their *myōshu* titles confirmed and would be called *shōjitō* when a *sōjitō* was appointed. In these circumstances Sokua, as a *myōshu* holder, is to honor the superior authority of the *sōjitō*, and, in accordance with precedent, is to be responsible for the fixed annual tax and other services.

Item: Concerning the *sōjitō's* residence [*yashiki**] and grant lands [*kyūden**].

According to Yasufusa's statement: "It is the practice in various places for a *sōjitō* to receive an official residence and grant fields. However, in Kanbara the grant lands are only one *chō*, and there is no residence. Jirōmaru has neither a residence nor grant lands. Let the land registers be called in and examined."

According to Sokua's statement: "In the matter of the grant lands and residences, during five generations of *sōjitō* there have been no suits seeking changes [*shingi*]."

In response to Sokua's claim that this was a suit seeking changes in established practice, Yasufusa made no rejoinder. Therefore, [the matter] need not be dealt with. . . .[11]

By command of the Kamakura lord, the foregoing points are decreed as stated.

      2d year of Hōji [1248], 9th month, 13th day

                      sakon no shōgen, Taira ason[12] (monogram)
                      Sagami no kami, Taira ason[13] (monogram)

SOURCE: *Murozono monjo* 1248/9/13 Kantō gechijō, *Hennen Ōtomo shiryō*, 1: 382–86, doc. 444 (*KBSS*, 1: 84–87, doc. 81).

    1. A court trial before the Bakufu in which the two sides had to confront one another. See Glossary.

    2. I.e., Sokua had asked that the *sōjitō shiki* be granted to someone else. Interpretation confirmed by Seno Seiichirō.

    3. Amano Tōkage, the Bakufu deputy for Kyushu, 1186–95.

    4. Nakahara Chikayoshi, successor to Amano Tōkage.

    5. Nakahara Suetoki, successor to Chikayoshi.

    6. Literally, "a private confirmation asking how there could be disturbances in the future."

7. I.e., it predated the *sōjitō* investiture. Yasufusa was arguing that the later investiture nullified the *shōjitō* appointment.

8. The reference to western provinces here probably means Kyushu. See Glossary.

9. The Bakufu was refusing to intrude in a matter dealing with rear-vassals. Interestingly, the authority of the local *sōjitō* was not so precluded. Equally intriguing is the lowly Tsunemura's taking his case all the way from Kyushu to Kamakura.

10. Sōjitō Chikayoshi, in other words, was calling his *shōjitō* counterpart Ieshiki, a mere deputy *jitō*—i.e., his own vassal.

11. Half-line summaries of eight other unrelated items follow here.

12. Hōjō Tokiyori, Kamakura regent.

13. Hōjō Shigetoki, Kamakura cosigner.

DOCUMENT 46

The Bakufu Settles Another Dispute Between Sōjitō and Shōjitō, 1227

Two points emerge from this interesting document: the equal division of income between *sōjitō* and *shōjitō* (unlike that in the previous example), and the nonhereditary nature of the *sōjitō* post. Kamakura's diligence in trying to discover the truth in this case is also noteworthy.

ORDERED: to the residents of Saga Estate, Hizen Province.

That forthwith the disruptive innovations [*shingi no ranbō*] carried out in Sueyoshi Myō by *sōjitō* Hasunuma Saburō Tadakuni shall cease, and that duties be performed according to precedent. [Also] concerning Takagi Nanjirō Sueie's accusation that the *shōjitō*'s income share [*tokubun*] has been seized.

On the occasion of a trial confrontation [*taiketsu**] between Sueie's retainer Suemasu and Tadakuni, Suemasu stated: "The practice on this estate is a rent [*kajishi**] of 1 *to* [one-half bushel] per *tan* of rice land, with 5 *shō* [i.e. half] going to the *sōjitō* and 5 *shō* to the *shōjitō*. However, after Tadakuni was appointed *sōjitō*, he appropriated the whole amount, leaving us helpless. Since the time of the late *utaishō* lord, the successive *sōjitō*—Izu *minbu nyūdō*;[1] *kamon no kami nyūdō*;[2] *kami no shōji*; Hori Tōji; Amano *saemon no jō; uemon no daibu*; and Nakamura Gorō—have each taken 5 *shō*. Now, however, Tadakuni holds the post, and he has attempted to seize [the full amount]. When a complaint was lodged last year [1226], the former *sōjitō*, Amano *saemon no jō*, was questioned; and the [Da]zaifu,[3] ordered to act as magistrate, handled

interrogation of the estate's small *jitō* and *jikinin*.* Our cosigned petition [*rensho* no *mōshijō**] is presented herewith."

Tadakuni stated: "This place was granted me as a reward of merit.
Since I did not know the particulars [of the post], I inquired them of
Amano *saemon no jō*, who issued a document citing an emolument of
1 *to* for the *sōjitō*. I am exercising authority in accordance with this document. Also in the 4th month of last year a [Kantō] edict [*ongechijō*]
was granted [confirming] the 1 *to* per *tan*."

Since Tadakuni, in his defense, has claimed to exercise authority in
accordance with former *sōjitō* Masakage's document, Masakage has
been summoned and questioned.[4] According to his deposition [*ukebumi**]: "I have no knowledge concerning the said emolument. A decision might best be rendered in accordance with the practices of other
shōjitō [*jiyo no shōjitō*] within this estate."[5] Given this statement, it is
difficult for Tadakuni to use Masakage's document as a standard. Not
only that, but according to the record of 2d Karoku [1226], cosigned
by the *shōjitō* and *jikinin* and presented by Suemasu, it is recorded that
the *sōjitō*'s share be 5 *shō* and the *shōjitō*'s share 5 *shō*, out of a rent levy
[*kajishi*] of 1 *to* per *tan*. Also, according to the yearly rent receipts
[*san'yōjō**] of the *sōjitō*, similarly presented, the original tax-producing
fields [of the estate were listed] at 5 *shō* per *tan*, and newly opened
fields at 2 *shō*, 5 *gō* [i.e. 2.5 *shō*] per *tan*. In view of this, the disruptive
innovations [*shingi no samatage*] of Tadakuni are forbidden; and following precedent, [*jitō*] duties are to be discharged without interruption. By command of the Kamakura lord, it is so decreed.

3d year of Karoku [1227], 3d month, 19th day

> Musashi no kami seal
> Sagami no kami seal

SOURCE: *Ryūzōji monjo*, 1227/3/19 Kantō gechijō an, *Saga ken shiryō shūsei*, 3:
7–8 (*KBSS*, 1: 34–35, doc. 42).

1. Amano Tōkage, first Bakufu deputy to Kyushu, ca. 1186–95.
2. Nakahara Chikayoshi, a court noble who supported Yoritomo; closely linked
to Kyushu affairs on behalf of the Bakufu after 1195.
3. Imperial headquarters in Kyushu; under total Bakufu control by the 1220's.
4. Masakage is the Amano *saemon no jō* referred to earlier.
5. Saga Estate had multiple *shōjitō*, one for each *myō*. See *Ryūzōji monjo*,
1226/2 Saga goryō nai shōjitō tō mōshijō, *Saga ken shiryō shūsei*, 3: 3–6 (also in
Dazaifu-Dazaifu Tenmangū shiryō, 7: 393–97).

THE LIMITS OF KAMAKURA'S JURISDICTION

DOCUMENT 47

A Central Proprietor Warns Local Outlaws of Impending Kamakura Sanctions, 1191

During the turbulent 1180's the emerging Bakufu was eager to accept new responsibilities for peacekeeping around the country. It was soon recognized, however, that the burden was far more than Kamakura could handle on its own; landowners at court were giving the widest interpretation to this commitment, and in the process exhausting Kamakura's patience and resources. In this unsigned document, a proprietor warns that continued local disturbances, even by men who were not *jitō* or Bakufu-related, would nevertheless be dealt with in future by Kamakura.

[ORDERED: to] Moriie of Tōishi Branch Shrine, Suō Province, a holding [*ryō*] of [Iwashimizu] Hachiman Shrine.

The aforesaid Moriie, since taking the title of *jitō*, has seized all the proprietor's and estate custodian's revenues [*ryōke azukari dokoro no tokubun*]. Moreover, during the time of his father Morisada, Tokuzen and Suetake Ho, which were not held [by the branch shrine], were also [the objects of] unprecedented seizure attempts. Also, when shrine retainer Tomo-[1] . . . was wounded, a Kamakura lord's edict was conveyed to the proprietor [*ryōke*][2] through the retired emperor, and an ex-emperor's decree [*inzen**] was issued ordering an end to these [violations][3] and the banishment [of the miscreant].

Inasmuch as such lawlessness still continues, the proprietor has [again] appealed, citing the disruption of shrine affairs. If this is true, it is deplorable. In accordance with precedent, Moriie is not to interfere with the proprietor's or custodian's income. Henceforth his negligence is to cease. Should he still not comply, the Kamakura lord will be informed and steps taken to impose a punishment. This should be clearly understood. By command of the [shrine] administrator [*bettō**], it is so decreed.

2d year of Kenkyū [1191], 2d month, 10th day

SOURCE: *Iwashimizu monjo*, 1191/2/10 Iwashimizu Hachimangūji bettō gechijō an, *DNK, iewake* 4 (Iwashimizu monjo), 1: 350, doc. 159 (in *KI*, 1: 386, doc. 508).
1. The second half of this name is missing.
2. Tōishi Branch Shrine. Iwashimizu was evidently patron (*honke*).
3. Character lost due to paper deterioration. Such lacunae are very common.

DOCUMENT 48

The Bakufu Accepts Jurisdiction Over a Non-Jitō Case, But Refuses to Do So in the Future, 1205

By the mid-1190's Kamakura had determined to limit its jurisdiction to the actions of *shugo* and *jitō*. All other judicial matters would be referred back to Kyoto. A desire to restore traditional hierarchies as a step toward peace was the chief motive for this decision. In this selection Kamakura warns that all future trouble involving a certain estate will be handled by the court.

ORDERED: to the officers of Kogawa Temple, Kii Province.
That in accordance with directives of the retired emperors Toba and Go-Shirakawa,[1] generations of proprietor's covenants and orders originating with the Tokudaiji left minister's house,[2] and finally a judicial decision [*goseibai*] of the late *utaishō* house, the depredations of various local persons [*kō-otsu no tomogara**] are to cease forthwith. In accordance with precedent, Kurusu Estate of this province, a temple land, shall be under the jurisdiction [*shinshi*] of the temple.

According to the petition by temple authorities regarding the aforesaid: "Service levies were imposed on the temple during the age of Hōen [1135–41], when the Tokudaiji left minister's house held provincial authority [*kokumu**] over the estate.[3] When divine retribution occurred as a result, [Kurusu] was granted a tax-exempt status.[4] In that circumstance, repeated directives were issued by the retired emperors.[5] Later, on an occasion when no official custodian was in office and the temple itself was administering affairs, the priest Jikkaku stole some written records [*shōmon*] of Kurusu and after fleeing with them made donations here and there.[6] When this occurred, an appeal was made to the late *utaishō* house, and the misdeeds were brought to a halt. However, in recent days numerous lawless persons unmindful of these precedents have appeared. We therefore request a [Kantō] order that will provide us with written proof."[7]

Details can be found in the documents [that have been submitted]. In accordance with two generations of retired emperors' directives, as well as several generations of proprietor's covenants, and by virtue of a judicial decision of the late *utaishō* house, the unprecedented acts of these various local persons are to cease, and the temple is to have ownership [*ryōchi**] of this estate, as before. Any additional details should be directed to the court, and a judgment [*saikyo*] will be reached [there].[8] By command of the Kamakura lord, it is so decreed.

2d year of Genkyū [1205], 5th month, 27th day

Tōtomi no kami, Taira seal

SOURCE: *Kōyasan Ikenobō monjo*, 1205/5/27 Kantō gechijō an, *Kōyasan monjo, kyū kōya ryōnai monjo* 1, 9: 93–95, doc. 49 (in *KI*, 3: 239–40, doc. 1,548).

1. Successive retired emperors, 1129–92.

2. Fujiwara Saneyoshi, a ranking member of ex-emperor Toba's entourage.

3. I.e., when the estate was still in the "public" sector. For a reference to Kurusu Estate's status as a *ho* (unit of public governance) before the Hōen period, see *Kōyasan Ikenobō monjo*, 1298/8/10 Kantō gechijō, *KBSS*, 1: 281, doc. 216.

4. It was commended to Kogawa Temple by Fujiwara Saneyoshi's son, Kin'yoshi, in 1138: *Kokokuji monjo*, 1138/3/25 sa kon'oe gon no chūjō Fujiwara Kin'yoshi kishinjō, *HI*, 5: 2016, doc. 2,384.

5. See, e.g., 1146/4/29 Toba In-no-chō kudashibumi an, *HI*, 6: 2176, doc. 2,575.

6. Meaning unclear. Jikkaku was obviously using the stolen documents to mount a challenge to Kogawa's proprietorship, but exactly how he proceeded with this effort remains uncertain.

7. I.e., a new Bakufu decree regarding the inviolability of Kurusu Estate.

8. This interpretation is confirmed by Seno Seiichirō.

DOCUMENT 49

The Bakufu Accepts a Non-Jitō Suit in the Troubled Years After Jōkyū, 1225

In this selection Kamakura accepts a suit refused twelve years earlier, but gives the actual proprietor authority in the matter.

The agent for Usa Shrine, Ujiyasu, has lodged a complaint concerning control of the pottery trade and the paddy and uplands in Takamura Myō. About the 3d year of Kenryaku [1213], when this matter first came up, it was decided that there would be no adjudication [*seibai*], since no *jitō* or *goke'nin* matter was involved. Nevertheless, Ujitada, Ujiyasu's elder brother, lodged a complaint, citing as a reference [Kamakura's] special agent [*otsukai* no zōshiki*] Munesato.¹ When a document of inquiry [*toijō**] was sent [to Ujiyasu] during this past 5th month, [the latter] stated that [Ujitada] had seized those rights unjustifiably, using this document.² This is most unseemly. Henceforth, in accordance with the shrine-patron's orders [*honke shake no gechi*],³ authority is to be held [by Ujiyasu]. In pursuance of this command, it is decreed thus.

1st year of Karoku [1225], 11th month, 23d day

Musashi no kami, Taira (monogram)
Sagami no kami, Taira (monogram)

SOURCE: *Takamure monjo*, 1225/11/23 Kantō gechijō, *Ōita ken shiryō*, 1: 227, doc. 235 (in *KI*, 5: 378, doc. 3,432).

1. Just what the connection was between Ujitada and Munesato is not explained.
2. In other words, Ujitada had used the inquiry from Kamakura as "proof" of the correctness of his suit.
3. Usa Shrine was *honke*, or "patron," of the affected estate.

DOCUMENT 50

Kamakura Accepts a Non-Jitō Suit Appealed by a Temple Under the Bakufu's Special Patronage, 1255

The Bakufu's protection of certain shrines and temples exceeded its normal jurisdictional limits. In a number of provinces shogunal "prayer centers" were designated for favored treatment. The Kinzanji of Bizen Province was one such temple.

Regarding the complaint by priests of Kinzan Kannon Temple, Bizen Province, that Mino Gorō *saemon no jō* Sukenobu has been calling himself local lord [*jinushi*] over the homelands of this temple, and has been aggrandizing his power.

According to the temple's appeal [*ge*] concerning this matter: "This temple was designated as a Kantō prayer center [*Kantō onkitōsho*]. According to a Kantō order of the 2d year of Kempō [1214], 9th month, 26th day:¹ 'Intrusion on this mountain by various persons for the purposes of hunting or cutting timber is a great crime. Under the *jitō's* authority a prohibition shall be laid down, and the priests made secure. In the event there are still violators, the *shugo* shall be informed and a list of names forwarded.' According to a similar order of the 3d year of Jōō [1224], 2d month, 3d day: 'This temple was designated a shogunal-house prayer center. A generation [*nenjō**] has passed since trespassing, hunting, and despoilments by warriors [*bushi*] and others [*kō-otsu no tomogara*] were prohibited. Nevertheless, persons committing these crimes have reportedly appeared. If this is true, it is most irregular. In accordance with earlier judgments, these depredations are to cease. If there continue to be violations of this prohibition, a list of names shall immediately be reported.'[2] Notwithstanding, Sukenobu, calling himself *jinushi*, has unlawfully entered temple precincts, forcibly extorted tributes and income shares, invaded the priests' quarters, commandeered private property, and seized many cows, horses, and other goods. In consequence, seven summonses were issued, but he still has not appeared. Regarding these losses, even if full restitution is made, we still desire that punishment be imposed for violating a [Kantō] order, and that future outrages be prohibited."

. . .

[Sukenobu's] claim to *jinushi* status over Ōharai,[3] a holding of the temple, is abolished, and his intrusions and plundering shall cease. It is so commanded.

7th year of Kenchō [1255], 5th month, 21st day

sakon no shōgen, Taira[4] (monogram)

SOURCE: *Kinzanji monjo*, 1255/5/21 Rokuhara gechijō, *Okayama ken komonjo shū*, 2: 10–11, doc. 16 (in *KBSS*, 2: 24–25, doc. 11).

1. The reference is to Document 87 below. Obviously, the present rendering is merely a Bakufu summary of that earlier edict.

2. The original of this document was dated the 2d year of Jōō (1223), not the 3d year as stated here. The contents are verbatim. *Kinzanji monjo*, *KI*, 5: 149, doc. 3,049.

3. Not further identified.

4. Hōjō Nagatoki.

DOCUMENT 51

The Bakufu Issues a Directive Concerning Aid to a Famous Shrine, 1298

Kamakura's support of great temples and shrines often took the form of urging responsible local authorities to perform services on their behalf—in this case

a construction project for Kitsuki Shrine in Izumo. Note that the proper chan-
nels are not being violated.

Regarding the construction¹ of Kitsuki Grand Shrine, there have been
repeated complaints to the court that the provincial office [*kokuga**]
has not discharged this responsibility for many years. Lord Saionji²
should be informed that a [Bakufu] order [*ongechi*] will be issued,
to the effect that this meritorious deed be carried out promptly. It is
conveyed herewith.

     6th year of Einin [1298], 5th month, 25th day

[To] Kōzuke zenji dono³   Mutsu no kami⁴ (monogram)
Sagami ukon no daibu, shōgen dono⁵   Sagami no kami⁶ (monogram)

SOURCE: *Kitajima monjo*, 1298/5/25 Kantō migyōsho, *Izumo Kokuzō ke monjo*,
doc. 28, p. 78.
    1. I.e., reconstruction.
    2. Saionji Sanekane, a friend of the Bakufu at court.
    3. Hōjō Munenori.
    4. Hōjō Noritoki, Kamakura cosigner.
    5. Hōjō Munekata. Munenori and Munekata were the Bakufu's two deputies in
Kyoto (*Rokuhara tandai**).
    6. Hōjō Sadatoki, Kamakura regent.

DOCUMENT 52

The Bakufu Refuses Jurisdiction, 1252

The Bakufu here refuses to involve itself in an internal affair of the Iwashimizu Shrine. The court was advised to dispose of a case in which Kamakura
had no interest.

Your petition [*mōshijō**] concerning the *bettō shiki*¹ has been considered. Since such matters are the concern of Kyoto [Kyoto *no onhakarai*],
there can be no [Bakufu] intercession [*gokunyū**]. Matters such as this
are surely to be judged equitably. It is so conveyed.

     4th year of Kenchō [1252],² 12th month, 12th day

[To] Hachiman gon no bettō,   Sagami no kami (monogram)
    hōin gobō   Mutsu no kami (monogram)

answered respectfully³

SOURCE: *Iwashimizu monjo*, 1252/12/12 Kantō migyōsho, *DNK*, *iewake* 4 (Iwashimizu monjo), 6: 73–74, doc. 51.
    1. A chief administrator's office.
    2. In half-sized characters; probably added later.

3. The Bakufu was replying to an appeal lodged by the acting chief (*gon no betto*) of the shrine. For an almost identical refusal to a temple in Kyushu, see *Maeda ke shozo monjo*, 1253/3/25 Kanto migyosho, *KI*, 10: 350, doc. 7,530.

DOCUMENT 53

A Proprietor Orders the Cessation of a Local Warrior's Depredations, 1204

In the thirteenth century, with increasing regularity, estate holders began to reassert their traditional jurisdictions over *shoen*. The present document, using Bakufu-type language, seeks to end disturbances by a local outlaw. Whether such efforts were effective remains uncertain. The climate of 1204 was much different from that before 1180.

The Kangaku-in chancellery orders: to Uno Estate, Yamato Province.
    That forthwith the depredations of the accused, Shigeharu, shall cease.

Regarding the aforesaid, an edict from the retired emperor's chancellery was issued during the 8th month, stating that the distress caused to estate notables by Shigeharu's constant accusations was to cease. He has still not complied, however, and his lawlessness is most unseemly.[1] By decree of the head abbot, it is hereby ordered that the said Shigeharu's lawlessness shall cease forthwith. Do not be remiss. Wherefore, this order.
    1st year of Genkyu [1204], 11th month, 8th day

betto, sachuben, Fujiwara ason seal   chiinji, sa shisho, Takahashi seal
                                           daizen no shoshin, Fujiwara seal
                                           onshi, Fujiwara

SOURCE: *Kasuga Jinja monjo*, 1204/11/8 Kangaku-in mandokoro kudashibumi an, *Kasuga Jinja monjo*, 1: 351–52, doc. 306 (in *KI*, 3: 216–17, doc. 1,506).
    1. Presumably, Shigeharu's complaints were accompanied by other acts.

DOCUMENTS 54-55

Governors Issue Orders Against the Outrages of Provincial Officers, 1203

The authority of provincial governors was also restored, with the same uncertain effectiveness. In our first example the governor of Iyo, acting on behalf of the imperial house, orders his nominal subordinates in the Iyo provincial office to cease violating an estate's boundaries. This particular effort may well have ended in failure, since the Iyo headquarters was dominated at this time by the powerful Kamakura vassal house of Kōno. Even the Bakufu could not readily control this family.[1] In our second example the governor of Sanuki attempts to end provincial officers' interference with a local temple.

54

Governor's edict: to the absentee provincial office.

That intrusion by agents and the ill treatment of Yuge[shima] Estate shall cease forthwith.

Petition from the estate appended herewith.[2]

The aforesaid estate has for many years been a holding of Senyōmon-in.[3] An edict from Go-Shirakawa's house chancellery and a former governor's exemption writ make this clear. Nevertheless, a complaint has arisen that provincial agents have trespassed and plundered. This is deplorable. Forthwith, in accordance with precedent, provincial headquarter agents [kokuga no tsukai] are to cease [such intrusions]. It is decreed thus. Wherefore, this edict.

　　　3d year of Kennin [1203], 4th month,　day

ōsuke, Fujiwara ason (monogram)[4]

55

Governor's edict: to the absentee provincial office.

That Zentsū-Mandara Temple shall, as of old, be a branch [matsuji*] of Tōji Temple.

The aforesaid temple has reportedly passed many years as a branch of the Tōji. Nevertheless, there is now a complaint of repeated violations committed by the provincial headquarters [kokuga].[5] In accordance with past practice, [this temple], as a branch of the Tōji, shall be immune from violations by the provincial headquarters. It is so decreed. The absentee provincial office shall take note and act accordingly. Wherefore, this edict.

　　　3d year of Kennin [1203], 6th month, 20th day

ōsuke

SOURCES: Document 54: Tōji monjo, 1203/4 Iyo kokushi chōsen an, Nihon engyō taikei, shiryō hen, kodai-chūsei, 1: 83, doc. 20 (in KI, 3: 90, doc. 1,357). Document 55: ibid., 1203/6/20 Sanuki kokushi chōsen an, KI, 3: 93, doc. 1,363.

　　1. See Document 172.

　　2. See Tōji hyakugō monjo, 1203/4/7 Yugeshima-no-shō satanin hyakushō tō ge, Nihon engyō taikei, 1: 82–83, doc. 19 (in KI, 3: 88–89, doc. 1,352).

　　3. A daughter of ex-emperor Go-Shirakawa and a person of great influence at

court. Her estates were considered part of the larger portfolio of the imperial house. A register of Senyōmon-in holdings is extant, though it is undated: *Shimada monjo*, Senyōmon-in shoryō mokuroku, *Nihon engyō taikei*, 1: 83–87, doc. 21.

4. The version in *Nihon engyō taikei* cited above is the original of this document; hence the monogram. The *KI* version is a copy (*an*) and contains only the word *ōsuke* (see Glossary); the remaining part of the signature is omitted.

5. I.e., the immunity accruing to the local temple as a branch of the Tōji had been violated.

DOCUMENT 56

A Temple Proprietor and Local Residents Formally Agree to Cooperate, 1203

An interesting product of the post-Gempei years was the more explicit alliance of absentee and local interests to protect their mutual holding, the *shōen*. Though it is not apparent in the present document, such efforts were often directed against *jitō*.

Agreement cosigned [*renshojō*] by the peasants [*hyakushō tō*] of Yokawakami Estate.[1]

Regarding the foregoing, the intent is that no one shall be faithless to Hōkōji Temple. In the event of unforeseen difficulties, whether involving mountains, plains, or "lamp oil" paddy and uplands, estate officers and temple priests, acting as one, will direct their laments to the court. The agreement is thus.

3d year of Kennin [1203], 8th month, 5th day

For the temple: For the estate:
Priest Ryōzen (monogram)   Takamuko Yukitoshi (monogram)
Priest Sōken (monogram)   Hayashi Morishige (monogram)

SOURCE: *Hōkōji monjo*, 1203/8/5 Yokawakami-no-shō hyakushō tō keijō, *KI*, 3: 100, doc. 1,373.
   1. In Harima Province.

DOCUMENT 57

Local and Central Interests Engage in a Traditional Shiki Exchange, 1186

A clear indication that court guarantees of land rights had never been entirely abandoned emerges from this contract of 1186. As described here, this is precisely the way exchanges of local income for central legitimacy had been taking place for centuries. The creation of new *shōen*, a usual product of such transactions, did not cease with the emergence of the Kamakura Bakufu.

The chancellery of Hachijō-in¹ orders: to Yoshii Estate, in Ōuchi Gō, Tango Province.

That the lady Ben-no-tsubone shall be custodian [*azukari dokoro*].

The aforesaid estate, as the hereditary private land [*shiryō*] of Ben-no-tsubone, has had its guarantor's title [*honke shiki*] commended to Hachijō-in as a safeguard against difficulties [*rōrō*] in the future. Except for payment of the fixed annual tax, the authority of the custodian shall not change. Should problems be caused by some [outside?] claim of historic rights [*yuisho*], the effect of this commendation will be ended.² In pursuance of the petition,³ it is hereby ordered that the [custodial authority] be hereditary with [Ben-no-tsubone's] descendants. Estate personnel shall take note, and shall not be remiss. Wherefore, this order.

2d year of Bunji [1186], 10th month, 16th day

bettō, jū-sammi, Fujiwara ason seal   sakandai, san-i, Ōe ason seal
kura no kami, Fujiwara ason seal

SOURCE: *Tōji hyakugō monjo*, 1186/10/16 Hachijō-in-no-chō kudashibumi, *KI*, 1: 112–13, doc. 185.

1. A daughter of ex-emperor Toba who became the guarantor (*honke*) of many estates.

2. Interpretation of this sentence remains speculative. The implication seems to be that outside claims will upset the division of interests between *azukari dokoro* and *honke*, but other readings are possible.

3. I.e., the petition accompanying the commendation.

DOCUMENTS 58-61

An Estate Experiences Twenty Years of Recovery After the War Period, 1186, 1195, 1199, 1205

Shōen that had been badly ravaged during the middle 1180's often regained their stability. Nukata Estate in Kaga Province seems to be a case in point. In 1186 the Bakufu saw fit to issue an order against various incursions there, but nine years later the proprietor had apparently regained control. In 1205, the central holder was given total jurisdiction when the Bakufu announced a *jitō*-free estate. In effect, the pre-1180 hierarchy was restored.

58

Kamakura utaishō[1]
seal

ORDERED: to the residents of Nukata Estate, Kaga Province. That forthwith Itazu *no suke* Narikage and Sōshin *hosshi* shall cease their incursions upon Hatta and Nukata Gō, holdings of this estate; that Heita Sanetoshi, deputy [*daikan*] of the attendant [*toneri**] Tomomune, shall also cease his trespassing; that Katōji Narimitsu shall cease committing misdeeds on the pretext of being a *jitō*; and that the proprietor shall exercise overall authority [*shinshi*].

Regarding the foregoing, Hatta and Nukata Gō are later additions [*kanō**] to this estate. Even so, Narikage and Sōshin *hosshi* have disobeyed both chancellery orders of the retired emperor and decrees of the governor, and have encroached [on these lands]. Such violations of the imperial will cannot escape severe punishment. Furthermore, Tomomune's deputy, Sanetoshi, has removed markers and violated the southern boundaries of the estate's holdings. And although Tomomune has promised to desist, Sanetoshi still does not comply. The commission of such acts is intolerable. It is also reported that Katōji Narimitsu is guilty of fraudulently claiming the title of *jitō*. The deeds of all these persons are deplorable. Henceforth, the malicious scheming of these people shall cease, and the estate's proprietor shall have final authority [*shintai ryō-shō**].[2] It is commanded thus. Wherefore, this order.

2d year of Bunji [1186], 9th month, 5th day

59

The chancellery of the *go-in*[3] orders: to the officials of Nukata Estate, Kaga Province.

That forthwith *gyōbu no kyō* Tenji shall be custodian [*azukari dokoro*].

Regarding the foregoing, the said Tenji, as custodian, shall oversee collection and forwarding of the annual tax. The command is thus. Estate officers shall take note and obey this decision. Wherefore, this order.

6th year of Kenkyū [1195], 5th month, 27th day

bettō, sakyō no daibu,   azukari, saemon no shōjō,
   Fujiwara ason   Nakahara seal
udaiben ken chūgū no suke, Echizen gon no kami, Fujiwara ason seal
kura no kami ken Harima no kami, Takashina ason seal
udaiben ken monjō hakase, Noto gon no kami, Fujiwara ason
sachūben, Fujiwara ason

60

The chancellery of the retired emperor orders: to the officials of Nukata Estate, Kaga Province.

That in accordance with the last testament of *jū-sammi* Noriko, the Inaba governor Minamoto Michikata shall control [*chigyō*] estate affairs.[4]

In accordance with this testament, the aforesaid estate shall be the hereditary possession [*sōden ryōshō*] of Michikata. If in future there should be any challengers [of this right], they shall be treated as flouters of the imperial will. The order is thus. Estate officers shall take note, and shall not be remiss. Wherefore, this order.

    1st year of Shōji [1199], 12th month,   day

bettō, naidaijin ken ukon'oe taishō, Minamoto ason[5]
gon dainagon ken minbu no kyō, Fujiwara ason seal
gon dainagon, Minamoto ason
chūnagon, Fujiwara ason
chūnagon ken kōgōgū no daibu, Fujiwara ason seal
21 persons omitted

61

ORDERED: to the officials of Nukata Estate, Kaga Province.

    That forthwith the *jitō shiki* shall be abolished.

Regarding the aforesaid, a complaint has been lodged that a deputy *jitō*, upon various pretexts, has made false charges against local officials and peasants, has seized a portion of the annual tax, and has neglected tribute obligations [*kuji**]. Moreover, it is reported that no *jitō* has been appointed here in recent years. Hence it is ordered that the *jitō shiki* be abolished.[6] Wherefore, this decree.

    2d year of Genkyū [1205], 5th month, 28th day

                Kiyohara seal
                saki no ukyōshin, Nakahara seal
                saemon no jō, Taira seal
                saki no daizen no daibu,
                    Nakahara ason seal

SOURCES: Document 58: *Hiramatsu monjo*, 1186/9/5 Minamoto Yoritomo kudashi-bumi an, *Kano komonjo*, p. 36, doc. 53 (also in *KI*, 1: 107, doc. 171). Document 59 also from *Hiramatsu monjo*, 1195/5/27 goin-no-chō kudashibumi an, in *Kano komonjo*, p. 37, doc. 55 (*KI*, 2: 142, doc. 790). Document 60: *Hiramatsu monjo*, 1199/12 Go-Toba In-no-chō kudashibumi an, *Kano komonjo*, pp. 38–39, doc. 59 (*KI*, 2: 369, doc. 1,095). Document 61: *Nakanoin ke monjo*, 1205/5/28 shōgun ke

mandokoro kudashibumi an, in *Kano komonjo*, p. 40, doc. 62 (*KI*, 3: 240, doc. 1,549).
    1. In half-sized characters; obviously added later.
    2. The terms *shinshi* and *shintai ryōshō* are equivalent in this document.
    3. A retirement palace established by a ruling emperor (see Glossary). Go-Toba had not yet "retired" at this time.
    4. It is possible that Michikata was being invested with the custodianship held several years earlier by *gyōbu no kyō* Tenji. However, this is not made explicit.
    5. Minamoto Michichika, the most influential power in Kyoto at this time.
    6. Interpretation here is difficult. Perhaps a *jitō* had once been appointed but never reconfirmed. Clearly, though, a deputy of some sort was still present. At all events, the Bakufu was now granting the estate permanent exemption from a *jitō shiki*. This would also have voided any deputy's claim to special status.

DOCUMENT 62

An Estate Custodian Appoints a Local Manager, 1258

Although our documents have so far implied a situation of universal chaos, a great many Kamakura *shōen* in fact suffered no apparent dislocations by *jitō* or any other military types. The holdings of the Katsuragawa Myōō-in Temple seem to be a case in point. Here the hierarchy of proprietor, custodian, manager, and peasant cultivator remained essentially viable.

ORDERED: to Katsuragawa.
    Concerning reappointment to the *kumon shiki*:
    Fujii Morizumi.

The aforesaid person, as rightful heir, is reappointed to the *kumon* shiki*. Regular and emergency [tribute] levies are to be faithfully discharged [by him]. He shall likewise receive title to the rice fields of Nukui Myō. Residents shall take note, and shall not be remiss. Wherefore, this order.

2d year of Shōka [1258], 12th month, 19th day

azukari dokoro, ajari dai hosshi (monogram)

SOURCE: *Katsuragawa Myōō-in monjo*, 1258/12/19 azukari dokoro kudashibumi, *Katsuragawa Myōō-in shiryō*, p. 846.

THE GESU SHIKI AND
COURT-BAKUFU RELATIONS

DOCUMENT 63

A Traditional Estate Custodian Assigns a Gesu Shiki, 1179

The managerial post of *gesu* assumed a special importance in Kyoto-Kamakura relations. Since a *gesu* was normally the equivalent of a *jitō* in both income and authority, the post came to be viewed as subject to a landowner's control, just as *jitō* were controlled by the Bakufu. In effect, the *jitō/gesu* separation became a kind of jurisdictional boundary between Kyoto and Kamakura. Before the Bakufu's founding, and again after the turbulent 1180's, *gesu* were appointed and controlled directly by estate holders. The present document is a typical pre-Kamakura *gesu* investiture.

ORDERED: to Tamai Estate.
That forthwith Ki Sukekane shall hold the *gesu shiki*.

Regarding the aforesaid, Sukekane, as *gesu*, is to manage estate affairs, and is not to neglect the fixed dues owed to the patron [*honke*] and the custodian [*azukari dokoro*].[1] It is so commanded.

3d year of Jishō [1179], 11th month,   day

seal

SOURCE: *Kano Kōkichi shi shūshū monjo*, 1179/11 Yamashiro no kuni Tamai-no-shō azukari dokoro kudashibumi an, *HI*, 8: 2,986, doc. 3,894.
1. The lack of any reference to a "proprietor" [*ryōke*] may mean that a cus-

todian had all but assumed that authority. He might simply have been of insufficient court rank to receive investiture as a *ryōke* legally.

DOCUMENT 64

Yoritomo Confirms a Gesu Shiki, 1186

During the middle 1180's much of the old central administrative apparatus ceased to be effective, and warriors simply took matters into their own hands. One result was that Yoritomo often became concerned with *shōen* where he held no lawful jurisdiction.

seal[1]

ORDERED: to the residents of Yano-no-befu,[2] Harima Province.

That forthwith Ebina Shirō Yoshisue's despoilments are to cease, and management [*shinshi*] is to lie with the *gesu*.

The aforesaid place is a Kankikō-in land. However, a recent edict of the retired emperor states that Yoshisue, without any clear historical claim, has committed outrages and has failed to obey the authority [*shintai*] of the temple. It is hereby ordered that these violations shall cease immediately; and that the annual taxation shall be conducted under authority of the *gesu* Morishige. Let no one be remiss. Wherefore, this order.

2d year of Bunji [1186], 6th month, [25th?] day

SOURCE: *Ebina monjo*, 1186/6 Minamoto Yoritomo kudashibumi, *KI*, 1: 81–82, doc. 118. See also *AK*, 1186/6/25.
  1. Minamoto Yoritomo.
  2. Land added to an estate—in this case Yano-no-shō—after incorporation.

DOCUMENTS 65-66

The Bakufu and an Estate Custodian Make Appointments to a Gesu Shiki, 1193, 1201

It was normal practice for the Bakufu to replace the *gesu* of confiscated lands with *jitō*, or sometimes to change a vassal's office from *gesu* to *jitō*. In both instances, the perquisites and responsibilities of a *shiki* would not change, only the ultimate legitimizing authority. During the Bakufu's early years, however, occasional references can be found to Yoritomo's appointment or confirmation of *gesu shiki*. Document 65, the most explicit example of this type, suggests that the *jitō/gesu* separation had not become fully established as yet. Document 66 reveals an estate evidently free of Bakufu influence.

65

The chancellery of the shogun's house orders: to the residents of Yasuda Ho, Suō Province.
 Concerning appointment of a *gesu shiki*:
 Fujiwara Tamesuke.

The aforesaid person is appointed to this *shiki*. It is commanded thus. Residents shall take note, and shall not be remiss. Wherefore, this order.
 4th year of Kenkyū [1193], 4th month, 16th day

ryō, ōkura no jō, Fujiwara (monogram)   anzu, Kiyohara (monogram)
bettō, saki no Inaba no kami,   chikeji, Nakahara (monogram)
     Nakahara ason (monogram)
san-i, Fujiwara ason (monogram)

66

ORDERED: to the residents of Yoshinari [and] Kitajima [Gō], Kayajima Estate.
 Fujiwara Yoshimura.

The aforesaid person was previously appointed to the *gesu shiki* of the western [part of this] estate. Now it is again ordered, herewith, that the two gō of Yoshinari and Kitajima be added to this appointment. Estate officers shall take note, and shall not be remiss. Wherefore, this order.
 1st year of Kennin [1201], 4th month, 10th day

azukari dokoro, hokkyō seal
 Two agents:[1]
 zōshiki, Sadakuni
 Chūkei hosshi

SOURCES: Document 65: *Mōri ke monjo*, 1193/4/16 shōgun ke mandokoro kudashibumi, *DNK*, *iewake* 8, 1: 1, doc. 1 (in *KI*, 2: 73, doc. 668). Document 66: *Katsurabara monjo*, 1201/4/10 azukari dokoro kudashibumi an, *KI*, 3: 8, doc. 1,193.
 1. I.e., the investiture was conveyed by these two agents. Written in half-size characters.

DOCUMENT 67

An Estate Custodian Issues an Order in a Matter Involving a Gesu, 1206

By the first decade of the thirteenth century *gesu*-related lawsuits (and lawlessness) were once again being handled through traditional estate machinery.

In contrast to the Bakufu's intercession in Document 64, the matter presented here was resolved by a proprietor and his deputy.

ORDERED: to the shrine attendants at Hirahama Branch Shrine.
That priest-administrator [sōkengyō*] Takayoshi shall forthwith be confirmed as of old.

In response to an accusation by gesu Hidenobu, it was ordered that Takayoshi accompany a special agent to the capital so that the details might be investigated. Unauthorized foraging in myō fields under pretext of their being [part of] Yawata Estate, as well as the expulsion [of residents] from the estate itself, are crimes without parallel. Forthwith, [those expelled] shall be restored to their homes, the harvest shall be gathered in accordance with precedent, and divine obligations shall be performed as before. [Takayoshi] must come to the capital to report particulars.[1] It is so commanded.[2]

    1st year of Ken'ei [1206], 8th month,   day

                azukari dokoro (monogram)

SOURCE: Aoki Motoi shi monjo, 1206/8 azukari dokoro kudashibumi, Shinshū shimane kenshi, shiryō hen, 1, p. 374, (KI, 3: 286, doc. 1,633).
    1. Obviously, the confirmation of Takayoshi's position in the first part of the document is not followed through. Perhaps, as Professor Seno suggests, the confirmation was being given in the form of an admonition to return to the status quo ante.
    2. A reference to this document in my Warrior Government, p. 139, l. 6, is incorrect. The corrected sentence should read: "A certain local officer was accused of depredations by the gesu, and ordered to come to the capital."

DOCUMENT 68

The Bakufu Hears a Gesu's Suit, 1225

As mentioned earlier, the immediate post-Jōkyū years saw the Bakufu involving itself in matters it normally would have avoided (cf. Document 49). In the present selection, Kamakura resolves a dispute in which the main principals are gesu and kumon on one side, and an azukari dokoro on the other. The Bakufu, of course, held jurisdiction over none of these, and the document specifically names the proprietor as the ultimate authority.[1]

Concerning a dispute between the custodian hokkyō Shōsen of Tarumi Estate, Settsu Province, and the gesu Fujiwara Ieyuki and kumon Fujii Shigetsuna, over this estate's annual tax.

According to a *monchūjo*[2] report of the 1st year of Gennin [1224], 11th month: "Although the points made by both sides are many, in essence Shōsen has stated: 'This domain is a revolving estate [*watari no shō*] subject to changes [in who administers] Tōji services. Although the *gesu* and *kumon* hold hereditary rights by virtue of confirmatory edicts granted by the estate headquarters [*honjo*],[3] their failure to heed the custodian's orders and their willful sequestering of the annual tax are most unreasonable.' Ieyuki rejoined: 'There is no dispute regarding status as a revolving estate. Therefore, although [responsibility] for temple services may shift, the *gesu* and *kumon*, as *shiki* over many generations, have become hereditary. The edicts that have been granted by the estate headquarters are [merely] designed to illustrate this fact and to forestall any changes [*shingi*] in the future. Since long ago, the forwarding of the annual tax and other tributes has been the responsibility of the *gesu* and *kumon*; but Shōsen, citing his authority as custodian, now acts improperly by arguing for direct payment.'"

Although Shōsen's explanation seems to have some justice behind it,[4] both parties agree [that the area is a] revolving estate. Moreover, Ieyuki states that taxes have long been a *gesu* and *kumon* responsibility, but Shōsen does not refer to this, instead citing the confirmatory edicts. Despite this argument, however, supervisors of temple services have exercised their authority for single generations only, whereas the estate's *gesu* and *kumon* have clearly been on the land from ages past. Since custodians are appointed only once, it is difficult to challenge hereditary local authority.[5] Shōsen's unjust [claim for] direct payment of taxes is disallowed; and Ieyuki and Shigetsuna shall have that responsibility, as before. By this command, it is so decreed.

2d year of Gennin [1225], 4th month, 2d day

Musashi no kami, Taira seal

SOURCE: *Tōji hyakugō monjo*, 1225/4/2 Kantō gechijō an, *KBSS*, 1: 30–31, doc. 37 (in *KI*, 5: 350, doc. 3,362).

1. At least one of the disputants (*gesu* Ieyuki) was a Kamakura vassal, but this would not normally have entitled him to the Bakufu's protection in a purely local dispute. Only *jitō* enjoyed a special immunity.

2. Chief investigative agency of the Bakufu.

3. I.e., by virtue of repeated confirmations by the proprietor or by the successive *azukari dokoro*.

4. We do not get this impression; but then, Shōsen's statement is presented here only in summary.

5. In fact, the Bakufu itself had earlier caused trouble on Tarumi Estate by dispossessing the original *gesu* family in the aftermath of the Gempei War. Later on, that *gesu* was restored (see Document 34).

DOCUMENT 69

A Proprietor Moves to Curtail a Gesu's Violations of Precedent, 1228

In this document an estate owner cites Yoritomo's delimitation of a *gesu* vassal's authority: the offender was violating both *shōen* law and a decree from his own military chieftain. It is clear, however, that once again it was the estate owner who held final jurisdiction.

The chancellery of the *zenjō jū-ni-i* house orders: to the officials of Tannowa Estate, Izumi Province.

That the lawlessness [*hihō*] of the *gesu*, *saemon no jō* Kaneshige, shall cease forthwith.

The said Kaneshige's flouting of precedent and interference with the fixed annual tax is most disturbing. Likewise, concerning the upland wheat tax, the customary practice has called for a surtax [*kachō**] of 2 *shō* for each *tan* of land. Under [present] custodian Kujō *risshi's* tenure, lenience has been shown; but now, reportedly, it is proposed to increase [the rate] to 5 *shō* per *tan*. If this is true, it is most irregular. Also, an order from the time of the late Kamakura *utaishō* house states: "*Saemon no jō* Kaneshige is not to be concerned as *gesu* with any matters beyond his 4 *tan* of grant fields [*kyūden*]." At present Kaneshige is violating this decree; and his persecution of the residents and delay of the annual tax are lawlessness of the most serious kind.

Forthwith, in accordance with the shogunal house order, Kaneshige is to have no involvement beyond his fixed grant lands. This estate is especially small, and if such outrages do not cease completely it will be difficult for the peasants to feel secure.[1]

Also, concerning Fujimatsu Myō, it is reported that the *risshi* has met with recalcitrance. This is indeed outrageous. Henceforth, cultivation shall take place under the supervision of the custodian. It is so ordered. Officials and peasants take note, and do not be remiss. Wherefore, this order.

2d year of Antei [1228], 5th month,   day

bettō, saki no Oki no kami, Minamoto   anzu, sa shishō, Ki (monogram)
    ason (monogram)   chikeji, u kajō, Ki (monogram)
saki no Bingo no kami, Minamoto
    ason (monogram)

SOURCE: *Tannowa monjo*, 1228/5 Kon'oe ke mandokoro kudashibumi, *KI*, 6: 85–86, doc. 3,747.

1. In fact, Kaneshige's disobedience was only beginning: six years later, he attempted to pass himself off as a *jitō*. Since this would effectively have removed him from the proprietor's jurisdiction, the latter, with Kamakura's assistance, moved immediately to reaffirm Kaneshige's status as a *gesu*. See *Tannowa monjo*, 1234/5/20 saki no sadaijin ke mandokoro kudashibumi, *KI*, 7: 125, doc. 4,662.

DOCUMENT 70

The Bakufu Adjudicates a Dispute Over Control of a Gesu Shiki, 1258

The significance of the separation between *jitō* and *gesu* is clearly seen in this document. A Heike partisan had had his *gesu* title annulled by the Bakufu, which then set up a *jitō shiki*. Two decades later Kamakura relinquished its interest in the affected estate by dismissing its appointee and allowing the restoration of the original *gesu*. In the 1250's, however, the fate of the *gesu* office once again came into dispute.

Concerning a dispute over the *gesu shiki* of Suita Estate, Settsu Province, between the Nanto [Nara] Kōfukuji priest Kō and others and Senpuku Maru.

Following an earlier hearing, the two sides were once again summoned for judgment. Though the arguments were many, with numerous details, a [Kantō] order of the 1st year of Genkyū [1204], 11th month, stated: "Ordered to the residents of Suita Estate, Settsu Province: that forthwith the *gesu shiki* of Munesue *ason*, governor of Buzen, shall be as before. Regarding the aforesaid, this estate's *jitō* rights were confiscated by special constable [*tsuitōshi**] Kajiwara Heizō Kagetoki because of the Heike affiliations of Munesue's younger brother, *saemon no jō* Munetoki during the war of Bunji.[1] After that, [Taira] Moritoki was appointed [to the post], and subsequently Takayoshi became *jitō*. However, owing to Kōfukuji's petition, a Fujiwara order [*denka no ōse*] was issued, and this has now arrived.[2] Henceforth, Munesue may be appointed to the *gesu shiki*, as before."

Munesue held the original of this document, and it was passed down to his descendants. But then Senpuku Maru's father, Muneari, was dismissed by the proprietor's headquarters.[3] Muneari brought suit; and after much litigation there were judgments [*seibai*] in the 3d and 5th years of Kenchō [1251 and 1253] that Senpuku Maru, as *gesu shiki*, should serve temple interests.[4] Now, because of the temple's appeal [*osso**], the present investigation has been undertaken. According to the edict of Genkyū, it was decided that Munesue should be appointed here. . . .[5] But according to this document [also], it was the proprietor's recommendation that led to the edict's being issued. The temple's suit has much justice in it. In accordance with this [1204] document, jurisdiction [*shinshi*] is to lie with the temple.[6] By command of the shogunal house, it is so decreed.

2d year of Shōka [1258], 12th month, 25th day[7]

Musashi no kami, Taira ason seal
Sagami no kami, Taira ason seal

SOURCE: *Kasuga Jinja monjo*, 1258/12/25 Kantō gechijō an, *Kasuga Jinja monjo*, 1: 278–79, doc. 223 (*KBSS*, 1: 120–21, doc. 102).

1. It was not, of course, a *jitō shiki* that was confiscated, but rather the estate's managerial authority: Kamakura could easily convert a *gesu* post of this kind to a *jitō shiki*. The phrase "war of Bunji" refers to the final stages of the Gempei fighting.

2. Evidently, Kōfukuji Temple was the proprietor (*ryōke*) and the Fujiwara senior branch the patron (*honke*). The former was appealing to the latter to petition Kamakura for a cancellation of the Suita *jitō shiki*.

3. I.e., the Kōfukuji. Authority over a *gesu* lay not with Kamakura but with a central estate owner.

4. In other words, the original *gesu shiki* was restored, once again under authority of the temple. Nevertheless, Kōfukuji, which had earlier dismissed the *gesu*, was evidently displeased with this settlement and took steps to bring its own suit before the Bakufu.

5. The last part of this phrase is corrupt, as noted in *KBSS*, p. 121.

6. We should review the major events here. In 1204 the temple had sought to dismiss a *jitō* and replace him with a *gesu*, and had called on the Bakufu to expedite this. Then, in the 1250's, the proprietor, no longer needing the *gesu*, moved against him. The Bakufu was once again called in, this time on behalf of the *gesu* against the temple. The *gesu* was restored to office, prompting a countersuit by the proprietor. Victory was awarded to the latter, on the grounds that both *honke* and *ryōke* had requested the restoration of 1204. Final authority would hereafter lie with the temple as proprietor. We may conclude, therefore, that Kōfukuji's earlier control over a local post had once again been confirmed: the *gesu* would no longer be able to turn to the Bakufu for protection. This was the essence of the *jitō-gesu* distinction.

7. None of the documents referred to in the text are extant.

DOCUMENT 71

The Bakufu Judges a Case Involving Jitō and Gesu, 1262

Whether a local holder was recognized as *jitō* or as *gesu* was a critical question for all parties concerned. Unfortunately, the arguments in the present document are so complicated that it has been necessary to omit the more obfuscatory passages. What is left is a dispute over the proper titles for land

and men. The key issue is whether the land units of Yamada and Hirose are separate and discrete. If not, then an order canceling Yamada's *jitō shiki* should also have applied to Hirose.

The terms of dispute between Kōjō [and Kōen], proprietor's deputies [*zasshō**] of Hirose, Ishikuro Estate, Etchū Province, an Enshūji holding, and [*jitō¹*] Sadatomo, *sakon no shōgen* Tokisada, and Fuji Shirō Munesada.

ITEM: Concerning the *jitō shiki*.
On the occasion of a trial confrontation, Kōen stated: "Hirose is within Yamada Estate. Long ago it was under the estate proprietor's jurisdiction [*ryōke no shinshi*]; but during the time of the late *utaishō* house and the *saemon no kami dono*,² Iino Saburō Yasuie, Ni[?]³ Shirō Korenori, and Shibuya Saburō Arimasa were granted the *jitō shiki*. However, owing to a suit by the patron, Omuro,⁴ the [post] was later abolished. But because the grandfather of Sadatomo, Sadanao, had meanwhile become a follower of the temple, he was appointed by that *ryōke* to the *gesu shiki*. Sadanao presented a personal pledge [*kishōmon**], a promise of good intentions [*taijō**], and pedigree register [*myōbu*]. Also, it was stated in a [Kantō] directive of the 3d year of Genkyū [1206] that if any lawsuit should arise, the *jitō shiki* would be abolished. By contravening these various documents, [Sadatomo] has antagonized the proprietor and usurped authority over the *gō*. Therefore, in accordance with the [1206] understanding Sadatomo's *jitō shiki* should be abolished and [his authority] assigned to the proprietor."⁵
According to Sadatomo's defense: "Hirose is an independent land unit and is by no means within Yamada Gō. The two *gō* of Yamada and Hirose form a single estate [*shō*]. Upper, Middle, and Lower Ishikuro form another *shō*; and the five *gō* of Yoshiie, Ōumi, Inbayashi, Naoumi, and Daikōji form yet another. In short, there are three discrete *shō*. How, then, can a waiver of claim to Yamada Gō be used as evidence for Hirose Gō? Next, as to the claim that Sadanao was appointed *gesu* by the proprietor: since this occurred during the time of the Heike, there is no need to consider it.⁶ Since we received a confirming edict from Kiso *sama no kami*,⁷ followed by generations of shogunal investitures [in my family's capacity] as Kantō vassals, details do not seem necessary. Next, as to the Genkyū [1206] directive, it is suspect because the date was affixed [later]"....⁸
Kōen stated: "The fact that Hirose is within Yamada Gō is clear from a Taira Iemasa[...?]⁹ of the 5th year of Kōwa [1103], the personal pledge [*kishōmon*] of Sadanao, and other documents. Moreover, it is

the height of deceit for [... ?] in the middle of an investigation. The [1206] directive [and ... ? the Kantō] investiture decree [should be?] requested [for examination?]."

Sadatomo [answered?]: "It is clear from the Genkyū [1206] directive and other evidence that no incursions were to take place and that [... ?]. Next, in Sadanao's personal pledge, 'Yamada-no-shō Hirose' is written. Since the character for 'within' is missing, this is insufficient proof. The Genkyū [1206] directive was issued in response to former custodian Benkei's document of accusation. On his petition [the words] 'within Yamada' are noted only in the margin; the text itself records that long ago the two *gō* of Yamada and Hirose formed one estate. The fact that they are separate is undeniable. As to Sadanao's promise of good intentions [*taijō*], since the year period is unknown and the seal is suspect, it is patently a forgery."[10]

. . .

According to [Kantō] directives of the 6th month, 16th day—1st year of Genryaku [1184][11]—from the *utaishō* house, and of the 24th year of Genkyū[12] from the *saemon no kami* house, as well as a [Kantō] edict [*gechijō*], it is ordered that the Yamada Gō *jitō shiki* be abolished.

According to Sadanao's pedigree register of the 3d year of Kenkyū [1192]: "Fujiwara Sadanao, senior sixth rank, upper grade."

According to [Sadanao's] personal pledge of the 3d year of Kennin [1203]: "Concerning the pledge of *gesu* Sadanao of Hirose Gō, Yamada Estate, henceforth there will be no violations of orders, whether from patron or proprietor or from agents sent by the capital. . . ."

According to the accusation by Benkei, dated the 2d year of Genkyū [1205], 12th month: "Sadanao violated his pledge and is exercising authority illegally. The two *gō* of Yamada and Hirose once formed one estate. When the Yamada Gō *jitō shiki* was abolished,[13] why should there have remained a separate *jitō* for the Hirose sector?"

. . .

According to a provincial government [*rusudokoro*] [edict] of the 5th year of Jishō [1181], 8th month, and a Kiso *sama no kami* [investiture] of the next year, 2d month, both submitted by Sadatomo: "Sadanao shall hold the Hirose village [*mura*] *gesu shiki*."[14]

According to a Hiki Tōnai Tomoshige[15] [decree] of the 6th month, 14th day, year unrecorded: "By command of the Kamakura lord, estate notables shall exercise the Yamada authority. As for Hirose, it is another matter."

. . .

According to a [Kantō] directive of [1204], 7th month, 10th day:

"In regard to Korenori, the *jitō* of Yamada Gō, that *shiki* is hereby abolished, at the request of Omuro. As to the lack of a *jitō* cancellation in Hirose Gō, in the absence of any pretext, how can a vassal of no particular guilt have his holding terminated?"

. . .

Concerning the Genkyū directive submitted by Kōen: since the first part of it quotes from a document of accusation, it would appear to be a request for information [*toijō*].¹⁶ Likewise, the final sentence states, "If a suit should arise [again], that *shiki* will be cancelled"; these are clearly the words of an admonition. How, based on this document, can we revoke the two confirming directives of Kennin and Genkyū? Next, a promise of good intentions, a pedigree register, and a personal pledge were written out and given to the proprietor. While Kōen has thus been asserting a proprietary jurisdiction, generations of [Kantō] directives have been handed down. Inasmuch as the statute of limitations [*nenjo**] has expired during the rule of three generations of *jitō*, further details are unneeded. . . .

     2d year of Kōchō [1262], 3d month, 1st day

                              Musashi no kami, Taira ason
                              (monogram)
                              Sagami no kami, Taira ason
                              (monogram)

SOURCE: *Kanazawa toshokan shozō monjo*, 1262/3/1 Kantō gechijō, *KBSS*, 1: 123–26, doc. 106.

1. Several characters are missing in these phrases; names and titles drawn from text.

2. I.e., during the rules of Yoritomo and Yoriie.

3. Character missing.

4. I.e., Ninnaji Temple in Kyoto.

5. The implication here is that Hirose and Yamada were indeed separate; only the Yamada post had been canceled. But Kōen is not looking at it this way. He is arguing that the cancellation of the Yamada *jitō shiki* and the Bakufu's 1206 warning regarding the Hirose post within Yamada clearly justified a return of the entire region to proprietary control.

6. I.e., since this occurred so long ago, it has no bearing on present circumstances. The allegiance of Sadatomo's family to the proprietor, he is arguing, has long since lapsed. This is supported in the document's next sentence.

7. Kiso Yoshinaka, a cousin of Yoritomo who was politically active in the region of Etchū Province during the early stages of the Gempei War.

8. Sadatomo's argument continues, but the references become obscure.

9. Characters are missing at several points in the following passage.

10. From this point on the Bakufu presents the various documents submitted in

evidence. I include here only those that are of significance or interest. When one had a losing case, it was a common tactic to attempt to cloud the issue by presenting irrelevant documents. None of these are extant.

11. The year name here is written in half-size characters and is probably inaccurate: certainly there was no Yamada *jitō shiki* in 1184; nor was there yet a Kamakura *utaishō* house.

12. Obviously an error. The correct date is evidently the 3d year of Genkyū (1206).

13. In 1204, as we shall see shortly.

14. In 1181, Etchū Province was under the control of the local provincial office: hence this *rusudokoro* decree from early in the Gempei War. By 1182, Kiso Yoshinaka had taken over in the region.

15. Tomomune, a special agent (*kannōshi*) of Yoritomo assigned to the Hokuriku region early in 1184. We see here one means by which Kamakura expanded its influence: authorizing local warriors to seize power. For another reference to Hiki's wartime activities in Hokuriku, see Document 7.

16. The Bakufu renders judgment here; the interpolation continues beyond the translated passage, but adds nothing substantive to the points already made.

DOCUMENT 72

The Bakufu Confirms a Jitō in a Gesu's Previous Land Rights, 1288

The transition from *gesu* to *jitō* is vividly shown in this document. It is also noteworthy that during the early Kamakura period the proprietor's representative was titled *azukari dokoro*, whereas later practice favored *zasshō*. Both terms appear in this document, suggesting a greater degree of cooperation between proprietor and agent than had formerly been the case.

> The points of a dispute between Jitsugen, the proprietary deputy [*zasshō*] of Numata Estate, Aki Province, and Suishin, representative of the nun Jōren, daughter of the *jitō* of Nashiba Gō, Kobayagawa Mimasaka *no kami hosshi*, priestly name Honbutsu.
>
> · · ·

ITEM:[1] concerning Gakuonji rice land. In the matter of the aforesaid, Jitsugen asserted that numerous *chō* of the estate's rice fields had been taken over in excess of the original exempt area.[2] Suishin rejoined that [the temple][3] was established by the original *gesu* during the era of Tenkei [938–47]. After Doi Jirō Tōhira's Ken'ei-period [1206–7] appointment as *jitō*, [he continued,] there was no custodial [*azukari dokoro*] interference [with Gakuonji], since it had now become the *jitō* clan temple [*ujidera*]. During successive land surveys [*kenchū*] over the years no inspection of [its holdings] was ever made.[4]

In the matter of this inspection issue, Jitsugen presents no evidence [concerning the omission]. Moreover, although Jitsugen claims that [Gakuonji] is not the *jitō* clan temple, he does not say who, other than the original *gesu*, might have established it. In consequence, there is no specific proof of a proprietary jurisdiction [*ryōke no shinshi*] over it. Next, although [Jitsugen] alleges that estate rice lands have been appropriated, numerous documents have shown these fields to be within the temple confines. For land located within the temple boundaries, no repossession may take place, even if [the total area] exceeds that originally exempted. The claims of the proprietary deputy will therefore not be acted upon. By command of the Kamakura lord, the two aforementioned matters are resolved thus.

11th year of Kōan [1288], 4th month, 12th day

> saki no Musashi no kami, Taira ason seal
> Sagami no kami, Taira ason seal

SOURCE: *Gakuonji monjo*, 1288/4/12 Kantō gechijō an, *KBSS*, 1: 231–32, doc. 169.

1. The first item in the document is omitted here.
2. I.e., Jitsugen asserted that the *jitō* had encroached upon normal tax-yielding fields that were not part of Gakuonji's original enclave.
3. I.e., the temple and its accompanying exempt fields.
4. The summary of Suishin's defense statement ends here, and the Bakufu's decision begins.

DOCUMENT 73

The Bakufu Resolves a Dispute Between Jitō and Gesu, 1245

One of the presumptions of the division between *jitō* and *gesu* was that the two posts would be mutually exclusive and could not coexist in cases where they had equal authority. In this sense *jitō* and *gesu* were really "consecutive," in that the appointment of one involved supersession of the other.[1] Thus only when holding office on adjacent estates could *jitō* and *gesu* become antagonists.[2]

The points of a dispute between Yūba Saburō Tadamoto, *jitō* of Kogi Gō, Izumi Province, represented by the priest Chōkan, and the *gesu*, *saemon no jō* Minamoto Motomitsu, of Abiko Tribute

Estate [*mikuriya**], an "imperial table" land. The remaining issues are omitted here.

I T E M : concerning Kogi Bay.

According to Chōkan's statement regarding the aforesaid: "In the age before Jōkyū [1219–21] the full tribute quota was derived from 36 *chō* lying within this table land. However, the quota could not be maintained at this rate; in consequence, gift fields [*kyūden*³] to the amount of 65 *chō* were set aside from this province, of which 13 *chō*, 5 *tan*, were located within this *gō*. From the 3d year of Jōkyū [1221] through the 2d year of Jōō [1223], a total of 3 years, authority over this bay area was exercised entirely by the *jitō*. Then, following a fair and equitable decision by the Kantō, a 50-50 division of authority [*hambun sata*] was achieved. However, as regards Tsuruhara and Sano estates, lying on this bay, Motomitsu had no rights of interference. Pursuant to this practice, his involvement there should be terminated. Failing this, a surtax [*kachō**] might be collected, despite the area's status as gift lands.⁴ Should this also prove impractical, [the exempt fields] could be switched to another place."⁵

According to Motomitsu's statement: "During the age of emperor Daigo [897–930] this bay was established as an imperial rice tribute area. In addition, 165 *chō* of land were exempted from miscellaneous provincial dues [*zōmen**]. Because of difficulties, however, the exemption was withdrawn during the Shōji period [1199–1200], and 65 *chō* of fully exempt land [*fuyu menden**] were granted [instead]. It is clear from generations of imperial commands and orders from the retired emperor's chancellery, that [the status of] both the bay land and the gift fields has not changed. Why should there be any change [now]? Similarly, from the 3d year of Jōkyū until Jōō [1221–23] authority lay entirely with Motomitsu.⁶ There is no justification for the [*jitō*'s] usurpation under the pretext of an order for 50-50 division after the 2d year of Jōō [1223]. Details of this have been made clear in Rokuhara's letters of inquiry [*toijō*].⁷ In accordance with [a succession of] imperial decrees, the encroachments must cease. Moreover, as regards Tsuruhara and Sano Estates, these were converted to private domains [*shō*] by Hōjōji Zenjō *denka*.⁸ How can a person [as lowly as] the deputy *jitō* cite these as examples?"

Regarding both the bay lands and the gift fields:⁹ inasmuch as no changes have occurred since the issuance before Jōkyū of imperial commands and orders from the retired emperor's chancellery, why should these gift lands be switched to another place? Also, why should the surtax be collected? If Chōkan still harbors complaints after this judgment, he may petition the Kantō.[10] As for the bay lands, each side is to exercise authority in accordance with the "equitable order" [of 1223] and the rights of possession that have existed for more than 20 years.[11] The foregoing points are so ordered.

3d year of Kangen [1245], 7th month, 17th day

Sagami no kami, Taira ason seal

SOURCE: *Kōyasan monjo*, 1245/7/17 Rokuhara gechijō an, *DNK, iewake* 1 (Kōyasan monjo), 6: 564–65, doc. 1,471 (*KBSS*, 2: 23–24, doc. 10).

1. One result of this was a constant effort by proprietors to resurrect *gesu shiki*, and by *gesu* to acquire immunity through promotion to *jitō* (see Document 105). The division between these offices began to break down only in late Kamakura times.

2. The exact location of the *jitō* and *gesu* in this document is not altogether clear. The *jitō* was assigned to a *gō*, and the *gesu* to a tribute estate. Presumably the estate was located within the *gō*, but this does not mean that the *jitō* held lawful authority over it. The two units were *functionally* separated; indeed, this is what the *jitō* is complaining about.

3. Or simply "assigned fields." *Kyūden* is normally used in an entirely different context (see Glossary).

4. I.e., the *jitō* might be permitted to collect a surtax from lands otherwise exempt. The overall thrust of this argument is not clear. If Tsuruhara and Sano were outside *gesu* Motomitsu's legitimate sphere of influence, why would the *jitō* have been willing to compromise? We are not told. At all events, it is clear that the *gesu* is an agent of proprietary interests, whereas the *jitō* is working to further his own ends.

5. The actual text reads "switched to another practice" (*ta no rei*). However, at the end of the document, the phrase appears as I have rendered it.

6. Note the basic disagreement on this point.

7. I.e., the questionnaires sent out by Rokuhara had been returned.

8. The imperial regent, Fujiwara Tadamichi.

9. The Bakufu's decision begins here.

10. Kamakura was clearly the tribunal of last resort. It was for this reason that Rokuhara, which had been established in 1221 as a Bakufu branch in Kyoto, was generally ineffective as a judicial agency. For more on Rokuhara, see Document 98.

11. See Glossary under *nenjo*.

DOCUMENTS 74-75

A Jitō Appoints a Gesu Shiki, 1229, 1231

Occasionally a *gesu shiki* would be subject to a *jitō*'s authority, either in whole or in part. This suggests that *gesu* could coexist with *jitō* if the two were not on the same level. The jurisdiction of a *jitō* in this case did not imply direct Bakufu jurisdiction.

74

ORDERED: concerning the *gesu shiki* of Kimoto Island.
Okinaga Morisada is appointed.

By right of hereditary succession, the circumstances of this *gesu shiki* are clear. Forthwith, the additional tax share [*jōbun**] and regular tributes shall be paid without negligence. The local notables and peasants shall not be remiss. Wherefore, this order.

1st year of Kangi [1229], 9th month, 11th day

jitō, Tachibana seal   otsukai, Ōya Iesada seal

75

ORDERED: to the peasants of Kimoto Tribute Estate [*mikuriya*], Shima Province.
That forthwith Okinaga Yoshimori[1] shall be *gesu*.

Owing to this person's possession of valid documents [*shōmon*] and his explanation of the details, he is appointed to this *shiki*. Regarding the additional tax share and other dues, he shall carry out these responsibilities without negligence. It is so commanded. Local residents shall take note, and shall not be remiss. Wherefore, this order.

3d year of Kangi [1231], 11th month, 14th day

jitō, danjōchū Minamoto (monogram)
(monogram)[2]

SOURCES: Document 74: *Noda monjo*, 1229/9/11 jitō-otsukai rensho bu'ninjō an, *KI*, 6: 142, doc. 3,868. Document 75: *Noda monjo*, 1231/11/14 jitō Minamoto bō kudashibumi, *KI*, 6: 331, doc. 4,245.

1. A document of 1230 makes it clear that Yoshimori and Morisada (Document 74) were rivals for the post of *gesu*; Morisada was confirmed on that occasion. See *Kii zoku fudoki*, 1230/4/30 bō kudashibumi, *KI*, 6: 202, doc. 3,984. The switch to Yoshimori a year later is not explained.

2. The different *jitō* signatures on these two documents are puzzling. Perhaps a new *jitō* was moving to appoint his own candidate. The second monogram is not identified.

JITŌ STRENGTHS AND WEAKNESSES

DOCUMENTS 76-77

A Proprietor and a Jitō Issue Joint Edicts, 1248, 1293

As a perquisite of his appointment a *jitō* often gained jurisdiction over some of an estate's local officials. This authority could be shared with a proprietor or his deputy, or it could be exercised over specifically named offices. In either case the *jitō's* powers might include appointments, dismissals, and general supervision. In the two documents here we see examples of cooperative control: the *jitō* was virtually the equal of the proprietor, and the two sides were able to work together.

76

Concerning a dispute between the Tagarasu official [*satanin**] Gen *daibu* and Hon *daibu*.

In accordance with the purport of pledges [*kishōmon*] received from both men, the official¹ shall henceforth make the peasants secure, treating them compassionately. Likewise, Hon *daibu*, pursuant to orders from the official, is to have authority over personal assessments [*kuji**], causing no anxieties and showing no favoritism. Above all, local residents shall be suitably assigned to the vacated lands of peasants who have fled, and levies from *kuji* to emergency imposts shall be discharged without neglect. It is so ordered.

2d year of Hōji [1248], 7th month, 16th day

> proprietor's agent (monogram)
> *jitō's* agent (monogram)

77

Appointment: to the acting assistant head priest [*gon no dai-kannushi*] of the Lower Shrine:
Sōshichi Genshu.

The aforesaid person is appointed to this *shiki.* Shrine priests and other religious officers within the estate shall take note, and shall not be remiss. The edict of appointment is thus.

1st year of Einin [1293], 12th month, 7th day

> bettō (monogram)
> jitō, Minamoto (monogram)

SOURCES: Document 76: *Hata monjo,* 1248/7/16 ryōke-jitō rensho gechijō, *Wakasa gyoson shiryō,* pp. 297–98 (also *Echizen Wakasa komonjo sen,* pp. 780–81). Document 77: *Sado Hachimangū monjo,* 1293/12/7 gon no dai-kannushi bu'ninjō, in *Sado Honma ibun Sakurai ke monjo,* p. 199, no. 14.
1. I.e., Gen *daibu.*

DOCUMENT 78

The Bakufu Judges a Dispute Over Control of Estate Officials, 1293

Not surprisingly, the existing documents provide considerably more evidence of contention than of cooperation in the matter of controlling an estate's officers. Jurisdiction over local *shiki* meant more than just the power of appointment: it entailed domination of the land itself. In the present example, Isaku Estate was quite literally divided between a *jitō* and an estate deputy on the basis of control over local officials.

> Concerning a dispute over the *gesu* and *myōshu shiki* between Ryōi, agent for the *jitō* Shimotsuke Hikosaburō Tadanaga of Isaku Estate, Satsuma Province, and the estate deputy [*zasshō*] Shōdō.

The *zasshō's* suit regarding various estate matters was previously taken up [by the Kantō]. When a judgment was reached, in the 2d year of

Kōan [1279],[1] the said titles were assigned to the proprietor, thereby leading to a *jitō's* appeal [*osso**]. The matter was taken up again. But last year, on the 30th day of the 11th month, a compromise document [*wayojō**] was presented by the two sides.[2] According to this, "The *jitō's* suit regarding the two *shiki* is permanently ended. However, the *myōshu* titles of Miyauchi, Iyokura, and Imada *myō*, plus the shrine headship [*kannushi**] (but minus the temple and shrine support lands [*busshinden*]) together with the *kumon* and *tadokoro* [titles], as well as residences, and paddy and upland fields, are consigned to the *jitō*. There shall be no neglect of the annual tax and other payments."[3]

Further details need not be taken up. In pursuance of this document, authority is to be exercised mutually, with no future disturbances. By command of the Kamakura lord, it is so decreed.

6th year of Shōō [1293], 1st month, 13th day

> Mutsu no kami, Taira ason (monogram)
> Sagami no kami, Taira ason (monogram)

SOURCE: *Shimazu ke monjo*, 1293/1/13 Kantō gechijō, *DNK, iewake* 16 (*Shimazu ke monjo*), 1: 192–93, doc. 199 (*KBSS*, 1: 255, doc. 193).

1. The date of this document (1279/2/15) can be ascertained elsewhere, as well as the fact that it was extremely detailed. But full information on this complex dispute is denied us, since the decree itself is not extant. See the reference to it in *Shimazu ke monjo*, 1289/11/17 Isaku-no-shō zasshō-jitōdai wayojō, *Sappan kyūki zatsuroku, zempen*, 7: 117–19, doc. 571.

2. As indicated by the 1289 document, *ibid.*, this was not the first compromise between these disputants. The Bakufu reviewed and confirmed the earlier agreement in 1290 (*ibid.*, 1290/2/12 Kantō gechijō, 7: 120, doc. 573; also in *KBSS*, 1: 245, doc. 180). Obviously, this arrangement broke down, leading to the present accord of 1292 (see Note 3).

3. A *wayojō* of 1292/11/30 is extant, but it fails to confirm the summary offered here: there is no reference to the three *myōshu shiki* consigned to the *jitō*. *Shimazu ke monjo*, 1292/11/30 Isaku-no-shō nai Hioki-kita Gō wayojō, *Sappan kyūki zatsuroku zempen*, 7: 142–44, doc. 599. One possible explanation is that this document is the only one surviving from a series of accords reached for different subdivisions of Isaku Estate; hence its specific reference to Northern Hioki Gō (see also Document 43). The Bakufu's confirmation, then, merely highlights the main features of the overall agreement, leaving out specifics.

DOCUMENT 79

A Proprietor Grants a Jitō's Request to Open New Fields, 1229

If a *jitō* and a proprietor were to cooperate, some element of common interest was required. The opening of new land was one possible area for joint effort.

For an estate owner, the conversion of waste fields to cultivated acreage promised greater revenues. For a *jitō*, the supervision of such a project led to greater local authority. The document offered here is unusually vivid in its detail.

seal

ORDERED: to the *jitō* headquarters of Fukunaga Myō in Matsuura Estate.[1]

That forthwith undeveloped areas shall be opened and taxes [*shotō*] paid from them.

Regarding this, a petition from the *jitō* and others states: "This estate is populous, but has too few paddy and upland fields. Accordingly, new fields should be opened, and taxes produced." In essence, the restoration of smoke from every house[2] will mean prosperity for the village, and will also ensure the peace. You may open new land, as requested. However, during the first year of development, taxes will be waived. For the next year the rate will be one *to* per *tan*, by item,[3] with an increase of one *to* the following year, and ultimately a rate of three *to*. As regards the miscellaneous obligations [*manzō kuji**], a [similar] exemption will be in force. Should the newly opened fields become a pretext for the desolation of established ones, payment quotas will conform to those of the old fields, even in newly cultivated areas. As for the stipulated regular taxes, these will be paid, without fail, into the estate warehouse. Also, the number of workers engaged in developing the new land is to be reported each year when [the proprietor's] agents conduct their [annual] survey. In response to the petition, it is so decreed.

3d year of Antei [1229], 2d month, 21st day

SOURCE: *Isshi monjo*, 1229/2/21 Matsuura-no-shō ryōke kudashibumi, *Hirado Matsuura ke shiryō*, pp. 148–49 (in *KI*, 6: 117–18, doc. 3,812).
1. In Hizen Province.
2. Literally, "from the people."
3. I.e., one-half bushel per .294 acre of whatever the commodity being grown.

DOCUMENTS 80-82

The Bakufu Comes to the Aid of Beleaguered Jitō, 1206, 1227, 1227

Not all *jitō* were men of parts who moved irresistibly toward greater local control. There were always a few who had all they could do merely to fend off local rivals. The three selections here provide glimpses of such situations.

80

Regarding the complaint lodged by *jitō* Yukinao of Horio Estate
that an official of Nagaoka Estate has violated long-established
boundaries in an effort to annex rice land.

"Although Horio Estate and Nagaoka Estate are both Fujiwara holdings [*denka goryō**], each has a separate *shōen* title, and there is no
mixing of land. From the first, boundaries were clearly marked, and
no disputes over borders have ever occurred. But now, as a result of
boundary violations by a Nagaoka official, there exists an effort to de-
tach Horio lands, against all precedent."

If this [complaint] is true, there has been grave misconduct [*ransui**].
Forthwith, this [lawlessness] is to cease, and [the borders] are to be
fixed as before. By command of the Kamakura lord, it is so decreed.

1st year of Ken'ei [1206], 7th month, 4th day

> Koremune seal
> minbu no jō, Nakahara seal
> san-i, Fujiwara ason seal
> shohakase, Nakahara ason seal
> san-i, Ōe ason seal

81

Regarding the complaint lodged by the deputy *jitō* of Hachijō
Estate, Yamato Province, of depredations by Ryōken and Jungen.

According to the petition: "Because of [Ryōken and Jungen] the *jitō's*
administrative office [*mandokoro**] was destroyed by fire, and paddies
and uplands confiscated." If this is true, it as a terrible offense. The Fujiwara [*denka**] have been respectfully notified that the aforesaid persons should be summoned for trial.[1] In the meantime, their plundering
is to cease, and the deputy *jitō* shall be made secure. It is so ordered.

3d year of Karoku [1227], 8th month, 24th day

[To] the deputy *jitō* of Hachijō Estate   shuri, gon no suke seal
                                               kamon, gon no suke[2] seal

82

Concerning the ravaging of an outlaw band [*akutō*][3] in Toyokuni
Estate, Yamato Province.

The complaint of *jitō* Nagafuse Shirō Shigeyasu, along with the petition of the deputy *jitō*, is sent herewith.[4] There have been repeated
orders that particulars of this matter be ascertained; but the summonses have not been heeded, and outrages have been committed.

This is a serious crime, and most reprehensible. The Fujiwara administrative headquarters shall duly be informed of this; and former *gesu* Yukisue, custodian Chōchū *goshi*, and their immediate followers, shall be sent posthaste to the Kantō.[5] Let there be no delay. Furthermore, as concerns deputy *jitō* Mitsushige, he is to be made physically secure.[6] By command of the Kamakura lord, this order is so conveyed.

3d year of Karoku [1227], 9th month, 7th day

[To the] kamon no suke dono and	Musashi no kami (monogram)
shuri no suke dono[7]	Sagami no kami (monogram)

SOURCES: Document 80: *Sangun yōryaku shō no ge shihai monjo*, 1206/7/4 Kantō gechijō an, *KBSS*, 1: 10, doc. 15 (in *KI*, 3: 282, doc. 1,626). Document 81: *Kasuga Jinja monjo*, 1227/8/24 Rokuhara migyōsho an, *KI*, 6: 43, doc. 3,654. Document 82: *Kasuga Jinja monjo*, 1227/9/7 Kantō migyōsho, *Kasuga Jinja monjo*, 1: 277, doc. 222 (in *KI*, 6: 48–49, doc. 3,663).

1. Note that Ryōken and Jungen, who were not vassals, remained under the jurisdiction of the proprietor.

2. The Bakufu's two Kyoto deputies (Rokuhara *tandai*), Hōjō Tokiuji and Hōjō Tokimori.

3. This is an early use of a term that assumed much wider currency—with strong sociological connotations—around the 1260's. See Glossary.

4. For the original of the *jitō*'s document see *Kasuga Jinja monjo*, 1227/8 Taira Shigeyasu gejō, *Kasuga Jinja monjo*, 1: 539–42, doc. 448 (in *KI*, 6: 45–47, doc. 3,658).

5. Here, then, is an incident involving the same province, proprietor, and period as that described in the previous document, but with a different resolution. The explanation probably lies in the repeated failure of a more localized justice (Fujiwara and Rokuhara) to end the Yamato troubles. At all events, Kamakura is clearly advising Rokuhara to inform the Fujiwara headquarters regarding the steps that were being taken.

6. As the person on the scene in Toyokuni Estate, Mitsushige was obviously in some danger.

7. The two Rokuhara *tandai*.

DOCUMENTS 83-84

Jitō Issue Documents of Investiture to Local Officers, 1191, 1214

In some instances *jitō* enjoyed unusual authority in their appointment areas from the outset. For example, the Bakufu councillor Ōe Hiromoto effectively acted as an *azukari dokoro* for a Suō Province estate owned by the Fujiwara. The special circumstances here were Hiromoto's Kyoto origins and the close relationship that existed in 1191 between Yoritomo and the Fujiwara scion Kanezane. In our second example the presence of a shogunal prayer center in Ōya Estate added to the *jitō's* power and prestige.

83

seal

A Fujiwara holding:
Yashiro Estate.

Concerning appointment of a *kumon*-in-chief [*sōkumon shiki*]: *san-i* Abe Morizane.

The aforesaid person, as *kumon*-in-chief, shall administer[1] estate affairs [*shōmu*] and supervise the miscellaneous estate payments, without negligence and in accordance with precedent. Estate officials shall take note, and shall abide by this. The appointment is thus.

> 2d year of Kenkyū [1191], 3d month, 22d day

> > jitō, Nakahara[2] seal

84

ORDERED: to Saikōji, in Southern Shimi Village, Ōya Estate.[3]
Concerning appointment of a temple abbot:
the priest Keishin.

Under this *shiki* the aforesaid person shall exercise authority over temple affairs [*jimu**]. However, this temple is a prayer center of the Kamakura lord. The deputy *jitō*, resident notables, and local peasants are to create no disturbances. Wherefore, this order.

> 2d year of Kempō [1214], 8th month,   day

> > jitō seal[4]

SOURCES: Document 83: *Seijun shiryō gaihen*, 1191/3/22 Suō no kuni Yashiro-no-shō sōkumon shiki bu'ninjō an, *KI*, 1: 397, doc. 524. Document 84: *Saikōji monjo*, 1214/8 jitō bō kudashibumi an, *Kano komonjo*, pp. 142–43, doc. 68, (in *KI*, 4: 142–43, doc. 2,123).

1. An incorrect character is here, but the meaning is clearly "administer."
2. Ōe Hiromoto. In 1226, Hiromoto's heir threatened to divest the *sōkumon* of his *shiki* unless its duties were performed more effectively. Recorded in *Kushibe monjo*, 1226/6 Suō no kuni Yashiro-no-shō ryōke sadamebumi an, *KI*, 5: 410–11, doc. 3,502.
3. In Noto Province.
4. See Document 86.

DOCUMENT 85

A Jitō's Headquarters Issues an Order, 1208

The extent of a *jitō's* authority could be measured in different ways. The existence of a regular administrative office (*jitōsho*) was one such indicator. In the present instance the headquarters of a gō-level *jitō* directs local officials to reassign a certain property.

The *jitō's* headquarters orders: to the officials of Minami Gō.[1]

That forthwith the residence [*yashiki**] of Chiyomatsu's mother shall be confirmed as of old.

The aforesaid residence shall be assigned, as of old, to Chiyomatsu's mother. It is hereby ordered that officials take note of this and effect the assignment. Know this, and do not be remiss. Wherefore, this order.

2d year of Jōgen [1208], 3d month, 3d day

jitō seal

SOURCE: *Haseba monjo*, 1208/3/3 jitōsho kudashibumi an, *Sappan kyūki zatsuroku*, 2: 15, doc. 113 (in *KI*, 3: 342, doc. 1,717).
1. In Satsuma Province.

THE JITŌ AS ESTATE CONSTABLE

DOCUMENTS 86-87

A Jitō Prohibits Hunting and the Cutting of Timber, 1197; The Bakufu Invests a Jitō With Similar Prohibitory Powers, 1214

Jitō commonly assumed some level of police authority within their areas of jurisdiction. The issuing of prohibitory orders was one element of this responsibility, notably in regard to the precincts of officially sponsored temples. In Document 86 a *jitō* is already exercising this authority. In Document 87, a *jitō* is given powers in response to a temple's request for assistance in safeguarding its lands.

86

Concerning the borders [*shishi**] and residence fields [*yashikiden*]¹ of the Saikōji, within Southern Shimi Village, Ōya Estate.

Totals: borders [described here]; 2 *tan* of residence fields.

Within the borders of the said Saikōji, hunting shall be prohibited, and there shall be no cutting of the temple's timber. Persons who disregard this protection will be fined. It is so decreed.

8th year of Kenkyū [1197], intercalary 6th month, 9th day

jitō, hyōe no jō seal

87

The chancellery of the shogun's house orders: to the priests of Kinzan Kannon Temple, Bizen Province.

That forthwith hunting and the cutting of dead trees by various persons shall cease inside the borders of temple land.

According to the temple's petition: "Various persons have intruded on this mountain for the purposes of hunting and cutting down dead trees. Prohibitions have gone unheeded, and these evil acts go on continuously; hence there is no peace for the temple, and Buddhist ways are upset." If this is true, it is most reprehensible. In future, under the authority of the *jitō*, prohibitions for the borders of the temple lands shall be laid down, and the priests shall be made secure. In the event there are still violators, the *shugo* is to be informed and a list of names forwarded. The command is thus. Wherefore, this order.[2]

2d year of Kempō [1214], 9th month, 26th day

ryō, zusho no shōjō, Kiyohara   anzu, Sugano (monogram)
   (monogram)   chikeji, Koremune (monogram)
bettō, Sagami no kami, Taira ason
   (monogram)
Tōtomi no kami, Minamoto ason
Musashi no kami, Taira ason
   (monogram)
shohakase, Nakahara ason (monogram)
san-i, Fujiwara ason (monogram)

SOURCES: Document 86: *Saikōji monjo*, 1197/int.6/9 jitō gechijō, *Kano komonjo*, p. 38, doc. 58 (in *KI*, 2: 228, doc. 917); some question exists concerning this document's authenticity. Document 87: *Kinzanji monjo*, 1214/9/26 shōgun ke mandokoro kudashibumi, *Okayama ken komonjo shū*, 2: 7, doc. 9 (in *KI*, 4: 144, doc. 2,128).
   1. Evidently an immune enclave intended to support the temple.
   2. See Document 50 for a similar prohibition 40 years later.

DOCUMENT 88

The Bakufu Settles a Dispute Over Policing Rights, 1243

The formal authority for policing and adjudication (*kendanken*[*]) was often an object of contention between *jitō* and estate proprietors. A major reason for this was that exercise of the *kendan* privilege carried with it the right to confiscate the property of criminals. In this document we see the lengths to which a proprietor's agent might go in order to secure a portion of that authority. Not only is his argument proved to be a tissue of lies and deceit, but his actions seem to have included the murder of a key witness. Unfortunately, several of the references to persons and documents remain obscure.¹ What does emerge is the extent of the Bakufu's effort to discover the truth.

ORDERED: to the residents of Ushigahara Estate, Echizen Province, a Daigoji land.

    Orders regarding three matters.²

    ITEM: concerning the *kendan* [authority].

On the occasion of a trial confrontation, the proprietor's agent [*zasshō*], Morikage, stated: "During the tenure of former *jitō* Tosa Saburō Hiroyoshi the *kendan* authority rested two-thirds with the proprietor [*ryōke*] and one-third with the *jitō*. In the aftermath of the Jōkyū treachery,³ when the present *jitō* was appointed, a [Kantō] decree [*gechijō*] was issued stating that authority should be exercised jointly by the former deputy, Sukemoto,⁴ and the proprietor, as earlier. However, the subdeputy [*mata daikan*] and others failed to heed this; and when a complaint was lodged with the *jitō*, [this officer] handed down a decree in the 3d year of Jōō [1224] urging that the former *jitō's* practices be followed. But even after Sukemoto had been replaced, and Masanori and [then] Shinnen appointed as deputy *jitō*, orders were still not obeyed. As a consequence, an appeal was made to the Kantō in the 11th month of last year, and a [Bakufu] directive was dispatched to the *jitō*. According to the *jitō's* decree of the 12th month of last year, the practices of former *jitō* should be investigated and the truth determined. Although it was so ordered, this has not been done. We therefore appeal for an order that the authority of the proprietor, in accordance with precedent, constitute a two-thirds share, and the authority of the *jitō* a one-third share."

    According to the statement of deputy *jitō* Shinnen and his agent Shinren: "Jūen *hosshi*, an expert in the old customs of this domain, has clearly stated that during the [*jitō*] tenures [*chigyō*] of the late Tōtomi *nyūdō*, Yamashiro *nyūdō*, and Tosa Saburō, the proprietor had no share in this estate's *kendan* authority; the *jitō* exercised full control [*shinshi*].⁵ During the more than 20 years from Jōkyū until the present, the *jitō's* authority has [also] been total. As concerns Sukemoto's edict,⁶ it is not an edict of the *jitō*. Moreover, as deputy for the estate's southern part [Sukemoto] was hardly administrator of the whole domain;⁷ circumstances merely allowed him to issue this document.⁸ Although [Sukemoto's] decree states that authority should be exercised as in the past, the lack of any precedents [favoring a proprietor's *kendan* share] makes this contention untenable. Next, an order was issued by the *jitō* in the 3d year of Jōō [1224] that no changes should occur regarding this authority. If any precedents had existed, why, given this [1224] document, was the proprietor's agent not exercising a [*kendan*] involvement during these years? Considering the murder of the expert in local customs, Jūen, distortions such as we have seen presented here are entirely groundless."⁹

Morikage, citing former deputy *jitō* Sukemoto's edict, claims a two-thirds authority for the proprietor and one-third for the *jitō*. [By contrast,] Shinnen asserts total *jitō* authority, citing the precedents described by Jūen *hosshi*. But a final statement [*okijō*] by Jūen has not been produced. Moreover, although repeated *jitō* decrees state that the earlier *jitō* arrangements should be adhered to, these practices remained unclear. At this juncture, Shinano *minbu daibu* Yukimori *hosshi* was asked to present any surviving documents from Yamashiro *nyūdō*'s tenure [as *jitō*]. His reply of the 5th month, 1st day, however, stated: "Because of deteriorating paper, during the age of the late Shinano *zenji* Yukimitsu *hosshi*, these documents [*komonjo*] were thrown away, and I did not inherit any records" . . . .¹⁰

The former *jitō* Tosa Saburō Hiroyoshi *hosshi*, priestly name Jitsunen, was [then] interrogated. According to Jitsunen's sworn statement of the 6th month, 24th day: "During the tenures of Tōtomi *nyūdō* and Yamashiro *nyūdō* the *jitō* exercised full *kendan* authority over this estate. Because he was so informed, Jitsunen exercised authority in accordance with that precedent." Other depositions are omitted here.¹¹

Forthwith, in accordance with precedent, the *jitō*'s authority shall be as before [i.e. total].¹²

. . .

1st year of Kangen [1243], 7th month, 19th day

Musashi no kami, Taira ason
(monogram)

SOURCE: *Hōon'in monjo*, 1243/7/19 Kantō gechijō, *DNK, iewake* 19 (Daigoji monjo), 1: 219–24, doc. 212 (*KBSS*, 1: 67–70, doc. 72).

1. The role of former deputy *jitō* Sukemoto is especially difficult to fathom. My best guess is that after his dismissal by the *jitō* he became an ally of the *zasshō*, remaining in some kind of official capacity.

2. Since this document is unusually long, I have omitted two of the three items.

3. "Jōkyū *rangyaku*." This is the standard designation for the Jōkyū War.

4. The word "former" must refer to the present. At the time of the events being discussed, Sukemoto was still deputy *jitō*.

5. Jūen *hosshi's* statement ends here. The references are to the successive *jitō* in the period before Jōkyū. "Tōtomi *nyūdō*" refers to Hōjō Tokimasa, and "Yamashiro *nyūdō*" to Nikaidō Yukimasa, a major Bakufu figure. The third name cannot be identified. Cf. Document 116.

6. This is the first reference to Sukemoto's edict (Sukemoto *no gechijō*). The circumstances surrounding its issuing remain obscure, though it is clear that the *zasshō* was basing much of his argument on what this document contained.

7. This reference to a separate deputy for the estate's southern part is confirmed by a Kamakura decree of 1222; see Document 116. The statement of *zasshō* Morikage in the present document ignores this arrangement and assumes that Sukemoto had full authority.

8. Obviously, Sukemoto had been able to exceed his authority in the absence of the estate's chief *jitō*, who was an absentee figure.

9. Shinnen's defense statement clearly ends here; the character signifying the end of a quotation has been obliterated by a wormhole.

10. A sentence with several missing characters comes here. The references to Yukimori *hosshi* and Yukimitsu *hosshi* are to members of the prestigious Nikaidō family. At the time of this incident Yukimori was assistant head (*shitsuji*) of the shogun's chancellery (*mandokoro*). His ancestor Yukimitsu had at one time been *jitō* of Ushigahara Estate.

11. This sentence written in half-size characters.

12. This is the only possible interpretation. See the headnotes in *DNK, iewake* 19, 1: 219, and *KBSS*, 1: 68.

DOCUMENT 89

The Bakufu Settles Another Kendan Dispute, 1247

In this instance Kamakura imposed a compromise solution. Although the proprietor seems to have had the stronger case, the lack of clear precedents prompted a 50-50 settlement.

The terms of a dispute between priest Jōen, the agent [*zasshō*] for Tara Estate, Wakasa Province, and Jōsai *hosshi*, representing the *jitō* Wakasa Shirō Tadakiyo.

.   .   .

I T E M:[1] concerning the *kendan*.
Jōen stated that when this *ho* was public land [*kokuryō**], and [later] when it was called *shō*[*en*], authority lay totally with the proprietor or governor [*kokushi**]. Jōsai countered that from the time of the former *utaishō* [Yoritomo], authority lay with the *jitō*. A local peasant was summoned for questioning, and according to his statement: "During the tenure of former *jitō* Chūjō *uemon no jō* Ienaga the *kendan* lay with the custodian [*azukari dokoro*].[2] As for fines, I do not know to which side they were paid. The present *jitō*, Tadakiyo, exercises full authority." According to this statement, the authority of the custodian is confirmed.

However, it does not say that the *jitō* did not also participate. Given this circumstance, the two sides are to exercise a mutual, 50-50 authority. . . .[3]

By command of the Kamakura lord, the aforementioned five points are decreed thus.

1st year of Hōji [1247], 10th month, 29th day

> sakon no shōgen, Taira ason seal
> Sagami no kami, Taira ason seal

SOURCE: *Tōji hyakugō monjo*, 1247/10/29 Kantō gechijō an, *KBSS*, 1: 81, doc. 79.
  1. This is the second item in the document; I have omitted the first.
  2. Once again (see Document 72) we see *azukari dokoro* and *zasshō* referred to consecutively. A custodian had given way to a proprietor's agent.
  3. Three other items are omitted here.

DOCUMENT 90

A Local Shrine Seeks to Retain a Three-Way Division of the Kendan, 1229

When the *jitō* on lands belonging to Hitachi Province's Yoshida Shrine moved to upset the traditional *kendan* balance, the response of the shrine's estate agent was to seek a restoration of the original division. Presumably, if such efforts failed, the next stage would be appeal to the Bakufu.

ORDERED: to Yoshida Shrine, in Hon Gō.
    That authority over criminals shall henceforth be exercised in accordance with precedent.

Concerning the fines exacted from criminals, there are to be three shares —a proprietor's share, a *jitō's* share, and a *tadokoro** agent's share. Details appear in the edict of lord Mibu.[1] In recent years the total lapse of this arrangement has been most suspicious. Henceforth, when criminals appear, the *jitō*, in cooperation with *tadokoro* Naritsune, shall exercise jurisdiction in accordance with precedent. It is so ordered.[2]

1st year of Kangi [1229], 7th month, 9th day

> azukari dokoro, shami (monogram)

SOURCE: *Yoshida Jinja monjo*, 1229/7/9 Yoshida sha azukari dokoro kudashibumi, *Yoshida Jinja monjo*, pp. 19-20, doc. 26 (in *KI*, 6: 133, doc. 3,844).
  1. Not identified.
  2. Fifteen years later the shrine, on its own authority, directly condemned the same *jitō* for commandeering the full amount. See *Yoshida Jinja monjo*, 1244/3 Yoshida sha bō kudashibumi utsushi, *KI*, 9: 72, doc. 6,301.

THE JITŌ SEEKS LOCAL CONTROL

DOCUMENT 91

Yoritomo Prohibits a Jitō's Terrorism, 1191

From the very beginning of Kamakura's rule there were *jitō* who abused their privileges in many ways. In one incident of 1191 a *jitō* tried to seize not only land and its produce but also its cultivators.

The former *utaishō* house chancellery orders: to Sasage Kigo Chikanaga.
    That the taxes in kind from Shiojiri Saijō, a holding of Suwa Lower Shrine, shall forthwith be paid.
    Appended herewith: a [Kantō] order.

Hori Shirō *daibu* Moritsugu¹ has lodged a complaint that despite extensive farming, the taxes in recent years have not been paid, upon the pretext of crop failure. If this is true, it is most irregular. Payment should certainly be made. In addition, a complaint has been lodged that local residents have been arrested and their possessions seized; and that 17 male and female servants [*shojū**] of Moritsugu, who reside in this *gō*, have been imprisoned upon some pretext. If this is true, restitution shall take place at once. It is commanded thus. Wherefore, this order.
    2d year of Kenkyū [1191], 2d month, 21st day

ryō, kazue no jō, Fujiwara	anzu, Fujii (monogram)
(monogram)	chikeji, Nakahara (monogram)
bettō, [saki no Inaba]² no kami,	kamon no jō, Koremune (monogram)
Nakahara ason	Fujiwara

SOURCE: *Suwa Jinja monjo*, 1191/2/21 saki no utaishō ke mandokoro kudashibumi, *Suwa shiryō sōsho*, 15: 99, doc. 219 (in *KI*, 1: 387, doc. 511).
    1. The *Suwa shiryō sōsho* version reads "Morii," and that in *KI* "Morie"; both seem to be incorrect. Later in the document there is a clear reference to "Moritsugu," and a third text (*Shinano shiryō*, 3: 423) has both names this way.
    2. Characters missing but inserted.

DOCUMENT 92

The Bakufu Resolves a Proprietor's Suit Against a Jitō's Lawlessness, 1207

The document offered here is unique for its detail on an early *jitō*'s privileges and plans for aggrandizement, and the Bakufu's reasoning on each point deserves close attention. Unfortunately, the first part of the document has been lost.

. . .

A miscellaneous tribute levy [*zōji**] of 6 *to* is not a regular practice. Henceforth, it should be stopped. However, as regards firewood within this tribute [category], a reduced [levy] should be followed.

> I T E M: that the laborers conscripted for trout fishing be treated in accordance with the practice of Tokisada *hosshi*.[1]

Although a precedent for [recruiting] such workers exists, it should be handled during the harvest season in such a way as to avoid disturbing the harvesters. In essence, it is to follow the practice of Tokisada *hosshi*.

> I T E M: that the *jitō*'s requirement of hunting service from peasants be abolished during the silkworm culture season.

According to a peasants' petition [*ge*]: "If extra services are suspended during the silkworm culture season, the payment of tribute [i.e., in silk] can [take place] without difficulty." According to the *jitō*'s defense statement: "For more than ten years important [working] seasons have been observed in spite of [extra] service and without any formal complaint." Let this same custom be followed.[2]

> I T E M: that service in growing indigo likewise be ended.

Although indigo culture was once a Nii[3] tax obligation, under the authority of the provincial office [*kokuga*], when [the area] became a *shō*[*en*] the proprietor [*ryōke*] granted an exemption. Therefore, the *jitō* should not, on his own, concern himself with indigo. Let it be stopped.

ITEM: that caring for the horses of the deputy *jitō* and his men shall similarly be stopped.

As concerns providing for one or two horses belonging to the *jitō* himself, peasants shall not submit complaints. However, regarding horses belonging to the deputy and his men, [such service] is not required. When the *jitō* visits [the estate], providing such things as hay, firewood, and various greens involves no burdensome expense. Beyond that, the various necessities arising from travel by [the *jitō*'s] children and his deputy are to be borne by the *jitō myō*.[4]

ITEM: that the *jitō*'s harvesting of peasants' flax be similarly abolished.

According to the *jitō*'s defense statement: "I have never interfered with flax fields. As for mountain hemp, first the *jitō* harvested it, and next the peasants were exempt.[5] But henceforth all hemp harvesting shall cease." Of course it shall be thus.

ITEM: that the levying of men and horses [to assist in journeys] across Kizu and to the capital be similarly abolished, with the exception of taxes being transported from [*jitō*] demesne lands [*tsukuda**].[6]

Regarding men and horses [for journeys] across Kizu and to the capital, peasants shall discharge this service [only] when carrying taxes derived from *jitō* demesne lands. In addition, the service will be performed only once a year, on a system of rotation. It will be unlawful for labor and horses from this estate to be used in transporting goods from other places to Kyoto. However, any precedents should be followed.[7]

ITEM: that of the rice to be paid in lieu of labor and horses owed to the Kantō, half shall be gathered from the *jitō*'s own income share [*tokubun**].[8]

According to the *jitō*'s defense statement: "[Peasants] have met this obligation for the more than 10 years since my appointment." During more than 10 years the absence of any relief from [a commutation rate of] six *koku* of rice in place of each person's labor service shows the strictness of the *jitō*. Henceforth, for [commutation of] both labor and horses, half the cost in harvested rice shall be drawn from the *jitō*'s income share.

ITEM: that three services imposed by the [*jitō*'s] wife and deputy shall be abolished.

The *jitō* has agreed to terminate the supplying of miscellaneous services [*zōji*] to followers of the deputy, Zenke *hosshi*, [and also] to end such services, along with maid duty and the like, for Megi Rokurō's family, his deputy, and others.[9] This goes without saying. There is nothing in the *jitō's* defense statement about send-offs and welcomes for his wife, though according to the peasants' appeal this practice has involved high costs. Let these be reduced.

ITEM: that the proprietor and the *jitō* shall divide [equally] the lands and homestead areas [*zaike**] of peasants who have fled. There is great truth in the peasants' complaint that the homestead areas of fleeing persons have been seized, and their paddy and upland fields subsumed within the *jitō myō* lands. Accordingly, the *jitō* has agreed that there will be parity.[10] However, as regards the actual houses of these persons, a petition has been lodged that the proprietor exercise full control. Though so stated, when peasants flee and leave behind two homestead areas, the proprietor and the *jitō* shall divide them equitably, and shall invite unattached persons [*rōnin**] to settle there.

The foregoing points are summarized thus. As a land intended to furnish important expense funds for the nobility [*kuge*], this estate should have its residents made secure and free of distress. In the matter of the *jitō's* exercise of estate affairs [*shōmu*], in essence his actions shall be in accordance with the practices of the former *jitō*, Tokisada *hosshi*. By command of the Kamakura lord, it is decreed thus. Wherefore, this order.

1st year of Jōgen [1207], 12th month,   day

> Koremune (monogram)
> saki no zusho no jō, Kiyohara (monogram)
> san-i, Nakahara ason (monogram)
> san-i, Fujiwara ason
> shohakase, Nakahara ason (monogram)

SOURCE: *Mibu monjo*, 1207/12 Kantō gechijō, *Mibu shinsha komonjo*, pp. 48–50 (in *KI*, 3: 334–36, doc. 1,709).

1. Inaba *gon no kami* Tokisada, a local lord of Kunitomi Estate (and much of the rest of Wakasa Province) until his dispossession by the Bakufu in 1196.

2. What custom (or example = *rei*)? All sides agree that a precedent did exist. Is this not a call, then, for lenience rather than abolition? For a similar injunction, see the next-to-last "item."

3. Probably a unit within the larger Kunitomi area.

4. Lands directly administered by a *jitō*, from which only the annual rice tax (*nengu*) was owed to the estate proprietor.

5. I.e., there was an alternating labor arrangement.

6. This is hard to understand, since *tsukuda* fields were by definition exempt from all taxes. See Glossary.

7. I.e., if precedents exist that qualify this prohibition, they should be heeded.

8. Although *jitō* owed no regular land taxes to the Bakufu, they were obligated to provide labor and horses. When distances were great, these services were usually commuted to rice or cash payments. In the present instance, the *jitō* is being advised that no more than half of this obligation could be foisted off on the peasantry.

9. Megi Rokurō's identity is not explained.

10. I.e., a 50-50 division of these lands between proprietor and *jitō*.

DOCUMENT 93

The Bakufu Resolves Another Series of Complaints, 1216

The fundamental weakness of Bakufu justice is revealed here: after any action short of actual dismissal, lawless *jitō* were free to begin a new round of offenses. Kamakura disposed of most of the suits it heard with fairness and with some imagination. It was in the area of sanctions against its own men that it had to move cautiously.

The chancellery of the shogun's house orders: to Kunitomi Estate, Wakasa Province.

Instructions regarding sixteen matters.

ITEM: that cultivation of the *jitō's* demesne [*tsukuda*] shall henceforth follow the practices of the former *jitō*, Tokisada *hosshi*.

ITEM: that the *jitō* agent's monthly receipt of tribute goods is to cease.[1]

. . .

The foregoing 11 matters appear in a chancellery order of this house from the 1st year of Jōgen [1207], 12th month,   day. It was therein ordered that [these] lawless actions [*shingi hihō*] were to cease. However, according to domain petitions of the 4th year of Kempō [1216], 1st month,   day, from this imperial prayer center's table service office and from Enshūji:[2] "The resident deputy *jitō* has completely disobeyed [the earlier judgment], and year by year grows more lawless." If this is true, it is very disturbing. Why, contrary to this document, have illicit practices been engaged in? Forthwith, authority shall be exercised in accordance with the earlier judgment.

ITEM: regarding the deputy *jitō* Arimori's arresting the *kumon* and peasants and forcing them to sign pledges [*kishōmon*].[3]

According to the same complaint document:[4] "A judgment of these matters was rendered pursuant to the lawsuit of the 1st year of Jōgen[1207]. However, [this edict] was not complied with; and [the *jitō*], fearing future consequences, detained the *kumon*, Ienaga *hosshi*, as well as local peasants, in the 3d year of Jōgen [1209], 2d month, 29th day, compelling them to sign pledges." Inasmuch as the two sides were not summoned for trial, it is [now] difficult to ascertain the truth or falsity of this charge. But if it is true, it is very disturbing. Forthwith, these pledges are to be returned.

I T E M : concerning special service levies with no relief.
According to the same document: "The service demands on *kumon* and peasants have been excessive with regard to [five construction projects[5]]." As *jitō*, why should he not give orders concerning service payments? Nevertheless, for imposts of unusual severity, leniency should be shown to the residents.

I T E M : regarding the fining of peasants without cause.
According to the same document: "Despite the absence of specific crimes, fines are imposed upon the smallest pretext. Even worse, those fined and their relatives are all arrested." When criminals appear, their guilt or innocence should be determined and action taken accordingly. This matter of fining residents on some minor pretext is most disturbing. Forthwith, such lawlessness is to cease.

I T E M : regarding the flight of papermaker Tsunetoshi because of burdens imposed by the *jitō*.
According to the same document: "Tsunetoshi, who is not a common peasant, was enlisted for service out of sympathy by the proprietor. However, the *jitō* imposed various services [on him], and he fled." According to this document, justice has been forsaken. As before, this person is to be made secure. For the future, such lawlessness is to cease.

I T E M : concerning the [*jitō*'s] desire to convert various persons into dependents [*hikan**] because of the crime of a peasant named Kida.
According to the same document: "The *jitō* has confined innocent persons on the pretext that they collaborated with this thief, who has since fled." After the criminal absconded, why would even his relatives have been punished, if no guilt had been determined and no stolen goods had turned up? In the event clear proof is lacking, these persons shall be made secure.

In pursuance of the earlier [Kantō] edict, and in conformity with precedent, the aforementioned lawless acts shall be ended. The command is thus. Wherefore, this order.[6]

4th year of Kempō [1216], 8th month, 17th day

ryō, zusho no shōjō, Kiyohara (monogram)	anzu, Sugano
bettō, Mutsu no kami, Ōe ason (monogram)	chikeji, Koremune
daigaku no kami, Minamoto ason	
Sagami no kami, Taira ason (monogram)	
uma gon no kami, Minamoto ason	
saemon no gon no shōjō, Minamoto ason	
minbu, gon no shōyū, Ōe ason	
Musashi no kami, Taira ason (monogram)	
shohakase, Nakahara ason (monogram)	
Shinano no kami, Fujiwara ason (monogram)	

SOURCE: *Mibu monjo*, 1216/8/17 shōgun ke mandokoro kudashibumi, *Mibu shinsha komonjo*, pp. 51–55 (in *KI*, 4: 227–29, doc. 2,258).

1. The nine items that follow the two presented here are those that appear in full in the judgment of 1207 (Document 92). Item 1 and a portion of item 2 are missing from the 1207 record.

2. Rendering speculative.

3. These would be pledges of personal subordination to the *jitō*, or pledges confirming the validity of his claims to authority.

4. I.e., the complaint of 1216/1.

5. I omit the detailed list here. One of the five was the rebuilding of the *jitō*'s residence, which had been destroyed by fire. The other four involved Buddhist and Shinto buildings.

6. Even this second Bakufu edict did not bring peace to troubled Kunitomi Estate. In the wake of the Jōkyū War the new Rokuhara headquarters in Kyoto was called on to issue a further desist order. See *Shokoku shōho monjo*, 1221/int.10 Gyōkan gokigansho kudashibumi an, *KI*, 5: 67, doc. 2,880.

DOCUMENT 94

The Bakufu Settles a Dispute Over a Kantō Jitō's Lawlessness, 1209

Jitō were often quite resourceful in manufacturing pretexts and disguises to cover their illegal acts. In the present document, we find regular tax lands placed in a tax-exempt category, local products seized as provincial tributes, and a determination of the official hierarchy of Katori Shrine. Unfortunately, the language of this document is unusually turgid and repetitive.

ORDERED: to the *jitō* and the officers of [Katori] Shrine, Shimōsa Province.

Instructions in various matters.

ITEM: that Aine Village shall cease to be a *jitō* residence area [*hori no uchi**].

In response to a complaint by shrine administrator Hirofusa regarding this village, the deputy *jitō* Nobuhiro was summoned for trial. The charge of Hirofusa was not unfounded. Likewise, an edict of the Fujiwara house chancellery is clear in urging that the incursions of the *jitō* should stop.[1] Henceforth, the collection and delivery of the fixed taxes and tributes shall be under the authority of the shrine administrator.[2]

ITEM: that the enlistment of shrine officials for Kyoto and Kamakura labor services shall cease.

Upon the summoning for trial of the two sides, the statement presented by the shrine administrator and various other officials was not without justice. Forthwith, in accordance with precedent, labor services by shrine officials are to cease.

ITEM: that the willful seizure of paddy, upland, and homestead areas from among the vacated holdings [*ato*] of shrine officials who have fled shall cease.

Upon the summoning for trial of the two sides, the statement of shrine administrator Hirofusa showed justice. Likewise, the edict of the Fujiwara house chancellery is clear in urging that seizures by the *jitō* shall cease in regard to the vacated lands of deceased and departed shrine officials. Henceforth, these *jitō* seizures are to stop.

ITEM: that appropriations by the *jitō* shall cease, and that shrine fields [*shinden*] and added tax fields [*jōbunden**] shall be under the authority of the shrine administrator.

Upon the summoning [of the two sides] for trial, the statement of shrine administrator Hirofusa was not without justice. Forthwith, seizures by the *jitō* shall cease, and the shrine administrator is to exercise jurisdiction [*shinshi*].

ITEM: that hereditary Fujiwara fields [*watariden*[3]] shall be under authority of the shrine administrator, according to precedent.

Upon the summoning [of the two sides] for trial, the statement of shrine administrator Hirofusa was not without justice. Forthwith, seizures by the *jitō* shall cease, and authority is to be exercised in accordance with precedent.

ITEM: that the commandeering of bamboo from the 8 *chō* surrounding the treasure-house [*hōden*] shall cease.

Upon the summoning of the two sides for trial, *jitō* Tanemichi cited provincial business [*kuni no gyōji*] [as the justification] for his willful commandeering of this bamboo. Such an action is most disturbing. An

existing governor's edict is clear, in regard to provincial matters, that
authority shall be exercised by shrine administrator Hirofusa. Despite
this, Tanemichi has failed to obey and has seized [the bamboo]. The
edict of the Fujiwara house chancellery calls for such action to cease.
In accordance with this document, the authority of the *jitō* shall be
terminated; and shrine administrator Hirofusa shall exercise authority
over provincial matters.

ITEM: that the *jitō* shall cease to decide the seating arrangement
[*zaseki*⁴] for shrine officials.
Upon the summoning [of the two sides] for trial, the statement of shrine
administrator Hirofusa was not without justice. Henceforth, in accordance with precedent and with the edict of the Fujiwara house chancellery, the *jitō's* discretion [*seibai*] in this matter shall cease, and authority
shall be exercised by the shrine administrator.

ITEM: that taxes and tributes shall be paid forthwith from Shiba-
zaki and Jingūji.⁵
Upon the summoning [of the two sides] for trial, the edict of the Fujiwara house chancellery made it clear that [tax] seizures [by the *jitō*]
were to end. In accordance with precedent and with this document, the
taxes and tributes shall be paid.

ITEM: that taxes from the oilseed fields [*tōyuden*] shall be forwarded by Tamata Village.
Upon the summoning [of the two sides] for trial, the statement of shrine
administrator Hirofusa was not without justice. Since designated oilseed fields are now under cultivation, why is this service not being discharged? In accordance with the edict of the Fujiwara house chancellery, lamp oil shall be provided for.

By command of the Kamakura lord, the foregoing matters are decreed
thus. Wherefore, this edict.

3d year of Jōgen [1209], 3d month, 17th day

> Koremune seal
> saki no zusho no jō, Kiyohara seal
> san-i, Nakahara ason seal
> san-i, Fujiwara ason seal
> shohakase, Nakahara ason seal

SOURCE: *Katori sha kyū Ōnegi ke monjo*, 1209/3/17 Kantō gechijō an, *Chiba ken
shiryō, chūsei hen, Katori monjo*, pp. 68–69 (*KBSS*, 1: 13–15, doc. 17).

1. Katori Shrine was under the special protection of the main Fujiwara line. For
this Fujiwara edict, see *Katori sha kyū Ōnegi ke monjo*, 1207/10 kampaku ke mandokoro kudashibumi, *KI*, 3: 329–32, doc. 1,703.

2. By claiming that the Aine region was a personal residence area, the *jitō* was

attempting to block a new tax survey (*kenchū*) there by the proprietor. For details, see *ibid.*

3. This interpretation is speculative. The term *watariryō* is sometimes used to refer to a special group of estates held by the Fujiwara house chieftain. See Glossary under *denka goryō*. In this case, however, the Fujiwara head's own chancellery states that these *watariden* belong under shrine supervision (*sata*). Cf. the document cited in Note 1. Perhaps the affected lands were merely possessed by the Fujiwara at the level of *honke*.

4. I.e., the hierarchy.

5. The names of bay areas (*ura*) in the vicinity. See the document cited in Note 1.

DOCUMENT 95

The Bakufu Issues a Desist Order to Three Neighboring Jitō, 1222

The incident described here involves a fragmented *shōen*, with its lands scattered within three larger *gō* units. And each *gō* has a *jitō* who wishes to extend his authority into the divided estate.

That the incursions into lands belonging to Nii Estate, Tajima Province, an Omuro[1] domain—by the *jitō* of Taki [Gō], Numata Saburō; the *jitō* of Mikata Gō, Shibuya Saburō; and the *jitō* of Hikage Gō, Koshio *uma no jō*—shall cease forthwith.

A letter of accusation concerning the foregoing has stated: "The holdings of this estate include 1 *chō*, 7 *tan* in lower Taki Gō, over 7 *chō* in Mikata Gō, and 7 *tan* in Hikage Gō.[2] But upon the pretext that each [holding] was *gō* land, violations were committed, and estate residents were made weary under a double burden.[3] Their will to work the land was lost, and the temple holdings fell into ruin." If this is true, the appropriation of Nii Estate lands by the *jitō* of these *gō* is most unseemly. These willful acts must certainly stop: the Nii Estate lands shall be as before, and their residents are to be made secure. By this command, it is so decreed.

1st year of Jōō [1222], 7th month, 7th day

Mutsu no kami, Taira (monogram)

SOURCE: *Ninnaji monjo*, 1222/7/7 Kantō gechijō, *KBSS*, 1: 23, doc. 26 (*KI*, 5: 115, doc. 2,973).

1. I.e., Ninnaji Temple of Kyoto.

2. To complicate matters, a document of 1223 (Document 96) lists the total paddy holdings of Nii Estate as 18.883 *chō*, whereas the total here (paddy not specified) is only 9.4 *chō*. Also, a Nii Estate *jitō* is referred to who is not one of the three

gō-level *jitō* mentioned here. Discovery of this second document necessitates a small emendation to my remarks regarding Nii Estate in *Warrior Government* (p. 197, l. 7): "consisted of" should read "contained."

3. I.e., were confronted with levies by both the proprietor and these three *jitō*— by *shō* and *gō* assessments.

DOCUMENT 96

Kamakura Orders a Jitō to Cease His Lawlessness, 1223

Between mid-1222 and the end of 1223 conditions clearly worsened on Nii Estate (see Document 95). In addition to pressures from the neighboring *jitō*, Nii now began to have trouble with its own *jitō*, who had been newly appointed. For the second time Kamakura was called on to assist a beleaguered *shōen*.

That the illegal acts of the *jitō* of Nii Estate, Tajima Province, an Omuro holding, shall cease forthwith.

According to the letter of accusation in this matter: "Of the total paddy fields of 18 *chō*, 8 *tan*, 300 *bu*,[1] the taxable lands [*jōden**] are 13 *chō*, 7 *tan*, 120 *bu*. Of the total upland field count of 12 *chō*, 9 *tan*, 16 *bu*, the taxable lands are 8 *chō*, 7 *tan*, 96 *bu*. Nevertheless, the newly appointed *jitō* Utada Shirō Iemori,[2] by ignoring custom and figuring from the total field area, has increased the burden of the surtax [*kachō**] to an unendurable amount." If this is true, it is most disturbing. Forthwith, such willful acts are to cease; and both surtax and grant lands [*kyūden**], according to a court edict, shall be based on the taxable fields only. By this command, it is so decreed.

2d year of Jōō [1223], 12th month, 24th day

saki no Mutsu no kami, Taira (monogram)

SOURCE: *Ninnaji monjo*, 1223/12/24 Kantō gechijō, *KBSS*, 1: 29–30, doc. 36 (*KI*, 5: 253, doc. 3,193).

1. I.e., 18.883 *chō*; 1 *chō* = 10 *tan* = 3,600 *bu*.
2. Obviously this was an officer appointed after the Jōkyū War.

DOCUMENT 97

The Bakufu Orders the Replacement of a Jitō, 1216

In this fascinating episode, a native *goke'nin* had become a *jitō* after promising the dutiful collection of taxes. Later, after thoroughly abusing his office, he refused to recognize the proprietor's attempt to dismiss him independently, since only the Bakufu could take such action.

The chancellery of the shogun's house orders: to Gakuenji, Izumo Province.

That former *jitō* Takamoto's encroachments shall cease forthwith, and that Kura Takayuki shall be *jitō*, in accordance with an order from the main temple.

According to a petition by officials of Ryōgon Sammai-in: "Regarding the *jitō shiki* for lands belonging to Gakuenji, a branch of this temple. Takamoto was appointed to this *shiki* by virtue of his entreaty that under this title he would forward, without negligence, the fixed annual tax and other levies. However . . .[1] as though forgetful of his name,[2] he has failed entirely to pay these obligations [*shotō**]. Moreover, the annual tax and dues owed to the temple priests were sequestered at his pleasure; and the entire quota from the past two years of both upland taxes and household family cloth [*zaike nuno*] has not been paid. [Also], a male servant [*shojū**] named Fuji Jirō, who belonged to Tsuina— real name unknown[3]—the former estate custodian, had his family arrested and his house taken over, without any specific guilt [on his part]. Then the servant himself was murdered in Hōki Province. In consequence of this, the *jitō shiki* was cancelled; but [Takamoto], claiming to possess a shogunal house edict, disregarded the main temple's order and expanded the scope of his lawlessness."

The utter ingratitude for the main temple's favor apparent in these outrages is totally reprehensible. Forthwith, in accordance with the main temple's order, Takamoto's evil deeds [*mudō*] are to cease, and Takayuki shall become *jitō*. By this command, it is ordered thus. Wherefore, this edict.

4th year of Kempō [1216], 5th month, 13th day

ryō, zusho no shōjō, Kiyohara
   (monogram)
bettō, Mutsu no kami, Nakahara ason
   (monogram)
daigaku no kami, Minamoto ason
Sagami no kami, Taira ason (monogram)
uma gon no kami, Minamoto ason[4]
saemon no gon no shōjō, Minamoto ason (monogram)
minbu gon no shōyū, Minamoto ason (monogram)[4]
Musashi no kami, Taira ason (monogram)
shohakase, Nakahara ason (monogram)
Shinano no kami, Fujiwara ason (monogram)

anzu, Sugano (monogram)
chikeji, Koremune (monogram)

SOURCE: *Gakuenji monjo*, 1216/5/13 shōgun ke mandokoro kudashibumi, *Shinshū Shimane kenshi, shiryō hen* 1, pp. 332–33 (*KI*, 4: 215, doc. 2,231).
    1. The text is corrupt here.
    2. I.e., his *jitō* title.
    3. In half-size characters.
    4. The two names cited here are omitted in the *Shinshū Shimane kenshi* version but included in *KI*.

DOCUMENT 98

Rokuhara Orders a Jitō to Follow Precedent, 1233

After the Jōkyū War the Bakufu established a branch office in the Rokuhara sector of Kyoto. This agency was expected to judge suits relating to central and western Japan. In practice its settlements were rarely considered final, and appeal to Kamakura, as indicated here, was always a possibility. The resolution in this case—an admonition to follow unspecified precedents—gives little promise of effective justice.

Concerning the *jitō's* income [*tokubun*] and administrative authority [*shomu*] in Ōbu Estate, Harima Province.

Details were investigated in response to a seven-point appeal made by the estate deputy. [According to the *jitō's* statement:] "The *jitō shiki* of this estate does not involve a new Jōkyū land.[1] Since the appointment in the 3d year of Kempō [1215] there have been no changes [*shingi**] in either administration or income share." When the estate agent was questioned concerning this, he stated: "The foregoing is correct;[2] however, our suit is the result of the *jitō's* lawlessness." It is difficult, given these arguments, to determine right and wrong. In essence, authority should be exercised, mutually and in accordance with precedent, by both the estate agent and the *jitō*. Beyond this, should grievances remain on either side, the Kantō shall be informed. The order is thus.

2d year of Jōei [1233], 2d month, 29th day

kamon no suke, Taira seal
Suruga no kami, Taira seal

SOURCE: *Tōdaiji monjo*, 1233/2/29 Rokuhara gechijō an, *KBSS*, 2: 6, doc. 5 (*KI*, 7: 13, doc. 4,453).
    1. See Glossary under *shimpo jitō*.
    2. I.e., the *jitō* appointment indeed predated Jōkyū and had experienced no lawful increases in authority or perquisites.

DOCUMENT 99

Rokuhara Resolves Another Dispute, 1238

The document presented here has no peer among Rokuhara settlement decrees for richness of detail and intrinsic interest. Though various references remain obscure, the history of a *shōen* and those who hoped to dominate it emerges in bold relief.

The points of a dispute between the priest Kakushū, agent [*zasshō*] for Sasakibe Estate, Tamba Province, a Matsuo Shrine land, and the *jito, saemon no jō* Ōya Mitsunobu.

ITEM: concerning tax arrears for the *jitō myō*.¹
When the two sides were summoned for trial, many details emerged. In essence, Kakushū stated: "In the 2d year of Tenshō [1132] shortages [in the payments] for daily ceremonies and shrine offerings became frequent on this estate. By imperial order, the shrine authorities were given total jurisdiction; and, according to their own decision, appointed various persons [*kō-otsu no tomogara**] to the estate offices of *gesu, kumon,* and *anzu.*² At the time of the Jishō treachery,³ when *jitō* were appointed countrywide, the former shrine administrator, Sukeyori, owing to the merit of his prayers toward ending future trouble, was granted a Kantō order in the 2d year of Bunji [1186].⁴

"During the period in which Kajiwara Kagetoki served as deputy [*jitō*]⁵ he took no rights, in conformity with the original managerial practice, beyond the possession of 2 *chō* of grant fields and 8 *chō* of *myō* fields. However, after Kagetoki's downfall Iida Daigorō Kiyoshige was appointed to the *jitō shiki*, claiming [Kagetoki's] inheritance [*ato*].⁶ But because it was stated in the investiture edict that estate administration should follow precedent, the original managerial practices [*honshi no rei*] remained unaltered. Although Sukeyori protested that the grant to the shrine had [in fact] been changed, he was now in his 80's and had been ill for many years. Because he had not been able to state his case effectively,⁷ the years passed for him in sadness, even though estate administration, following Kagetoki's practice, had not [yet] been interfered with.

"After Jōkyū, however, the *jitō*'s activities became extremely lawless; and a Kantō edict of the 2d year of Jōō [1223] asked that all disruptive acts cease. In consequence, no further disturbances occurred,⁸ although taxes from the *jitō*'s *myō* fields now came to be held back on an annual basis. Under a tax assessment in excess of 25 *koku* a year, a little over

120 _koku_ of the total 427 set aside as shrine rice were paid during the 17-year period from the 3d year of Jōkyū [1221] through the 3d year of Katei [1237]; thus more than 300 _koku_ have been withheld. As 'pledged fields' [_kishōden_] of long standing,[9] this estate had never had taxes withheld. However, [taxes from] the _jitō's myō_ fields [now] went unpaid, and [this prompted] our effort to appeal the shortages in the vital daily shrine [rice]. In this present year, moreover, on the pretext of attendance on the shogun,[10] [the _jitō's_] disobedience became excessive; it was virtually as though the power of the Jōō [1223] order had vanished.

"To conclude, then, we petition for one of two judgments: the assignment of the _jitō_ title to the shrine, according to the order of Bunji [1186];[11] or payment of the [_jitō's_] mounting tax deficit, the remedying of shrine shortages, the cessation of lawless acts, and a quieting of estate officers' complaints."

Mitsunobu offered this defense: "At the time of Kajiwara's overthrow, my father, Kiyoshige, was granted this estate's _jitō shiki_ by virtue of his loyalty in the Takahashi Battle.[12] However, it was a small and distant place; and when a retainer [_ge'nin*_] was dispatched there [he found] only scattered paddy and dry fields lying desolate in a marshy area. Inasmuch as this grant land was called the 'original officer legacy' [_honshi no ato*_], the _jitō's_ income from it [_tokubun_] was obviously in name only.

"Out of the 10 _chō_ of _myō_ fields, 3 _chō_, 5 _tan_, and 30 _shiro_[13] had been unworked for more than 30 years. However, since it is stated that there was no unpaid tax before Jōkyū, there is no need to answer [for that period]. After Jōkyū, [an additional] 6 _tan_, 30 _shiro_, of paddy fell to waste, and taxes were not paid at all from this sector. It is a lie that for some 20 years before Jōkyū 25 _koku_ in taxes were being delivered [annually].[14] Let the receipts be called in. Moreover, concerning the years after Jōkyū, such figures cannot be found at all. The two or three persons appointed as deputy [_jitō_] have each stated that there was never any difficulty.

"Finally, although the Jōō [1223] order may have been issued, the fact that it was not sent to the then _jitō_ shows the unfortunate position of Mitsunobu. Without being informed of details, he is suddenly rebuked for a liability accumulated over many years. If payment cannot be managed, the plan is evidently to have him removed from his [_shiki_]. On the question of whether any arrears exist, the [_jitō's_] _myō_ fields should be surveyed, and if any facts are uncovered the deputy [_jitō_] should be summoned and interrogated."

Kakushū rejoined thus: "On the occasion of a general survey in the

2d year of Bunji [1186], there was a register by *tsubo*[15] of the *gesu's myō* fields. In accordance with this, Kajiwara exercised his authority during those years.[16] In pursuance of that legacy [*ato*], the present *jitō*, as is clear from the provincial register [*zuchō*],[17] has held [these fields] now for several decades. How, then, can [our demands] be called unprecedented [*shingi*]? Finally, on the occasion of last year's inspection" —the 3d year of Katei [1237][18]—"the *jitō myō* was not at all desolate. If taxes were not warranted, why, over the years, have there not been calls for an inspection?" This is point one.[18]

"Next, there is the minor contention that taxes were never requested, and that the rebuke came suddenly. [In fact] this requisition was made every year. . . ."[19] This is point two.[18]

"Next is the false claim regarding the 25 *koku*. It was requested that the receipts be called in. In response, receipts from the 3d year of Kenryaku [1213], the 2d year of Kempō [1214], and the 3d year of Kempō [1215] have been presented for examination. In that regard, the *jitō* has claimed that *jitō myō* fields lay desolate for more than 20 years before Jōkyū and 18 years after, a total of [nearly] 40 years. The 25-*koku* figure appears in the receipts as the [*jitō*] *myō* assessment before Jōkyū. However, after the [Jōkyū] treachery, the receipts decreased. And because no more than 5 or 6 *koku* [were delivered] every year thereafter, the arrears are now several hundred *koku*. [Moreover,] there is no justification for blaming this on the deputy *jitō*. According to the [Jōei] Code, 'If the proprietor's annual tax is withheld, blame is to lie with the master even if it is the act of a deputy.'[20] In regard to these arrears, then, since authority lay with Mitsunobu, he should pay." This is point three.[18]

"Next, regarding the claim that the Jōō order was not sent to Mitsunobu: because the original document [*shōmon**] constituted important evidence, it has been held by the shrine since its arrival; but a copy [*anmon*] was sent to the deputy *jitō*, and he ceased his lawlessness. How, then, can [Mitsunobu] falsely claim that the directive was never sent?" This is point four.[18]

"Next, concerning inspection [*kenmi*] of the *myō* fields, regular surveys [*shōken*] were made during Bunji [1186] and Katei [1237]. But even in years when special investigations [*naiken**] were conducted into [crop] loss, payments were withheld by the deputy *jitō*. Why should we have still another inspection?" This is point five.[18]

Mitsunobu rejoined: "As to the existence of an [earlier] suit alleging [overt] *jitō* lawlessness and several hundred *koku* in tax arrears, I have no knowledge of this, since the directive [*migyōsho*][21] that was issued was not sent to me. Still, not having submitted an acknowledgment [*ukebumi**] of this order, I feel mixed grief and fear. In the event of any [future] suits alleging tax default on this small and distant holding, where I have no personal involvement in administration, I will interrogate the deputy at once and take care of [the matter].²² Because the [1223] directive was not sent [to me], I must now admit that several hundred *koku* [in arrears] accumulated between Jōō and last year. But please understand that I was not aware of the instruction that a *shiki* holder must bear responsibility for the acts of his deputy."

[The Bakufu renders judgment:]
During the time of shrine administrator Sukeyori, the shrine was assigned the *jitō shiki* because of the merit of [his] prayers. Because Kagetoki was appointed deputy at the same time, after his repudiation the legacy [*ato*] was assigned to [a new *jitō*,] Kiyoshige. Given the circumstances, although a *jitō* holding a Kantō appointment should not have been patterned after a *gesu* under shrine patronage,²³ it was recorded [in the edict] that [the *jitō's*] authority be exercised in accordance with precedent. Two generations, a period of 40 years, have now passed under Kiyoshige's and Mitsunobu's authority [*ryōchi*] with no changes whatsoever. At the time of Jōkyū, of course, a suit was presented alleging misconduct by the deputy *jitō*; [but] a prohibitory [Kantō] edict was issued in response. After that, no lawlessness occurred until this year, when, on the pretext of accompanying [the shogun] to Kyoto, a series of "new practices" [*shingi*] were reportedly introduced.²⁴ There is not the slightest justification for this.

In pursuance of precedents for the *jitō's* authority extending from the 2d year of Shōji [1200] through the 3d year of Jōkyū [1221], there are to be no changes. As for the taxes, these provide for an important daily rice offering [by the shrine]. In accordance with the pre-Jōkyū payment custom, there will be no further peculation [*taikan**]. As to the more than 300 *koku* of accumulated debt, it is to be paid off within three years.²⁵

. . .²⁶

4th year of Katei [1238], 10th month, 19th day

Echigo no kami, Taira (monogram)
Sagami no kami, Taira (monogram)

SOURCE: *Higashi monjo*, 1238/10/19 Rokuhara gechijō, *KBSS*, 2: 9–12, doc. 7 (in *KI*, 7: 410–15, doc. 5,315).
  1. Lands assigned to a *jitō* but owing the annual rice tax (*nengu*).
  2. See Glossary. Obviously, the imperial order had granted Matsuo Shrine an unrestricted proprietorship.
  3. A standard term for the Kantō rebellion of 1180–83, but curious in a lawsuit

brought before the Bakufu. Was it "treachery," after all, that had inspired the Minamoto movement? Also, we know that *jitō* were not appointed "countrywide" until 1186 and beyond.

4. I.e., Sukeyori was granted a *jitō shiki*.

5. This appointment by Yoritomo of one of his closest advisors as deputy *jitō* was highly unusual. In the event, Kagetoki was to serve virtually as a *jitō*. For the time being, however, Matsuo Shrine's jurisdiction over estate officers (but not their deputies) was to remain inviolate. Kagetoki was the most hated of Yoritomo's confidants, and within months of the Kamakura lord's death in 1199 a conspiracy brought him down.

6. In other words, the Bakufu had dropped the facade of a deputy *jitō* and appointed its man to the title itself.

7. Speculative; several characters missing here.

8. That is, blatant illegalities.

9. Fields earmarked long ago (1132?) exclusively for the support of Matsuo Shrine.

10. The shogun Yoritsune made a pilgrimage to Kyoto early in 1238. For details, see *AK* 1238/1/28, 2/17, *et seq.*

11. I.e., a cancellation of the *jitō* title, which would restore the shrine's full authority over the estate.

12. The incident that resulted in Kajiwara Kagetoki's death.

13. A total of 3.56 *chō*; 50 *shiro* = 1 *tan*.

14. Evidently, Mitsunobu was trying to prove that the tax figure of 25 *koku* was inaccurate. That is: since such a high figure was never paid before Jōkyū, and since there were no claims of arrears for that period, how could the estate agent base his present calculations on 25 *koku*?

15. A square measure of this period equal to one *chō*.

16. Here is the standard *jitō/gesu* distinction: before the 1186 appointment, Sasakibe Estate had a *gesu* manager under proprietary authority. Then a *jitō* was appointed, who replaced the *gesu* and fell heir to his perquisites. What was different in this case was that during the first generation it was "deputy" *jitō* Kajiwara who received the inheritance.

17. See Glossary under *zudenchō*.

18. Phrase in half-size characters; possibly an interpolation by the Bakufu.

19. Several characters have been lost here.

20. Notice that the estate agent was here seeking to use Kamakura's own laws, the Jōei Code of 1232, against a Bakufu retainer.

21. One might wonder why the *jitō* calls this document a "directive," which is in effect for only a short time, rather than a "settlement edict" (*gechijō*). Elsewhere, the document is referred to by the latter term, which is clearly correct.

22. Speculative; several characters missing.

23. Here the Bakufu seems to be admitting its own mistake in converting, without justification, a *gesu* legacy under shrine jurisdiction into a *jitō shiki* under its own authority.

24. Here, as throughout the document, there is a clear distinction between overt lawlessness (referred to as *shingi hihō*, or either of these words alone) and tax default (referred to, with some change in nuance, as *taikan*, *yokuryū*, or *mishin*).

25. Article 5 of the Jōei Code prescribes this three-year repayment rule.

26. The document continues with other matters.

DOCUMENTS 100-106

The Bakufu Is Called on to Settle a Long-Standing Dispute Over a Jitō Shiki, 1205–33

The seven documents in this series form an absorbing jigsaw puzzle. Clearly, some of the pieces are missing, but enough remains to tell a fascinating story. The major issues are the failure for some years to clarify the status of an interior *myō* unit within a *jitō's* appointment area, an attempt by the proprietor to reclassify a *jitō* as a *gesu*, and the importance to the *jitō* of placing land rights under the protective immunity of his *shiki*.

100

That forthwith, in accordance with the testament of his father, Toshihira, [Iehira][1] shall possess Matsuyoshi Myō, on the western side of Kutsuna Island, Iyo Province.

According to Iehira's statement regarding the foregoing: "Mutō Myō, on the eastern side of this island, was given to my elder brother Kanehira. Although Matsuyoshi Myō, on the western side, was given to me, Kanehira has interfered there." If this is true, it is most irregular. Forthwith, Kanehira's interference is to cease; and, in conformity with the testament, Iehira shall have possession. By command of the Kamakura lord, it is so decreed.

2d year of Genkyū [1205], 5th month, 6th day

Tōtomi no kami, Taira seal

101

udaijin house[2]
seal

ORDERED: to the residents of Kutsuna Island, Iyo Province.
Concerning appointment to a *jitō shiki*:
Fujiwara Kanehira.[3]

The aforesaid person is appointed to this *shiki*. It is commanded thus. Wherefore, this order.

2d year of Genkyū [1205], 11th month, 12th day

102

Concerning the *jitō myō* [lands] and the grant paddy and upland fields [*kyūdenpata**] on Kutsuna Island, Iyo Province. Upon receipt of a petition, the Kamakura lord instructed that no changes should occur, and that precedents should be observed. Accordingly, it is hereby so conveyed.

2d year of Ken'ei [1207], 5th month, 6th day

san-i (monogram), magistrate[4]

103

ORDERED: to the residents of Kutsuna Island, Iyo Province.
Concerning appointment to a *jitō shiki*:
Fujiwara Kunishige.

The aforesaid person, in accordance with the testament of his father, Kanehira, is to exercise authority under this *shiki*, pursuant to precedent. By command of the Kamakura lord, it is so decreed. Wherefore, this order.

2d year of Jōgen [1208], intercalary 4th month, 27th day

Koremune (monogram)
saki no zusho no jō, Kiyohara (monogram)
san-i, Nakahara ason
san-i, Fujiwara ason seal
shohakase, Nakahara ason seal

104

Concerning the *jitō shiki* of Kutsuna Island, Iyo Province. The aforesaid *shiki*, in accordance with hereditary right and an order from the late *udaijin*, is confirmed [*ando*] to Fujiwara Kunishige.[5] Moreover, the paddy and uplands of Matsuyoshi Myō within this island are similarly to be administered without change. By this command, it is so decreed.

3d year of Jōkyū [1221], intercalary 10th month, 12th day

Mutsu no kami, Taira seal

105

Regarding the petition of Iyo Province vassal Kunishige concerning the *jitō shiki* and Matsuyoshi Myō of Kutsuna Island, same province.

Citing an estate agent's report [*zasshō no ge*] that the *gesu* of this island, Kunishige, had engaged in cunning plots and had seized Matsuyoshi Myō, the proprietor lodged a suit.[6] In response, a document of inquiry [*toijō**] was sent [to Kunishige]. However, [the latter] claimed that the estate agent, citing this document, had himself violated Matsuyoshi Myō.[7] According to a Kantō order of the 3d year of Jōkyū, intercalary 10th month, 12th day, in Kunishige's possession: "Concerning the *jitō shiki* of Kutsuna Island, Iyo Province. The aforesaid *shiki*, in accordance with hereditary right and an order from the late *udaijin*, is confirmed to Fujiwara Kunishige. Moreover, the paddy and uplands of Matsuyoshi Myō within this island are similarly to be administered without change." As to the allegation that Matsuyoshi Myō was seized by the *gesu* holder, this is a totally false claim by the agent. At all events, in conformity with the order of Jōkyū, this island's *jitō shiki*, as well as Matsuyoshi Myō, shall be held by Kunishige in accordance with precedent. It is thus.

> 1st year of Jōei [1232], 7th month, 27th day

> > Kamon no suke, Taira seal
> > Suruga no kami, Taira seal

106

The *jitō shiki* of Kutsuna Island, Iyo Province, was granted to Kanehira in the 2d year of Genkyū [1205] by an investiture from the *udaijin*. In the second year of Jōgen [1208] *sama no jō* Kunishige was issued a similar order in accordance with the testament of his father. Moreover, in the 3d year or [Jōkyū[8]] an edict was issued that Matsuyoshi Myō of the *jitō*'s holding should continue without change.[9] In response to the proprietor's suit[10] that in the present year Kunishige had seized Matsuyoshi Myō and failed to pay the annual tax, an inquiry document was sent by Suruga *no kami* and *kamon no suke*.[11] [The *jitō*], however, claimed that the estate agent used this record to seize the *myō* himself. According to Kunishige's defense summary [*chinjō*]: "Since the time of my grandfather Toshihira's commendation [of Kutsuna Island] to Chōkōdō [Temple],[12] paddy and upland taxes in excess of 200 *koku* have been paid [annually]. Apart from the 3 *chō* of paddy and 13 *chō* of dry land composing Matsuyoshi Myō, I have drawn neither surtax nor grant fields [*kachō kyūden*]."[13] Evidently no change is warranted now. Forthwith, in accordance with repeated judgments, authority shall be exercised without interference. By command of the Kamakura lord, it is so decreed.

> 1st year of Tempuku [1233], 12th month, 10th day

> > Musashi no kami, Taira seal
> > Sagami no kami, Taira seal

SOURCES: Document 100: *Kutsuna ke monjo*, 1205/5/6 Kantō gechijō an, *Ehime ken hennenshi*, 2: 200 (in *KI*, 3: 237, doc. 1,539). Document 101: *Chōryūji monjo*, 1205/11/12 Minamoto Sanetomo kudashibumi an, *Ehime ken hennenshi*, 2: 206 (in *KI*, 3: 262, doc. 1,588). Document 102: *Kutsuna ke monjo*, 1207/5/6 Kantō migyōsho, *Ehime ken hennenshi*, 2: 214 (in *KI*, 3: 315, doc. 1,683). Document 103:

ibid., 1208/int.4/27 shōgun ke mandokoro kudashibumi, *Ehime ken hennenshi*, 2: 14 (*KI*, 3: 356, doc. 1,740). Document 104: *Chōryūji monjo*, 1221/int.10/12 Kantō gechijō an, *Ehime ken hennenshi*, 2: 245–46 (in *KI*, 5: 65, doc. 2,874). Document 105: *ibid.*, 1232/7/27 Rokuhara gechijō an, *Ehime ken hennenshi*, 2: 259–60 (*KBSS*, 2: 5–6, doc. 4). Document 106: *ibid.*, 1233/12/10 Kantō gechijō an, *Ehime ken hennenshi*, 2: 263 (*KBSS*, 1: 50–51, doc. 54).

1. Characters lost, but inferred by translator.
2. Minamoto Sanetomo. This name must have been added later, since Sanetomo did not become *udaijin* until 1218.
3. Why, six months after issuing a desist order to Kanehira as the aggressor, did the Bakufu promote him to *jitō* over the whole island? The fate of the younger brother is unknown, though it is clear that Matsuyoshi Myō did not immediately become a full possession of Kanehira.
4. Nikaidō Yukimasa, an officer of the Bakufu. The identity of the addressee is unknown.
5. Unlike many vassals from Iyo Province, Kunishige remained loyal to Kamakura in the Jōkyū War. The present document is merely a reaffirmation of his *jitō shiki.*
6. The *zasshō's* reference to Kunishige as a *gesu* points up the critical importance of the *jitō/gesu* distinction.
7. I.e., the deputy had used the *toijō* as proof of his position.
8. The text actually says "3d year of Ken'ei" (1208), but the reference is probably to the 3d year of Jōkyū (1221); see Document 104. The Ken'ei era had no 3d year.
9. This is the first time that Matsuyoshi Myō is being placed explicitly *under* Kunishige's *jitō shiki.* The 1221 record referred to here does not actually make this placement.
10. I.e., the suit presented to Rokuhara the previous year.
11. The two Rokuhara deputies, Hōjō Shigetoki and Hōjō Tokimori.
12. According to Kunishige's house genealogy this was in 1182. See *Kutsuna ke monjo, Iyo shiryō shūsei* 1, p. 22.
13. It is possible that the last part of this sentence should read: "I have drawn both surtax and grant fields." All but one of the several printed versions of this document leave out the character "not," thereby making it a positive statement. However, the basic thrust of Kunishige's argument seems better served by the negative implication; see the transcription in *Ehime ken hennenshi*, 2: 14. For the omission of "not," see the *KBSS*, *KI*, and *DNS* versions. A second possibility is that the drafters of the record intended the negative meaning but omitted it in error (just as the reference to an earlier edict was apparently misdated; cf. Note 8). Unfortunately, the original of the present an is not extant.

DOCUMENT 107

A Governor Issues an Order Regarding a Jitō's Violations, 1232

The *kachō* surtax was a special rice levy exacted by estate officers. In Kamakura times it became a regular perquisite of the *jitō.* In the present instance we see a governor attempting to retain an earlier *kachō* ratio for a unit of public land. Note that this edict is sent to the absentee governor's office, not to the *jitō*, who was outside the governor's jurisdiction.

seal

Governor's decree: to the absentee office.

That in accordance with precedent, the *jitō*'s surtax violations in Yoda Ho shall cease forthwith.

The said *jitō*'s surtax [*kachōmai*] has long been paid at the rate of 3 *shō* of early rice per *tan* of original fields. Reportedly, no payment was made for new fields. This is clear, also, from an edict[1] dating from the time when provincial affairs [*kokumu*] were under the late priest Shōbō.[2] It is hereby decreed, in accordance with precedent, that surtax payments in excess of the 3 *shō* per *tan* of original fields shall cease forthwith. The absentee office shall take note, and shall act accordingly. Wherefore, this edict.

1st year of Jōei [1232], 11th month,   day

ōsuke, Fujiwara ason

SOURCE: *Tōdaiji monjo*, 1232/11 Suō kokushi chōsen an, *KI*, 6: 413, doc. 4,408.

1. The term is *ongechijō*, the standard for a Bakufu edict. However, we cannot be certain that this is the meaning here.

2. Probably, Shunjōbō Chōgen, a priest-administrator who was put in charge of Suō and Bizen Provinces when they were designated as Tōdaiji proprietorships [*chigyōkoku*°]. Chōgen died in 1206.

THE JITŌ AND HIS DEPUTIES

DOCUMENTS 108-10

A Jitō House Appoints Deputy Jitō, 1197, 1247, 1264

Most Kantō vassals who received *jitō shiki* appointed members of their own families or bands as deputies (*jitōdai*); they themselves remained at home. Thus *jitō* authority was largely exercised by proxies. These deputies, moreover, were the vassals only of their immediate lords; Kamakura had no direct jurisdiction over them. The three documents presented here show deputy appointments of different types:[1] an administrative assignment, a reward for valor in battle,[2] and an assignment to a widow. It was not until the fourteenth century, when warfare increased dramatically, that women came to be denied both *jitō* and *jitōdai* titles.

108

(monogram)

ORDERED: to Kama Tribute Estate [*mikuriya**].
Concerning an appointment to the *jitōdai shiki* of Upper and Lower Kama Gō:
Minamoto Kiyonari.

The aforesaid person, as holder of this title, shall conduct administration [*shomu*]. It is so commanded. Residents shall take note, and shall not be remiss. Wherefore, this order.
8th year of Kenkyū [1197], 6th month,　day

109

(monogram)

ORDERED: to Taira Mitsuhiro.

That forthwith he shall hold the *jitōdai shiki* for Hajizuka Gō, Natori District, Mutsu Province.

The aforesaid person, as a reward for meritorious service, shall hold this title. It is commanded thus. Wherefore, this order.

1st year of Hōji [1247], 7th month, 18th day

110

(monogram)

Concerning the *jitōdai shiki* for Iwatate Village, Hiraga District, Mutsu Province.

The nun-widow of Soga Daijirō shall possess [this title], as of old.[3] It is so commanded.

1st year of Bun'ei [1264], 5th month,   day[4]

SOURCES: Document 108: *Kama Jimmyōgū monjo*, 1197/6 Hōjō Tokimasa kudashibumi, *Shizuoka ken shiryō*, 5: 823–24 (in *KI*, 2: 233, doc. 921). Document 109: *Saitō monjo*, 1247/7/18 Hōjō Tokiyori kudashibumi, *Nambu ke monjo*, p. 244, doc. 194 (*KI*, 9: 390, doc. 6,856). Document 110: *Saitō monjo*, 1264/5 Hōjō Masamura andojō, *Nambu ke monjo*, p. 282, doc. 264 (also in *Iwate ken chūsei monjo*, 1: 7, doc. 24).

1. Yet they are all issued by scions of the house of Hōjō. Although deputies were universally used, only the Hōjō (and later the Ashikaga) seem to have been of sufficient standing to assume a right of formal investiture. See Satō Shin'ichi, *Komonjogaku nyūmon*, p. 132.

2. The Miura War of 1247.

3. I.e., shall retain the title held by her husband. Widows in Kamakura times commonly received Buddhist orders.

4. The *Nambu ke monjo* version specifies "10th day," as does an early transcription in *Aomori kenshi* (1: 30). However, the more recent transcription in *Iwate ken chūsei monjo* is probably the correct one.

DOCUMENT 111

A Jitō Deputy Confirms a Tadokoro Shiki, 1209

Very few documents by deputy *jitō* survive. In this instance an estate official appointed by the *jitō* was "endorsed" by the deputy. It was this *jitōdai* who was actually present on the estate.

ORDERED: to Tokunaga Estate [*goryō*],[1] Sawara District.
Concerning confirmation of a *tadokoro shiki* appointment:
Mibu Yoshinaga.

The aforesaid person has been appointed to this *shiki*. Resident notables and peasants shall take note, and shall not be remiss. The command is thus. Wherefore, this order.

3d year of Jōgen [1209], 3d month, 9th day

jitōdai, Minamoto (monogram facsimile)

SOURCE: *Iimori Jinja monjo*, 1209/3/9 jitōdai Minamoto bō kudashibumi, *Fukuoka ken shiryō*, 8: 115–16 (in *KI*, 3: 375, doc. 1,782).
  1. See Glossary. This estate was in Chikuzen Province.

DOCUMENT 112

The Bakufu Settles a Suit Involving a Deputy Jitō's Lawlessness, 1222

The *jitō* was held responsible for all acts by a deputy. This is clearly illustrated in the present document, which highlights a *jitōdai*'s effort to subsume new fields under the *"jitō*'s share."

That forthwith, the deputy of *jitō* Akimoto Jirō *hyōe no jō*, of Kushibuchi Branch Shrine, Awa Province, shall cease his violations of estate administration [*shōmu*], his seizure of the hereditary fertile fields [*nōden*] of shrine personnel, and his despoiling of agriculture [*nōgyō*].

According to the letter of accusation: "The deputy of the new *jitō*, Akimoto Jirō *hyōe no jō*, has seized the hereditary fertile fields of shrine personnel, labeled them as the *jitō*'s share [*jitō bun*], and then exploited them. The less fertile remaining fields were neglected, and agriculture has halted." If this is true, the *jitō*'s acts are most willful. Beyond his original grant fields and his original *myō* share, why should he disrupt estate administration and selfishly appropriate other *myō*? In strict accordance with precedent, such despoilment is to cease, and local peasants shall be made secure. By this command, it is so decreed.

1st year of Jōō [1222], 7th month, 24th day

Mutsu no kami, Taira (monogram)

SOURCE: *Iwashimizu Tanaka ke monjo*, 1222/7/24 Kantō gechijō, *Awa no kuni chōko zasshō*, pp. 73–74 (*KBSS*, 1: 24, doc. 28).

DOCUMENT 113

The Bakufu Orders a Deputy Jitō to Cease His Lawlessness, 1205

It was unusual for Kamakura to take direct action against a deputy *jitō*; normally this was done through the *jitō* himself.[1] Perhaps the importance of the *shōen* in this case was a consideration.

ORDERED: to the headquarters of the deputy *jitō* of Inoe Estate, Kaga Province.

That willful plundering cease forthwith; that the welfare of the people be attended to; and that orders of the proprietor be obeyed.

The aforementioned estate differs from other domains in the importance of its services. Nevertheless, there has been a complaint that because of the deputy *jitō's* penchant for lawless innovation local persons [*domin*] are insecure, and tributes have become difficult to pay. Forthwith, such willful despoilments are to cease, and authority shall be exercised in accordance with precedent. By command of the Kamakura lord, it is so decreed.[2]

2d year of Genkyū [1205], 6th month, 5th day

Tōtomi no kami, Taira (monogram)

SOURCE: *Kanshūji monjo*, 1205/6/5 Kantō gechijō, *Kano komonjo*, p. 40, doc. 63. In *KI*, 3: 240, doc. 1,550 this document is cited as belonging to the Sonkeikaku holdings (*Sonkeikaku shozō monjo*).
    1. In the later Kamakura period the exclusiveness of the *jitō* caste deteriorated, and we find rather numerous instances of direct Bakufu involvement with deputies.
    2. In an earlier incident involving a *jitō's* violations of Inoe Estate the Bakufu had warned that any future trouble would lead to a dismissal of that officer; but for unexplained reasons Kamakura did not carry out this threat. See *AK*, 1190/5/13 Minamoto Yoritomo migyōsho (in *KI*, 1: 360, doc. 447).

DOCUMENT 114

The Bakufu Orders a Jitō to Replace His Deputy, 1205

The outcome in this incident is fully in line with normal practice. Only the *jitō* could dismiss or appoint a deputy.

An appeal [ge] from Koyama-Izumi Estate, Echizen Province, has been received. An order [gechi] will immediately be issued that the deputy *jitō* is to be dismissed in favor of someone else. Respectfully.

7th month, 8th day[1]

ukon no chūjō (Sanetomo's monogram)

SOURCE: *Sonkeikaku shozō monjo,* 1205/7/8 Minamoto Sanetomo shojō, *KI,* 3: 241–42, doc. 1,554.

1. The following phrase appears on the reverse side of the document: "Arrived on the 2d year of . . . 7th month, 27th day." This information combined with Sanetomo's elevation to the title of *ukon no chūjō* in 1205 (the 2d year of Genkyū), gives us the year here.

DOCUMENT 115

Rokuhara Resolves a Dispute Between Two Deputy Jitō, 1251

When the deputies of individual *jitō* found themselves in contention, the Bakufu had to step in. This was not interference in the *jitō-jitōdai* relationship, but rather an involvement in a matter lying outside the *jitō's* authority. In effect, the dispute was between two *jitō.*

The deputy *jitō* of Miyagawa Ho, Wakasa Province, has stated: "The deputy *jitō* of Saitsu Ho, calling himself a Miyagawa retainer, has dismissed Moritaka, the *tone*[1] of Tagarasu Bay, arrested his family, seized generations of documents, and imposed a fine." Details appear in the document, which is presented herewith. If this is true, it is most disturbing. Forthwith, this person shall be confirmed, and his lost property restored.[2] Should there be additional details, let these be reported. The order is thus.

3d year of Kenchō [1251], 10th month, 13th day

[To] the jitōdai   sakon no shōgen seal

SOURCE: *Hata monjo,* 1251/10/13 Rokuhara gechijō an, *Wakasa gyoson shiryō,* p. 298, doc. 7.

1. Evidently a harbor chief, in this instance; see Glossary.

2. A document of two months later did just that: the Tagarasu Bay *tone* was confirmed in his original *shiki.* Although the issuing authority is not identified, it was clearly not the Bakufu. See *Hata monjo,* 1252/1 Tagarasu-no-ura tone shiki ando kudashibumi, *Wakasa gyoson shiryō,* p. 298, doc. 8.

DOCUMENT 116

The Bakufu Orders the Cessation of Outrages by a Jitō's Deputies, 1222

In this graphic account a *jitō* has exploited the deputy privilege by appointing one of his followers to each of an estate's villages. The Bakufu counters by issuing an order against their excesses and by directing that there be only two deputies.

> That the lawless innovations of *jitō* Tokimori's deputies on Ushigahara Estate, Echizen Province, a Daigoji holding, shall cease forthwith.
> Appended herewith: an order of the shogunal house from the 1st year of Jōgen [1207]; the original *jitō's* income register.

According to the letter of accusation regarding the above: "Nine deputy *jitō* from the villages of this estate, five *sōtsuibushi* and *kumon*, and more than 100 of their followers have been entering [the homes] of estate families. Besides [commandeering] supplies, with no respite, they have condemned the smallest flaws. The people, entirely blameless, have been unable to endure these hardships and have lost all security. As a consequence, the temple's annual tax, labor services, and miscellaneous tributes have fallen into complete collapse." If this is true, it is most disturbing. Concerning the *jitō's* income share, a register [of perquisites] was granted to Hiroyoshi in accordance with the legacy of Yukimasa *hosshi*.[1] At present, the *jitō* totally [disregards[2]] this precedent, and his unceasing outrages are most wrongful. Henceforth, of the two deputies [that shall be permitted], one will be assigned to the southern sector, the other to the northern. As for the income share, there will be no increases or decreases, pursuant to the original register. Finally, if this judgment is violated and there are further crimes, severe sanctions will be imposed. By this command, it is so decreed.

4th year of Jōkyū [1222], 4th month, 5th day

Mutsu no kami, Taira (monogram)

SOURCE: *Sanbōin monjo*, 1222/4/5 Kantō gechijō, *DNK, iewake* 19 (Daigoji monjo), 2: 38–39, doc. 302 (*KBSS*, 1: 21–22, doc. 24).

1. As we saw in Document 88, Ushigahara Estate had received a succession of three *jitō* in the period before 1221: Hōjō Tokimasa (Tōtomi *nyūdō*), Nikaidō Yukimasa (Yamashiro *nyūdō*), and Tosa Saburō Hiroyoshi. The new *jitō*, Tokimori, was appointed in the wake of the Jōkyū War. Cf. Document 88 and *Daigoji monjo* 1222/1 Daigoji ge an, *KI*, 5: 84–87, doc. 2,922.

2. Speculative; character missing.

SETTLEMENTS WITH JITŌ: WAYO, UKESHO, SHITAJI CHŪBUN

The Bakufu Approves a Compromise Settlement, 1263

Though not unknown in early Kamakura times, compromise agreements between *jitō* and proprietors become much more common after about 1250. This suggests an admission by proprietors that *jitō* could no longer be treated merely as land managers but had become rivals for hegemony over estates. In the future *jitō* would increasingly be dealt with directly rather than through Kamakura. It is interesting that the Bakufu concurred in this, reducing its judicial pronouncements to approval rather than settlement. However, not all disputes could be resolved by the contending parties themselves, and thus Kamakura justice remained important.

Concerning the dispute over Yamaguchi:[1] between *hokkyō* Jitsuzen, agent for *jibe no kyō risshi* Raiei—protégé of the priest Raiken[2]—the chief administrator of Gakuenji, Izumo Province; and the *jitō* Yorimasu, of the same province's Uga Gō.

According to the Rokuhara report of the 6th month, 13th day, concerning this matter: "In compliance with a [Kantō] directive [*migyōsho*] of the 1st year of Shōka [1257], a trial proceeding was initiated; but a compromise settlement was reached." According to Yorimasu's compromise document [*wayojō**] of the 1st year of Bun'ō [1260], 11th month, 29th day: "One person for each household [*zaike**] under the temple's main residents is to serve the *jitō* 25 days per year. However, during the peak agricultural seasons [*kannō no toki*], 15 persons daily—that is, 3 persons per homestead[2]—are to serve [the *jitō*] in 3-day shifts. Yamaguchi itself is to be exempt from this service; and hunting service has also been prohibited. Should either side act contrary to these instructions, there will be strict sanctions." According to Jitsuzen's document of the same day: "Concerning Yamaguchi, in Uga Gō, the *jitō*'s compromise proposal has been received. There will be no further suit." According to Raiei's document of the 4th month, 29th day—year unrecorded[2]— "A [Kantō] edict should be granted [as protection] for the future." In accordance with the compromise document, authority shall be exercised without irregularities by either side. By command of the shogun's house, it is so decreed.[3]

   3d year of Kōchō [1263], 8th month, 5th day

       Musashi no kami, Taira ason (monogram)
       Sagami no kami, Taira ason (monogram)

SOURCE: *Gakuenji monjo*, 1263/8/5 Kantō gechijō, *Gakuenji monjo no kenkyū*, pp. 272–73, doc. 18 (*KBSS*, 1: 140, doc. 109).
 1. Place name not further identified.
 2. Phrase in half-size characters.
 3. A reference to this document in *Warrior Government* (p. 187) is incorrect. Line 28 should read: "reveals *a variation of* the latter." Also, l. 30: "*However*, *during* the busy agricultural periods. . . .*"

DOCUMENTS 118-19

Agreement to and Authorization of an Ukesho, 1232

Ukesho, or "receipt," became a dominant mode of compromise between *jitō* and proprietors after the mid-thirteenth century. This arrangement involved a release to the *jitō* of full administrative powers over an estate, in return for the *jitō*'s pledge to collect and remit all stipulated taxes. *Jitō ukesho* had its origins in the Kantō, where estate owners were most vulnerable, but it later spread throughout the country.

118
          (monogram)

Regarding Tsunemasa Myō in Kumagai Gō, Musashi Province, a holding of Tsurugaoka Hachiman Shrine, from the legacy [*ato*] of the late Heinai *saemon no jō* Naokuni.

Entrance by the custodian is hereby prohibited. Under the *jitō*'s authority, the fixed annual tax and the various personal revenues shall be paid without fail. Likewise, all regular and extraordinary shrine services are to be discharged according to precedent. In the event of neglect or nonpayment, the *jitō's* authority shall be revised, and an agent of the shrine shall conduct administration. By command of the chief priest, the order is conveyed thus.

1st year of Jōei [1232], 8th month, 21st day

[To] Kumagai Heinai saemon   moku gon no suke, Fumimoto—
Jirō dono   secretary

119

Regarding Kumagai Gō, Musashi Province, a Tsurugaoka Hachiman shrine-temple land.

Agents of the shrine are denied entrance. The fixed annual tax shall be paid under a *jitō ukesho*. In the event of neglect, shrine agents may enter. By this command, it is so decreed.[1]

1st year of Jōei [1232], 11th month, 4th day

Musashi no kami, Taira (monogram)
Sagami no kami, Taira (monogram)

SOURCES: Document 118: *Kumagai ke monjo*, 1232/8/21 Tsurugaoka Hachimangū migyōsho, *Kumagai ke monjo*, p. 32, doc. 12 (in *KI*, 6: 394, doc. 4,363). Document 119: *Kumagai ke monjo*, 1232/11/4 Kantō gechijō, *Kumagai ke monjo*, p. 33, doc. 13 (in *KI*, 6: 410, doc. 4,400).

    1. This second document refers to the whole of Kumagai Gō, whereas the first mentions only a *myō* within this holding. Perhaps separate *ukesho* accords were made for each of Kumagai's component *myō*, and only one of these records is extant. At all events, the Bakufu obviously approved an *ukesho* agreement embracing the entire *gō*.

DOCUMENT 120

The Bakufu Issues a Directive Concerning the Transfer of an Ukesho, 1216

The transfer or inheritance of an *ukesho* agreement normally required Bakufu approval. Once Kamakura had given its initial endorsement, the agreement became part of that estate's customary law, and the Bakufu then became the guarantor of that law. In the present instance, a formula had apparently been worked out for boosting tax assessments if new fields were opened.

Concerning Northern Takei Gō, Kazusa Province. Since the time of the late *utaishō* house, a generation [*nenjo**] has passed, during which, under an *ukesho* of Yoshikiyo, the former *jitō*, 600 *tan* of second-class

cloth was paid [annually] into the capital [i.e., Kyoto] warehouse. Instructions were set down regarding the opening of new fields, and also
regarding the *jitō's* own residence lands [*hori no uchi**]. Nevertheless,
this inheritance [*sono ato*] has [now] been granted to Kage . . . ,[1] and no
changes shall occur [in its provisions]. By command of the Kamakura
lord, the order is conveyed thus.

> 4th year of Kempō [1216], 8th month, 26th day
>
>   zusho no jō, Kiyohara

SOURCE: *Kujō kebon sasshibon Chūyuki Gen'ei gannen Aki no maki ura monjo,*
1216/8/26 Kantō migyōsho an, *KI,* 4: 229, doc. 2,260.
  1. Character missing.

DOCUMENT 121

A Proprietor Agrees to an Ukesho, 1223

Continued pressure from a *jitō* was the normal reason behind an *ukesho* agreement. More unusual was the experience described here.

ORDERED: to the residents of Akanabe Estate.
    That henceforth the annual tax shall be paid under a *jitō ukesho.*

Regarding the above, this estate has found it difficult, under the custodian's administration, to pay the 100 rolls of cloth and 1,000 *ryō* in
cash. Consequently, the annual tax will be paid under authority of the
jitō, in accordance with the [*ukesho*] agreement document. Residents
shall take note, and shall not be remiss. It is commanded thus. Wherefore, this order.

> 2d year of Jōō [1223], 8th month,   day
>
> bettō, sōjō, saki no hōmu seal

SOURCE: *Tōdaiji monjo,* 1223/8 Tōdaiji bettō kudashibumi an, *Gifu kenshi shiryō
hen, kodai-chūsei,* 3: 181, doc. 148 (in *KI,* 5: 218–19, doc. 3,143).

DOCUMENTS 122-23

A Jitō Confirms the Inheritance of His Deputy's Ukesho, 1222, 1223

The documents here reveal the same *ukesho* principles that obtained between
proprietor, *jitō,* and Bakufu. The inheritance of certain powers is confirmed,

and the interference of estate authorities is prohibited. In northern Japan, where there were few actual *shōen,* "estate authorities" were usually public officials.

122

(monogram)[1]

Concerning the holdings within Hiraga Gō, Tsugaru-Hiraga District,[2] of Soga Gorō Jirō. In accordance with the practice of his father, Soga Kogorō, the fixed taxes shall be paid, without default, under a "direct" *ukesho.*[3] It is so ordered.

4th year of Jōkyū [1222], 3d month, 15th day

123

(monogram)

Concerning the villages that constitute the holdings [*chigyōbun*] of Soga Gorō Jirō Koreshige within Tsugaru-Hiraga's principal *gō.* In accordance with the practice of his father, Soga [Ko]gorō, intrusion by officers of the district police [*kebiisho*[4] *mandokoro no shimobe*] is to cease, and local peasants shall be made secure. It is so ordered.

2d year of Jōo [1223], 8th month, 6th day

SOURCES: Document 122: *Saitō monjo,* 1222/3/15 Hōjō Yoshitoki andojō, *Iwate ken chūsei monjo,* 1: 1, doc. 2 (in *KI,* 5: 90, doc. 2,932). Document 123: *Saitō monjo,* 1223/8/6 Hōjō Yoshitoki andojō, *Iwate ken chūsei monjo,* 1: 1, doc. 3 (in *KI,* 5: 219, doc. 3,144, cited there as *Soga monjo*).
   1. Hōjō Yoshitoki, *jitō* of Hiraga Gō.
   2. The meaning here must be the Hiraga subsector of Tsugaru District. The district's official name was Tsugaru, not Tsugaru-Hiraga.
   3. I.e., without having to arrange things through the *jitō.*
   4. This term taken from the *KI* version; an incorrect word appears in *Iwate ken chūsei monjo.*

DOCUMENT 124

The Bakufu Resolves an Ukesho Dispute, 1244

Once an *ukesho* was sanctioned, it was expected to be permanent and unchanging. Thus a proprietor's attempt to acquire the right of periodic resurveying might logically be objected to by a *jitō.* Here, a suit by a proprietor is dismissed by the Bakufu, and the *jitō's* four-year-old *ukesho* is reaffirmed.

Regarding a dispute over [the right of] land survey [*kenchū*] between *danjōchū* Moritō, estate agent of Okuyama Domain,

Echigo Province, and the *jitō* thereof, Takai *hyōe* Saburō Toki-shige *hosshi*.

Concerning the above, Moritō's letter of accusation states: "In response to the compromise document issued by former estate agent Naonari, a [Kantō] edict of the 1st year of Ninji [1240], 10th month, 10th day, clearly notes, for four out of five matters, of which the first was the land survey [*kenchū*], that there should be no interference.[1] As for the survey [itself], no instructions are written.[2] It is clear, therefore, that surveys following new appointments [*shonin kenchū*][3] may be undertaken by the proprietor."

According to Tokishige *hosshi*'s rebuttal: "The five matters beginning with the survey are listed in the Kantō edict [issued] in response to the compromise document. It is written further that by virtue of this *ukesho* future generations shall experience no change. If [new] surveys were to be conducted, why was it recorded that no changes affecting descendants were to take place?"

In response to Naonari's compromise,[4] the [Kantō] edict that was granted to Tokishige *hosshi* in the 1st year of Ninji includes the heading "concerning the *kenchū*"; also, "concerning the *ukesho*, there are to be no changes for descendants." Thus, although [explicit] instructions are not recorded, the inclusion of these words renders it unnecessary to adjudicate the matter. Forthwith, Moritō's arbitrary suit [*ranso**] is terminated; and, in accordance with the earlier edict, there will be no further surveys, by virtue of the *ukesho*. By command of the Kamakura lord, it is so decreed.

2d year of Kangen [1244], 7th month, 21st day[5]

Musashi no kami, Taira ason (monogram)

SOURCE: *Nakajō ke monjo*, 1244/7/21 Kantō gechijō, *Okuyama-no-shō shiryōshū*, p. 100, doc. 11 (*KBSS*, 1: 75–76, doc. 76).

1. I.e., involvement by the estate agent.

2. That is, only the survey procedure, among the five matters listed, did not carry a specific prohibition against future involvement by the agent. The 1240 document itself, however, does not bear this out: none of the five matters mentioned in its preamble carries a specific prohibition, and none is mentioned again; instead, the prohibition was all-inclusive. The *zasshō*, in other words, was simply lying. See *Nakajō ke monjo*, 1240/10/10 Kantō gechijō, *Okuyama-no-shō shiryōshū*, pp. 98–99, doc. 8.

3. Meaning unclear, but probably a reference to surveys occurring with each testamentary passage to a new *jitō*.

4. For the original accord, see *ibid.*, 1240/9/27 azukari dokoro Fujiwara Naonari wayojō, p. 98, doc. 7. The *jitō* had obligated himself to transmit either 100 *koku* of rice or 600 *mon* cash for each *koku*, plus an unrecorded amount of cotton figured

at 800 *mon* cash for each 10 *ryō*. The custodian was not permitted to enter the *shōen* or to conduct business of any kind with Okuyama Estate.

5. It is interesting that even 60 years later the proprietor of Okuyama was still hoping to retrieve his lost privileges—this time by an outright cancellation of the *ukesho*. The Bakufu rejected his petition. *Ibid.*, 1304/12/26 Kantō gechijō, p. 108, doc. 36.

DOCUMENT 125

A Proprietor Agrees to a Less Onerous Ukesho, 1327

In Document 124 a proprietor was trying to tamper with an *ukesho*. It was much more common for *jitō* to try evading or altering such an agreement; and since their only obligation was the remission of various taxes, violations inevitably occurred here. In the present document a proprietor has renegotiated an *ukesho* in hopes of salvaging something. To be noted also is that payment was now to be made in cash. This became the regular practice on many estates during the late Kamakura period. It also became a new source of trouble between proprietors and *jitō*, since there were constant disagreements over shifting rates of exchange.

Concerning the annual tax due the proprietor from Tomita Estate, Owari Province.

Regarding the above, the annual tax was to be collected in accordance with a Hōjō lord's *ukebumi*[1] dating from the 5th year of Jōgen [1211]. However, owing to continual defaults, even though lawsuits had been entered, a [new] *ukebumi* was issued [as follows]: that 110 *kammon** be forwarded to Kyoto in the 11th month of each year, whether or not [crop] losses had occurred.[2] In consequence, suits concerning arrears [*mishin**], as well as the entrance of outside tax inspectors, were terminated. However, as regards the 3 *chō* of [proprietary] demesne [*tsukuda**], which has been outside the scope of the agreement from the beginning, the estate agent's authority cannot now be questioned. If, in violation of this accord, crimes involving late payment should occur, the original suit will be revived; and authority shall be exercised in conformity with the original *ukebumi* of Jōgen. For the future, [this agreement] shall be thus.

2d year of Karyaku [1327], 5th month, 18th day

Arimune (monogram)

SOURCE: *Engakuji monjo*, 1327/5/18 Owari no kuni Tomita-no-shō ryōke zasshō keijō, *Kamakura shishi, shiryō hen*, 2: 130–31, doc. 74 (*Kanagawa kenshi, shiryō hen 2, kodai-chūsei*, 2: 807–8, doc. 2,622).

1. I.e., an *ukesho* document.
2. Implicit in most *ukesho* agreements was the promise to deliver full tax quotas whatever the actual harvest on an estate. This was partly to forestall *jitō* who might use the pretext of a crop failure to withhold taxes (see, for example, Document 91)

DOCUMENT 126

The Bakufu Approves a Compromise Division of Lands, 1256

Shitaji chūbun, the outright division of estates, was another important method of settling disputes between proprietors and *jitō.* Most such cases evolved out of compromises reached privately by the two sides, which were then ratified by Kamakura.

Regarding a complaint of *jitō* lawlessness from the local holder of three villages in Horie Estate, Etchū Province, a Kanshin-in domain.

A summons to trial was issued; but, in response to a petition from the two sides, an order has now been given that there shall be a division [*chūbun*].[1] We beg that an announcement of this intention be made. Respectfully conveyed.

8th year of Kenchō [1256],[2] 6th month, 12th day

Sagami no kami, Tokiyori seal
Mutsu no kami, Masamura seal

SOURCE: *Yasaka Jinja monjo,* 1256/6/12 Kantō ukebumi an, *Yasaka Jinja monjo,* 2: 418, doc. 1,638 (also in *Toyama kenshi, shiryō hen,* 2: 81, doc. 91).
1. A Kantō directive of several days earlier had specified the exact villages involved and had ordered that boundary markers be posted. See *ibid.,* pp. 417–18, doc. 1,637.
2. The year is missing from this *an,* but can easily be inferred.

DOCUMENT 127

The Bakufu Rejects a Proprietor's Appeal for an Estate Division or Ukesho Revocation, 1287

In this document the proprietor's interests attempt, through legal trickery, to persuade Kamakura to cancel both an *ukesho* and the *jitō shiki* involved in it; or, failing this action, to divide the estate. The Bakufu, as might be expected, upholds the status quo.

The matters in dispute between the agent [*zasshō*] of Ōyama Estate, Tamba Province, a Tōji holding; and *jitō* Nakazawa Saburō *saemon no jō* Motokazu [and his brothers] Rokurō Nobumoto and Shichirō Motomura.

I T E M : concerning the *ukesho*.¹

The plaintiff and defense statements along with accompanying documents [*gusho**], as forwarded by Rokuhara, contain many details. In essence, however, the agent's complaint is as follows:² "The fact of *zasshō* control of estate administration between the 3d year of Ninji [1242] and the 2d year of Bun'ei [1265] is clear from the tax records [*san'yō no jō**] of local peasants. Nevertheless, the *jitō* Shōren—deceased father of Motokazu³—negotiated with the then agent and reached an *ukesho* accord. Inasmuch as this was a 'private *ukesho*,' it should be revoked, and the *jitō shiki*, following old custom, should revert to temple personnel.⁴ Failing this, the land should be divided."

According to Motokazu's statement of defense: "Since Nakazawa Kojirō *saemon no jō* Motomasa received this estate⁵ as a reward for Jōkyū service, there has been no change for three generations of *jitō*. Also, a Rokuhara decree from the 2d year of Ninji [1241] clearly states that there shall be an *ukesho*. Given this, [the pact] can hardly be revoked."

According to the Rokuhara order presented by Motokazu, dated the 2d year of Ninji, 5th month, 29th day: "Concerning Ōyama Estate, Tamba Province, a Tōji holding, a directive of the chief priest--and other documents³—has been sent. According to this communique, 'With regard to the *jitō*'s lawlessness, trial proceedings were initiated in response to a Kantō directive; but a *jitō ukesho* was then arranged. This agreement states that the annual tax and other services due the temple shall be discharged without fail, and in conformity with a land register of the 6th year of Kyūan [1150]. In consequence of that, the matter⁶ is closed.' The terms of this compromise appear most equitable. In accordance with the essence of the *ukebumi*, authority shall be exercised without infringement by either side."

Since the Ninji order, a generation has passed under this *ukesho*. Because of the difficulty of altering this [1241] judgment, the arbitrary suit [*ranso*] of the agent is terminated.

. . .

By command of the Kamakura lord, the aforementioned matters are decreed as stated.

10th year of Kōan [1287], 12th month, 10th day⁷

saki no Musashi no kami, Taira ason (monogram)
Sagami no kami, Taira ason (monogram)

SOURCE: *Tōji monjo*, 1287/12/10 Kantō gechijō, *Ōyama sonshi, shiryō hen*, pp. 64–66, doc. 71 (*KBSS*, 1: 228–30, doc. 167).

1. The document covers five separate points of dispute, but only the first is translated here.

2. "The agent's complaint was thus" appears at the end of the quotation in the original document.

3. In half-size characters.

4. The "old custom" intended is apparently that obtaining before Jōkyū.

5. I.e., this estate's *jitō shiki*.

6. I.e., the suit.

7. The Tōji renewed its suit in 1294, complaining that the *jitō* was still not delivering taxes in the agreed amounts. This time the dispute ended with a division of the estate. *Tōji hyakugō monjo*, 1294/10/23 Kantō gechijō an, *KBSS*, 1: 258–59, doc. 196.

DOCUMENT 128

The Bakufu Approves a Compromise Land Division, 1296

Land divisions followed no set pattern. They could be total or partial, even or uneven; and they could result from compromise or from unilateral petition.[1] The reference in this document to a "partial *jitō*" (*ippō jitō*) concerns the divided inheritance system:[2] by late Kamakura times many *jitō shiki* had become fragmented as they were passed on.

> Regarding the administrative matters [*shomu no jōjō*] in dispute between the *zasshō* for Urunuma Gō, Izumo Province, a Hie Shrine land, and *saemon no jō* Yukiyasu, agent for the partial *jitō* Jibe *gon no tayū* Akimune *ason*.[3]

In pursuance of plaintiff and defense statements regarding the above, there was a desire for judgment [in this matter]. However, on the 27th day of last month a compromise statement was issued by the two sides. According to this document: "One *chō* each of paddy and upland is first to be given to the *jitō*; all remaining land is to be [equally] divided." In consequence, possession [*ryōchi*] shall be in conformity with this document. By command of the Kamakura lord, it is so decreed.[4]

4th year of Einin [1296], 9th month, 5th day

Mutsu no kami, Taira *ason* (monogram)

Sagami no kami, Taira *ason* (monogram)

SOURCE: *Gakuenji monjo*, 1296/9/5 Kantō gechijō, *Gakuenji monjo no kenkyū*, p. 285, doc. 32 (*KBSS*, 1: 270, doc. 206).

1. For details, see my "Jitō Land Possession in the Thirteenth Century," in John W. Hall and Jeffrey P. Mass, eds., *Medieval Japan: Essays in Institutional History* (New Haven: Yale University Press, 1974), pp. 170–71.
2. The standard term is *ichibu jitō* (see Glossary). The exact meaning of *ippō jitō* is not clear.
3. The *jitō*'s name is in half-size characters.
4. Despite this accord, trouble between the contending interests did not end. Within months Kamakura was once again asked to adjudicate the matter. See *Gakuenji monjo*, 1297/1/12 Kantō gechijō, *KBSS*, 1: 273–74, doc. 208.

DOCUMENT 129

The Bakufu Decides Between Ukesho and Land Division, 1298

A popular theory holds that land division usually resulted from the failure of an *ukesho*. In the present instance, however, we see the reverse: a *jitō*'s attempt to convert a 60-year-old *chūbun* into an *ukesho*.

Concerning a dispute over Ōeda Gō, a holding of [Kashima] shrine, between the Kashima priest [*ōnegi*[1]] Tomochika and Nomoto Shirō *saemon no jō hosshi*—Buddhist name Gyōshin.[2]

Although both plaintiff and defense have submitted many details regarding the above, it is evident that the land of this *gō* was divided in the 3d year of Katei [1237], by mutual agreement. Nevertheless, Gyōshin now argues that because this compromise was effected through negotiations with an uninformed deputy [*jitō*], the land should be totally controlled [by the *jitō*], with taxes paid to the shrine. Relative to the [original] compromise document, the statute of limitations [*nenjo*] has passed, with dual possession dating from the age of Katei; it is thus very difficult to attempt to disrupt things now. Therefore, authority will be exercised in accordance with the document [of Katei]. . . .[3] By command of the Kamakura lord, it is so decreed.

6th year of Einin [1298], 2d month, 3d day

Mutsu no kami, Taira ason (monogram)
Sagami no kami, Taira ason (monogram)

SOURCE: *Kashima ōnegi ke monjo*, 1298/2/3 Kantō gechijō, *Kashima Jingū monjo*, p. 686, doc. 16 (*KBSS*, 1: 277, doc. 212).
1. See Glossary under *negi*.
2. In half-size characters.
3. An unrelated matter follows.

DOCUMENT 130

A Provincial Governor Issues an Order Regarding a Bogus Jitō, 1216

In this final selection relating to *jitō* we encounter the true meaning of Kamakura's monopoly over that post. Although Tomokane is initially referred to as a *jitō*, he actually holds no investiture from Kamakura. He has merely adopted the title on his own, or perhaps received it from someone else. Both acts were legal impossibilities.

ORDERED: to the absentee office.

According to a complaint, *jitō* Tomokane's acts have been most irregular. Without holding a Kantō edict, and lacking a governor's endorsement,[1] under what pretext does he call himself a *jitō* and commit such outrages? Kantō-appointed *jitō* do not do such things: how then could an unattached *jitō*?[2] This should not be allowed. If there are other persons who acquiesce in this, they shall be punished. By command of the governor, it is so decreed.

    4th year of Kempō [1216], intercalary 6th month, 2d day

chikara no kami ken san hakase,
Miyoshi ason seal

SOURCE: *Tōdaiji monjo,* 1216/int.6/2 Suō no kuni kokusen an, *KI,* 4: 222, doc. 2,245.

    1. See Documents 22 and 23 for a governor's endorsement of a *jitō* appointment made by the Bakufu.
    2. Or "self-styled *jitō*" (*jiyū no jitō*).

THE EMERGENCE OF SHUGO AND
THE TAIBON SANKAJŌ

Documents Relating to an Early Shugo, 1184

The episode described here provides our closest contemporaneous view of an early *shugo*, or provincial constable. Despite several unclear references, the points to be noted are the *shugo*'s native roots in his appointment area,[1] his prominence within the Kii provincial office, and his clear preoccupation with the men and materiel of war.

131

We acknowledge that the estates of Denpōin [Temple], Kii Province, are to be exempt from the commissariat levy [*hyōrōmai**]. This order will be given. When Toshihira, a government official [*chōkan*], went down [to Kii], the exemption was put in force.[2] Therefore, resident officials [*zaichō**] should know this. [However,] the *shugonin*[3] Teshima Tarō Aritsune fails to obey the governor. An order should immediately be issued concerning this state of affairs. Respectfully submitted.[4]

1st year of Genryaku [1184],[5] 8th month, 5th day

shikibu, gon no shōyū, Norisue[6]

132

The chancellery of the retired emperor orders: to the resident officers of Kii Province.

That general tax [*shotō**], militia [*hyōji**], and commissariat rice [*hyōrō**] levies shall forthwith cease for the estate holdings of Denpōin [Temple].

Since long ago this temple has performed services without interruption and without negligence. In recent days, especially, prayers have been requested,[7] and [the temple's] service has been virtually continuous. [In consequence,] it is hereby ordered that the gathering of soldiers and commissariat rice, as well as foraging by warriors, shall be ended. Resident officials shall take note, and shall not be remiss. Wherefore, this order.

1st year of Genryaku [1184], 8th month, 8th day

[signatures of chancellery members follow]

133

Governor's edict: to the absentee office.

That in accordance with the order of the retired emperor, the requisitioning of supplies and tributes from Denpōin lands by the *shugonin* Teshima Tarō Aritsune shall cease forthwith.

Regarding the aforesaid supplies and tributes, it is hereby decreed that in accordance with an order of the retired emperor, [the requisitioning] is to cease. The absentee office shall take note, and by virtue of this edict act accordingly. Wherefore, this decree.

1st year of Genryaku [1184], 8th month, 8th day

kami, Fujiwara ason

134

Acknowledgment of Teshima *uma no jō*.[8]
Respectfully received.
    Concerning the directive.

A directive of the 24th day arrived on the 29th day.[9] I respectfully acknowledge what has been instructed. Concerning the intrusion of [*shugo*] agents into Denpōin lands, this matter is [already] as enjoined. Even before the [recent] order regarding commissariat rice and tributes, an exemption was in force for the estate holdings of Kōya Denpōin. In the matter of recruiting soldiers, a similar exemption was in force for the residents of these estates, except for vassals of the Kamakura lord and persons with the capacity [to serve].[10] Now, however, your instruction has been presented and I am deeply thankful. How could I neglect such an order? I beg you to convey this. Respectfully submitted by Aritsune.[11]

1st year of Genryaku [1184],[5] 8th month, 29th day

Taira Aritsune—acknowledgment[8]

SOURCES: Document 131: *Negoro yōsho*, 1184/8/5 Kii kokushi Fujiwara Norisue ukebumi an. Document 132: 1184/8/8 Go-Shirakawa In-no-chō kudashibumi an. Document 133: 1184/8/8 Kii kokushi chōsen an. Document 134: 1184/8/29 Kii no kuni shugo Teshima Aritsune ukebumi an. All in *HI*, 8: 3142–43, 3147, docs. 4,189, 4,191, 4,192, 4,204.

1. This is the only known instance (outside the Kantō) for the entire Kamakura period. With this one exception, *shugo* were always easterners.

2. The original exemption came in late 1180 when a special constable [*tsuitōshi*] was sent to Kii to gather men and supplies. See the reference in *Negoro yōsho*, 1184/2 Denpōin shoshi ge an, *HI*, 8: 3118–19, doc. 4,141. Possibly Toshihira was that constable. The exemption was later confirmed by the Bakufu. See Document 2 above.

3. A common alternative for *shugo*.

4. This document was obviously directed to the court. Document 132 is the retired emperor's response.

5. Date missing in original.

6. The governor of Kii Province.

7. An obvious reference to the disorder of the war years.

8. In half-size characters.

9. This directive cited the continued noncompliance of warriors with the earlier orders and reemphasized the imperial immunity that had been granted. It was personally addressed to "acting governor" [*gon no kami*] Teshima. *Negoro yōsho*, 1184/8/24 Oribe no kami Kagemune hōsho an, *HI*, 8: 3146, doc. 4,201.

10. In other words, the *shugo* was claiming an unrestricted right to recruit fighting men within tax-exempt lands. For a discussion of the Teshima and other Gempei War *shugo*, see Mass, *Warrior Government*, chap. 4.

11. Several months later Aritsune essentially reiterated this pledge in response to a further complaint. It was easy to make empty promises. See *Negoro yōsho*, 1184/12/29 Kii gon no kami hōsho an, *HI*, 8: 3158, doc. 4,225. The final outcome is unknown.

DOCUMENTS 135-36

Yoritomo Issues Directives Relating to the Imperial Guard Service, 1192, 1196

The Kamakura *shugo* institution, as later defined in law, took shape only in the 1190's. The documents here describe one dimension of that process: the recruitment of Kamakura vassals for the Kyoto guard service (*ōban'yaku*[*])

under the supervision of Bakufu-appointed provincial commanders. The administration of this guard duty would soon become the responsibility of all *shugo.* Also to be noted is the charge to the Mino commander to determine who merited inclusion in the Kamakura band.

135

The chancellery of the former *utaishō* house orders: to the housemen [*ke'nin*] of Mino Province.

That recruitment calls by Koreyoshi, the governor of Sagami,[1] shall forthwith be obeyed.

Among the *jitō* within the *shōen* of this province, those under obligation as housemen[2] are to obey the recruitment calls of Koreyoshi and serve loyally. In particular, there is a report of looting within the capital during recent days. In order to suppress these insurgents, [housemen] shall make ready to go to the capital for palace guard duty. However, if there are any among these who should not be housemen, details shall be reported at once. Also, in the public lands [*kōryō*], there is to be no mustering.[3] In addition, the retainers [*rōjū**] of the former Sado [Province] governor, Shigetaka, shall be recruited for this service.[4] Persons concealing their residences shall have their names reported. It is so commanded.

3d year of Kenkyū [1192], 6th month, 20th day

ryō, minbu no shōjō, Fujiwara   anzu, Fujii
bettō, saki no Inaba no kami, Nakahara   chikeji, Nakahara
saki no Shimōsa no kami, Minamoto ason
san-i, Nakahara ason

136

The chancellery of the former *utaishō* house orders: to the housemen of Izumi Province.

That the imperial guard [service] shall forthwith be discharged in conformity with the recruitment calls of *saemon no jō* Taira Yoshitsura.

The aforesaid housemen will perform the imperial guard service without negligence, following the recruitment calls of Yoshitsura. It is commanded thus. Wherefore, this order.

7th year of Kenkyū [1196], 11th month, 7th day

ryō, ōkura no jō, Fujiwara seal   anzu, Kiyo[hara seal][5]
bettō, hyōgo no kami, Nakahara   chikeji, Nakahara [seal][5]
  ason seal
san-i, Fujiwara ason seal

SOURCES: Document 135: *Azuma kagami*, 1192/6/20 saki no utaishō ke mandokoro kudashibumi (in *KI*, 2: 19, doc. 596). Document 136: *Nigita monjo*, 1196/11/7 saki no utaishō ke mandokoro kudashibumi an, *KI*, 2: 206, doc. 881.

    1. Ōuchi Koreyoshi, civil governor of Sagami Province, was now made *shugo* of Mino.

    2. The reference to *jitō* in this passage is difficult to understand, since *jitō* were by definition housemen of Kamakura. Perhaps *jitō* is used here in the general sense of "prominent warriors."

    3. This was probably a temporary order in deference to the recently deceased retired emperor, who had been "proprietor" of Mino. Go-Shirakawa died on the 13th day of the 3d month.

    4. Shigetaka was a vassal who had recently been purged by the Bakufu. In other words, Kamakura was hoping to convert the followers of a fallen "enemy" into its own housemen.

    5. Missing character(s) added.

DOCUMENT 137

The Bakufu Issues Instructions to an Incipient Shugo, 1197

Here we see an investiture that embraces both the supervision of vassals and a limited criminal jurisdiction. These would become the *shugo*'s major areas of legal authority.

The chancellery of the former *utaishō* house orders: to *sa hyōe no jō* Koremune Tadahisa.

    Elements of the duties to be discharged forthwith by the vassal administrator [*ke'nin bugyōnin**] for Ōsumi and Satsuma Provinces.

ITEM: that [men for] the palace guard service shall be mustered. Housemen recruited from these provinces are to serve.

ITEM: that the buying and selling of persons shall be ended. Repeated imperial decrees have ordered that this practice be banned. Nevertheless, there are reports of this crime among persons in remote areas. Forthwith, it is to cease. Violators shall be severely punished.

ITEM: that murder and other outrages shall be ended. Murder and despoilment are strictly forbidden. The provinces shall be protected, and [these crimes] stopped.

    The foregoing points are so ordered. Tadahisa is not, under some pretext, to cause distress to innocent persons. At the same time, housemen are not to oppose the administrator's orders under cover of [Kantō's] leniency. When unexpected matters arise, all are to show their loyalty. Wherefore, this order.

8th year of Kenkyū [1197], 12th month, 3d day

ryō, ōkura no jō, Fujiwara (monogram)   anzu, Kiyohara
bettō, saki no Inaba no kami,   chikeji, Nakahara
         Nakahara ason
san-i, Fujiwara ason (monogram)

SOURCE: *Shimazu ke monjo*, 1197/12/3 saki no utaishō ke mandokoro kudashibumi, *DNK, iewake* 16 (Shimazu ke monjo), 1: 8–9, doc. 11 (in *KI*, 2: 275–76, doc. 950).

DOCUMENT 138

The Shugo's Authority Is Described, 1199

A clear definition of the *shugo's* duties appears in an *Azuma kagami* entry for 1199. We encounter three specific elements: supervision of recruiting for the imperial guard service, suppression of rebels, and jurisdiction over murderers. For the duration of the Kamakura period this definition (called *taibon sankajō**) would remain essentially unchanged.

29th day:
Koyama[1] *saemon no jō* Tomomasa has been appointed to the *shugo* post of Harima Province. The housemen of this province are to obey Tomomasa, perform the imperial guard service, and in general show their loyalty. Tomomasa's authority is limited to rebels and murderers; he is not to interfere in provincial administration [*kokumu**] or judge the suits of the people. And he is not, under any pretext, to cause difficulties for the notables of this province. He has been apprised of these instructions.

SOURCE: *Azuma kagami*, 1199/12/29. This work has appeared in many editions. The most accessible is *Azuma kagami*, Ryō Susumu, ed., Iwanami bunko series, 5 vols. Tokyo, 1939–44.
      1. Or "Oyama."

DOCUMENT 139

The Bakufu Issues Its Definitive Statement Regarding the Shugo's Authority, 1232

This statement is taken from the *Goseibai shikimoku*, the Bakufu's well-known code of laws for housemen.

Concerning the duties of the country's *shugonin*:

During the age of the *utaishō* house these duties were defined as imperial guard recruitment [and the control of] rebels and murderers—[these crimes] to include night raiding, violent burglary, brigandage, and piracy.[1] In recent years, however, [*shugo*] deputies have been appointed to *gun* and *gō*, and tributes have been levied on private and public estates [*shō-ho*]. [*Shugo*] are not governors [*kokushi*], yet they interfere in provincial business. They are not *jitō*, yet they seek the profits of the land. Undertaking such acts is extremely unprincipled. Persons without up-to-date investitures may not be recruited for service, even if they are housemen of several generations' standing. Similarly, *gesu*, general estate officers [*shōkan*], and others in various places have reportedly called themselves housemen and then resisted the orders of governors and proprietors. Now, even if such persons should express a desire to perform services for *shugo*, recruiting them is strictly forbidden.

Forthwith, in accordance with practices from the time of the *utaishō* house, *shugo* authority beyond the imperial guard service, rebellion, and murder is prohibited. Should this regulation be contravened by excessive involvement, and if the violations are exposed by appeals from governors or proprietors, or by the complaints of *jitō* or local residents, the post will be reassigned and a more peaceable person appointed. Also, as concerns deputies, only one will be allowed.

SOURCE: *Goseibai shikimoku*, art. 3 (1232/7/10), *KI*, 6: 374–75, doc. 4,340.
  1. The additional list of crimes is in half-size characters.

SHUGO ENTRY INTO ESTATES

DOCUMENTS 140-42

The Bakufu Confirms a Shōen's Immunity From the Entry of Shugo, 1225, 1227, 1244

One of the most immediate problems relating to *shugo* was whether they should be permitted to enter an estate or religious area in pursuit of a major criminal. The Bakufu entertained requests for immunity from such intrusions literally from the start of the *shugo* institution. As we see in Documents 140 and 141, constant reminders were necessary.

140

Concerning entry by the *shugo* into Kongōji, Kawachi Province. According to the temple priests' petition: "During the time of the late *utaishō* lord it was judged that this temple should be free of the authority of the *shugo* headquarters, and that total jurisdiction should lie with temple personnel. After that there were no disturbances. However, since the recent treachery,[1] the *shugo* has been entering temple precincts in search of minor faults and then issuing directives." In accordance with precedent, these willful intrusions are to cease. It is so ordered.

2d year of Gennin [1225], 4th month, 5th day

[To] the deputy *shugo*   Sagami no kami, Taira (monogram)

141

Concerning the suit by Kongōji, Kawachi Province, a branch of the Kita-in.

An Omuro communique has been sent—along with testimonials, copies of proof records, and a register of confiscated goods.² According to this document: "Because this temple is a prominent seat of learning, a judgment was issued during the time of the late *utaishō* lord that the authority here of the *shugo* headquarters be terminated, and that total jurisdiction lie with temple personnel. This was confirmed in a decree of the Sagami governor³ dated the 2d year of Gennin [1225]. Nevertheless, against precedent and in contravention of this order, the [temple's] boundaries were violated on the 15th day of the 1st month, upon the pretext of minor crimes; one cow, one horse, two persons, clothing, and various valuables were seized."

If this is true, the import of such acts is most unsettling. Forthwith, total restitution shall be made. In accordance with the intent of previous orders, henceforth the *shugo* headquarters shall not presume to authority [within Kongōji], and jurisdiction shall lie with temple personnel. It is so ordered.

3d year of Karoku [1227], 2d month, 14th day

[To] the deputy *shugo*   Taira (monogram)
kamon, gon no suke (monogram)

142

Regarding entry by agents of the *shugo* headquarters into Hisanaga Estate, Iwami Province, a holding of Kamowake Ikazuchi Shrine; also regarding the tribute obligations of exiles from Kōyasan.

The petition of the shrine—with accompanying documents²—is presented herewith, and details appear in this record. In brief, according to a Kantō decree of the 2d year of Jōgen [1208], 10th month, 15th day: "This estate has been under total shrine jurisdiction since its commendation during the time of the late *utaishō* lord. The authority of the *shugo* headquarters is now terminated. As for the imperial guard service, it shall be performed in accordance with precedent;⁴ other services are to be excused."⁵

Subsequent to its issuance in the 2d year of Jōgen, this edict came to be violated [by the *shugo*] without cause. In accordance, therefore, with the intent of this decree, entry by [the *shugo*'s] agents is to cease, and the tribute obligations of exiles [settled there] are excused. It is so ordered.

2d year of Kangen [1244], 6th month, 3d day

[To] the deputy *shugo*   Sagami no kami seal

SOURCES: Document 140: *Kongōji monjo*, 1225/4/5 Rokuhara migyōsho, *DNK*, *iewake* 7 (Kongōji monjo), pp. 92–93, doc. 52 (in *KI*, 5: 351, doc. 3,364). Document 141: *ibid.*, 1227/2/14 Rokuhara migyōsho, *DNK*, *iewake* 7, pp. 103–4, doc. 56 (in *KI*, 6: 6, doc. 3,574). Document 142: *Kamowake Ikazuchi Jinja monjo*, 1244/6/3 Kantō migyōsho an, *KI*, 9: 95, doc. 6,327.

1. I.e., the Jōkyū War of 1221.
2. Phrase in half-size characters.
3. I.e., Document 140.
4. Clearly, Hisanaga Estate contained a Kamakura vassal who would continue to owe guard service. What this implied for the *shugo* is not certain.
5. The original of this record is not extant.

DOCUMENTS 143-44

The Bakufu Limits a Shugo's Authority to Extradition, 1203, 1229

In many instances where *shugo* were barred from an estate, the estate's own constabulary officials were obliged to deliver rebels and murderers to the *shugo*'s headquarters.

143

The chancellery of the shogun's house orders: to the residents of Ōbu Estate and Ozumi Harbor, Harima Province.

That forthwith agents of the *shugo* shall cease their intrusions.

The aforesaid places have been illegally entered by these agents; and because of disturbances to the people, there is no peace. When criminals[1] appear, they are to be apprehended and delivered up by estate personnel. The prayer office of Tōdaiji has requested that the agents' intrusions be prohibited. Accordingly, it is hereby ordered that the *shugo*'s agents cease their intrusions. Wherefore, this edict.

3d year of Kennin [1203], 5th month, 17th day

ryō, uhyōe no shōjō, Fujiwara seal   anzu, Kiyo[hara]
bettō, saki no daizen daibu,   chikeji . . .[2]
      Nakahara ason seal
san-i, Fujiwara ason seal

144

That entry by agents of the *shugo's* headquarters into Kamibayashi Estate, Tamba Province, shall cease forthwith.

In accordance with repeated [Kantō] orders, the entry of these agents is prohibited. If rebels or murderers appear, they should be apprehended and turned over to the *shugo's* headquarters under the authority of estate personnel. By command of the Kamakura lord, it is so decreed.

1st year of Kangi [1229], 4th month, 10th day

> Musashi no kami, Taira (monogram)
> Sagami no kami, Taira (monogram)

SOURCES: Document 143: *Naikaku bunko shozō zatsu komonjo*, 1203/5/17 shōgun ke mandokoro kudashibumi an, *KI*, 3: 90, doc. 1,358. Document 144: *Jingoji monjo*, 1229/4/10 Kantō gechijō, *KI*, 6: 126, doc. 3,830.

1. I.e., murderers and rebels.
2. Several characters are missing.

DOCUMENTS 145-46

The Bakufu Issues Further Orders Regarding Shugo's Trespassing, 1223, 1231

The question of access to estates was taken up case by case, and numerous variables could influence a decision. The two *shōen* here happened to possess *jitō*. In the first, *shugo* and *jitō* were ordered to divide the policing authority; and the *shugo* could enter only in the performance of his regular duties. In the second, the *jitō* was given full authority.

145

That agents of the Iga Province *shugo* shall forthwith cease their intrusion into that province's Nagata Estate.

The *jitō* has petitioned that during the terms of previous *shugo* their agents did not enter this estate. Except for matters involving the imperial guard service, rebellion, and murder, these agents are not to enter. By this command, it is so decreed.

2d year of Jōō [1223], 8th month, 6th day

> saki no Mutsu no kami, Taira (monogram)

146

That agents of the *shugo* shall forthwith cease their intrusion into Miri Estate, Aki Province.

Entry by these agents is prohibited. When criminals appear, they are to be apprehended and turned over under the authority of the *jitō*. By command of the Kamakura lord, it is so decreed.

    3d year of Kangi [1231], 2d month, 13th day

> Musashi no kami, Taira ason (monogram)
> Sagami no kami, Taira ason (monogram)

SOURCES: Document 145: *Shimazu ke monjo*, 1223/8/6 Kantō gechijō, *DNK, iewake* 16 (Shimazu ke monjo), 1: 16, doc. 23 (in *KI*, 5: 219, doc. 3,145). Document 146: *Kumagai ke monjo*, 1231/2/13 Kantō gechijō, *Kumagai ke monjo*, doc. no. 10, p. 30 (in *KI*, 6: 245, doc. 4,099).

DOCUMENT 147

A Shugo Attempts to Expand the Authority of His Own Headquarters, 1215

Another problem concerned crimes other than murder and rebellion. Normally, *shugo* had no authority here; but in the present instance a *shugo* is asserting his right to extradite incendiaries and those who have inflicted serious injury.

Intrusion by agents of the *shugo* headquarters was prohibited in Tajiri and Ōba, Mitama [Shrine] holdings. However, as concerns the arrest of murderers, those guilty of bloodshed, and incendiaries, apprehension and delivery shall be under the authority of Lord Kokuzō. For the future, it is so decreed.

    3d year of Kempō [1215], 7th month,   day

> sa hyōe no jō, Minamoto[1] (monogram)

SOURCE: *Kitajima monjo*, 1215/7 Izumo no kuni shugo Minamoto bō gechijō, *Izumo Kokuzō ke monjo*, pp. 8–9, doc. 8 (in *KI*, 4: 185, doc. 2,173).
    1. Probably the *shugo* or his deputy. Cf. *Izumo Kokuzō ke monjo*, p. 9.

DOCUMENT 148

The Bakufu Condemns an Illegal Entry, 1223

The right of entry could be complicated by the failure of a *shugo*'s agents to heed their master's orders. This seems to be the case in the document presented here. Koyama Tomomasa, the scion of a great Kantō house, was probably little concerned with the day-to-day activities of his provincial headquarters in distant Harima.

That in accordance with a previous [Kantō] order, the intrusion of the *shugo's* agents into Yamagami-sakamoto¹ of Hiromine Shrine, Harima Province, branch shrine of Gion,² shall cease forthwith.

According to the appeal: "Pursuant to an acknowledgment by Yukimitsu in the 4th year of Kempō [1216],³ a [Kantō] order was issued in the 11th month of last year.⁴ Then, in the 4th month of the present year the *shugo* Koyama *hangan* Tomomasa accorded formal recognition [to this order]; but the deputy [*daikan*] did not abide by it. By illegally entering the private residences of functionaries and shrine officials, he has caused the most severe distress, which is exceedingly unprincipled."

If this is true, the entrance of the deputy *shugo*, in violation of a [Kantō] order, is most unseemly. Forthwith, trespass by these agents is to cease, in accordance with the earlier order. By this command, it is so decreed.

2d year of Jōō [1223], 10th month, 25th day

saki no Mutsu no kami, Taira (monogram)

SOURCE: *Hiromine Jinja monjo,* 1223/10/25 Kantō *gechijō, Himeji shishi, shiryō hen,* 1: 3–4, doc. 4 (*KI,* 5: 228, doc. 3,166).

1. A place name.
2. I.e., Yasaka Shrine in Kyoto.
3. The Bakufu, through its officer Nikaidō Yukimitsu, first prohibited entry by the *shugo* in 1216: *Hiromine Jinja monjo,* 1216/8/28 Kantō *migyōsho an, Himeji shishi, shiryō hen,* 1: 3, doc. 1 (not in *KI*).
4. Not extant, but obviously a reiteration of the 1216 prohibition.

DOCUMENTS 149-51

The Bakufu Restricts Entry to Shogunal Prayer Centers, 1229, 1232, 1241

Special Bakufu patronage of a temple carried no guarantee that Kamakura's own men would honor its status. In fact, the Bakufu's sponsorship of a religious institution often prompted requests for immunity from—rather than protection by—*shugo* and *jitō.*

149

That agents of the *shugo's* headquarters and other persons shall forthwith cease their intrusions into Kashioyama, Kai Province.

The aforesaid temple is registered as a prayer center for this house.¹

In accordance with a previous [Kantō] order,[2] intrusions into this temple are to cease. By command of the Kamakura lord, it is so decreed.

1st year of Kangi [1229], 8th month, 7th day

> Musashi no kami, Taira ason seal
> Sagami no kami, Taira ason seal

150

Regarding the appeal of two matters by the resident priests of Kinzan Kannon Temple, Bizen Province, a shogunal house prayer center.

The letter of accusation is appended herewith. In essence, neither the deputy *shugo* nor the deputy *jitō* is to engage in willful excesses [*jiyū no shingi*]. In accordance with repeated Kantō orders granted on behalf of the temple's priests,[3] no despoilments are to take place. Even if there are additional details, let these matters be reported.[4] It is so commanded.[5]

1st year of Jōei [1232], intercalary 9th month, 26th day

> kamon no suke, Taira (monogram)
> Suruga no kami, Taira (monogram)

151

Regarding the appeal by resident priests of Kinzan, Bizen Province, that *shugo* and *jitō*, under some pretext, have caused distress to travelers, the letter of accusation is appended herewith. Why do such things occur? If what is stated is true, these disturbances are to cease. Should there be any special details, let them be reported. It is so commanded.

2d year of Ninji [1241], 6th month, 11th day

[To] the deputy at the *shugo's*   Echigo no kami (monogram)
    headquarters   Sagami no kami (monogram)

SOURCES: Document 149: *Daizenji monjo*, 1229/8/7 Kantō gechijō, *Kōshū komonjo*, 1: 264, doc. 614 (in *KI*, 6: 139, doc. 3,860). Document 150: *Kinzanji monjo*, 1232/int. 9/26 Rokuhara migyōsho, *Okayama ken komonjo shū*, 2: 9, doc. 13 (in *KI*, 6: 406, doc. 4,390). Document 151: *ibid.*, 1241/6/11 Rokuhara migyōsho, *Okayama ken komonjo shū*, 2: 9, doc. 14 (in *KI*, 8: 282, doc. 5,886).

1. I.e., the shogunal house.

2. See *Daizenji monjo*, 1213/12/29 Kantō gechijō an, *KI*, 4: 109, doc. 2,075. According to this document, the immunity from entrance was first granted by Yoritomo.

3. See Document 87.

4. The words "even if" are clearly expressed here, but make little sense in context. Compare the final injunction in Document 151.

5. The addressee is not identified. Presumably, it was the *shugo's* headquarters.

DOCUMENTS 152-55

The Bakufu Has Difficulties With a Deputy Shugo, 1284–85

Ōmi was one of the few provinces with a hereditary *shugo*—the house of Sasaki. The extent of that family's *shugo*-derived powers, however, remains unclear. For example, a full 90 years after the initial Sasaki investiture, the Bakufu clearly expected compliance in a matter involving an agent's violations. In no sense had the Sasaki become territorial overlords. However, there was evidently no way for Rokuhara to override the deputy's delaying tactics. Satisfaction in the matter would depend on how hard the Sasaki wished to press the issue. Unfortunately, we do not know the ultimate resolution.

152

The priests of Chikubujima Temple, Ōmi Province, have stated: "In violation of repeated orders the deputy *shugo* of this province's Asai Gun has illegally entered Hayazaki Village, a temple holding, and seized personal wealth including cash (*senka*)." The letter of accusation and accompanying papers are presented herewith. Why do such things happen? Forthwith, [this matter] shall be investigated, and the true conditions reported. This order is so conveyed.

    7th year of Kōan [1284], 12th month, 22d day

[To] Sasaki Bitchū zenji dono¹   Musashi no kami seal

153

The priests of Chikubujima Temple, Ōmi Province, have stated: "In violation of repeated orders the deputy *shugo* of this province's Asai Gun has illegally entered Hayazaki Village, a temple holding, and seized personal wealth including cash." A renewed accusation and accompanying documents are presented herewith. When earlier requests for information [*toijō**] were sent, depositions were not forthcoming; and reportedly, encroachments continued to increase. Why do such things happen? An order is to be issued² to come to the capital at an early date and explain matters. It is so conveyed.

    8th year of Kōan [1285], 2d month, 24th day

[To] Sasaki Bitchū zenji dono   shuri no suke seal
                                           Musashi no kami seal

154

The priests of Chikubujima Temple, Ōmi Province, have stated: "In violation of repeated orders the *shugo*'s agent³ for this province's Asai

Gun has illegally entered Hayazaki Village, a temple holding, and seized personal wealth including cash." The renewed accusation and accompanying documents have been received. In accordance with these instructions, I have issued an order calling for appearance in the capital and an explanation. The agent Shigeyuki is in possession of a defense statement [*chinjō*] and is on his way there. I beg you to make this announcement. Respectfully reported.

[8th year of Kōan,] 4th month, 22d day

saki no Bitchū no kami, Yoritsuna
[monogram on reverse side
of document]

155

The complaint document of the Chikubujima administrator [*zasshō*] has been given [to us].[4] When the *shugo*'s agent for the area returns to this province, he shall be summoned at once and made to explain. Respectfully reported.

[8th year of Kōan,] 6th month, 4th day

Kimitsuna (monogram)[5]

SOURCES: All documents from *Chikubujima monjo*: 1284/12/22 Rokuhara migyōsho an; 1285/2/24 Rokuhara migyōsho an; 1285/4/22 saki no Bitchū no kami ukebumi; 1285/6/4 Ōmi no kuni shugodai ukebumi. All in *Higashiasai gunshi*, 4: 195.

1. The *shugo* of Ōmi, Sasaki Yoritsuna. Notice that Rokuhara has routed its complaint through the *shugo*. In numerous other provinces, it simply issued orders to an offending deputy.

2. I.e., by the Ōmi *shugo*.

3. The Bakufu's two documents (152–53) both refer to lawlessness by a deputy *shugo* (*shugodai*). In the present document the *shugo* himself refers to an agent (*tsukai*). Perhaps he was taking account of Kamakura's ban against more than one deputy (see Document 139). Or perhaps he merely wished to place the blame at a lower level. See Document 155.

4. The accused deputy *shugo* finally responds. Evasion is the substance of his reply.

5. Surviving documentation ends here. Six months had passed since the original Rokuhara order, but the incident was not yet resolved.

SHUGO AND THE IMPERIAL
GUARD SERVICE

DOCUMENTS 156-57

A Shrine Orders Resistance to Imperial Guard
Recruiting, 1197, 1215

We have seen that the question of entry by *shugo* was a major source of re-
sentment and difficulty for estate owners. This was not merely with regard
to criminal jurisdiction, but with regard to recruiting and other matters as
well. Document 156, when read side by side with Document 157, clearly
seems to be objecting to the sudden presence of *shugo*. The second document is explicit; *shugo* service or conscription calls were to be ignored.

156

The records office [*kumonjo**] of Hachiman Shrine-Temple orders: to
Suda Estate.

That military service [*hyōjiyaku*] shall henceforth follow customary practices.

Regarding the above, the lands of this shrine are located in various provinces. Nevertheless, there has been no recruiting on them, either for the
imperial guard service or for labor service on the Tōdaiji construction
project. But now such an authority [*sata*] is reportedly claimed.[1] By
force of precedent [*senrei*] and in pursuance of customary practice

[*bōrei**], it is hereby ordered that there be no performance [of these services].[2]

8th year of Kenkyū [1197], 1st month,   day

> dōtatsu, hosshi (monogram)
> gon no zaichō, hosshi
> gon no jishu, hosshi (monogram)
> gon no jishu, hosshi (monogram)
> jōza, hokkyō, jōnin-i (monogram)

157

The records office of Hachiman Shrine-Temple orders: to Suda Estate. That in pursuance of precedent and customary practice, estate officers and shrine personnel, except by order of the proprietor [*honjo**], shall not answer the *shugo*'s muster calls.

Regarding the above, when the priest Komatsu *hōin* of Kumano returns for periods of residence at the main shrine, the warriors of Kii are [customarily] directed to muster and proceed there. However, it is now reported that the officers and shrine personnel of this estate, at the behest of the *shugo*, have [similarly] been ordered to muster. Precedent and customary practice that would sanction such action are entirely unheard of. During the time of the *utaishō* lord, although the imperial guard service was made incumbent on Kamakura housemen, estate officials on shrine lands, and especially those who had had no formal audience of submission [*kezan**] [with Yoritomo], were declared exempt. All the more reason, then, that unrestricted recruiting calls by the *shugo* should not be obeyed. By command of the chief administrator, it is so decreed.[3]

3d year of Kempō [1215], 8th month, 24th day

> mokudai, hosshi (monogram)
> san-i, Fujiwara (monogram)
> san-i, Nakahara (monogram)
> gon no jishu, hosshi (monogram)
> gon no jishu, hosshi (monogram)
> jōza ken shō bettō, dai hosshi
>   (monogram)

SOURCES: Document 156: *Suda ke monjo*, 1197/1 Iwashimizu Hachimangū kumonjo kudashibumi, *Wakayama kenshi, shiryō hen*, 1: 33–34, doc. 8 (in *KI*, 2: 213, doc. 896). Document 157: *ibid.*, 1215/8/24 Iwashimizu Hachimangū kumonjo kudashibumi, *Wakayama kenshi, shiryō hen*, 1: 63–64, doc. 71 (in *KI*, 4: 185, doc. 2,175).

1. I.e., the Bakufu, through its *shugo*, has begun to impose these levies.

2. During the same month the deputy *shugo* of Kii Province granted an immunity

from vassal services and various payments [*goke'ninyaku zōji rōryō*] to several estate holdings of Kōyasan. See *Kōyasan monjo* 1197/1/17 Kii shugodai menjō, *KI*, 2: 212, doc. 893. Obviously, Iwashimizu Shrine felt that it too deserved similar treatment in Kii, the site of Suda Estate.

3. This may well be the clearest documentary expression of principles central to the Bakufu's systems of *shugo* and *goke'nin*.

DOCUMENTS 158-59

The Bakufu Regulates Guard Service, 1215, 1214

The Kyoto guard service varied in length up to six months. Document 158 is an order to the *shugo* of Satsuma to assemble Kamakura vassals for service in Kyoto. Document 159 hints that Settsu Province had no *shugo* in 1214,[1] or perhaps that the Bakufu reserved to itself the grant of guard duty exemptions.

158

Additional order:

If in defiance of past practice recalcitrants should appear, a list of names shall be reported.[2]

Concerning next year's palace guard duty [*dairi ōban**], the housemen of Satsuma Province shall serve from the 5th month to the 7th month, 15th day. Likewise, [the housemen of] Hyūga, Ōsumi, and Iki Island are to be mustered. An order to this effect should be given. By command of the Kamakura lord, it is so conveyed.

3d year of Kempō [1215], 10th month, 4th day

respectfully, to Shimazu,   zusho no jō, Kiyohara seal
saemon no jō dono[3]

159

Concerning the imperial guard duty and other services that have been appealed by *gesu* Ieyuki of Tarumi Estate, Settsu Province. In accordance with his entreaty, he is to be exempted.[4] It is thus.

2d year of Kempō [1214], 11th month, 4th day

Sagami no kami (Yoshitoki[5]) seal

SOURCES: Document 158: *Sappan kyūki zatsuroku,* 1215/10/4 Kantō migyōsho an, *Sappan kyūki zatsuroku,* 2: 24–25, doc. 124 (in *KI*, 4: 189, doc. 2,182). Document 159: *Tōji hyakugō monjo,* 1214/11/4 Kantō migyōsho an, *Toyonaka shishi,* p. 17, doc. 26 (in *KI*, 4: 145, doc. 2,131).

1. For a similar suggestion, see Hyōgo kenshi henshū semmon iinkai, comp., *Hyōgo kenshi* (Hyōgo, 1975), 2: 121. Our first reference to a Settsu *shugo* comes in 1221 (cf. Document 173). But this is hardly conclusive.

2. The "addendum" ends here.

3. Koremune (Shimazu) Tadahisa, *shugo* of Satsuma. See Document 137.

4. *Gesu* and other non-*jitō* vassals were fully liable for *goke'nin* services, even though their duties on the land were under the proprietor's jurisdiction.

5. Appears next to the signature in smaller characters, obviously added to this copy as a clarification. No addressee is cited.

SHUGO AS AGENTS OF THE BAKUFU

Kamakura Orders Its Shugo to Conduct Local Investigations, 1225, 1205

A major duty of *shugo* was as liaison between the Bakufu and its vassals. This could take many forms. One task was assisting Kamakura in its disposal of lawsuits, either before or after the actual trial.

160

Concerning the complaint of Tosa Province vassal Katayama *ko-daibu* Sanetoki that the *kumon* rights of Katayama Estate [*goryō**] had been seized by the priest Kenkai.

The accusation document has been sent, and details appear therein. This *shiki* was recorded in a shogunal house decree of the 1st year of Genkyū [1204], now in Sanetoki's possession.[1] If Kenkai had had any historical claims to it, he should have been the beneficiary of a judgment [*saidan*] to that effect. Instead, without a sound, why has he simply seized it? Forthwith, both sides shall be summoned for investigation; and a report, as well as documentary evidence, shall be forwarded. By this command, it is so decreed.[2]

1st year of Karoku [1225], 12th month, 15th day

[To] the Tosa Province *shugo*   Musashi no kami (monogram)
     headquarters   Sagami no kami (monogram)

161

Concerning an appeal by the officers of Sōsha Shrine, Izumo Province, regarding plundering by Ieshige, deputy *jitō* of Ōkusa Gō.

The shrine officials' document of complaint was delivered to the Ōkusa Gō *jitō*, Sukemitsu, and his defense statement is presented herewith. The positions of the two sides are contradictory; hence it is difficult to reach a decision. In brief, however, it is argued that Sukemitsu cease his arbitrary seizures beyond Ōkusa Gō, and that shrine officials not commit outrages [*rangyō*] upon the pretext of overseeing divine matters. Forthwith, under the authority of the *shugo*, details on both sides should be investigated, and these despoilments prohibited in accordance with justice. By command of the Kamakura lord, it is so decreed.

2d year of Genkyū [1205], 4th month, 22d day

[To] the Izumo Province *shugo*   Tōtomi no kami (monogram)
headquarters

SOURCES: Document 160: *Maeda ke shozō monjo,* 1225/12/15 Kantō gechijō, *KI,* 5: 380, doc. 3,439. Document 161: *Kitajima monjo,* 1205/4/22 Kantō gechijō, *Izumo Kokuzō ke monjo,* p. 4, doc. 5 (in *KI,* 3: 234, doc. 1,532).

1. I.e., the *shiki* was confirmed as belonging to Sanetoki or one of his forebears.

2. There are several possible explanations for the Bakufu's involvement in this non-*jitō* case. (1) Katayama Estate was a Kamakura proprietorship; hence the use of the designation *goryō,* though this is not conclusive (see Glossary). (2) The incident was taking place in the troubled years after Jōkyū, at a time when jurisdictional boundaries had become blurred. (3) The plaintiff was a *goke'nin* whose *kumon shiki* had once before been confirmed by Kamakura; the present appeal would be natural under these circumstances.

DOCUMENT 162

The Bakufu Issues a Directive That Includes a Charge to a Shugo, 1236

In this document a shrine under Bakufu patronage is advised to pass on future complaints through the Izumo *shugo* headquarters, which will assume jurisdiction and then report to Kamakura.

Concerning the petition of Tsunetaka, son of priest-administrator [*kannushi**] Takatsuna of Kitsuki Grand Shrine, Izumo Province, regarding this shrine's *kannushi* post.

During the time of the *utaishō* house, it was stipulated that there be [no][1] interference here by warrior houses [*buke*]. Nevertheless, because of Tsunetaka's claim to succession by right of primogeniture,[2] administrative authority [*shomu*] shall be under this *shiki*; the standard services for the proprietor shall be performed without negligence; and divine affairs are to be carried out without omission. If there should appear unruly persons who commit violations under some pretext, the *shugo* headquarters is to be informed; and after suppressing them [it] will report details to the Kantō. By command of the Kamakura lord, the order is so conveyed.

2d year of Katei [1236], 6th month, 5th day

Musashi no kami, Taira (monogram)
Sagami no kami, Taira (monogram)

SOURCE: *Kitajima monjo*, 1236/6/5 Kantō migyōsho, *Izumo Kokuzō ke monjo*, pp. 15–16, doc. 14 (in *KI*, 7: 285, doc. 4,996).
1. The editors of *Izumo Kokuzō ke monjo* assume a negative sentence here. *KI* omits this reading, but a document of 1184 shows the negative to be correct. In the midst of the Gempei War, Yoritomo outlawed warrior trespasses against Kitsuki Shrine. See *Kitajima monjo*, 1184/10/28 Minamoto Yoritomo kudashibumi, *Izumo Kokuzō ke monjo*, pp. 1–2, doc. 2.
2. The connection between this and the first sentence is not clear.

DOCUMENT 163

The Bakufu Orders a Shugo to Report on Local Disturbances, 1205

In this incident a *shugo* is directed to take action against local outrages, but to seek a deposition from the accused in the event of extenuating circumstances.

A copy [of a petition] by Kasuga Shrine has been sent. According to this document: "Shrine lands[1] have been invaded, and crimes have greatly increased." Particulars appear in this record. The despoilments of this lawless person are to be stopped.[2] In the event of any further details, a defense statement [*chinjō*] should be forwarded. By command of the Kamakura lord, it is so conveyed.

2d year of Genkyū [1205], 5th month, 19th day

[To] Sasaki, nakatsukasa nyūdō dono[3]   Tōtomi no kami seal

SOURCE: *Ōhigashi ke monjo*, 1205/5/19 Kantō migyōsho an, *Kasuga Jinja monjo*, 3: 210 (in *KI*, 3: 238, doc. 1,542).
1. Tsuda Island in Awa Province. Cf. Document 18.
2. A *sōtsuibushi** had invaded Tsuda Island and committed outrages. See Document 18, Note 1.
3. Sasaki Tsunetaka, *shugo* of Awa.

DOCUMENTS 164-65

The Shugo Endorses a Jitō's Claim in a Land Dispute, 1226; a Shugo Participates in the Dismissal of Jitō, 1248

At the behest of Kamakura, a *shugo*'s "good offices" might be used in other ways. In our first document, a *shugo*'s endorsement assists a *jitō* when the latter takes his case to Kyoto (Rokuhara). In the second document we see the opposite: the cancellation of *jitō shiki* after a *shugo*'s investigation.

164

In the matter of the Tosa Province *jitō* Kōsokabe Munemichi, I have been notified. Although a rival, Morifusa, had mounted a claim [to this office], a quitclaim [*saribumi**] was forwarded to us after details had been explained.[1] In accordance with the last testament of [Munemichi's] father, a new investiture should be granted when Munemichi goes up to the capital; he will explain full details. Respectfully reported by Yoshimura.

2d year of Karoku [1226], affixed,[2] 9th month, 22d day

saki no Suruga no kami, Yoshimura
(monogram)

165

... After Jōkyū [1221], when resident provincial officers [*zaichō**] were questioned by the magistrate [*bugyō*], *shugo* Hemmi nyūdō,[3] a report [*kanjō**] was sent on stating that [the lands in question] had been exempt areas since long before Jōkyū. As a consequence, the *jitō* of six *gō* were dismissed. ...

SOURCES: Document 164: *Kōsokabe kaden shōmon*, 1226/9/22 Miura Yoshimura shojō, *Kōsokabe shiryō*, p. 146, no. 8 (in *KI*, 5: 430, doc. 3,530). Document 165: extracted from a much longer Bakufu edict dealing with another matter, *Kumedadera monjo*, 1248/12/15 Kantō gechijō, *Izumi Kumedadera monjo*, p. 12, no. 2 (*KBSS*, 1: 87, doc. 82).

1. I.e., Morifusa had renounced his claim. In *Warrior Government* (p. 224, l. 23), the phrase "explaining his position" should read "relinquishing his claim."
2. I.e., the year was affixed later.
3. I.e., the *shugo* of Izumi Province, acting as agent for the Bakufu.

DOCUMENTS 166-69

Various Shugo Ratify Jitō Assignments by Kamakura, 1208, 1213, 1257, 1265

Kamakura grants or confirmations of *jitō shiki* were commonly endorsed by *shugo*, who would issue documents supporting the formal Kamakura investitures. This served notice that a local authority was on watch against irregularities. A relatively large number of these *shugo* verifications survive.

166

The *shugo*'s headquarters[1] orders: to four places within Kōzuma Estate, namely, Imahirochi, Kushibe, Mitsutomo, and Kitada.

That forthwith, in accordance with a directive [*migyōsho*] of the Kamakura *chūjō dono*,[2] Iemune shall possess [these areas], as of old.

Regarding the above, a directive of the 2d year of Ken'ei [1207], 8th month, 28th day, arrived here this 2d year of Jōgen [1208], 1st month, 17th day.[3] It states: "The seven places held by Kōzuma Jirō *daibu* Iemune are clear from an order of the late *utaishō*. Among these, Imahirochi, Kushibe, Mitsutomo, and Kitada are to be returned to Iemune, as before. The remaining three shall await further instructions.[4] By command of the Kamakura *chūjō dono*, the order is so conveyed." In acknowledgment thereof: the four places, in pursuance of this directive, shall be held, as of old, by Iemune. The remaining three, in compliance with the Kamakura lord's directive, shall be subject to further instructions. It is so commanded.

2d year of Jōgen [1208], 1st month, 17th day

saemon no jō, Fujiwara[5] seal

167

The *shugo*'s headquarters of Chikugo Province orders: to the residents of Kōzuma Estate.

That in accordance with a Kantō edict, Iemune shall forthwith hold the *jitō shiki* for these villages.

Regarding the above, a [Kantō] edict of the 2d year of Kenryaku [1212], 12th month, 13th day, arrived here on the 3d year [1213], 5th month, 3d day. Details appear in this document. As regards the village *jitō shiki* that have been ordered, Iemune shall hold the *jitō* titles in accordance with this [Kantō] edict. It is so decreed. Wherefore, this order.

3d year of Kenryaku [1213], 5th month, 3d day

shugosho no saemon no jō, Fujiwara seal

168

Concerning five places in Mitsuie District, Satsuma Province: Hishijima, Kawada, Nishimata, Jōmaeda, and Uehara-no-sono.

Tarō Sukenori holds these lands, in accordance with the last testament of *hokkyō* Eison, dated the 5th year of Kenchō [1253], 7th month, 10th day,[6] as confirmed by a decree [*ongechi*] and a directive [*migyōsho*] from the Kantō. In consequence, no challenge can be raised.[7] It is so commanded.

1st year of Shōka [1257], 8th month, 22d day

[To] Hishijima Tarō dono   saki no Ōsumi no kami[8] (monogram)

169

Concerning the notice that Izumo Yasutaka shall possess, in accordance with his father's testament, the *jitō shiki* of Ōba and Tajiri *ho*, Mitama Shrine lands, Izumo Province. In pursuance of a [Kantō] edict of the 8th month, 22d day,[9] this [circumstance] shall be known. It is so commanded.

2d year of Bun'ei [1265], 9th month, 6th day

shugonin, saki no Shinano no kami,
Minamoto (monogram)

SOURCES: Document 166: *Kōzuma monjo*, 1208/1/17 Chikugo no kuni shugosho kudashibumi an, *Zōho teisei hennen Ōtomo shiryō*, 2: 13–14, doc. 21 (in *KI*, 3: 337, doc. 1,712). Document 167: 1213/5/3, *ibid.*, 2: 28–29, doc. 44 (in *KI*, 4: 77, doc. 2,006). Document 168: *Hishijima monjo*, 1257/8/22 Satsuma no kuni shugo shigyōjō, *Sappan kyūki zatsuroku, zempen*, 4: 99, doc. 333. Document 169: *Kitajima monjo*, 1265/9/6 Izumo no kuni shugo shigyōjō, *Izumo Kokuzō ke monjo*, p. 73, doc. 23.

1. Of Chikugo Province in Kyushu.

2. Minamoto Sanetomo.

3. A delivery period of nearly four months from Kamakura to Kyushu (five months in the next document) seems unusually slow. Cf. *Kōzuma monjo*, 1207/8/28 Kantō migyōsho an, *KI*, 3: 327, doc. 1,696, for Kamakura's directive.

4. These, too, were eventually confirmed to Iemune. The reason for the delay was a dispute over house property between Iemune and one of his kinsmen. The

challenger, however, remained dissatisfied, and brought suit in 1212. Once again Iemune was confirmed. See *Kōzuma monjo*, 1212/12/13 shōgun ke mandokoro kudashibumi an, *KI*, 4: 50–51, doc. 1,958. The *shugo's* endorsement of this Kamakura decision appears as Document 167.

5. Probably the deputy *shugo*.

6. See *Hishijima monjo*, 1253/7/10 Eison yuzurijō, *Sappan kyūki zatsuroku, zempen*, 4: 86–87, doc. 315.

7. Several younger brothers of Sukenori had also received portions of the family inheritance. Presumably, this admonishment was designed to forestall any future trouble. See *ibid.*, 1253/7/10 Eison okibumi, 4: 85, doc. 314.

8. Shimazu Tadatoki, *shugo* of Satsuma.

9. *Kitajima monjo*, 1265/8/22 Kantō gechijō, *Izumo kokuzō ke monjo*, p. 72, doc. 22.

DOCUMENT 170

A Shugo Issues a Judicial Edict, 1258

Kamakura *shugo* did not possess an independent judicial authority over Bakufu vassals. Occasionally, however, a *shugo* did issue a preliminary judgment. In such cases it was understood that disputants might appeal upward. Few of the details in the present example can be explained easily; but it is clear that the judgment was merely an affirmation of points agreed to between the disputants themselves.[1]

The matters in dispute between Ōsumi Province houseman Sata Kurō Munechika and his elder brother, Shirō Chikatsuna.

Item: concerning the statement[2] that tribute obligations be discharged from the Ōtomari Bay region.[3]

Item: concerning the statement about foraging in shrine fields and newly developed fields within the widow's land allotment.[4]

Item: concerning the statement about the destruction of old roadways and the building of new roads through Munechika's lands.

Item: concerning the statement about Chikatsuna's outright seizure of the uplands granted to the *jitō* when the governor was first appointed.[5]

Item: concerning the statement that Takeyasu Myō, because it is heavily burdened with service obligations, should have its dues paid to the household head [*sōryō**] as a legacy from his late father.[6]

Item: concerning two female bequests.

Item: concerning the statement about the seizure by Munechika's deputy, Tamesada, of Jizō's wife and her two children.[7]

In accordance with the compromise document of this past 9th month,

21st day, there are to be no changes concerning these seven items. It is so decreed.

2d year of Shōka [1258], 10th month, 18th day

saki no Owari no kami, Taira[8]

(monogram)

SOURCE: *Nejime monjo*, 1258/10/18 Ōsumi no kuni shugo gechijō, *Nejime monjo*, 1: 48–49, doc. 62.

1. The compromise settlement itself appears in *ibid.*, 1258/9/21 Tarube Chikatsuna wayojō, pp. 47–48, doc. 61. Unfortunately, both documents contain points that are obscure.

2. I.e., the clause in the compromise document.

3. These obligations are specified in the *wayojō*.

4. The dispute involved an inheritance arrangement that was not satisfactory to all parties. This item refers to incursions by one of the sons upon his mother's inheritance share.

5. Upon the governor's appointment he authorized the transfer of 1.5 *chō* of upland area to the Sata *jitō* family. This was seized in its entirety by Chikatsuna, prompting a complaint from his brother. A compromise ensued, and one-third of the total was relinquished to Munechika.

6. It was the traditional practice during Kamakura times for the chieftain to collect all tributes [*kuji*] from his brethren that were owed to the Kantō.

7. Note that Munechika (through his deputy) was also guilty of lawless acts. Hence the need to grant concessions and compromise.

8. Nagoe (Hōjō) Tokiaki, *shugo* of Ōsumi.

LIMITATIONS AND POTENTIAL OF THE SHUGO

DOCUMENT 171

Kōfukuji Lays Claim to Provincial Police Powers, 1300

The police authority in Yamato Province was exercised during Kamakura times by Kōfukuji Temple. Technically, this made the *shugo* office superfluous there, and no such official was ever appointed. In this circumstance the disputes over rights of entry that might have involved *shugo* redounded instead to Kōfukuji.

The lower officers of Kōfukuji, Rinken and others, have stated: "Concerning the petition of the agent [*zasshō*] Sōen, of Hiranodono Estate, in this province [Yamato], a Tōji holding, that the district agent's incursions are to cease.[1] This claim is a false charge [*ranso**] contradictory to the facts. For the entire province of Yamato, governor and *shugo* duties were long ago terminated and assigned to this temple-shrine. Thus it is an age-old custom that the police and related authorities [*kendan* ika*] be under this temple's control [*shinshi*], even for the holdings of elite central houses [*kemmon seika* no ryō*].[2] Moreover, it is clear that from ages past this estate has been subject to entrance by public persons.[3] How can a false charge of innovation be brought? . . .[4]

2d year of Shōan [1300], 12th month, 26th day

geshoshi, Rinken tō

SOURCE: *Tōji hyakugō monjo*, 1300/12/26 Kōfukuji geshoshi tō mōshikotoba, *Nihon no komonjo*, 2: 396–97, doc. 635.
  1. The district agent referred to is a deputy of the Kōfukuji.
  2. I.e., Kōfukuji held the *kendan* privilege for all non-immune *shōen* within Yamato, even those belonging to the ranking landholding powers of the capital. See Glossary.
  3. I.e., entry by representatives of the "state," in this instance agents of the Kōfukuji.
  4. The document continues on to another matter.

DOCUMENT 172

The Bakufu Repeals a Shugo's Authority, 1205

In Document 171 it was hinted that *shugo* were not uniformly appointed to all provinces. In some places (e.g., Mutsu, Dewa, Yamashiro, and Yamato) *shugo* were never appointed. In others, special conditions led to the temporary removal of either the *shugo* themselves or some portion of their authority. One example of the latter occurred in Iyo Province. So influential was the local notable Kōno Michinobu that Kamakura felt compelled to transfer immediate supervision of its own vassals to his jurisdiction. However, Michinobu was not made a *shugo*. A cardinal rule of the Bakufu was to deny that title to all non-Kantō figures.

(monogram)

Concerning Michinobu and the vassals who appear on the name register:[1] [32 names follow].

The aforesaid housemen shall no longer be under the jurisdiction of the *shugo's* headquarters, but will perform their obligations under the authority of Michinobu. However, if criminals appear, they shall be summoned and sent on [to the Kantō] under Michinobu's direction.[2] By command of the Kamakura lord, it is so decreed.

  2d year of Genkyū [1205], intercalary 7th month,   day

SOURCE: *Ōyamazumi Jinja monjo*, 1205/int.7 Kantō gechijō, *KI*, 3: 248–49, doc. 1,570.
  1. Registers of provincial housemen were drawn up during the 1190's. See Mass, *Warrior Government*, p. 152.
  2. The meaning here seems to be that Michinobu will not have the power to prosecute rebels or murderers, since he is not a *shugo*; he must send them on to Kamakura.

DOCUMENT 173

Kamakura Awards a Shugo Shiki, 1221

Shugo investiture decrees are extremely scarce. A major reason for this is that written evidence was required only when land perquisites, which affected others, were included in an appointment package. The small number of these documents suggests that land rights very rarely accompanied *shugo* assignments.[1]

That Fujiwara Munemasa shall forthwith assume the Settsu Province *shugo* headquarters [*shugosho**] and the Ai Estate *jitō shiki*.

The aforesaid person shall hold these *shiki*. By this command, it is so decreed.

3d year of Jōkyū [1221], 6th month, 25th day

Mutsu no kami, Taira (monogram)

SOURCE: *Minagawa monjo*, 1221/6/25 Kantō gechijō, *Toyonaka shishi, shiryō hen* 1, p. 18, doc. 30 (in *KI*, 5: 20, doc. 2,761).
    1. I am able to cite only three other examples: (1) The assignment of Fujiwara Munemasa to the Awaji Province *shugo* post and two *jitō shiki* (*Minagawa monjo*, 1221/7/20 Kantō gechijō, *KI*, 5: 26, doc. 2,779). (2) The assignment of Shimazu Tadahisa to the Echizen *shugo* post (*Shimazu ke monjo*, 1221/7/12 Kantō gechijō, *KI*, 5: 20–21, doc. 2,764; a *jitō shiki* was granted by a separate document, *ibid.*, 1221/5/13 Kantō gechijō an, *KI*, 5: 14, doc. 2,745). (3) The transfer of Nakahara Chikazane from the Suō Province *shugo* position to the same office in Aki Province (*Itsukushima monjo*, 1235/5/9 shōgun ke mandokoro kudashibumi, *KI*, 7: 180, doc. 4,757; the additional *shiki* were assigned by a separate document, *ibid.*, 1235/6/5 Kantō gechijō, *KI*, 7: 182, doc. 4,763). A number of references to *shugo* appointments appear in *Azuma kagami*. But there are almost no documents of this type. In *Warrior Government* (p. 227, fn. 88) the words "all include" should more accurately read "tend to include."

DOCUMENT 174

A Bakufu Directive Refers to Shugo Lands, 1326

Only in the last third of the Kamakura period do we find occasional references to *shugo* lands.[1] It is doubtful, however, whether the *shugo* office was changing its essential character. The *shugo* as territorial magnate was a product of the Nambokuchō period.

Concerning the *shugo's* land allotment [*shugo no bunryō*] within Ninomiya Estate, of which chief priest Kunitame and other officials [of Iminomiya Shrine], Nagato Province, have complained.

This shrine is a major spiritual center, but has fallen [of late] into serious decay; moreover, the [*shugo's*] portion constitutes an important part of it.[2] The substance of what is reported, which makes it difficult to ignore this petition, is hardly unreasonable. As a fully exempt shrine land once again,[3] divine matters shall be carried out in accordance with former practice, and prayers will be said faithfully. Shrine officials are to be duly informed of this. By this command, it is so conveyed.

1st year of Karyaku [1326], 3d month, 20th day

[To] Kōzuke zenji dono[4]   Sagami no kami (monogram)
                                         shuri no daibu (monogram)

SOURCE: *Iminomiya Jinja monjo*, 1326/3/20 Kantō migyōsho, *Shōen shi shiryō* (undated ed.), p. 36.

1. I have now identified four such references: in the present document; in Document 177 below; and in *Kanazawa bunko komonjo*, 1278/12/25 Rokuhara gechijō and 1314/18/27 Rokuhara gechijō, *Kanazawa bunko komonjo* (1937 ed.), 1:7, doc. 6, and 1: 34, doc. 30. In three of these four cases the *shugo* concerned were members of the house of Hōjō. A fifth reference is in a document that appears to be a forgery: *Ōtomo monjo*, 1256/8/11 Kantō gechijō an, *Hennen Ōtomo shiryō*, 1: 402–3, doc. 469.

2. This sentence evidently summarizes the shrine's petition.

3. By favoring a return to full exemption, Kamakura was effectively cancelling the *shugo's* share in Ninomiya Estate.

4. Hōjō Tokinao, *shugo* of Nagato.

DOCUMENT 175

The Bakufu Directs a Shugo Headquarters to Suppress an Outbreak of Local Violence, 1286

During the years after the Mongol Invasions the Hōjō came to dominate the Bakufu completely. Among other things, they accelerated their takeover of *shugo* posts, and by the end of the Kamakura period they held roughly half the national total. Hōjō-controlled *shugo* offices, moreover, tended to assume a greater share of provincial governance. Though never formally revoked, the older limitations on types of crimes under *shugo* jurisdiction gradually fell into obsolescence. Here we encounter one Hōjō-controlled agency (Rokuhara) directing a second (the Harima Province *shugo* office) to assume total jurisdiction in a local disturbance.

Concerning the depredations of warrior retainers and neighboring local notables, as appealed by priests of the Taizanji, Harima Province. The accusation document and accompanying papers are presented herewith. As they report: "In violation of prohibitions, temple land has been invaded, trees and bamboo cut and taken, and fish caught."[1] If this is true, it is a most serious offense. Forthwith, [such lawlessness] shall be checked. It is so commanded.

9th year of Kōan [1286], intercalary 12th month, 25th day

[To] the deputy *shugo*   shuri no suke (monogram)
                                            Musashi no kami (monogram)

SOURCE: *Taizanji monjo,* 1286/int.12/25 Rokuhara migyōsho, *Harima Taizanji monjo,* p. 8, doc. 8.
    1. None of these misdeeds is included in the regular definition of *shugo* jurisdiction.

DOCUMENTS 176-77

The Bakufu and a Shugo Issue Orders Concerning a Special Tax, 1293

The levying of a household tax (*munabetsu*[1] *sen*) became a regular practice of *shugo* in the second half of the fourteenth century, after the fall of the Kamakura Bakufu. Here we have perhaps the earliest reference to an impost of this kind, as well as a reference to a *shugo*'s land rights. Equally significant, however, is that Tada-in was a proprietary holding of the Kamakura Hōjō house. This meant that all four orders mentioned as being issued (from the court, the Kantō, the Rokuhara office, and the Tango Province *shugo*) were for the benefit of the Bakufu's dominant family.

176

Regarding the construction of Tada-in, Settsu Province.

According to an imperial order of the 1st month, 19th day,[2] held by priest Ryōkan: "Although the details are many, in essence cash [*senka*] to the amount of 10 *mon* per household within this province[3] shall be collected and used as a repair fund for the main temple and other buildings." Pursuant to this edict, *shugo, jitō,* and *goke'nin* will discharge this obligation. By command of the Kamakura lord, it is so decreed.

6th year of Shōō [1293], 3d month, 2d day

                    Mutsu no kami, Taira ason (monogram)
                    Sagami no kami, Taira ason (monogram)

177

Regarding the construction of Tada-in, Settsu Province.

According to a Kantō decree of this year's 3d month, 2d day, and a Rokuhara enforcement order of the 6th month, 6th day: [4] "Cash to the amount
of 10 *mon* per household within Tango Province shall be collected and
used as a repair fund for the main temple and other buildings." Following the intent of this order, the *shugō's* land allotment [*ryōbun*] will discharge this obligation. [5] It is thus.

1st year of Einin [1293], 9th month, 9th day

shuri no suke, Ōe ason (monogram)

SOURCES: Document 176: *Tada-in monjo*, 1293/3/2 Kantō gechijō, *Chō komonjo*,
1: 507–8. Document 177: *ibid.*, 1293/9/9 Tango no kuni shugo shigyōjō, *Nihon
no komonjo*, 2: 137, doc. 185.

1. Commonly read also as *munebechi* or *munabechi*; see Glossary.

2. See *Tada-in monjo*, 1293/1/19 kan senshi, *Komonjo ruisan*, pp. 69–70.

3. The actual imperial order refers to eight provinces but does not name them.
Tango was one, as we see in Document 177. Another was Settsu, in which Tada-in
was located. See *Tada-in monjo*, [date missing] Kasuga Jinja mandokoro kudashibumi, *Komonjo ruisan*, p. 108 (this is an order urging payment of the special repair
tax by Kasuga's estate holdings in Settsu). The remaining six provinces are unknown, but most likely all were in the central region.

4. *Tada-in monjo*, 1293/6/6 Rokuhara shigyōjō an, *Chō komonjo*, 1: 509. Evidently a Rokuhara draft order (*an*) was sent to the *shugo* of each of the eight
provinces. The original of the enforcement decree was dated four days earlier; see
Tada-in monjo, 1293/6/2 Rokuhara shigyōjō, *Komonjo ruisan*, p. 139.

5. Here, the *shugo* was in effect agreeing not to exclude his own lands from this
emergency levy.

DOCUMENT COLLECTIONS
REPRESENTED IN THE TEXT

As with the labeling of documents, there is no uniformly acceptable way to list collections. A recent trend (in *KI*) has been to place the province name ahead of the collection. But this would have made alphabetization meaningless. Another uncertain area involves documents traditionally associated with some well-known collection but now in private hands. Most editors give credit to both sources: e.g., "Satō Kiyoshi shi shozō Tōji monjo." A third difficulty occurs when a document's ownership has changed recently or is simply attributed differently in different books. Scholars have yet to agree on a single system of identification. Finally, there are the many instances in which documents survive only in chronicles or diaries or on the reverse sides of such sources. Complicated classification schema abound. The present listing follows a somewhat abbreviated method, concentrating on main or "core" sources. The numbers cited here refer to documents, not pages.

CHRONOLOGICAL INDEX OF
DOCUMENTS TRANSLATED

This list is offered for quick identification. The actual year periods—eras—appear in the translations themselves. In a few instances, years have been determined from context and then inserted. The user should bear in mind that the labeling of documents is often imprecise. For example, there are numerous records that are *kudashibumi* in style but *bu'ninjō* in content. Which designation should we use, then? Even within single volumes compilers regularly switch from one form to the other. There are also the many instances in which documents are not clearly of *any* style. Rokuhara edicts, especially, seem to combine attributes of *gechijō* and *migyōsho*.

GLOSSARY

akutō 悪党. Literally, "evil bands"; groups of peasants and minor warriors who perpetrated local crimes, generally looting and foraging. Became a distinct social phenomenon after about 1260. For an early reference, see Document 82.

an 案. Draft or copy of a document, normally identifiable by the absence of an authorizing monogram (*kaō*). Considered by historians as hardly less valuable than a signed document. The term *anmon* often appears in document texts in contradistinction to *shōmon*, which is a document original. Cf. the references in Document 99.

andojō 安堵状. Document of confirmation for land rights or some other legal transaction. Always issued by a higher authority to a lower (e.g. the Kamakura Bakufu's confirmation of a *jitō's* rights after each generation). The term *ando* by itself often conveys the meaning of guaranteeing or providing general security. For *andojō* examples, see Documents 21 and 104.

anzu 安主. Middle-level officer of a noble family's administrative headquarters (*mandokoro*); often involved with preparing documents or recording decisions. Performed such duties for the Kamakura Bakufu's *mandokoro*. Also, an administrative officer within a *shōen*.

ari han 在判. A term appearing under the signature (or signatures) on documents that are copies (*an*). Signifies that a formal monogram (*kaō*) appears on the original.

ason 朝臣. A hereditary imperial rank, held by certain prestigious warriors.

ato 跡, see *honshi no ato*

atsujō 圧状. Literally, "forced document." Such was the importance of written evidence in Kamakura litigation that disputants often compelled inferior officials to sign depositions favoring their arguments. If so identified, records were deemed inadmissible as evidence.

azukari dokoro 預所. Literally, "custodial office," but actually the office name (*shiki*) commonly given by absentee proprietors to large-scale commenders of land. In time, this title came to have the additional meaning of a proprietor's deputy, that is, an officer representing the domain owner's interests. Sometimes, also, central families not of the highest status were called *azukari dokoro* over hereditary estates. In such instances they would be virtual proprietors (*ryōke*): above them would stand only a "patron" (*honke*).

baiken 売券. A contractual agreement finalizing the sale of land; issued by the seller.

befu 別符. Newly opened land that was duly recognized by the provincial office as being part of an already existing estate.

benzaishi (or *bezaishi*) 弁済使. A "financial officer" of private estates or public lands. Common in Kyushu.

betsu-in 別院. A branch temple or detached Buddhist structure. The term *betsu-gū* (branch shrine) also appears.

betsunō (or *bechinō*) 別納. Direct payment of taxes without going through a *jitō* or other estate officer.

bettō 別当. A chief administrator, whether of a house chancellery (*mandokoro*), a local religious institution, or (sometimes) an estate headquarters.

bonge 凡下. Commoners; general population.

bōrei 傍例. Customary practices; unwritten precedent.

bōsho 謀書. A fraudulent document.

bu'ninjō 補任状. An appointment document. *Shiki* were commonly assigned (from higher to lower) by this vehicle. See, for example, Documents 11–13, 62–63, 65–66, 74–75, 83–84, and 108–10.

bushidan 武士団. General term for a warrior band, used for groups of all sizes. Bands were held together by a mixture of kinship (fictive or real) and ties of vassalage centering on the head of the group's dominant lineage.

chakushi 嫡子. The designated heir to a family headship, though not necessarily the eldest son. Until late Kamakura times the *chakushi* and his brothers and sisters generally divided the family's wealth according to the specifications laid down in their father's final testament. A trend toward unitary inheritance began in the late thirteenth century.

chigyō 知行. Minimally, the right to income from land; maximally, the right of territorial possession. Thus *chigyō* could refer to a *shiki* holding, especially during Heian and Kamakura times, or to a fief holding during the Ashikaga period.

chigyōkoku 知行国. A province held in "proprietorship" by a ranking court noble or religious institution during late Heian and Kamakura times. Provincial proprietors enjoyed the right to nominate governors (*kokushu*), as well as the right to receive income from the cultivated "public lands."

chigyōkokushu 知行国主. A provincial proprietor.

chinjō 陳状. A document summing up the rebuttal of a defendant in a lawsuit. See the references in Documents 36, 106, and 163.

Chinzei 鎮西. Traditional name for Kyushu.

Chinzei bugyō 鎮西奉行. A designation for the two Kamakura commissioners for Kyushu. Purportedly held by the Ōtomo and Shōni (originally Mutō) families, though recent scholarship raises many questions concerning this title. Superseded by the Chinzei *tandai*.

Chinzei tandai 鎮西探題. The two Kamakura deputies for Kyushu, established in the 1290's with full powers of jurisdiction over that island. Exercised much greater authority than the Chinzei *bugyō*. Held by members of the Hōjō house.

chō 町 (or 丁). A basic unit of land area. Was 2.94 acres until Hideyoshi reduced the size to 2.45 acres (about 1 hectare).

chōsen 庁宣. A provincial governor's decree. Many were issued from Kyoto by absentee governors to the provincial headquarters (*rusudokoro*). See Documents 54–55.

chūshinjō 注進状. A documentary form used to list something or to report to a higher authority. Tax registers (e.g. *kechige* or *san'yōjō*) are one type of *chūshinjō*.

dairi ōban 内裏大番. Imperial palace guard service in Kyoto. Organized on a province-by-province basis during Heian times, with the responsibility for duty falling on major local warriors. From early Kamakura times on, only vassals of the new Bakufu discharged this service.

dajōkan (or *daijōkan*) 太政官. The imperial state council and highest legitimizing agency, composed of the ranking ministers at court.

Dazaifu 太宰府. The government-general for Kyushu, founded in the seventh century. Located in Chikuzen Province (Fukuoka Prefecture). Responsible for foreign affairs and the supervision of Kyushu governance. Later fell under control of the Bakufu.

denka goryō (or *tenka goryō*) 殿下御領. A collection of estates passed on by inheritance to the head of the main Fujiwara line (i.e. the regent's line). Totaled about 150 domains in the late Kamakura period. See the references in Documents 4 and 80.

denpata 田畑. Paddy and upland (rice and dry fields). *Ta* plus *hata*.

fukkanjō 覆勘状. Documents acknowledging the performance of guard duty or military service. Issued in large numbers by *shugo* during the Mongol invasion crisis of the 1270's and 1280's. Contributed to a blurring of the distinction between Kamakura vassals and others.

funshitsujō 紛失状 . A document issued as replacement for an original record that had been lost, stolen, or destroyed. The significant contents of the original would be reproduced, and the new document had full force in law. See Document 25.

fusen 府宣 . A decree issued by the Dazaifu (*q.v.*). See the reference in Document 15.

fuyu menden 不輸免田 . Land exempt from public taxation and jurisdiction. Used in reference to fully immune *shōen*.

gebumi 解文 (*gejō* or *ge*). A common documentary form used to petition (or simply offer a statement) from a lower to a higher authority. See the references in Documents 6, 92, and 114.

gechijō 下知状 . A documentary form used in matters requiring long-term efficacy. Judicial decisions commonly used this pattern. Both Bakufu and central proprietors issued numerous *gechijō*. One of the three basic documentary styles (along with *kudashibumi* and *migyōsho*) used by the Kamakura regime. See Document Originals, pp. 14–23.

gedai 外題 . A "marginal notation" added by a legitimizing authority to a petition or valid document. Used by Kamakura principally as a confirmation device. See Documents 42 and 44.

gejō 解状 , see *gebumi*

ge'nin 下人 , see *shojū*

gesu 下司 . An estate manager, commonly one of the major commenders of the land composing a *shōen*. The particular office most often replaced by a Kamakura-appointed *jitō*. See especially Documents 63–75.

gimonjo 偽文書 . A forged document.

goin 後院 . A palace established by an active emperor for his retirement. See Document 59.

goke'nin 御家人 . A vassal, or "houseman," of the Kamakura Bakufu. Without the honorific *go* the term connotes a retainer of any lord, whether civil or military.

gokunyū chi 御口入地 . Estates on which Kamakura vassals who were not *jitō* held interests, hence lands over which the Bakufu claimed no jurisdiction. The word *kunyū* or *gokunyū* means "benevolent intercession," usually of a judicial type. See Document 52.

goryō 御領 . Lands held by some especially prominent family or institution. Thus Kantō *goryō* were estates held in proprietorship by the Kamakura Bakufu, and *denka goryō* were domains belonging to the regent's line of the Fujiwara.

Goseibai shikimoku 御成敗式目 . The Bakufu's law code of 1232. Also known as the Jōei Code, after the year period in which it was promulgated. An excerpt appears as Document 139.

gōshi (or *gōji*) 郷司 . Chief of a *gō*-level (village-sized) administrative unit.

The public land equivalent of a private estate manager. Many *gōshi* in fact became estate managers after a *shōen* was formed.

gunji 郡司. Chief of a *gun* (district-sized) administrative unit. Provinces included from two to two dozen *gun*, nine or ten being the average.

gusho 具書. The sequence of documents submitted in support of a legal claim or petition. See Document 127.

hashi uragaki 端裏書. Writing appearing on the reverse side of a document. This was added by the recipient of the record and consisted of brief identifying data—e.g. "Rokuhara gechijō." The object here was simple convenience, since documents were normally kept rolled up and tied.

hikan 被官. A personal follower or retainer of insignificant rank.

hompo jitō 本補地頭. A post-Jōkyū *jitō* whose perquisites were those of a displaced *gesu*-level officer. A *hompo jitō* became "heir" to a *honshi no ato.*

honjo 本所. A term connoting the proprietor (*ryōke*) or—from the twelfth century—the patron (*honke*) of a *shōen*. Also used to refer to the administrative headquarters of a *shōen*.

honke 本家. The patron or guardian of an estate. The ranking title in the *shōen* hierarchy. Only the highest nobility and most prestigious religious institutions could be *honke*.

honryō ando 本領安堵. The confirmation of a family's right to its homelands, either by the assignment of a new *shiki* (e.g. a *jitō shiki*) or by the simple "reinvestiture" of an old *shiki*.

honshi no ato 本司跡. Literally, "original officer legacy." Used to connote inherited land rights and the customary procedures limiting them. Occasionally refers to a "successor" himself. Appears in many contexts, but especially in Kamakura's judicial edicts, which commonly order wayward *jitō* to "follow *honshi no ato*." Often the term *ato* is used alone. *Honshi no ato, ato,* and *honshi no rei* (another variation) all appear in Document 99.

hontaku ando 本宅安堵. Confirmation of a family's possession of its residence and the immediately adjacent land (i.e. its homestead).

hōō 法皇. A retired emperor who had taken Buddhist vows. This did not imply any diminution of his political authority.

hori no uchi 堀内. "Within the moat"; the personally owned area immediately surrounding an estate officer's residence. No taxes were due from this land category. See Documents 94 and 120.

hoshi 保司. Chief of a *ho*-level (hamlet-sized) administrative unit. *Ho* were the smallest units in the sequence *ho-gō-gun-kuni.*

hōsho 奉書. A document acknowledging that an order would be carried out.

hosshi (or *hōshi*) 法師. A common honorific Buddhist title, held by large numbers of warriors.

hyōji (or *heishi*) 兵士. Local militia; estate officers, *myōshu,* or even peasants impressed into military service. The term is a complex one. See Documents 2, 132, 134, and 156.

hyōjōshū 評定衆. The major deliberative council of the Kamakura Bakufu, established in 1225.

hyōrōmai (*hyōrō, rōmai, hyōranmai*) 兵粮米（兵粮，粮米，兵乱米）. The commissariat rice tax levied during major wars (e.g. Gempei and Jōkyū) by the opposing sides. Often used as a pretext to tax otherwise exempt estates. See Documents 2 and 131.

ichibu jitō 一分地頭. A "fractional" *jitō*. By late Kamakura times the system of divided inheritance had led to an extreme subdivision of some holdings; hence the distribution to heirs of partial *jitō shiki*.

ichien 一円. Complete or total. Often used in the sense of total jurisdiction over land.

ichigo 一期. "One generation." Used to connote a limited inheritance period for female heirs. To prevent portions of a house's patrimony from falling into alien hands, land rights granted to female heirs reverted to the main line after the recipient's death; hence "life tenure."

ichinomiya 一宮. "First shrine." The principal state-supported shrine within a province. By Kamakura times most *ichinomiya* had become private estate-holding institutions.

in 院. A retired emperor; palace of a retired emperor or imperial lady; imperial temple; territorial unit; etc.

in-no-chō 院庁. The administrative headquarters of a retired emperor (and sometimes of a court lady or imperial temple). For decrees of the retired emperor's chancellery, see Documents 7, 59, and 132.

insei 院政. The term used by historians for the governmental form of the late Heian period, postulating control over affairs of state by retired emperors.

inzen 院宣. A retired emperor's directive. See the references in Documents 4 and 7.

jike 寺家. Temple administrators or authorities; sometimes, the temple itself.

jikinin 直人. An administrative officer of a *shōen* or a provincial headquarters (*kokuga*).

jikkenshi 実験使. An investigating officer, often concerned with agricultural conditions or alleged local disturbances. Normally dispatched by an absentee proprietor.

jimu 寺務. Temple affairs or administration. Used especially in reference to local temples. Lawless warriors often interfered with *jimu*.

jinushi 地主. The generic term (Heian and Kamakura) for a prominent local holder of land rights. Many *jinushi* became *gesu* or Kamakura *jitō*.

jishi 地子. Payments from land categories other than rice paddy. The regular tax from paddy land was called *nengu*.

jitō 地頭 . An estate steward or manager appointed by the Kamakura Bakufu; chiefly concerned with tax collection and local police duties. Historically, the most important local figure during Kamakura times.

jitōdai 地頭代`. A deputy *jitō* appointed by the *jitō* from among personal relatives, private retainers, or local notables. See especially Documents 108–16.

jitōsho 地頭所 . The administrative headquarters of a *jitō* within an estate.

jiyaku 寺役 . Services and tributes owed to a temple.

jōbun 上分 . Rice that was payable as tax to the proprietor over and above the regular annual rice levy (*nengu*). See, e.g., Document 74.

jōden 定田 . Paddy fields whose economic yield was not earmarked for local consumption or otherwise tax-exempt; hence the fields from which payment was due to an absentee proprietor.

Jōei shikimoku 貞永式目 , see *Goseibai shikimoku*

Jōkyū rangyaku 承久乱逆 . The "Jōkyū treachery." Refers to the court's attempt to destroy the Kamakura Bakufu by force in 1221, the third year of the Jōkyū era. The phrase appears in many Bakufu and proprietors' documents.

jungyōjō 遵行状 . A document issued by *shugo* to enforce Bakufu decisions relating to land. Used during the late Kamakura period, but became a standard document form only in early Ashikaga times.

jūnin 住人 . "Residents." A general term signifying local notables or men of prominence. Orders or announcements from a proprietor or the Bakufu were commonly addressed to a region's *jūnin*.

kachōmai (*kachō*) 加徴米 . Originally, a surtax collected over and above the regular annual tax. Under the Bakufu it was regularized as a special perquisite of *shimpo jitō* (*q.v.*). Collection was always at a fixed and uniform rate from designated fields. See Documents 69 and 107.

kaieki 改易 . Revocation of a *shiki* and assignment of that "office" to someone else.

kaihotsu (or *kaihatsu*) *ryōshu* 開発領主 . Heian-period local notables recognized as owners of the land they had brought under cultivation. Later, such "public holdings" were often commended to central nobles, producing the division into proprietary (central) and managerial (local) authorities. The "original ownership" was thus passed to an aristocratic *shōen* holder.

kajishi 加地子 . The land rent collected by prominent local holders (*shiryōshu*) from resident cultivators. Viewed as a kind of on-the-land *nengu*, alongside the regular *nengu* owed to the *shōen* proprietor. Commendation transactions antecedent to a *shōen* incorporation often strengthened the commender's right to *kajishi*. For a reference to *kajishi*, see Document 46.

Kamakura dono no otsukai 鎌倉殿御使 . A pair of special agents of Minamoto Yoritomo assigned to Kyōto early in 1185. See Document 4.

kami 守, see *kokushu*

kanjō 勘状. In general, a deposition or report submitted to a higher authority in an investigative matter. Under the Kamakura Bakufu, *kanjō* were pretrial summaries by subordinate agencies, upon which judicial decisions were then based.

kanmon 貫文. A unit of cash: *kan* plus *mon*.

kanmotsu 官物. Tribute goods paid as taxes or tithes.

kannō 勧農. An improvement program to increase an estate's agricultural productivity; an agricultural reorganization, usually centering on a redistribution of cultivation rights. The person, family, or institution overseeing an area's *kannō* generally controlled that region. An ambiguous term, also used to refer to the busy agricultural seasons. See Document 117.

kannōshi 勧農使. A title granted to Minamoto Yoritomo's special deputy in the Hokuriku region after 1184. The holder of this office was Hiki Tōnai Tomomune, and his authority included overseeing vassals and restoring cultivation in "public lands." See Document 7.

kannushi 神主. The head priest-administrator of a shrine.

kanōden 加納田. Public fields adjacent to a *shōen* that were worked by residents of the *shōen* and then came to be recognized as part of the estate.

kaō 花押. A monogram (or monograms) affixed to a document and representing the name(s) of the issuing authority or his chancellery officers. The format and shape of *kaō* changed over time, having little bearing by Kamakura times to one's actual name. See *ari han*.

kebiishi 検非違使. Originally, a police captain for the central capital; later, a designation for provincial law-enforcement officials.

kechige 結解. Tax assessment and collection registers. Prepared annually by estate officials for submission to the proprietor.

keijō 契状. A document form used to establish an agreement or contractual arrangement between two or more parties, commonly cosigned by all of them. See Documents 56 and 125.

kemmon seika 権門勢家. "Influential houses and powerful families." A common designation for central landowning institutions. See the reference in Document 171.

kenchū mokuroku 検注目録. A land register for *shōen* or public lands. Included were such data as cultivated acreage, field types, tax exemptions, and local holders. An estate's total payments would be calculated from this. The term *kenchū* by itself refers to a land survey.

kendanken (*kendan*) 検断権. The right of jurisdiction in criminal matters. This privilege included rights of pursuit, incarceration, judgment, and confiscation. It could be divided among local authorities and central proprietary interests on any basis: by type of crime, by territorial boundaries, or by percentage of any fines levied. See especially Documents 86–90, 140–51.

kengen 権限 . The authorized limits of authority beyond which a *shiki* holder could not lawfully go; the perquisites and privileges of any office.

ke'nin 家人 , see *goke'nin*

ke'nin bugyōnin 家人奉行人 . A term applied in 1197 to the Bakufu's overseer of vassals in southern Kyushu, Koremune Tadahisa. Later subsumed under the title of *shugo*. See Document 137.

kezan (or *gezan; genzan*) 見参 . Originally a personal audience before a court figure, which led to a patron-client relationship; later, the act of swearing loyalty to a military lord. See the references in Documents 15, 40, and 157.

kirokujo 記録所 . A central office for the screening and review of *shōen* charters. First established in 1069 and then periodically revived. Functioned during the early Kamakura period as a court-controlled judicial agency.

kishinjō 寄進状 . A document for the commendation (endowment) of land. A *kishinjō* conveyed ownership rights to some higher authority, such as a temple or noble house, often preparatory to *shōen* incorporation. As a result of such commendations, donors were generally confirmed in a managerial-custodial authority, and recipients became proprietors (*ryōke*).

kishōmon (*kishō*) 起請文 . Written pledges promising certain duties or obligations; also, affidavits, depositions, or other evidence held as proof against some legal claim. See the references in Documents 10, 71, and 76.

kōden 公田 . Public paddy lands duly registered for taxation. The essential tax base of the central government and nobility, whether as public lands (*kokugaryō*) or as *shōen*.

koken 沽券 , see *baiken*

kokuga 国衙 . The administrative headquarters of a province. Control of these provincial offices fell into the hands of a militarized local elite during the late Heian period.

kokugaryō 国衙領 . "Provincial lands." Lands privately held but still subject to the governor's jurisdiction and to taxation. The public counterpart of private *shōen*. The term *kokuryō* also appears.

kokumu 国務 . Provincial affairs or administration; the purview of the governor and his subordinates.

kokushu 国守 . The governor of a province.

kokuyaku 国役 . Labor services under the jurisdiction of provincial authorities: e.g. construction or repair levies for local temples and shrines.

kokyakujō 沽却状 , see *baiken*

kompon ryōshu 根本領主 , see *kaihotsu ryōshu*

kondei 健児 . The provincial militia units that grew up in the late eighth century after the failure of the universal conscription system. *Kondei* headquarters were established in the different provincial capitals, and *kondei* fields were set aside to provide rations. By mid-Heian times these official guard units were being displaced by the more private *bushidan*; yet the term *kondei* survived for several more centuries.

kō-otsu no tomogara 甲乙輩 . The general population, especially the peasantry. However, the meaning might also include those capable of leading local disturbances, hence "lower gentry." The term *tomogara* alone, with the same meaning, is also common.

kudashibumi 下文 . An edict of permanent application issued from a higher to a lower authority; one of the three basic document types. Appointment decrees commonly used this format. See Document Originals, pp. 14–23.

kugen 公験 . A governor's edict acknowledging the limits of locally held rights, especially when land (*shiki*) was being sold or transferred. See the reference in Document 7.

kugyō 公卿 . The three highest ranks of the court aristocracy; sat in council during Heian times and "governed" the country.

kuji (or *kūji*) 公事 . The complement of dues levied on individuals, in contradistinction to the *nengu*, which was levied on land. Payment might be in agricultural and commercial products, labor services, or money.

kumai 供米 . Special tribute rice owed to religious institutions. The term often appears with the honorific prefix *on*.

kumon 公文 . A native officer of a *shōen*; duties undefined, though often dealing with tax collection. Generally ranked just below *gesu*.

kumonjo 公文所 . During Heian times, the agency within a provincial headquarters responsible for drafting documents. Established as one of the three organs of the emerging Bakufu, it later evolved into Kamakura's central administrative board, the *mandokoro*.

ku'nin 公人 . Functionaries of a house's administrative agency (*mandokoro*). Also, lower court officials.

kurōdo 蔵人 . Originally an archivist for the storehouse in which imperial edicts and other records were kept; later, an archivist or secretary for any ranking central family.

kyōkyō kingen 恐々謹言 . A closing phrase in many private documents. Professes respectful submission or deference to the addressee, even though he might be inferior in rank.

kyōmyō 交名 . A list of names, usually collected in reference to local disturbances of the peace. Kamakura-appointed *shugo* were constantly directed to forward such registers. See Documents 2 and 87.

kyūdenpata (*kyūden, kyūhata*) 給田畑 . The paddy and upland fields granted as a perquisite to estate officers; hence "grant" or "allotment" fields. The taxes that would normally have gone to the proprietor went instead to the recipient officer. These were lands, then, to be exploited economically; estate officials did not come to "own" *kyūdenpata* with a corresponding right of alienation.

mandokoro 政所. The headquarters for the administration of a great temple's or family's political and economic affairs. During early Kamakura times the main executive organ, or chancellery, of the Bakufu.

manzō kuji 万雑公事. The irregular, or miscellaneous, services or dues owed by local residents. Could be paid by labor, tribute goods, or money. See *kuji*.

matsuji 末寺. A branch temple. The great Buddhist centers of central Japan controlled networks of local *matsuji*.

menden 免田. Paddy fields exempt from taxes.

meshibumi 召文. A summons requesting the appearance of the accused in a lawsuit. Used extensively by the Kamakura Bakufu.

migyōsho 御教書. A standard documentary form for directives or communiqués with short-term effect. Issued from a higher to a lower authority, e.g. from the Bakufu to a *shugo*. A "letter of instruction." See Document Originals, pp. 14–23.

mikuriya 御厨. Tribute land for a shrine; a shrine estate. Originally created as a source of specialty products and ceremonial rice; later became indistinguishable from regular *shōen*. Most *mikuriya* were held by Ise Shrine. See Documents 9 and 108.

mishin 未進. Withheld or sequestered taxes. It became a common practice for *jitō* and other estate officials to hold back tax deliveries to absentee proprietors. The *mishin* amounts often climbed to astronomical figures over a period of years.

miuchi 御内. A personal retainer of the Hōjō family, the Kamakura Bakufu's dominant house.

mokkanryō 没官領. Land rights confiscated by Kamakura from the Taira leadership and its vassals. The great majority came from vassals and were managerial offices converted after 1185 into *jitō shiki*. The term appears only rarely in a context apart from the Taira.

mokudai 目代. Most commonly, the personal deputy of an absentee provincial governor. Often the most immediate link between central authority and the provincial office. The tension between *mokudai* and resident officers (*zaichōkanjin*) was a major impetus for the Gempei War.

monchū bugyōnin 問注奉行人. A judicial agent of the Kamakura Bakufu. These officers were occasionally sent to investigate a local matter, but never formed a regular official network.

monchūjo 問注所. The chief investigative agency of the Bakufu; it gradually lost much of its authority to the *hikitsuke-shū*, an organ established in 1249.

mondenpata 門田畑. Paddy and upland attached to an immediate homestead and therefore tax-exempt.

mōshibumi (*mōshijō*) 申文 (申状). General term for a request or petition submitted by a lower authority to a higher. See Document 52.

muhon 謀叛 . The general term for rebellion, though never clearly defined. The Kamakura Bakufu authorized its *shugo* to assume authority over cases of rebellion, and regularly appointed *jitō* to the lands of dispossessed rebels (*muhonnin*).

munebechi sen (or *munabetsu sen*) 棟別銭 . An emergency tax levied on households, generally for some construction or repair project. There is some evidence that late-Kamakura *shugo* had partial responsibility for this levy, but it became a regular means of taxation only in Muromachi times. See Documents 176–77.

myō 名 . The basic land unit of a local family's tenure. Taxes and services came to be determined by *myō*, and the regular administrative units (e.g. *shōen* and *gō*) were considered as constituting so many *myō*.

myōden 名田 . Literally, rice fields in local possession. The regular annual tax (*nengu*) was due from all *myōden*, whether held by local farmers (*hyakushō*) or by estate officers (*shōkan*). *Myōden* were an area's primary productive base.

myōshu 名主 . "Headman." A generic name for local holders who were no longer cultivators but who also were not members of the official class. The lands exploited by a *myōshu* were registered under his name, and he was the basic element in local administration. An estate's fiscal and service obligations were apportioned by *myōshu* among their own tenants. Collection would then be made from the aggregate of *myōshu*.

myōzu 名頭 . A type of *myō* headship found especially in Kyushu.

naiken 内検 . An emergency land survey conducted by representatives of the proprietor in the event of a crop failure or some natural disaster. See Document 99.

negi 禰宜 . A shrine officer ranking below *kannushi*. A common title in documents relating to Ise, Katori, and Kashima shrines.

nengu 年貢 . The annual rice tax payable to estate proprietors. After the mid-thirteenth century, often commuted to cash.

nenjo 年序 . A twenty-year statute of limitations, after which no counterclaims would be recognized either to possession of a *shiki* or to the practices and perquisites attendant on that possession. Written into Kamakura's Jōei Code of 1232, though enforcement was only sporadic. The reference to *nenjo* in some documents means simply a period long enough to cast doubt on any charge. See the references in Documents 71 and 129.

nyūdō 入道 . A Buddhist title held by certain prestigious warriors.

ōban saisoku 大番催促 . The act of drawing up rosters for performance of the imperial guard service in Kyoto. A responsibility of Kamakura *shugo*. See especially Documents 135–39, 156–59.

ōban'yaku 大番役 . The imperial guard service in Kyoto. A Kamakura guard service (Kamakura *ōban'yaku*) was instituted after 1219 as a complement to the Kyoto *ōban*. The eastern service, however, was limited to vassals from that part of Japan. See *dairi ōban*.

ōbō 押妨. The violation of another person's land rights; incursion or trespassing.

okibumi 置文. A record expressing the intention to devise certain property (often movable property) in a particular way; the conveyance itself was effected by another document, the *yuzurijō*. Also used to establish regulations or house rules for the treatment of family wealth. Sometimes simply a farewell statement.

onchi 恩地. Land rights granted to vassals as a largess of their lord. In Kamakura law such holdings were not to be pawned or disposed of by sale.

ōryō 押領. One of several terms used to describe violations or unlawful seizure of land or land rights. The emphasis in most cases is on forceful seizure. See *rōzeki, ōbō, rannyū*.

ōryōshi 押領使. A public constable originally appointed for the duration of some provincial emergency. By late Heian times the post had become hereditary within certain prominent local-officer houses (*zaichōkanjin*). It declined in importance with the onset of Kamakura times and the creation of a *shugo* network.

Ōshū seibatsu 奥州征伐. The Kamakura Bakufu's 1189 military campaign against the Fujiwara of northern Japan.

Ōshū sōbugyō 奥州惣奉行. The Bakufu's two commissioners for northern Japan. The posts became hereditary in the families of Kasai and Izawa, both appointed by Yoritomo soon after 1189. The Kasai took responsibility for superintending Kamakura vassals and maintaining public order; the Izawa (later surnamed Rusu) exercised general provincial administration.

osso 越訴. A second-level appeal of a lawsuit verdict. When a Kamakura *shugo* or the Bakufu's branch headquarters at Rokuhara settled a dispute, verdicts were commonly appealed to Kamakura. But *osso* could also be heard by Rokuhara itself, or by Kamakura in cases it had originally adjudicated. See the references in Documents 70 and 78.

ōsuke 大介. Literally "great vice-governor." However, the title appears only in documents sent from the capital to an absentee provincial headquarters (*rusudokoro*). Most scholars assume, therefore, that *ōsuke* referred to the governor, who was simply not present. A much debated term.

ōtabumi 太田文. A provincial register of paddy fields and their local holders.

otsukai (or *ontsukai*) 御使. An emissary assigned to perform some special duty.

ranbō 濫妨, see *rōzeki*

rannyū 乱入. Illegal intrusion into estates.

ranso 濫訴. A false suit, or "arbitrary accusation." Central proprietors commonly brought unjustified complaints to the Kamakura Bakufu. When claims were identified as false, the warrior regime would dismiss them as *ranso*. But since Kamakura could impose no sanctions on offenders, false suits continued. See the dismissal of *ranso* in Documents 124 and 127.

ransui 濫吹. Misconduct or despoilment; false words, slander, or derogatory intent.

rensho 連署. Multiple signatures on a document. Sometimes this signified agreement on the part of normal rivals within an estate hierarchy. At other times it involved the signatures of various officers largely to strengthen the force of some order. Under the Bakufu, official decrees (*gechijō*) carried two signatures, one belonging to the Hōjō regent, the other belonging to a Hōjō "cosigner." For examples of *renshojō* (cosigned documents) of different types, see Documents 45, 56, 74, and 76.

rimu 吏務. A term suggesting provincial governance.

rinji 綸旨. The personal edict of an emperor.

rōjū 郎従, see *rōtō*

Rokuhara tandai 六波羅探題. The two Kamakura deputies for central and western Japan, headquartered in the Rokuhara Palace at Kyoto; first appointed after the Jōkyū War of 1221. These were counterparts of the later Kyushu deputies, though the latter were given greater powers.

rōnin 浪人. A term used since ancient times to mean an unattached person, normally a man with military training. Sometimes used to describe refugee peasant cultivators.

ronnin 論人. The accused in a legal action; a rival or challenger.

rōrō 牢籠. "Hard times," as opposed to prosperity. Appears in many documents.

rōtō (or *rōdō*) 郎等. Military retainers, normally men of some standing who were not personally related to their lord. A higher rank than *ge'nin* or *shojū*.

rōzeki 狼藉. The despoilment of land, usually implying the foraging of crops.

rusu shiki 留守職. The title to which the Izawa family was appointed by Yoritomo after the 1189 Northern Campaign; later, Rusu became that family's surname. The office handled regular administration in the two northern provinces of Mutsu and Dewa. See *Ōshū sōbugyō*.

rusudokoro 留守所. Absentee office. The agency within a provincial headquarters that received the orders and communiqués of governors who remained in Kyoto. Gained special prominence during the eleventh and twelfth centuries.

-ryō 領. A suffix meaning the land rights belonging to a family or institution. For example, Kasuga *sharyō* were the holdings of Kasuga Shrine.

ryōchi 領地. Normally interchangeable with *chigyō*.

ryōji 令旨. The personal edict of an imperial prince.

ryōke 領家. The proprietor of a *shōen*. During Heian and early Kamakura times the title was restricted to members of the high nobility and ranking religious institutions.

ryōshu 領主. The generic term for a local lord over land. See *kaihotsu ryōshu*.

saemon no jō 左衛門尉. A "lieutenant of the outer palace guards, left division." An honorary title held by many warriors.

saigoku 西国. The western provinces of Japan. Originally this meant only Kyushu, but it later came to imply the entire area west of the Kinki region (i.e. west of Harima Province).

saikyojō 裁許状. A judicial settlement edict. During Kamakura times these were issued by the three main Bakufu headquarters at Kamakura, Rokuhara, and Chinzei (Kyushu). Rokuhara produced the fewest *saikyojō*.

saisho 税所. The tax bureau within a provincial headquarters (*kokuga*). Control of this office was often expressed in terms of a *saisho shiki*.

saisokujō 催促状. A letter of urgent command; a peremptory request.

samurai dokoro 侍所. Originally, the military bureau of a ranking Heian noble or religious proprietor. Subsequently adopted by the Kamakura Bakufu and converted into an agency for controlling its vassals.

sanden 散田. Paddy fields assigned by a proprietor to peasants. They were heavily taxed and therefore often neglected by cultivators. Later came to refer to fields abandoned by peasants.

sanjō 散状. An informal written reply. See also *ukebumi*.

san'yōjō 散用状. Tax estimate reports; tax receipts. Cf. *kechige*.

saribumi 避文 (去文). An affidavit acknowledging the relinquishment of land rights, whether by sale, exchange, passage through inheritance, or whatever. See Document 164.

sata 沙汰. Administrative authority, judicial competence, etc. The term has many meanings, and *shiki* holders "exercised *sata*" in a variety of contexts.

satanin 沙汰人. A general term for estate functionaries.

seibaijō 成敗状. A document authorizing punishment or sanction; sometimes a document disposing of some judicial or administrative matter. The term *seibai* alone, in reference to a Bakufu judgment, is very common. See Document 127.

sekkanke 摂関家. The regent's line of the Fujiwara house.

shake 社家. Shrine authorities or administrators; often the shrine itself.

shashi 社使. Agents of a shrine.

shigyōjō 施行状. An enforcement decree or edict of certification. Issued by an inferior officer (e.g. a Kamakura *shugo*) carrying out the directive of his superior (the Bakufu). See Documents 166–69.

shihai monjo 紙背文書, see *ura monjo*

shiki 職 . Originally a function or office with attached perquisites; later the right to designated income (with or without duties) under title of an "office." The bureaucratic (and therefore temporary) quality of *shiki* eventually gave way to that which was private and permanent, and the post often became hereditary. Several *shiki* levels might conjointly possess an individual unit of land.

shikken 執権 . The regent for a Kamakura shogun; this office was passed down to members of the house of Hōjō from about 1205 to the end of Kamakura rule.

shimpo jitō 新補地頭 . A *jitō* appointed after the Jōkyū War to an area whose confiscated revenues were not sufficient to serve as a *jitō's* perquisite and income share. The Bakufu invoked a uniform income formula in such cases.

shingi 新儀 . "New practices," or "innovations." *Jitō* were constantly admonished not to engage in innovative acts that would violate precedent or established local custom.

shinshi (1) 進止 . The right of primary jurisdiction over land or over some matter relating to land. Might be held either locally (e.g. by a *jitō*) or by an absentee proprietor.

shinshi (2) 参差 . A "contradiction" or discrepancy between stated positions. Appears in many judicial settlement decrees.

shintai 進退 , see *shinshi* (1)

shintai ryōshō 進退領掌 . A common phrase implying the administrative control of land.

shin'yaku 神役 . The services and tributes owed to a shrine.

shin'on jitō 新恩地頭 . A *jitō shiki* granted in an area that was not the recipient's homeland.

shiryō 私領 . Literally, "private landholding." Used in Heian and Kamakura times to designate the hereditary holding of a prominent local person. These *shiryō* might then be commended to a central proprietor and come to compose part of a *shōen*.

shisai 子細 . "Details." As part of the judicial process, the Kamakura Bakufu was constantly seeking out the particulars of a *shōen's* customary laws—i.e. its *shisai*.

shishi (or *shiishi*) 四至 . The boundaries or dimensions of an estate.

shitaji 下地 . The land itself, as opposed to the economic profits deriving from land.

shitaji chūbun 下地中分 . The territorial division of a *shōen* between competing central and local (*jitō*) claimants. See Documents 126–29.

shitsuji 執事 . Under the Kamakura Bakufu, an assistant headship (hereditary in the Nikaidō family) within the *mandokoro*. Also, headship of the *monchūjo* (hereditary in the Miyoshi family).

shobunjō 處分状 , see *yuzurijō*

shōji 荘司, see *shōkan*

shōjitō (or *kojitō*) 小地頭 . A "small *jitō*," or sub-*jitō*. A local notable of Kyushu granted a *jitō* post over his homeland. These officers were sometimes made subordinate to a chief *jitō* (*sōjitō*) from the Kantō appointed to the same land unit. See Documents 40–46.

shojū 所従. A personal servant who could be bought or sold, and could be forced to do whatever work was demanded by the lord. Similar in status to *ge'nin* (*q.v.*).

shōkan 荘官. A general term for *shōen* officials.

shōke 荘家. The local notables of a *shōen*; the administrative office of an estate.

shōkō 庄公. "Private and public": i.e. private estates and public holdings (*shōen* and *kokugaryō*).

shōmin 庄民. The general population of a *shōen*; the nonofficial class.

shōmon (1) 正文 . A valid, duly authorized document, as opposed to a draft. See the reference in Document 99.

shōmon (2) 證文 . The generic name for formal documents acceptable or intended as evidence; e.g. bills of sale (*baiken*). Took precedence over *kishōmon*, which were "hearsay" in nature. See the references in Documents 14, 44, and 45.

shomu 所務. Administration; often a specific privilege is implied, such as tax collection. Sometimes, revenue divorced from actual duties.

shōmu 荘務. Similar to the preceding entry, *shomu*, though here the reference is specifically to *shōen* administration.

shoryō 所領. The land rights from which profits derived, held by any *shiki* level. More than one person could thus claim *shoryō* over the same piece of land.

shoshi 所司. A general term for an official of a government agency. Also, the second-ranking post within the vassal-control board (*samurai dokoro*) of the Kamakura Bakufu; this became hereditary within the Nagasaki family. In Muromachi times *shoshi* was the chief post in the *samurai dokoro*.

shoshi (or *soshi*) 庶子. The siblings of a designated family heir (*chakushi*). Until late Kamakura times *shoshi* usually received a portion of the inheritance, but after that they were increasingly frozen out.

shotō 所当. The full complement of dues levied on the land and owed to the proprietor.

shugo 守護. In Kamakura times, a province-level "constable" appointed by the Bakufu. Acted as liaison officer between the Bakufu and its provincial vassals, and held primary responsibility for the suppression of local rebellion and major crimes. See *taibon sankajō*. In Muromachi times *shugo* came to mean a provincial military governor appointed by the Ashikaga Bakufu.

shugodai 守護代 . The deputy to a *shugo*. It was this officer who actually performed many of the *shugo*'s duties, since his master usually remained an absentee figure in the Kantō.

shugoryō 守護領. Land rights under a *shugo* title. The concept was in its infancy in late Kamakura times, and became fully developed only after the mid-fourteenth century. Appears in Documents 174 and 177 as *shugo no bunryō* and *shugo no ryōbun*.

shugosho 守護所. The provincial headquarters of a *shugo*.

sō- 惣 (総). A prefix used with many *shiki* titles; the meaning is often "chief *shiki*-holder."

sochinjō 訴陳状. The documents stating arguments for plaintiff and defendant in a lawsuit. See the reference in Document 127.

sōgesu 総下司. A provincial recruiting officer established by the Taira in 1181.

sōhei 僧兵. Literally, "armed monks." The designation of later writers for the fighting men employed by central and local temples. The contemporary term was *akusō*, "evil priests."

sōjitō 総地頭. A "chief *jitō*" appointed from among Kantō warriors to oversee land units in Kyushu that possessed native *jitō*. Occasionally appointed in other parts of Japan, but predominantly a Kyushu institution. See Documents 40–46.

sojō 訴状. An appeal or complaint document initiating a legal action. See the references in Documents 116 and 124.

sōkan 惣官. The military commander and general supervisor for central Japan. An office established by the Taira in 1181.

sōkengyō 総検校. A priest-administrator of shrines or temples; an office title found in many estates.

so'nin 訴人. The plaintiff in a lawsuit.

sōron 相論. The medieval term for "dispute," normally relating to land. The Kamakura Bakufu accepted certain categories of *sōron* for adjudication. See Documents 45, 68, 70, and 89, among others.

sōryō-sei 惣領制. The designation of historians for the system of divided inheritance of family property that prevailed during the thirteenth century. Other scholars use this term to connote a pattern of warrior organization in which, despite divided inheritance, general leadership over an extended family was retained by a single person. The term *sōryō*—family head—appears in numerous documents after the 1220's.

sōtsuibushi 総追捕使. Originally, a provincial police officer; later became an office within individual *shōen*. The title was granted to at least some provincial appointees of the nascent Bakufu in the 1180's.

tadokoro 田所. A *shōen* office generally concerned with land surveying or tax collection. Similar to *kumon*.

taibon (or *taihon*) *sankajō* 大犯三箇条. Literally, the "three regulations for great crimes." The legal limits of a Kamakura *shugo*'s authority. These were jurisdiction over murders, the suppression of rebellion, and responsibility for drawing up the imperial guard registers (*ōban saisoku*). Other crimes were added later; but the original *taibon sankajō* remained as the standard definition of a *shugo*'s duties. See especially Documents 135–39 and 156–59.

taijō (or *okotarijō*) 怠状. A document conveying an apology for crimes committed; a written expression of good intentions. See Document 71.

taikan 対捍. The defiance of lawful authority. Often used in reference to a failure to make tax deliveries.

taiketsu 對決. A court trial or hearing in which the two sides had to confront one another. Procedure adopted by the Kamakura Bakufu. See Documents 45, 46, and 71.

tan 反. One-tenth of a *chō* (*q.v.*); hence .294 (later .245) acre. One *tan* = 360 *bu*.

tetsugi no monjo 手継文書. A sequence of documents proving possession of land rights. The holding of such records virtually guaranteed victory in any legal action. See Document 25.

tō 党. A league of warrior bands (*bushidan*) with some common ancestry, which fought, when necessary, as a collective force. The absence of a strong single leadership characterized the *tō*.

toijō 問状. A document requesting information or an explanation, normally from someone accused in a lawsuit. See Documents 20, 49, 105, and 153.

tokubun 得分. The income that attended any *shiki*. See Documents 38 and 47.

tokusei 徳政. A Bakufu decree of 1297 limiting or nullifying certain commercial transactions involving lands that had been lost or sold by housemen. Subsequently, a general term for any decree, civil or military, that canceled a debt or sale.

tokusō 得宗. The term for the head of the Hōjō house during the later Kamakura period.

tone 刀禰. Among other things, this could mean a harbor official, an officer of the Ise or Kamo shrines, or a village chief.

toneri 舎人. Originally, military attendants on the imperial house. Some *toneri* later became the servants of different noble households, and others emerged as local families of distinction.

tōryō 棟梁. The chieftain of a warrior band.

tsubowake chūbun 坪分中分. The division of a *shōen* in terms of rights to component units of production. Generally, a less drastic measure than a "territorial division" (*shitaji chūbun*).

tsuibushi 追捕使 , see *sōtsuibushi*

tsuikahō 追加法. "Supplementary legislation" or amendments added to the main bodies of law under both the Kamakura and Muromachi regimes.

tsuitōshi 追討使. A "pursuit and punishment" officer; a special constable.

tsukuda 佃. Originally, the lands of an estate proprietor's personal demesne. A demesne of this kind was very small compared with the "home farms" of European estate owners. By Kamakura times both *azukari dokoro* and *jitō* sometimes held *tsukuda*. See the references in Documents 93 and 125.

ukebumi 請文. A document acknowledging receipt of an order or request; a document of reply. Also, an *ukesho* contract. See Documents 99 and 125.

ukesho 請所. A contractual agreement between a central proprietor and (usually) a *jitō* in which the latter assumed full responsibility for collecting and delivering the annual tax. In return, the proprietor agreed that his agents would not enter the estate. During Muromachi times, *ukesho* were arranged between central owners and *shugo* (the term then became *shugo uke*).

utaishō ke mandokoro 右大將家政所 . The chancellery of Minamoto Yoritomo, established in 1191. In 1192 Yoritomo became shogun and established a *shōgun ke mandokoro*. From 1195 he reverted to the earlier form. Cf. Documents 12, 13, 16, 17, 19, 65, 91, 136, and 137.

ura monjo 裏文書. A document copy (*an*) appearing on the reverse side of another document, a chronicle, a diary, or whatever. Owing to the scarcity of paper many early records were preserved in this fashion. Sometimes called *shihai monjo*. See Documents 80 and 120.

wayo 和与. A compromise agreement between central and local (usually *jitō*) interests leading to an adjustment of rights over *shōen*. See Documents 78, 117, 126, 128, and 170.

wayo chūbun 和与中分. A territorial division agreed to by compromise. The majority of *shitaji chūbun* cases were of this type. See Documents 125 and 128.

wayojō 和与状 . A compromise document. In some instances identical copies were made and signed by both sides. In other cases, each side would record its concessions in a separate document, and these would then be exchanged.

wayo saikyojō 和与裁許状 . A Bakufu document approving an agreed compromise. This gave the transaction binding force. See Documents 78, 117, and 128.

yashiki 屋敷 . In medieval documents this refers to the local residence and immediately adjoining land of an officer-level figure; hence a "warrior homestead." The term *yashikiden*, "residential paddy," also appears.

yosebumi 寄文. A document commending land. See *kishinjō*.

yose-gōri (or *yori-gōri*) 寄郡 . Mixed public and private lands: i.e. areas owing taxes to the regular provincial agencies as well as to a *shōen* head-quarters. The term *yose-gōri* (though not certain variations of the practice) was limited to southern Kyushu.

yōto 用途. A term connoting costs or expenditures, especially those relating to religious ceremonies or construction projects. Such costs had to be met by local levies.

yuisho 由緒. A historical or hereditary claim to land; traditional legacy; inherited privileges. See Documents 1 and 10.

yuzurijō 譲状. A testamentary record. The document form used to convey the will of a house head wishing to pass property (movable or immovable) to a son or daughter (or indeed, to any close relative). See the references in Documents 24, 25, 60, and 100.

zaichōkanjin (*zaichō*) 在庁官人. A resident provincial official. This official class came to dominate provincial headquarters and local administration in late Heian times. It was from the *zaichōkanjin* that Yoritomo drew his greatest support in 1180.

zaike 在家. A cultivator's residence and immediately adjoining land; became a taxation unit in medieval times. Also used to mean an agricultural tenant's family. A much debated term.

zasshō 雑掌. A centrally appointed *shōen* administrator; an alternative term for *azukari dokoro*. Also, a nonresident legal expert specializing in *shōen* rights and procedures.

zōji 雑事, see *kuji; manzō kuji*

zōmen 雑免, see *zōyakumen*

zōyakumen 雑役免. Exemption from all levies (labor or tribute) except the regular land tax (*nengu*). This did not necessarily benefit the local peasantry: it simply meant that *myōshu* or estate officers did not have to pass on to higher authorities what had been requisitioned or collected from below.

zōshiki 雑色. Lower functionaries within the imperial bureaucracy, and also within the great noble houses of Heian times. Minamoto Yoritomo assigned special duties to a class of *zōshiki* that had become his personal attendants. For references to *zōshiki*, see Documents 39 and 49.

zudenchō (or *zuchō*) 図田帳, see *ōtabumi*

zuryō 受領. "Tax manager." The middle and late Heian designation for the class of provincial governors.

PART TWO

Bibliography

BIBLIOGRAPHY

One often hears from graduate students, "Where can I find materials? How shall I begin research?" These questions are especially vital for the study of pre-1600 Japan. Although there are adequate bibliographies for secondary works and for nondocumentary sources,* Japanese scholars have done surprisingly little in one area: there is no satisfactory listing of published documents; and the lists we do have are fragmentary, exclude journal articles, and contain no annotations.† To fill this gap I

---

* Many recent monographs contain excellent lists of scholarly works. A particularly outstanding example is Abe Takeshi, *Nihon shōen shi* (Tōkyō, 1972), which presents 68 pages of *shōen* studies catalogued by locale. For current bibliography, there are two good sources: the early and medieval history sections (books and articles) in the monthly journal *Shigaku zasshi*, as well as the May issue of that periodical, which offers a review essay; and the journal *Nihon rekishi*, which presents regular listings of articles found in selected other periodicals. For local history, two (of many) sources may be cited: Azusaka Rintarō, ed., *Chihōshi bunken sōgō mokuroku* (3 vols., Tōkyō, 1973–76), which is a fairly comprehensive listing of unannotated book titles through 1970; and Chihōshi kenkyū kyōgikai, comp., *Nihon shi bunken nenkan* (2 vols. to date; published annually), which presents book and article titles from the preceding year. This last work can be especially recommended. For nondocumentary primary sources (diaries, chronicles, treatises, and infrequent document series), Endō Motoo, ed., *Kokushi bunken kaisetsu* (2 vols., Tōkyō, 1957–65), remains standard; although richly annotated, it lacks many titles, however.

† The two standard lists are: Kimura Tokue and Hayashi Hideo, eds., *Chihōshi kenkyū no hōhō* (Tōkyō, 1968), pp. 35–42; and Nagahara Keiji et al., *Chūsei shi handobukku* (Tōkyō, 1973), pp. 202–14.

have prepared the bibliography that follows. As we shall see, there are literally tens of thousands of printed records, many arranged for easy use.

Since this book deals with the Kamakura Bakufu, my first inclination was to limit the bibliography to documents from that period. It was obvious, however, that few volumes devoted themselves exclusively to the Kamakura age: most ended their coverage in 1600, not 1333. For that reason, it seemed a natural decision to expand treatment to the entire pre-Tokugawa age. A parallel decision was to eschew the format of a "selected" bibliography, that is, a listing in which the compiler's interests and impressions tend to shape the contents. In the case of the present list, the annotations would convey my own opinions of works; but a negative judgment would not disqualify them. The single requirement for inclusion in this bibliography is that a book or article present pre-1600 documents.

In my researches I used six university collections (at Stanford, Yale, Berkeley, Tōkyō, Kyūshū, and Tōhoku), as well as the private libraries of Professors Kawazoe Shōji, Toyoda Takeshi, Takeuchi Rizō, and Seno Seiichirō. I need hardly add that the resulting list is not complete. The number of potential source volumes is so great that the distinguished collections I consulted were simply missing certain promising titles. Nor were existing bibliographies much help in this regard. The information these contain is inadequate much of the time, and misleading often enough to undermine trust.* Even specialized bibliographic essays on local history commonly glide over major titles.† At any rate, I discovered no shortcuts; only those titles I was able to examine personally (with a few exceptions) could safely find a place in my listing. A scattering of city and township series are thus undoubtedly missing, along with many shorter collections concealed among the almost 1,200 local

---

* For example, the common practice of listing local history volumes by *shiryō hen* (source book) number tells us very little. More often than not the sources contained will postdate 1600 or will be nondocumentary in nature; but there is no way of knowing without more specific information. As for examples of misleading references, *Shiogama jinja shiryō* appears in the *Chūsei shi handobukku* listing (p. 203), even though that volume presents no documents; and "Tanegashima monjo" [577] is listed under the *kinsei* (Tokugawa) category, when in fact this article *does* contain medieval records (cf. *Nihon shi bunken nenkan*, 1976 ed., p. 371). The confusion in the second instance is that the materials in question range from the fourteenth to the seventeenth centuries.

† *Nihon shi bunken nenkan* (1976 ed.), for example, presents short essays summarizing recent publications and research trends in each prefecture of Japan. In the feature on Hyōgo (pp. 462–63), one of the most important source books of the decade, the *Himeji shishi, shiryō hen* 1 [390], is not even mentioned, although it is cited by title elsewhere (p. 293).

history journals.* But even with these limitations, the bibliography offered here is more inclusive than any listing with a similar purpose.

The number of published documents is a good measure of scholarly interest in this field. From the outset, compilers have worked to get the earliest materials into print first. As a result, virtually all known documents from the Nara and Heian periods have now been published. These appear in three massive series: *Nara ibun* [1], *Heian ibun* [2], and *Shōsōin monjo* [7]. Progress for the Kamakura age is not quite so impressive. It has been estimated that about 30,000 documents remain extant, of which somewhat more than half are now in print. For the pre-1253 period, however, the published total (ca. 8,000 documents) is over 95 percent. This is because 7,690 of these earlier records appear in a single series, the *Kamakura ibun* [3]. Eventually, this work will be all-inclusive.

When we view the figures regionally, we encounter marked variations. In Kyūshū, for example, some 95 percent of *all* Kamakura documents are in print, whereas in central Japan and some sections of western Honshū and Shikoku the proportions are much smaller. Discrepancies appear even in neighboring prefectures, such as Ehime and Kagawa in Shikoku: for Ehime (Iyo Province) we have a major series and several specialized works; but for Kagawa (Sanuki) there is simply nothing. Neither area, facing the Inland Sea, was historically "isolated"; it is merely that the Kagawa archives have not yet been tapped.

We must also consider discrepancies in the matter of documents' survival. Again, Kyūshū seems a special case, with 5,907 documents catalogued for the Kamakura period.† By contrast, the combined total for the Tōhoku and Shikoku regions is certainly much smaller, even though these areas were closer to the two great medieval power centers. In this instance, the Mongol Invasions in Kyūshū played an obvious role. But there must have been other contributing factors as well, for even *within* contiguous regions sizable discrepancies are often apparent. Thus—to cite one example—if Tottori and Yamagata have printed far fewer documents than neighboring Okayama and Fukushima, the fault may lie only partly with local scholars.‡

* See the list included in *Nihon shi bunken nenkan* (1975 ed.), pp. 365–419.
† See [466] in the Bibliography. Professor Seno lists 6,851 documents for the Nambokuchō age (1334–92).
‡ The present listing makes no attempt to include one major category of publication that would speak directly to this problem—catalogs of extant documents, or *monjo mokuroku*. There are literally hundreds of these works, whose purpose is to enumerate rather than transcribe. Obviously, the stage represented by most of these is that antecedent to the printing of the sources themselves.

When we turn to the Muromachi age, the estimates of extant documents vary widely. General opinion, however, places the figure at 300,-000, of which close to a third may be in print. Of this total, a majority date from the sixteenth century, and most source books clearly reflect this. On the average, 75 percent or more of the content of a document volume will be records dating from late Muromachi times. In this regard the student of *sengoku* history enjoys both advantages and disadvantages. The number of records at his disposal far exceeds the figure for earlier epochs; but there are also many more documents remaining to be transcribed. Similarly, it is evident that records relating to individual Muromachi *daimyō* are far more numerous than those dealing with Kamakura *jitō*; yet the Kamakura Bakufu is probably better documented than its Muromachi counterpart. The obvious implication of this is that governance in Japan was becoming multicentered. It also suggests that the written word never ceased to be important. The *sengoku* era may have witnessed constant warfare, but it also left us more than 150,000 documents.

For obvious reasons, the later Muromachi period—the "age of reunification"—has received a major share of attention from scholars. What is interesting, however, is that source books devoted specifically to the sixteenth century contain features not readily found elsewhere. A number of key studies treating the unifiers themselves and the great *daimyō* present Japanese readings of *kambun* documents (*yomikudashi*), with unusually thorough annotations. Unfortunately, there seems little hope of this trend becoming standard. Indeed, even *kaeriten* markings in document volumes are now increasingly rare.

It is clear, then, that vast resources exist for the study of early and medieval Japan; and, at least for Heian and Kamakura times, these materials have been identified and most of them printed. The researcher is dealing with a finite number of records. Moreover, even for the lengthy Muromachi age there are some provinces for which "complete" published collections now exist. Prefectural series may vary in quality, but some of the more recent ones clearly allow for exhaustive research on any pre-Tokugawa century. It should be noted, finally, that although a few previously unknown documents do come to light every year, breakthroughs in the sense of "missing links" are decidedly rare. When they do occur, they are normally well publicized. The problem of language training may still be an obstacle for the Western student, but there can be no argument regarding the adequacy or availability of sources.

The preparation of any lengthy bibliography involves many decisions regarding arrangement and citation. I have elected to divide all entries on a regional basis, using both provincial and prefectural designations. Though cumbersome in some respects, this arrangement seems necessary. The province is the contemporaneous unit of medieval times, even though certain source books, under prefectural sponsorship, fail to use it. At all events, I have given primacy to the province within a dual identification scheme; this places proper stress on the historical context but still allows for the location of sources within the modern system. The provinces (*kuni*) are grouped into major regions as shown in the accompanying list, and they correspond to the modern prefectures (*ken*) indicated in italics—obviously with some overlapping. Bracketed numbers refer to the Bibliography entries for each region.

TŌHOKU REGION [44–76]
  Mutsu: *Aomori, Iwate, Miyagi, Fukushima*
  Dewa: *Akita, Yamagata*

KANTŌ REGION [77–165]
  Kōzuke: *Gumma*
  Shimotsuke: *Tochigi*
  Hitachi: *Ibaragi*
  Shimōsa: *Ibaragi* (part), *Chiba* (part)
  Kazusa: *Chiba*
  Awa: *Chiba*
  Musashi: *Tōkyō, Saitama, Kanagawa* (part)
  Sagami: *Kanagawa*

TŌKAI-TŌSAN REGION [166–212]
  Kai: *Yamanashi*
  Shinano: *Nagano*
  Izu: *Shizuoka*
  Suruga: *Shizuoka*
  Tōtomi: *Shizuoka*
  Mino: *Gifu*
  Hida: *Gifu*
  Owari: *Aichi*
  Mikawa: *Aichi*
  Iga: *Mie*
  Ise: *Mie*
  Shima: *Mie*

HOKURIKU REGION [213–53]
  Echigo: *Niigata*
  Sado: *Niigata*
  Etchū: *Toyama*

Kaga: *Ishikawa*
Noto: *Ishikawa*
Echizen: *Fukui*
Wakasa: *Fukui*

KINKI REGION [254–397]
  Ōmi: *Shiga*
  Yamashiro: *Kyōto*
  Yamato: *Nara*
  Kii: *Mie* (part), *Wakayama*
  Kawachi: *Ōsaka*
  Izumi: *Ōsaka*
  Settsu: *Ōsaka* (part), *Hyōgo* (part)
  Tango: *Kyōto*
  Tamba: *Kyōto* (part), *Hyōgo* (part)
  Tajima: *Hyōgo*
  Harima: *Hyōgo*
  Awaji: *Hyōgo*

CHŪGOKU REGION [398–438]
  Bizen: *Okayama*
  Mimasaka: *Okayama*
  Bitchū: *Okayama*
  Inaba: *Tottori*
  Hōki: *Tottori*
  Bingo: *Hiroshima*
  Aki: *Hiroshima*
  Izumo: *Shimane*
  Iwami: *Shimane*
  Oki: *Shimane*
  Suō: *Yamaguchi*
  Nagato: *Yamaguchi*

SHIKOKU REGION [439–54]
  Sanuki: *Kagawa*
  Awa: *Tokushima*
  Iyo: *Ehime*
  Tosa: *Kōchi*

KYŪSHŪ REGION [455–584]
  Chikuzen: *Fukuoka*
  Chikugo: *Fukuoka*

Buzen: *Fukuoka* (part), *Ōita* (part)
Bungo: *Ōita*
Hizen: *Saga, Nagasaki* (part)
Tsushima: *Nagasaki*
Iki: *Nagasaki*
Higo: *Kumamoto*
Satsuma: *Kagoshima*
Ōsumi: *Kagoshima*
Hyūga: *Miyazaki*

The user of this bibliography should be aware of certain organizational difficulties. For example, in the case of temple and shrine collections, the criterion for placement in the listing will usually be the location of the particular institution cited, even though the materials themselves may deal with *shōen* scattered all across Japan. Thus hundreds or even thousands of transcribed documents may relate to a province that has had few, if any, of its "own" materials printed. Awaji and Sanuki provinces, for example, must be studied through printed sources residing entirely in "external" collections. Similarly, it is not possible to provide more than occasional cross-references, for individual collections, not to speak of whole volumes, commonly touch on a dozen or more provinces. Something of the same problem exists for city and prefectural series. These volumes generally collect documents actually housed in the particular area, even if the subject matter treats families or places at the other end of the country; however, they may also include documents bearing on the home area but residing elsewhere.

A different kind of problem arises in the case of family collections. For example, a warrior house may have originated in one province, experienced its early growth in a second, and enjoyed its age of prosperity in a third. Or perhaps the family began in the east but moved to the west and put down roots in several provinces. Consistency is difficult but I have tried, where possible, to follow the general identification schema of Japanese scholars. Once again, we are best off for Kyūshū; almost all collections are identified by province in Takeuchi Rizō, *Kyūshū chihō komonjo mokuroku* (Fukuoka, 1952). Finally, there are the many instances in which labeling by province simply has no meaning. For books that present documents by type or deal with a given time period, I have used the category "general."

In the matter of citation styles, there are still more difficulties. The identification of a primary editor or compiler is a common trouble area: should we give credit to a sponsoring research institute or to one (or all) of the several personal names that might be listed? For instance,

Dazaifu shiryō, jōsei hen [460] is sponsored by the Kyūshū bunka sōgō kenkyūjo, and edited by the Dazaifu chōsa bunken han, both of whose names appear on the front cover. It is well known, however, that the actual transcriber and compiler of the series was Takeuchi Rizō, and it is he who receives credit in bibliographies and footnotes. Yet his name is mentioned in the actual books only at the end of the Preface. Because of the uncertainty involved in cases like this I have thought it best to err in the direction of comprehensiveness: a full index of compilers, series names, and the like, appears on pp. 334–44. For easiest reference, Chinese characters for these names are placed there.

Another problem concerns the main titles of books. Subtitles in small letters often appear before a main title, whereas in other instances a series name will be given special prominence. Where I have found external listings for such volumes I have used those renderings. But the real problem comes when one encounters incomplete data. Privately distributed document pamphlets—of which quite a number exist—commonly fail to include publication pages. When this happens there can even be difficulty in distinguishing a "book" from a badly identified "offprint."

As one might expect, then, there are document collections whose very publication remains all but a secret. Such works are not advertised, and, while usually for sale, bear no price listings. They are *hibaihin*, i.e., "not for sale," which means simply that they can be obtained only by direct communication.* Moreover, since editions of 100–200 copies are common, pamphlets of this type regularly fail to reach major libraries. Only the most watchful of private scholars—and a few attentive book merchants—end up with these rare prizes. But it is not merely soft-cover *gariban*—as they are called—that university collections commonly lack. Similar problems can be noted for the abundance of local history series. The number of these new sets is too large—and the costs simply too high—to justify more than irregular purchase.† The result, at any rate, is that even Japan's major center for medieval research, the Historio-

---

* For the librarian or researcher wishing to assemble a medieval source collection, correspondence with individual compilers, local historical associations, and the like, becomes an absolute necessity. There are two convenient directories of active historians in Japan: *Shigakkai kaiin meibo*, a special number of *Shigaku zasshi* (1970/12); and *Nihon rekishi gakkai kaiin meibo*, a special issue of *Nihon rekishi* (1970). For local historical associations and journals, see the lists (with addresses) in *Nihon shi bunken nenkan* (1975 ed.).

† Local histories are indeed very expensive, commonly 5,000 yen or more per volume, in multivolume sets. This is the direct purchase price, plus postage. In Tōkyō's Kanda district, however, costs may be many times that figure—even before books go out of print. The banditry of these second-hand booksellers is legendary.

graphical Institute of Tōkyō University, is lacking many of the titles appearing in this bibliography.* For the Western student, shortcomings of this kind may seem to pose an additional burden. But at least a part of the problem—acquiring the knowledge that a source exists—will hopefully be resolved by the present listing.

In this regard, it must be stressed that all is not necessarily lost if a certain title cannot be located. Many document sequences appear in more than one book, and careful use of the present bibliography, with special reference to prefectural series, may supply an answer. In other ways, too, the value of duplication should not be lost. Transcriptions may vary from work to work, thereby alerting the researcher to an error or to the existence of dissimilar versions of the same document (see, for example, Documents 91 and 106 in Part I). Also, documents in different books often follow different arrangements. In one book they may be arranged chronologically, and in another they will be grouped by collection, subject, or locale. Additionally, there are the many volumes that provide valuable cross-references, indexes, or notes.

To provide a head start for the beginning researcher, I have marked entries of special interest or importance with a dot (·). The scarcity of the titles involved, however, has not normally affected these choices. All source entries have been numbered in a single sequence of 584 entries. For cross-listing purposes, the presence of a bracketed number, with or without a title, indicates the entry bearing that number. Thus [3] refers to *Kamakura ibun*, the major document series for the Kamakura period.

---

* This is one reason I do not cite library names alongside titles. Half or more of the works listed here derive from private collections, including my own. On the other hand, this does not mean that institutions do not *also* possess many of these works.

General Works

• 1
Nara ibun　寧楽遺文
Compiled by Takeuchi Rizō. 3 vols. Tōkyō, 1965–67.

Contains the most important Nara period records, except for the imperial codes and some major statutes: Included are the earliest *shōen* documents, local government reports, census registers, etc. There is a lengthy descriptive essay. A basic work for the study of early Japan. Supersedes an earlier two-volume series published in 1943–44 (same name).

• 2
Heian ibun　平安遺文
Compiled by Takeuchi Rizō. 13 vols. Tōkyō, 1963–68.

The indispensable document series for the Heian period. Contains all known records, arranged chronologically. Volumes 9 and 10 present documents missed in the earlier volumes. Of special interest is Volume 8, which covers the period of Taira ascendancy and the Gempei War years. Volume 11 is an invaluable index and reference guide containing descriptions of all document collections represented in Volumes 1–10, a chronological index of the documents themselves, and a comprehensive gazetteer that permits easy study of individual locales. Volume 12 contains tombstone inscriptions dating from Heian times. A truly seminal work.

• 3
Kamakura ibun　鎌倉遺文
Compiled by Takeuchi Rizō. 10 vols. to date. Tōkyō, 1971– .

Thirty or more volumes are projected for this first exhaustive document compilation of the Kamakura period. The ten volumes published so far cover 1185–1253 and are a model of exacting scholarship. The editors hope to continue at the rate of two new volumes each year. Unfortunately, there are no notes, and the index will come only at the end of the project. But the first ten volumes have already made an enormous contribution: the early Kamakura period can now be studied exhaustively. This series and its two predecessors, [1] and [2], are a tribute to the diligence and vision of Professor Takeuchi Rizō.

• 4
Dai Nihon shiryō　大日本史料
Compiled by Tōkyō daigaku shiryō hensanjo. Tōkyō, 1902– .

The largest of all collections of premodern source materials. It is divided into 11 series (pre-1600) with well over 200 volumes already published. Series 4 (17 volumes complete) and series 5 (24 volumes to date) deal with the Kamakura period but carry events only down to 1247. Includes all types of sources, many with brief editorial summaries. However, the reader must proceed with caution, especially for volumes published before the war, since the series contains many errors and gaps. Only a modest percentage of the extant documents are included. There is no published index beyond the *Shiryō sōran* [5].

5
Shiryō sōran　史料総覧
Compiled by Tōkyō daigaku shiryō hensanjo. 13 vols. Tōkyō, 1923–54.

The most comprehensive chronology of Japanese history, using summaries of basic source materials. The breakdown of volumes is keyed to the series divisions in the *Dai Nihon shiryō* [4]: Volumes 4 and 5, for example, deal with the Kamakura age. Massive in size but far from complete, since many documents have come to light in the years following its publication. Also, the series contains many gross oversimplifications and outright errors. It should be used only as a guide to other materials.

• 6

Dai Nihon komonjo, iewake series   大日本古文書，家わけ
Compiled by Tōkyō daigaku shiryō hensanjo. 86 vols. to date. Tōkyō, 1901– .

The great compendium of temple, shrine, and warrior family documents. This project is an ongoing one, with one or two new volumes published each year. Individual collections are listed separately. See [45, 77, 78, 79, 269, 274, 276, 279, 289, 315, 334, 345, 346, 398, 399, 414, 415, 535, 536, 547].

7

Shōsōin monjo   正倉院文書
Compiled by Tōkyō daigaku shiryō hensanjo (*Dai Nihon komonjo*). 25 vols. Tōkyō, 1901–40.

Contains the full complement of Nara-period records, which are housed mostly in the Shōsōin. Population registers, government reports, and the earliest *shōen* documents are presented. Though exhaustive, this series is not well arranged; the *Nara ibun* [1] is a better starting point.

• 8

Chūsei hōsei shiryōshū   中世法制史料集
Compiled by Satō Shin'ichi and Ikeuchi Yoshisuke. 3 vols. Tōkyō, 1969.

The basic compendium of warrior legal codes. Volume 1 contains Kamakura Bakufu statutes, Volume 2 the laws of the Muromachi regime, and Volume 3 the house laws of the great *daimyō*. A model of careful scholarship with extensive notes at the end of each volume.

• 9

Kamakura bakufu saikyojō shū   鎌倉幕府裁許状集
Compiled by Seno Seiichirō. 2 vols. Tōkyō, 1970–71.

The single most important work for studying the Kamakura Bakufu and the limits of its hegemony; a compendium of the regime's judicial decrees, drawn from dozens of different document collections. Volume 1 contains the decrees issued by Kamakura itself, whereas Volume 2 presents the edicts of the Rokuhara office in Kyōto and the Chinzei *tandai* in Kyūshū. A special feature of Volume 1 is a section that lists extant documents having some relationship to each of the Bakufu's judicial edicts. This is done also for the Rokuhara portion of Volume 2. For Chinzei, see [466].

• 10

Shōen shiryō   荘園志料
Compiled by Shimizu Masatake. 2 vols. Tōkyō, 1933.

A standard compendium of documents relating to *shōen*, covering over 5,000 medieval estates. The arrangement is by region, broken down into provinces and districts. A sentence or two of commentary introduces each *shōen*, followed by a sampling of sources (mostly documents) for that estate. A monumental work, though flawed by occasional transcription errors and by the unwieldiness of the page layouts: documents are squeezed in with only a small mark to designate a break. A reprint edition (1965) includes a third volume (*Shōen sakuin*, Takeuchi Rizō, comp.), which is an index of *shōen* names (with pronunciation guide) keyed to the main text. Together, these three volumes are basic to any research on the medieval estate system.

11
Shōen shi shiryō 荘園史資料
Compiled by Nishioka Toranosuke. Tōkyō, 1969.

The history of *shōen* through documents. Presents examples of documents representing each phase or aspect of *shōen* development, and covers the entire life of the estate institution from Nara times until *sengoku*. Unfortunately, responsibility for the project was placed in the hands of unqualified assistants, with the result that transcription errors abound. Although the format of the volume is admirable, the work itself cannot be recommended.

12
Shōen shi shiryō 荘園史資料
Compiled by Nishioka Toranosuke. Tōkyō: Waseda daigaku, n.d.

A privately distributed soft-cover work that served as the inspiration for [11]. Prof. Nishioka, one of the great authorities on *shōen*, used this book as a text for his own classes. It contains many materials not found in the published version; and, unlike that version, it is entirely reliable. However, there is no index or table of contents.

13
Komonjo ruisan 古文書類纂
Compiled by Hoshino Hisashi. Tōkyō, 1894.

A compendium of early and medieval records arranged by document type. Examples are very well chosen and illustrate the important stylistic changes occurring over time. There are many inserts containing facsimiles of original documents. No notes or index; but the excellent table of contents and the large, bold print used make this a worthwhile book. The weakness, as in many similar volumes, is the randomness of the selections.

14
Chō komonjo 徴古文書
Compiled by Kuroita Katsumi. 2 vols. Tōkyō, 1896–98.

An assemblage of documents from central Japan and the Tōkaidō circuit of eastern Japan, arranged by province. Contains many of the best-known and most interesting medieval records. Despite its age and occasional transcription errors, a useful work.

• 15
Hōsei shiryō komonjo ruisan 法制史料古文書類纂
Compiled by Takigawa Masajirō. Tōkyō, 1927.

A compendium of 460 early and medieval records, arranged by document type. Similar in format and function to [13]. Excellent of of its kind.

16
Shichō bokuhō 史徴墨宝
Compiled by Hennenshi hensangakari. 4 vols. Tōkyō, 1887–89.

Lithographs of more than 100 old documents, with explanations. The earliest compilation of its kind.

17
Komonjo jidai kagami   古文書時代鑑　♪
Compiled by Tōkyō teikoku daigaku shiryō hensanjo. 4 vols. Tōkyō, 1925.

Portfolio-size photographs of documents drawn selectively from Nara through Muromachi times. (Volumes 2 and 4 are mostly Tokugawa, but contain a handful of sixteenth-century records.) An accompanying booklet presents transcriptions of all documents, as well as brief discussions. The volumes themselves are in the traditional style and therefore most attractive. Recently reprinted, though very expensive.

18
Kyōto teikoku daigaku kokushi kenkyūshitsu shozō monjo shū
京都帝国大学国史研究室所蔵文書集
Compiled by Kyōto teikoku daigaku kokushi kenkyūshitsu. Kyōto, 1933.

A compendium of 60 or so photographic reproductions of well-known documents, with notes on each. Similar in intent to [17], but more modest.

19
Nakamura Naokatsu hakushi shūshū komonjo   中村直勝博士蒐集古文書
Compiled by Koki kinenkai. Tōkyō, 1960.

The private document collection of one of Japan's most famous medieval scholars. The documents (often with photographs) are presented in chronological sequence, followed by a separate section in which each record is discussed. Coverage is from late Heian into Tokugawa. An interesting volume, but limited by the fact that most of the records are unrelated to one another.

20
Kokushi shiryōshū   国史資料集
Compiled by Kokumin seishin bunka kenkyūjo. 4 vols. Tōkyō, 1940–43.

A history of Japan through source materials. Coverage is from ancient times through the sixteenth century. Records are drawn selectively from a wide variety of document collections, diaries, and chronicles. The project was interrupted by the war and never completed. Brief headnotes are included, and the materials themselves are interesting and valuable.

• 21
Nihon no komonjo   日本の古文書
Compiled by Aida Nirō. 2 vols. Tōkyō, 1954.

Volume 1 is the standard diplomatics text, with a thorough analysis of all aspects of that discipline. However, it is not nearly as readable as some other texts (e.g., [23]). Volume 2 contains a selection of documents arranged by type and covering the entire pre-Tokugawa age; a chronological list of all records is appended. A valuable work.

• 22
Nihon komonjogaku   日本古文書学
Nakamura Naokatsu. 2 vols. to date. Tōkyō, 1971– .

When the third and final volume of this work is published, the series will become the most exhaustive and authoritative in the entire field of premodern document study. The first two volumes have already made an enormous contribution and represent the culmination of a lifetime of research. Numerous examples are included, and the text is clear and precise. Massive in size; highly recommended.

• 23

Komonjogaku nyūmon 古文書学入門
Satō Shin'ichi. Tōkyō, 1971.

Easily the most accessible of the many diplomatics textbooks. Begins with a discussion of the study of old records and a review of the major document collections. Each document type is then expertly described and analyzed, and numerous examples are included. A natural starting point for anyone contemplating entrance into this field.

24

Enshū komonjo sen, kodai-chūsei hen 演習古文書選，古代 - 中世編
Compiled by Iyanaga Teizō et al. Tōkyō, 1971.

A recent diplomatics handbook with the unusual feature of having photographic reproductions of all documents presented. There are extensive notes for each document. The emphasis here is on learning to read unprinted originals.

25

Nihon chūsei komonjo no kenkyū 日本中世古文書の研究
Ogino Minahiko. Tōkyō, 1964.

A collection of short monographs dealing with a variety of document subjects, from the analysis of individual documents and collections to the study of old records engraved on wood. An essay treating the materials relating to Kō Estate in Ōmi Province is perhaps the most important historical contribution.

26

Gempei ōraiki 源平往来記
Zokuzoku gunsho ruijū 10: 707–33 (*kyōiku bu*). Tōkyō, 1908.

A collection of 23 documents dating from the period 1177–85. Includes key records bearing on the outbreak and course of the Gempei War. Highly interesting; drawn from several collections.

27

Muromachi ke gonaisho an 室町家御内書案
(*Shinkō zōho shiseki shūran* 12: 59–142). Kyōto, 1967.

An assemblage of documents that were sent by the Muromachi Bakufu to the great warrior houses of that age. Many of the famous names can be found here. There is thus much on the development of the *daimyō* and on the relations of these families with the Ashikaga. Coverage begins with the third shōgun, Yoshimitsu, and extends into the sixteenth century. Unfortunately, there are no notes and no index of names.

• 28

Nanzan junkaroku tsuika 南山巡狩録追加
(*Shinkō zōho shiseki shūran* 7: 369–542). Kyōto, 1967.

A major collection of documents bearing on the fortunes of the Southern Court during the fourteenth-century Nambokuchō wars. Chronological arrangement (1336–91), but no notes. There is also much of interest here on the rise of the Ashikaga. The documents themselves are drawn from a variety of collections.

29

Chōkei tennō sokkinsha jiseki kenkyū shiryō 長慶天皇側近者事蹟研究資料
Compiled by Rinji ryōbo chōsa iinkai. 1938.

Presents documents relating to the supporters of the Southern Court emperor

Chōkei (r. 1368–83) during the Nambokuchō wars. Arrangement is chronological, and there are occasional notes. A detailed table of contents serves as a summary of the materials contained. Interesting volume.

30
Kitabatake Chikafusa monjo shūkō　北畠親房文書輯考
Compiled by Yokoi Akio (Dai Nihon hyakka zenshokai). Tōkyō, 1942.

The documents and other materials bearing on the life of Kitabatake Chikafusa, the fourteenth-century imperial loyalist and author of the *Jinnō shōtōki*. Arranged chronologically, but incorporated in a text that is uncritically laudatory. A typical example of wartime scholarship. The documents, however, stand on their own merit.

• 31
Oda Nobunaga monjo no kenkyū　織田信長文書の研究
Compiled by Okuno Takahiro. 2 vols. plus addendum. Tōkyō, 1969–70.

A major contribution to scholarship. Volume 1 treats 1549–75; Volume 2 covers 1575–82. The format is ideal: the original *kambun* document, its rendering into Japanese, and copious notes. Appended to Volume 2 are indexes of personal names and document collections, as well as a section containing documents missed earlier. Indispensable for the period covered.

• 32
Tokugawa Ieyasu monjo no kenkyū 1–2　徳川家康文書の研究
Compiled by Nakamura Kōya (Gakujutsu shinkōkai). Tōkyō, 1965.

The career of the great Ieyasu in documents. Volume 1 covers up to 1590, and Volume 2 continues to 1600. The documents are followed by lengthy explanations, making this both a source book and critical work of scholarship. As important as Okuno's study of Nobunaga [31]. All that is needed now is a major Hideyoshi series.

• 33
Sōdōshū [or Sōtōshū] komonjo　曹洞宗古文書
Compiled by Ōkubo Dōshu. 3 vols. Tōkyō, 1961–72.

The land documents relating to estates held by the individual temples of the Sōtō sect. Coverage is overwhelmingly Muromachi, with many documents of considerable intrinsic interest. Sōtō temples and estates were located in all parts of Japan, and the arrangement is by individual collections.

34
Nichiren shū shūgaku zensho 18–23, shiden kyūki bu
日蓮宗宗学全書，史伝旧記部
Compiled by Risshō daigaku Nichiren kyōgaku kenkyūjo. Tōkyō, 1960–62.

Contains a vast number of medieval and early-modern documents, arranged by individual Nichiren temple. A great many of these records deal with economic and political matters, though locating specific documents is difficult. For the medieval period, the sixteenth century is best represented. Other volumes in the series may also contain documentary sources.

35
Nihon bukkyō keizai shi ronkō　日本佛教経済史論考
Compiled by Hosokawa Kameichi. Tōkyō, 1933.

The final section (ca. 130 pages) of this scholarly monograph contains selected documents relating to temple and shrine proprietorships. Most interesting are the

Munakata Shrine materials (northern Kyūshū), which contain a variety of Kamakura and Muromachi Bakufu records. See [471].

36
Goryōchi shikō 御料地史稿
Compiled by Ashida Ijin. Tōkyō, 1937.

Basically a historical study of imperial-house lands, but contains some important document-type materials. The 1191 estate register of the Chōkōdō, an imperial temple, is included.

37
Shinkan eiga 1 宸翰英華
Compiled by Teikoku gakushi-in. Tōkyō, 1944.

A selection of private letters by emperors. Coverage is from Shōmu to Go-Yōzei (i.e. from the eighth to the seventeenth century). Lengthy notes follow each entry. An extensive section of photographs is included.

38
Teihon Sen no Rikyū no shokan 定本千利久の書簡
Compiled by Kuwata Tadachika. Tōkyō, 1971.

Contains the private letters of the great sixteenth-century tea master Sen no Rikyū. Each letter is followed by an explanation, and there are numerous photographs; some 263 letters are included in all.

39
Komonjo nyūmon—hyakunin no shoseki 古文書入門―百人の書蹟
Compiled by Nagashima Fukutarō. Kyōto, 1965.

Calligraphic examples by famous men in Japanese history. The first 70 or so documents in this collection of 107 cover the Heian through Muromachi ages. Photographs of each document, transcriptions, and notes are included. Political, religious, and literary figures are represented. The photographs are superb.

• 40
Heian jidai kana shojō no kenkyū 平安時代假名書状の研究
Compiled by Kusogami Noboru. Tōkyō, 1968.

A monumental work of scholarship on one of the most difficult of all document types, private letters written in *kana*. Beautifully produced, with more than 200 photographs. Coverage is from Nara times into the early years of the Kamakura age. Full transcriptions of documents, copious notes, tables, and explanations. Of major importance.

41
Sorimachi monjo 反町文書
Compiled by Takahashi Masahiko et al. *Shigaku* 32.1, 32.2, 32.3, 33.1, 34.1 (1959–61).

A collection of 160 documents relating to warrior activities, mostly in central Japan. In the first group (32.1), six Kamakura records and 14 from the Nambokuchō age are presented. A large percentage of these concern the sale of land. Subsequent coverage is Muromachi into Tokugawa, with about 120 of the full total treating the Nobunaga age and beyond.

42
Matsugi monjo ni mieru Heian matsu-Nambokuchō ki no monjo ni tsuite
真継文書にみえる平安末－南北朝期の文書について

Compiled by Amino Yoshihiko. *Nagoya daigaku bungaku bu kenkyū ronshū* 56 (1972).

A collection of about 30 documents (mostly Kamakura), with a thorough analysis of each. Record after record here refers to the despoilments of *shugo* and *jitō*. Sequels are "Matsugi monjo ni mieru Muromachi ki no monjo" and "Matsugi monjo ni mieru sengoku ki no monjo (1)," *Nagoya daigaku bungaku bu kenkyū ronshū* 59 and 62 (1973, 1974). The total of nearly 100 documents deals with land problems in many provinces of Japan, though a number of these records are thought to be forgeries.

43
Benkan bu'nin shihai monjo　弁官補任紙背文書
Compiled by Tanaka Minoru. *Komonjo kenkyū* 1 (1968): 90–94.

Eight documents appearing on the reverse side of a traditional scroll. Coverage is late Heian and early Kamakura, and several Bakufu-related records are included.

Tōhoku Region

GENERAL

• 44
Ōshū Fujiwara shiryō　奥州藤原史料
Compiled by Tōhoku daigaku Tōhoku bunka kenkyūkai. Tōkyō, 1970.

The story of the Northern Fujiwara through source materials. Entries are mostly from diaries and chronicles, with only a few documents. No notes are included but valuable tables are appended—lists of governors for the two northern provinces (Mutsu and Dewa), names of the successive northern frontier military commanders, etc. There are also indexes of terms, persons, and materials cited. The indispensable source book on the subject.

• 45
Date ke monjo　伊達家文書
Compiled by Tōkyō daigaku shiryō hensanjo (*Dai Nihon komonjo, iewake* 3). 10 vols. Tōkyō, 1909–14.

A massive collection of documents tracing the rise of the great Date family of northern Japan. Coverage begins in 1333, and about one-third of the documents date from Muromachi and *sengoku* times. The remaining records are Tokugawa. The eventual headquarters of the Date was Sendai in Miyagi.

46
Sengoku monjo shūei—Date shi hen　戦国文書聚影－伊達氏篇
Compiled by Kobayashi Seiji and Ōishi Naomasa (Sengoku monjo kenkyūkai). Tōkyō, 1973.

Photographs of representative documents of the Date *daimyō* house, along with transcriptions and notes. The photographs are of the highest quality, and the overall production is excellent. Exclusively sixteenth century.

MUTSU PROVINCE (AOMORI PREFECTURE)

47
Aomori kenshi 1　青森県史
Compiled by Aomori kenshi hensan iinkai. Tōkyō, 1926.

The history of northern Mutsu through source materials arranged chronologically. Massive in size, but has major gaps. Coverage is from earliest times to 1687. Documents and other source excerpts included.

48
Nambu ke monjo　南部家文書
Compiled by Washio Yoritaka (Yoshino chō shiseki chōsakai). Tōkyō, 1939.

A useful document compendium relating principally to the restoration period of the 1330's and the struggles that followed. The Nambu, of Minamoto descent, had fought for Kamakura in the Northern Campaign of 1189 and were subsequently settled in that region. During Nambokuchō times they sided with the Southern Court and later emerged as a *daimyō* house of considerable power. Numerous photographs of original documents have been added, and there is a good table of contents and genealogical chart.

MUTSU PROVINCE (IWATE PREFECTURE)

• 49
Iwate ken chūsei monjo　岩手県中世文書
Compiled by Iwate ken kyōiku iinkai. 3 vols. Morioka, 1960–68.

A major compendium of documents on medieval Mutsu Province. Two tables of contents—one chronological, the other by collection name—assist the user. There are also numerous photographs of original documents. For the Kamakura period Volume 1 is best; Hōjō penetration of the north is detailed. With [57] and [66], this series is one of the three major source collections on northern Japan.

50
Iwate ken kinseki shi　岩手県金石志
Compiled by Iwate shi gakkai. Morioka, 1961.

Presents gravestone inscriptions from the Iwate portion of Mutsu Province. A considerable number of these date from the Kamakura period. Numerous photographs are included, and there are excellent notes.

• 51
Ōshū Hiraizumi monjo　奥州平泉文書
Compiled by Iwate ken kyōiku iinkai. Morioka, 1958.

Documents relating to the northern city of Hiraizumi. Coverage is from late Heian into Tokugawa times, with materials arranged chronologically. The documents of Chūsonji Temple are featured. Occasional notes assist the reader, and various photographs of records are appended. An important work.

Nambu ke monjo, *see* [48]

52
Morioka Nambu ke kankei monjo sonota　盛岡南部家関係文書その他
Compiled by Satō Hideo. Morioka, 1958.

Documents relating to two members of the Nambu *daimyō* house of northern Japan. About 125 records included in all, from the sixteenth and seventeenth centuries. Chronological arrangement, but no notes.

53
Morioka Hamada ke monjo　盛岡濱田家文書
Compiled by Tanaka Kitami. Morioka, 1958.

234 *Bibliography*

Pamphlet containing a few sixteenth-century documents relating to the Hamada family of northern Japan. Coverage is mostly Tokugawa.

54
Matsumoto monjo no kenkyū　松本文書の研究
Compiled by Koiwa Sueji. 1959.

Collection of 184 documents relating to a local family of Mutsu Province. Coverage is from early Kamakura times to the first years of Tokugawa, using a chronological arrangement. These materials seem not to be included in any larger compilation. There is a good table of contents, followed by a section that briefly summarizes each document. Mimeographed on low-grade paper.

55
Kitagami shishi 2, kodai-chūsei　北上市史，古代 – 中世
Compiled by Kitagami shi. Kitagami, 1970.

An excellent volume containing the documents and other sources, arranged chronologically, of this northern Japanese city. The format is ideal: each entry is followed by extensive explanatory notes and there are many photographs of documents. Essays on various topics make up much of the second part of the volume.

56
Takasu monjo　高州文書
Compiled by Kishida Hiroyuki. *Gekkan rekishi* 31 (1970): 7–10.

A collection of 16 documents (11 Kamakura) relating to *jitō* behavior in lands in Mutsu and Bingo provinces. The Mutsu documents (covering 1209–26) deal largely with the opening of new fields to cultivation; the Bingo records describe the passage of partial *jitō* rights within a main holder's family.

MUTSU PROVINCE (MIYAGI PREFECTURE)

•57
Miyagi kenshi 30, shiryōshū 1　宮城県史，史料集
Miyagi kenshi hensan iinkai. Sendai, 1965.

The major compendium of documents for the Miyagi sector of Mutsu Province. Treatment is from earliest times to 1600. There are two tables of contents, one chronological and the other arranged by collection name. Also, there is a separate photograph section. The volume is marred, however, by unreliable transcriptions and the absence of notes. Numerous errors detract from this important work. Should be used with Volume 1 of *Miyagi kenshi*, which is a history of the region during early and medieval times.

58
Sendai shishi 8　仙台市史
Compiled by Sendai shishi hensan iinkai. Sendai, 1953.

An excellent compendium of source materials (mostly documents) relating to the area around Sendai. Coverage is from earliest times to the end of the Tokugawa age with the heaviest concentration after 1600. No notes or index, but there is a table of contents listing all materials. Recently reprinted.

59
Sendai shishi, shiryō hen 1　仙台市史，史料編
Compiled by Sendai shishi hensan iinkai. Sendai, 1953.

A soft-cover version of [58], but stops at 1600. A useful work.

• 60

Rusu ke monjo　留守家文書
Compiled by Miyagi kenshi hensan iinkai. Sendai, 1952.

The documents of one of the Kamakura Bakufu's two commissioner families for northern Japan. Traces the rise of a lowly eastern house to a position of great prominence. Soft-cover on low-grade paper, and contains some errors. But the Rusu collection is one of the most important for a study of Kamakura's relations with the northern region.

61

Miyagi ken Nenoshiroishi sonshi　宮城県根白石村史
Compiled by Nenoshiroishi sonshi hensan iinkai. Sendai, 1957.

The history of a small area in northern Japan, with appendixes containing valuable documents. These records (the Hōzawa collection, a total of 16 documents) begin in the late Kamakura. Expert commentary is included, along with photographs.

62

Shiroishi shishi, 5, shiryō hen 2　白石市史，資料編
Compiled by Shiroishi shishi hensan iinkai. Shiroishi, 1974.

Contains some 90 pages of early and medieval records, arranged chronologically. All types of sources are presented.

63

Kuramochi monjo　倉持文書
Compiled by Sasaki Mitsuo. *Rekishi* 11 (1955): 64–71.

A major source of data on Ashikaga house development during Kamakura times. Also contains valuable documents relating to the success of that family during the fourteenth century. Should be used in conjunction with the Ashikaga-related records appearing in *Tochigi kenshi* [89]. The Kuramochi collection is held by Tōhoku University.

64

Ishikawa monjo　石川文書
Compiled by Ōishi Naomasa. *Tōhoku bunka kenkyūshitsu kiyō* 4 (1962): 69–88.

The Muromachi-period records of a warrior house in northern Japan. A total of 74 documents, with coverage beginning in 1333. A number of Ashikaga decrees are included. A genealogy and brief essay are appended.

For additional Mutsu Province sources, see [66–76]

DEWA PROVINCE (AKITA PREFECTURE)

65

Akita kenshi, kodai-chūsei shiryō　秋田県史，古代－中世資料
Compiled by Akita kenshi hensan iinkai. Akita, 1961.

Materials on Dewa Province, arranged chronologically. Relatively few documents from the Kamakura period, with coverage much better for later centuries. Many chronicle and diary excerpts. No notes, but there is a very detailed table of contents that summarizes each entry. Should be used with an accompanying volume: *Akita kenshi, kodai-chūsei hen.*

Mogi Chikugo kezō monjo—Jūnisho no kuchi Boshin sensō kankei monjo, *see* [91]

DEWA PROVINCE (YAMAGATA PREFECTURE)

No document publications encountered. The *Yamagata kenshi* now appearing has concentrated thus far on Tokugawa and modern times. A volume in the new *Yamagata shishi* series (shiryō hen 1, 1973) is reported to contain a small selection of sixteenth-century documents.

MUTSU PROVINCE (FUKUSHIMA PREFECTURE)

• 66

Fukushima kenshi 7, kodai-chūsei shiryō　福島県史，古代－中世資料
Compiled by Fukushima ken. Fukushima, 1966.

> A model with which other prefectural histories are often compared. More than 1,000 pages of documents, with transcriptions of the highest accuracy. Arrangement is by individual collection, but a chronological index of materials is appended. There is also a general description of each collection and a separate section for gravestone inscriptions. Easily the most important single source volume for the Tōhoku region. Should be used with the first volume of *Fukushima kenshi*, which is a history of the region from earliest times through the medieval period.

67

Shimpen Aizu fudoki　新編会津風土記
Dai Nihon chishi taikei 25–29. 5 vols. Tōkyō, 1970.

> An Edo-period compilation containing numerous medieval documents. These records, however, are buried in a gazetteer text and are thus difficult to find and use.

• 68

Fukushima shishi, genshi-kodai-chūsei shiryō
福島市史，原始－古代－中世資料
Compiled by Fukushima shishi hensan iinkai. Fukushima, 1969.

> The historical materials relating to Fukushima City, arranged chronologically. Helpful notes are included, along with lists of local temples, shrines, archaeological sites, etc. The materials contained are not limited to documents: chronicle and diary excerpts are also presented. Exemplary of its kind.

• 69

Aizuwakamatsu shishi 8, kodai-chūsei shiryōshū
会津若松市史，古代－中世史料集
Compiled by Takahashi Tomio et al. Aizuwakamatsu, 1967.

> Contains the historical materials relating to Aizuwakamatsu City. Beautifully produced with copious notes; chronologically arranged. Similar in appearance to [68] and highly recommended. Supersedes an earlier soft-cover version (*Aizuwakamatsu shi shiryōshū, kodai-chūsei hen,* 1964).

70

Kōriyama shishi 8, shiryō 1　郡山市史，史料
Compiled by Kōriyama shi. Kōriyama, 1973.

A massive volume of sources from earliest times through Tokugawa. The medieval section of 200 pages contains materials of all types, arranged chronologically. Very carefully annotated.

71
Yūki komonjo san　結城古文書纂
Compiled by Kokushi kenkyūjo. Tōkyō, 1963.

Various documents relating to the Yūki warrior house, Emperor Go-Daigo, and Kitabatake Chikafusa during the Kemmu and Nambokuchō periods. The format of the volume is very hard to follow, and the commentary that accompanies many of the documents is uncritical. There is no chronological index. See [30] for many of these same materials.

72
Iino oyobi Kunitama shiryō monjo　飯野及び国魂史料文書
Compiled by Morone Shōichi. Tōkyō, 1930.

Two important document collections from northern Japan. These records focus mainly on land disputes involving *jitō*. Arrangement is chronological, and there are helpful notes and accompanying essays. A worthwhile effort, with much of interest on the thirteenth and fourteenth centuries.

•73
Chūsei ni okeru Sōma shi to sono shiryō　中世に於ける相馬氏とその史料
Compiled by Toyoda Takeshi and Tashiro Osamu. *Nihon bunka kenkyūjo kenkyū hōkoku bekkan* 3 (Tōhoku daigaku, 1965).

A document assemblage of major importance, relating to an influential *daimyō* family of northern Japan. Coverage begins in the mid-thirteenth century, and there is much information on the changing nature of the inheritance system during late Kamakura and Nambokuchō times. An excellent descriptive essay is included.

74
Sōma shishi 5, shiryō hen 2　相馬市史，資料篇
Compiled by Sōma shishi hensankai. Sōma, 1971.

A large volume containing diaries and chronicles, along with 75 pages of documents. Of the three collections presented, the Sōma records are featured [73]. Chronological arrangement.

75
Kunimi chōshi 2, shiryō hen, genshi-kodai-chūsei-kinsei
国見町史，史料篇，原始－古代－中世－近世
Compiled by Kunimi chō. Fukushima, 1973.

A massive volume (ca. 900 pp.) of source materials, arranged chronologically. The medieval section is quite short, however, and is dominated by Muromachi records relating to the Date *daimyō* house. A beautifully produced volume with many photographs. Notes follow many entries.

76
Yatsuki monjo　八槻文書
Compiled by Kashiwano Harutake. *Tōhoku bunka kenkyūshitsu kiyō* 4 (1962): 89–113.

Collection of 104 fifteenth- and sixteenth-century shrine-related records from northern Japan. Interesting materials. A brief essay is appended.

Kantō Region

• 77
Uesugi ke monjo 上杉家文書
Compiled by Tōkyō daigaku shiryō hensanjo (*Dai Nihon komonjo, iewake* 12). 3 vols. to date. Tōkyō, 1931– .

Documents tracing the rise of the great Uesugi *daimyō* house. Beginning from a Kamakura Bakufu investiture in 1196, the Uesugi eventually became one of the most powerful warrior families in the land. A major collection.

• 78
Kumagai ke monjo—Miura ke monjo—Hiraga ke monjo
熊谷家文書－三浦家文書－平賀家文書
Compiled by Tōkyō daigaku shiryō hensanjo (*Dai Nihon komonjo, iewake* 14). Tōkyō, 1937.

The documents of three important eastern warrior houses, all of whom received *jitō* appointments in western Japan (the first and third in Aki Province, the second in Suō Province). Useful headnotes and genealogies enhance the worth of this volume. Contains many fascinating Kamakura records. For the Kumagai, see also [133].

• 79
Yamanouchi Sudō ke monjo 山内首藤家文書
Compiled by Tōkyō daigaku shiryō hensanjo (*Dai Nihon komonjo, iewake* 15). Tōkyō, 1940.

The documents of a warrior family that went from *jitō* in the Kamakura period to *daimyō* later on. Covers mostly the sixteenth century and beyond, but the earlier materials are of great interest too. The Yamanouchi, with their base area in the Kantō, were appointed *jitō* over an estate in Bingo Province. During the thirteenth and fourteenth centuries severe internal house disputes and trouble with the estate proprietor occurred. The family gained in strength and eventually emerged as one of the great military houses of the sixteenth century.

80
Yamanouchi Sudō ke monjo 山内首藤家文書
Compiled by Shōbara shi bunkazai hogo iinkai. 2 vols. No date.

The Yamanouchi collection in two soft-cover mimeographed volumes. A total of 567 records, with coverage from Kamakura into Tokugawa times. A detailed genealogical chart is appended to Volume 2. Brief headnotes. Another volume by the same compiler (*Shoshin shōmon—Yamanouchi ke shōmon nukigaki*. Shōbara, 1968) reportedly contains some 250 documents also relating to the Yamanouchi.

81
Kantō Nagao shi kankei monjo shū 関東長尾氏関係文書集
Compiled by Nerima kyōdoshi kenkyūkai. Tōkyō, 1968.

Documents relating to the activities of a major warrior house in service to the Uesugi [77]. Coverage begins in the 1330's, and useful notes follow each entry. Page citations to other works in which documents appear are included. Nicely organized.

82
Shoshū komonjo—Sōshū monjo shō　諸州古文書－相州文書抄
Compiled by Busō shiryō kankōkai. Tōkyō, 1962.

A scattering of documents from Sagami and several other provinces of the Kantō. These documents are generally available elsewhere.

KŌZUKE PROVINCE (GUMMA PREFECTURE)

• 83
Nitta Yoshisada kō kompon shiryō　新田義貞公根本史料
Compiled by Gumma ken kyōikukai. Maebashi, 1942.

A massive volume containing source materials bearing on the rise of the Nitta family of Kōzuke. There are numerous documents from the Kamakura period, but the heaviest concentration is on the early years of the Nambokuchō age, when the imperial loyalist Nitta Yoshisada was contending for power with the Ashikaga. Arrangement is chronological, and brief summaries preface the materials themselves. Recently reprinted under the title *Nitta shi kompon shiryō* (Tōkyō, 1974), edited by Chijiwa Minoru. An important work.

84
Masaki komonjo (Nitta Iwamatsu monjo)　正木古文書（新田岩松文書）
Compiled by Jōmō kyōdoshi kenkyūkai. Maebara, 1938.

The document collection of the Nitta warrior house of Kemmu Restoration fame. The handful of Kamakura materials contain *jitō* appointment decrees and testamentary records relating to that family's homeland, Nitta Estate. A majority of the latest documents are undated. An attractive volume in the traditional style.

85
Jōmō kinsekibun nempyō　上毛金石文年表
Compiled by Gumma ken. Gumma, 1937.

Stone, metal, and wood inscriptions either relating to or located in Kōzuke. Chronological arrangement, with coverage from Nara times to the early seventeenth century. Each entry is carefully annotated, and there are numerous photographs.

86
Tatebayashi shishi　館林市誌
Compiled by Tatebayashi shishi hensan iinkai. Tatebayashi, 1969.

A massive volume of more than 1,000 pages containing a brief document section with records relating to a certain Sanuki Estate. A total of 97 documents, of which about 15 date from Kamakura times. Various Kamakura and Muromachi Bakufu edicts are included. Interesting materials.

87
Kōzuke Nukinosaki jinja monjo　上野貴前神社文書
Compiled by Hashimura Hiroshi. *Rekishi chiri* 54.4 (1929): 101–5.

Brief collection of sixteenth-century documents belonging to a local shrine. These records carry the seals of two of the greatest *daimyō* of the age: the Takeda and the Uesugi. Fully annotated.

88
Gumma bunka　群馬文化
Published monthly by Gumma bunka no kai.

In the absence of an up-to-date Gumma prefectural history, various Kōzuke document collections have been introduced in this journal—e.g. the Nagao, Nawa, and Utsuki collections. Unfortunately, the journal itself is hard to find, and I have not been able to examine it.

SHIMOTSUKE PROVINCE (TOCHIGI PREFECTURE)

Kuramochi monjo, see [63]

· 89
Tochigi kenshi, shiryō hen, chūsei　栃木県史，史料編，中世
Compiled by Tochigi kenshi hensan iinkai. 2 vols. to date. Tochigi, 1973– .

The medieval documents of Shimotsuke Province in two large, handsome volumes. Volume 1 contains document collections presently housed in Tochigi Prefecture. Arrangement is by geographical district, with 90 percent of the coverage on Muromachi times. Indispensable for a study of the Ashikaga house, since Shimotsuke was that family's original base area. Volume 2 presents a portion of the documents relating to Shimotsuke that are housed in other parts of Japan. Arrangement here is by individual collection, and there is a valuable introductory essay. Coverage is principally the Muromachi age. Another volume in this series (*shiryō hen, kodai*) was published in 1974 and contains sources to the end of the Heian period.

90
Sano shishi, shiryō hen, genshi-kodai-chūsei
佐野市史，史料編，原始－古代－中世
Compiled by Sano shishi hensan iinkai. Sano, 1975.

A massive volume of sources treating the home region of the Sano *daimyō* house, covering prehistory through 1600. The final section presents about 160 pages of documents, arranged chronologically. Notes plus photographs. Handsomely produced.

91
Mogi Chikugo kezō monjo—Jūnisho no kuchi Boshin sensō kankei monjo
茂木筑後家蔵文書－十二所口戊辰戦争関係文書
Compiled by Ōdate shishi hensan iinkai. Ōdate (Akita), 1973.

Contains the documents of a local warrior house in Shimotsuke Province who early on became vassals of the Kamakura Bakufu. A collection of some importance, which appears also in Volume 2 of [89]. Later, the Mogi became a power in the Dewa region of northern Japan.

HITACHI PROVINCE (IBARAGI PREFECTURE)

· 92
Ibaragi ken shiryō, chūsei hen　茨城県史料，中世編
Compiled by Ibaragi kenshi hensan chūsei shi bukai. 2 vols. to date. Mito, 1970.

A major series containing documents housed in (Volume 1) and relating to (Volume 2) Hitachi Province. The Ibaragi portion of Shimōsa Province is also included. Of special interest are the Kashima Shrine collection (see [94]) and the Usuda records, both in Volume 1. Introductory essays describe each collection. Portfolio size and beautifully produced. Indispensable for the areas treated. A *kodai hen* volume has also appeared.

93
Shimpen Hitachi kokushi　新編常陸国誌
Compiled by Nakayama Nobuna. 2 vols. Mito, 1899–1901.

A traditional assemblage of historical materials and commentary, with numerous medieval documents. Contains many errors, however, and is superseded by the previous entry.

94
Kashima jingū monjo　鹿島神宮文書
Compiled by Kashima jingū shamusho. Kashima, 1942.

The documents of a major eastern shrine in close touch with the Kamakura Bakufu. A visually attractive volume, but marred by occasional errors in transcription. The documents themselves are among the most important for Kantō estate administration and the affairs of a local religious institution. The same materials appear in [92].

95
Kashima sha no monjo　鹿島社の文書
Compiled by Aida Nirō and Kojima Shōsaku. *Rekishi chiri* 54.5 (1929): 486–504; 55.3 (1930): 309–26.

A partial register of documents in the Kashima Shrine collection, along with brief data on individual records. Part 2 contains a small number of the documents themselves.

96
Sōsha jinja monjo　総社神社文書
Compiled by Miyata Toshihiko (*Ibaragi ken komonjo shūsei* 1). Mito, 1962.

The documents of a shrine in Hitachi Province. Expert commentary is added, and there are copious notes. More than half the 60 records date from Kamakura times. Excellent for relations between the Bakufu and Hitachi Province.

97
Saisho monjo　税所文書
Compiled by Miyata Toshihiko (*Ibaragi ken komonjo shūsei* 2). Mito, 1962.

The documents of a provincial official house in Hitachi. The Saisho became vassals of the Kamakura Bakufu and prospered in this dual capacity. The volume contains extensive notes and a genealogical chart. Most striking is the way Kamakura ruled in Hitachi through the provincial apparatus.

•98
Ibaragi ken komonjo shūsei　茨城県古文書集成
Compiled by Miyata Toshihiko. Kyōto, 1974.

Combines [96] and [97] in a handsome, hardcover volume. Interesting materials.

99
Hitachi Fuchū Saisho ke monjo　常陸府中税所家文書
Compiled by Ishioka shi kyōiku iinkai (*Ishioka shishi hensan shiryō* 10). Ishioka, 1960.

Generally superseded by [97] and [98], though of some value owing to different notes.

• 100
Yoshida jinja monjo 吉田神社文書
Compiled by Mito shishi hensan iinkai. Mito, 1962.

An important collection of documents relating to a shrine in Hitachi. Unusually rich materials on Kantō land administration and on a local proprietor's difficulties with *jitō*. Arrangement is chronological, and more than half the 97 records date from Kamakura times. There are no notes.

101
Yoshida Yakuō-in monjo 吉田薬王院文書
Compiled by Mito shishi hensan iinkai. Mito, 1962.

A total of 142 documents dealing mostly with the organization and administration of a shrine-temple in Hitachi. Coverage is Kamakura through *sengoku*, but only 15 documents date from before 1333. At least 60 of the later records are undated. Less interesting than the materials of Yoshida Shrine [100], which was placed administratively above the Yoshida Yakuō-in. There are no notes.

102
Mito shishi 1 水戸市史
Compiled by Itō Tasaburō. (Mito shishi hensan iinkai). Mito, 1963.

Fifty-three pages of medieval documents are appended to this first volume of the Mito city history. The records presented are ones referred to in some significant way within the text. For the Kamakura period, Yoshida Shrine materials predominate.

103
Hitachi no kuni ōtabumi 常陸国大田文
Zoku gunsho ruijū 33.1: 469–72. Tōkyō, 1958.

A field register of 1279 containing valuable data on the estates of Hitachi Province.

SHIMŌSA PROVINCE (IBARAGI PREFECTURE)

Ibaragi ken shiryō, chūsei hen, *see* [92]

Yūki komonjo san, *see* [71]

104
Yūki chihō saihō monjo 1–2　結城地方採訪文書
Compiler not identified. *Kokushigaku* 12–13 (1932/9, 1932/11): 67–70, 65–69.

Presents 62 Muromachi-period documents belonging to several different collections. These are mostly land records of unusual interest, though the complete absence of commentary or notes is a drawback.

• 105
Koga kubō shodai—Ashikaga Shigeuji monjo shū
古河公方初代－足利成氏文書集
Compiled by Satō Hironobu (Go-Hōjō shi kenkyūkai). Chigasaki, 1976.

Documents relating to the life and career of a major contender for power in the Kantō during the mid-fifteenth century. Shigeuji broke with the Ashikaga Bakufu and with the Kantō deputyship (*kanrei*) in Kamakura, establishing his own headquarters in the Koga region of Shimōsa. Henceforth Shigeuji's line came to be known as the Koga *kubō*. This volume contains some 290 documents, arranged chronologically, with a good name and place index.

106

Koga kubō nidai—Ashikaga Masauji monjo shū

古河公方二代－足利政氏文書集

Compiled by Satō Hironobu (Go-Hōjō shi kenkyūkai). Chigasaki, 1973.

Documents covering the years 1488–1520 and relating to the second-generation Koga *kubō*, Masauji. A total of 126 records are presented, arranged chronologically. A long essay is appended, plus a chronology of Masauji's life and a gazetteer.

107

Koga kubō godai—Ashikaga Yoshiuji monjo shū

古河公方五代－足利義氏文書集

Compiled by Satō Hironobu (Go-Hōjō shi kenkyūkai). Chigasaki, 1974.

Same features as the last two titles but relating to the fifth-generation *kubō*. Some 340 documents, with coverage beginning in 1553.

SHIMŌSA PROVINCE (CHIBA PREFECTURE)

• 108

Chiba ken shiryō, chūsei hen (Katori monjo)

千葉県史料，中世編（香取文書）

Compiled by Chiba kenshi hensan shingikai. Chiba, 1957.

One of the most important document collections for eastern Japan. The interplay between the Kamakura Bakufu, the Fujiwara house of Kyōto, and a prominent local landholder is the most interesting feature of these materials. The present volume corrects the many transcription errors of an earlier work, the *Katori monjo san* [109]. Unfortunately, there are no notes. Coverage is late Heian to Tokugawa.

109

Katori monjo san　香取文書簒

Compiled by Katori jingū shamusho. 17 vols. Chiba, 1906–8.

Essentially the same documents as the above in an attractive series of small volumes. But contains errors and is today not much used.

• 110

Chiba ken shiryō, chūsei hen (shoke monjo)　千葉県史料，中世編（諸家文書）

Compiled by Chiba kenshi hensan shingikai. Chiba, 1962.

The documents of the temples, shrines, and warrior houses of Shimōsa, Awa, and Kazusa provinces. A valuable compendium, though few materials date from Kamakura times. Occasional photographs and notes assist the reader. Each document collection is described briefly.

• 111

Chiba ken shiryō, chūsei hen (kengai monjo)　千葉県史料，中世編（県外文書）

Compiled by Chiba kenshi hensan shingikai. Chiba, 1962.

The documents relating to Shimōsa, Awa, and Kazusa provinces but held in collections outside those regions. Contains many valuable records, though the absence of notes (with a few exceptions) is a drawback. Heaviest concentration is on the *sengoku* period. A chronological index of records (by collection) is appended.

112
Bōsō sōsho 1　房総叢書
Compiled by Bōsō sōsho kankōkai. Chiba, 1940.

A compendium of medieval documents relating to Shimōsa, Awa, and Kazusa provinces. Although the major collections are represented and described briefly, the selection of materials is inadequate, and there are virtually no notes. Good distribution between Kamakura and Muromachi. Recently reprinted.

113
Kaburaya Ise hōki [Ichiki monjo]　鏑矢伊勢方記（樔木文書）
Compiled by Nishigaki Seiji. Tōkyō gakugeidai fuzoku kō, *Kenkyū kiyō* 4, 5 (1966–67): 15–46, 15–37.

The single most important collection of documents bearing on the limits of warrior power during late Heian times. These records tell the story of the Chiba family's failure to maintain satisfactory control over its homelands. Records begin with the year 1130 and are arranged chronologically. Coverage is into Tokugawa. The same collection is in [111] and [114].

• 114
Ichikawa shishi 5, kodai-chūsei shiryō　市川市史，古代 - 中世史料
Compiled by Ichikawa shishi hensan iinkai. Tōkyō, 1973.

Contains the Chiba-related documents and other records bearing on the development of warriors in eastern Japan. A volume of major importance, since it brings together in a convenient format many of the basic materials on Shimōsa Province. Arrangement is by individual collections, each presented chronologically. Coverage is from earliest times to the end of the sixteenth century.

• 115
Nakayama Hokekyōji shiryō　中山法華経寺史料
Compiled by Nakao Gyō. Tōkyō, 1968.

Documents relating to Shimōsa Province's Nakayama Hokekyō Temple, which received much of its initial support from the Chiba warrior house. Valuable for its portraits of the Nichiren sect and the activities of a great fighting family. The Nakayama Hokekyō Temple served as the guardian temple for the Chiba and received many commended lands. Coverage is Kamakura and Muromachi, with documents arranged chronologically by collection. A major flaw is the absence of notes.

116
Nichiren shū shiryōshū, chūsei hen　日連宗史料集，中世編
Compiled by Nakao Gyō. 2 vols. Tōkyō, 1963.

Generally superseded by the previous entry, but still of value owing to its arrangement of materials: Volume 1 contains documents, Volume 2 inscriptions on wood and stone.

117
Kampukuji monjo　観福寺文書
Compiler not identified. *Shichō* 5.3 (1935/10).

Collection of 47 documents belonging to a local temple in Shimōsa Province. Coverage is exclusively Muromachi. A three-page essay introduces these records.

KAZUSA and AWA PROVINCES (CHIBA PREFECTURE)

Chiba ken shiryō, chūsei hen (shoke monjo), *see* [110]

Chiba ken shiryō, chūsei hen (kengai monjo), *see* [111]

Bōsō sōsho 1, *see* [112]

MUSASHI PROVINCE (TŌKYŌ)

118
Bushū monjo 武州文書
Compiled by Busō shiryō kankōkai. 6 vols. Tōkyō, 1957–60.

A Tokugawa-period assemblage of documents relating to Musashi Province. Coverage is mid-Kamakura to about 1600; but distribution is very uneven. There are only two dozen records dating from Kamakura times. The haphazard arrangement of materials is mitigated by a chronological index appended to the last volume. Soft-cover and very scarce.

• 119
Shimpen Bushū komonjo 新編武州古文書
Compiled by Sugiyama Hiroshi and Hagiwara Tatsuo. 1 vol. to date. Tōkyō, 1975– .

Roughly the first half of [118] in a new hardcover series. A second volume, completing the set, will be published soon.

120
Shimpen Musashi no kuni fudoki kō 新編武蔵国風土記稿
Dai Nihon chishi taikei 7–18. 12 vols. Tōkyō, 1970.

An Edo-period gazetteer containing many of the documents found in [118]. Difficult to use because documents are interspersed with text and there is no index. Not recommended.

121
Musashi shiryō meikishū 武蔵史料銘記集
Compiled by Inamura Tangen. Tōkyō, 1966.

Stone, metal, and wood inscriptions dating from Nara times to the beginning of the Tokugawa age. Arrangement is chronological, and there are a number of photographs. Various tables are appended, as well as a map of the region.

122
Edo shi kankei monjo shū 江戸氏関係文書集
Compiled by Tōkyō to Chiyoda kushi hensan iinkai. Tōkyō, 1957.

A slim volume containing materials on the original warrior house named Edo. They were a prominent fighting family during late Heian times and subsequently became Kamakura vassals. Each document is followed by notes and an explanation.

123
Teshima—Miyagi monjo 豊島－宮城文書
Compiled by Nerima kyōdoshi kenkyūkai. Tōkyō, 1956.

A pamphlet containing 31 Muromachi-period *daimyō* records relating to Musashi

Province. Only 150 copies printed. No notes. A revised 1958 edition adds a few more documents.

124
Iami ke monjo shū　伊阿弥家文書集
Compiled by Nerima kyōdoshi kenkyūkai. Tōkyō, 1960.

A pamphlet containing the records of a sixteenth-century warrior house from Musashi. A genealogical chart and essay are appended. Only 15 documents, but the essay traces the family's roots and relates the house to the emerging Edo Bakufu.

125
Ōta shi kankei monjo shū　太田氏関係文書集
Compiled by Nerima kyōdoshi kenkyūkai. 6 vols. to date. Tōkyō, 1961– .

Mimeographed pamphlets presenting about 200 documents relating to the Ōta *daimyō* house of *sengoku* times. This family, originally from Tamba Province in central Japan, achieved prominence when it moved to the Kantō under sponsorship of the Uesugi. There are extensive notes and valuable essays.

126
Meguro ku shi, shiryō hen　目黒区史，資料編
Compiled by Tōkyō toritsu daigaku gakujutsu kenkyūkai. Tōkyō, 1962.

A massive volume covering primarily the Tokugawa period but containing a handful of sixteenth-century records. Of little value to the medievalist.

127
Setagaya ku shiryō 2　世田谷区史料
Compiled by Setagaya ku. Tōkyō, 1959.

A useful collection of materials relating to a region that later became part of Tōkyō. Coverage is late Kamakura to about 1600, with the sixteenth century predominating. The format is most attractive: documents are arranged by individual collection and presented chronologically; each document is followed by copious notes, often with a photograph of the original; and a comprehensive chronological index is appended. Valuable for the materials themselves rather than for a picture of the early Edo region. The documents are from temple, shrine, and warrior house collections, many available in other volumes.

128
Ōta ku no komonjo, chūsei hen　大田区の古文書，中世編
Compiled by Ōta ku kyōiku iinkai. Tōkyō, 1968.

An assemblage of documents relating to (or housed in) an area that is presently part of Tōkyō. Included are temple, shrine, and warrior-house records with coverage from the late Kamakura age into the sixteenth century. A variety of collections are represented, though the supposed connecting thread—reference to a common area—is strained. A coherent history hardly emerges. Still, a beautifully produced volume, with extensive notes and numerous photographs of documents.

129
Ōmori shūhen no bushi to nōmin—"Ōi monjo" nado o chūshin to shite
大森周辺の武士と農民—「大井文書」等を中心として
Compiled by Sugiyama Hiroshi. *Nihon shiseki ronshū* 2: 261–95 (Iwahashi Koyata hakushi kōju kinenkai).

Essay containing the records of the Ōi warrior house of Musashi. These materials appear also in [128], but they are given much more careful analysis here.

130

Machida shishi shiryōshū 4, chūsei hen 町田市史史料集，中世編
Compiled by Machida shishi henshū iinkai. Tōkyō, 1971.

The written sources and tombstone engravings relating to the medieval Machida region. Chronological arrangement, with useful notes.

131

Fuchū shi ni kansuru chūsei monjo 府中市に関する中世文書
Okuno Takahiro. *Fuchū shi shiryōshū* 4: 3–30. Tōkyō, 1964.

One study in a much larger series dealing with the premodern Fuchū region. Despite the title of this work, it is essentially a monograph built around sources rather than a presentation of documents. The same is true for the other essays in the series. Still, a valuable assemblage of critical studies individually authored by eminent historians. Many documents are contained.

MUSASHI PROVINCE (SAITAMA PREFECTURE)

Bushū monjo, *see* [118]

Shimpen Bushū komonjo, *see* [119]

Shimpen Musashi no kuni fudoki kō, *see* [120]

Musashi shiryō meikishū, *see* [121]

• 132

Saitama no chūsei monjo 埼玉の中世文書
Compiled by Saitama kenritsu toshokan. Urawa, 1965.

A handsomely produced compendium of Musashi Province documents. Photographs of originals are placed above transcriptions. Arrangement is by collection, with a chronological index of records appended. But there are surprisingly few Kamakura-period records, and virtually nothing relating to the Bakufu. Coverage is almost exclusively Muromachi.

• 133

Kumagai ke monjo 熊谷家文書
Compiled by Saitama kenritsu toshokan. Urawa, 1970.

The documents of an eastern warrior house that came to hold landed interests in western Japan under Kamakura Bakufu sponsorship. A collection of major importance. No notes are included, but photographs of each document are placed above the transcribed version. Arrangement is chronological, with one document per page. This is a handsome volume using expensive glossy paper. See also [78].

• 134

Ampo monjo 安保文書
Compiled by Matsumoto Shūji. Tōkyō, 1941.

Small but excellent volume containing the documents of an eastern warrior house that later obtained landed interests in several provinces. Covers the fourteenth century, both before and after the Kamakura Bakufu's demise. We are thus able to follow the shift in loyalties from one regime to the next. Each document is carefully annotated, and there is a well-produced photograph section. A genealogical chart is appended. A rare book.

135
Saido ke monjo　道祖土家文書
Compiled by Kawashima mura kyōiku iinkai. Kawashima (Saitama), 1971.

Sixteenth-century documents addressed to the locally powerful Saido family from the Ōta and Hōjō *daimyō* houses. Includes 26 documents, a historical essay, and explanations of original records, with photographs. Nicely produced short volume.

MUSASHI PROVINCE (KANAGAWA PREFECTURE)

Bushū monjo, *see* [118]

Shimpen Bushū komonjo, *see* [119]

Shimpen Musashi no kuni fudoki kō, *see* [120]

Musashi shiryō meikishū, *see* [121]

Kanagawa kenshi, shiryō hen, *see* [143]

· 136
Kanazawa bunko komonjo　金沢文庫古文書
Compiled by Seki Yasushi. 2 vols. Yokohama, 1937–43.

The documents of one of the great archives in eastern Japan. The records presented come close to being a Hōjō house document collection. Volume 1 contains materials relating to the Hōjō conduct of Kamakura Bakufu governance, and Volume 2 consists of the private letters of one of the last members of that clan before the Bakufu's downfall. Volume 1 also presents valuable materials on the Kamakura region (in adjacent Sagami) after 1333. Brief headnotes are included and the series is handsomely produced. These are rare books. See also [137] and [143].

· 137
Kanazawa bunko komonjo　金沢文庫古文書
Compiled by Seki Yasushi. 12 vols. Yokohama, 1952–61.

Volume 7 is an updated version of the original *Kanazawa bunko komonjo,* and Volume 1 is an update of the original Volume 2. Presents many new documents and corrects earlier errors. The other volumes in the series also contain medieval records, though Volume 7 is clearly the most important. No notes and no table of contents; but an index of personal names and place names was added later (*Kanazawa bunko komonjo sakuin,* 1964). Five other volumes (13–17) treat the Tokugawa age. An indispensable series, though difficult to use.

138
Kanazawa ibun　金沢遺文
Compiled by Ōya Tokushiro. 3 vols. 1934.

Only in Volume 3 are there materials that truly qualify as documents: private letters from members of the Kanazawa family, a branch of the Kamakura Hōjō. Unfortunately, the documents are not transcribed, and only photographs are presented. The first part of the volume, however, offers notes concerning each record. Beautifully produced but difficult to use. Portfolio size. A rare series.

139
Kanazawa bunko "Shingi hiden Hachiman" no shihai monjo
金沢文庫「神祇秘伝八幡」の紙背文書
Compiled by Nodomi Jōten. *Kanazawa bunko kenkyū* 154 (1969): 12–17.

Brief selection of documents copied on the reverse side of a traditional text. These records, which deal with Shintō practices, date from late Kamakura times. (The monthly journal *Kanazawa bunko kenkyū* regularly introduces or discusses newly transcribed documents.)

140
Bushū Shōmyōji komonjo 武州稱名寺古文書
Compiled by Seki Yasushi. Chiba, 1935.

Collection of late Kamakura and Nambokuchō documents from Shōmyōji Temple. Useful notes, with much on political conditions in the final years of the Kamakura Bakufu.

141
Yokohama shiritsu daigaku toshokan shozō no komonjo ni tsuite
横浜市立大学図書館所蔵の古文書について
Compiled by Fukuda Ikuo. *Yokohama shiritsu daigaku ronsō* 23.2 (1972): 75–96.

Description of the documents held by Yokohama City University, but also contains examples of the records themselves. Most come from the late Heian period, but there are several from the early Kamakura age.

142
Kawasaki shiiki ni kansuru chūsei shiryō ni tsuite
川崎市域に関する中世史料について
Compiled by Sawaki Eichi. *Miura kobunka* 13 (1973): 41–51.

Essay presenting documents from the region of Kawasaki City. Materials and analysis are divided by individual administrative units (*shōen* and *gō*). The records themselves range from the thirteenth to the fifteenth centuries.

SAGAMI PROVINCE (KANAGAWA PREFECTURE)

• 143
Kanagawa kenshi, shiryō hen, kodai-chūsei
神奈川県史, 資料編, 古代－中世
Compiled by Kanagawa ken kikaku chōsabu kenshi henshūshitsu. 3 vols. to date. Yokohama, 1971– .

An indispensable work for the study of the Kamakura Bakufu and eastern Japan in general. Sagami was the home province of the Kamakura regime. Coverage in Volume 1 is from earliest times to 1277, and Volume 2 carries the story to 1333, the year of the Bakufu's demise. Volume 3 continues to 1440. There are no notes, but the volumes are unusually comprehensive, containing both documents and other source excerpts. A description of all pre-Kamakura materials is included in a special section of Volume 1. A final Muromachi volume is expected soon.

• 144
Kamakura shishi, shiryō hen 鎌倉市史, 史料編
Compiled by Kamakura shishi hensan iinkai. 3 vols. Kamakura, 1956–58.

Indispensable for the study of the Kamakura region during medieval times. Contains the documents of the many religious institutions in that city. Of great value for understanding both the nature of the Hōjō hold over the Kamakura Bakufu, and the Kantō administrative office under the Muromachi regime. Arrangement is by individual collection, with useful headnotes. The various temples and shrines whose documents are presented are treated historically in a separate volume in this series, the *shaji hen*, or "shrine-temple volume." Appended to that book are 66 pages of documents not included in the main *shiryō* section. Recently reprinted.

145
Kamakura shishi shiryō shō 鎌倉市史史料抄
Compiled by Takayanagi Mitsutoshi. 10 vols. Kamakura, 1954–56.

Soft-cover mimeographed series that contains a significant portion of the documents appearing in [144], which supersedes it.

• 146
Kaitei shimpen Sōshū komonjo 改訂新編相州古文書
Compiled by Nuki Tatsuto. 5 vols. Tōkyō, 1965–70.

A Tokugawa-period compilation of documents relating to Sagami Province. Arrangement is by district, and only Volume 2 contains a sizable number of Kamakura-period records. The remaining volumes are almost wholly Muromachi, with the sixteenth century predominant. Volume 5 contains a chronological listing of all records. There are no notes.

147
Shimpen Sōshū komonjo 1 新編相州古文書
Compiled by Aida Nirō. Tōkyō, 1944.

The first volume in a *Sōshū komonjo* series that was never completed. Soft-cover. Includes the documents from Kamakura District (*gun*).

148
Shimpen Sagami no kuni fudoki kō 新編相模国風土記稿
Dai Nihon chishi taikei 19–24. 6 vols. Tōkyō, 1970.

An Edo-period work containing various medieval documents within a gazetteer text. Coverage is weighted in favor of the sixteenth century, though some Kamakura records appear. All of the documents presented appear also in [146]. Difficult to use, since there are no notes or index.

• 149
Azuma kagami 吾妻鏡
Shintei zōho kokushi taikei. 4 vols. Tōkyō, 1968.

The famous chronicle of the Kamakura Bakufu, covering the years 1180–1266. Contains numerous documents, which are reproduced in full. Interestingly, the period of greatest concentration for these records is the decade after 1185.

150
Tsurugaoka Hachimangū komonjo shū 鶴岡八幡宮古文書集
Compiled by Tsurugaoka Hachiman shamusho. 2 vols. Kamakura, 1928.

Photographs of documents from the patron shrine of the Kamakura Bakufu. The earliest record dates from 1183. Transcriptions of the full collection appear in [144] and [151].

151
Tsurugaoka Hachimangū monjo 鶴岡八幡宮文書
Compiled by Kamakura shishi hensan iinkai. Kamakura, 1958.

The Tsurugaoka-related portion of *Kamakura shishi, shiryō hen* 1 [144]. An extremely important collection, with much on the Bakufu and conditions in Kamakura. Coverage extends to Muromachi times.

152
Kamakura chihō zōzō kankei shiryō　鎌倉地方造像関係資料
Compiled by Miyama Susumu. 7 vols. to date. Kamakura, 1968– .

Pamphlets containing statue and tombstone inscriptions from the region of the Bakufu capital. Also contains chronicle and documentary references to statues being cast or presented. Chronological arrangement, with coverage beginning in Kamakura times.

153
Ōba mikuriya monjo　大庭御厨文書
Compiled by Nishigaki Seiji. *Fujisawa shishi kenkyū* (1972): 97–100.

Presents a handful of records relating to an Ise Shrine tribute estate in Sagami Province. The documents date from late Kamakura times. Interesting materials.

154
Sōunji monjo　早雲寺文書
Compiled by Fukuda Ikuo. *Hakone no bunkazai* 5. Hakone, 1970.

Pamphlet containing 23 documents from a small temple in Sagami. Coverage is exclusively Muromachi, mostly the sixteenth century. Special features are a photograph of each document presented, plus a rendering into Japanese, a summary, and an analysis. Sōunji was named after the progenitor of the Later Hōjō, Hōjō Sōun.

155
Odawara shi no komonjo—Renjōin monjo　小田原市の古文書－蓮上院文書
Compiled by Odawara shi kyōiku iinkai. Odawara, 1972.

A collection of 51 documents, of which roughly half date from the sixteenth century and half from Tokugawa times. An exemplary format: photograph, transcription, and analysis. The medieval records relate to the Later Hōjō.

156
Odawara oyobi Hakone shiryō　小田原及び箱根史料
Compiled by Ishino Ei. Yokohama, 1932.

Mostly Tokugawa materials and commentary, but contains a number of sixteenth-century records in a separate photograph section. These documents deal mostly with the Later Hōjō. Recently reprinted. (This volume is one of a ten-volume series entitled *Busō sōshō*. From their titles, several of the other volumes evidently contain medieval records; however, I have not been able to examine them.)

• 157
Hōjō Ujiteru monjo shū　北条氏照文書集
Compiled by Shimoyama Haruhisa (Go-Hōjō shi kenkyūkai). Tōkyō, 1970.

The sixteenth-century documents relating to *daimyō* Hōjō Ujiteru. Drawn from various collections, these records tell the story of the warrior whose elimination (with his brothers) in 1590 permitted Hideyoshi to dominate the entire country. Chronological arrangement, with an explanatory essay, a chronology, and an index.

• 158
Hōjō Ujikuni monjo shū　北条氏邦文書集
Compiled by Shimoyama Haruhisa (Go-Hōjō shi kenkyūkai). Tōkyō, 1970.

Same as [157], but centered around the life of Hōjō Ujikuni, a brother of the chief Hōjō *daimyō*, Ujimasa.

159
Sōshū Tamanawa jōshu—Tamanawa Hōjō shi monjo shū
相州玉繩城主－玉繩北条氏文書集
Compiled by Satō Hironobu (Go-Hōjō shi kenkyūkai). Tōkyō, 1970.

The sixteenth-century documents relating to the branch of the Later Hōjō whose
power centered in Tamanawa Castle. A lengthy essay is appended, along with a
chronology and name and place indexes.

160
Sengoku monjo shūei—Go-Hōjō shi hen 戦国文書聚影－後北条氏篇
Compiled by Sugiyama Hiroshi et al. (Sengoku monjo kenkyūkai). Tōkyō,
1973.

Photographs of representative documents of the Later Hōjō *daimyō* house, along
with transcriptions and notes. The photographs are excellent and the overall production is highly effective. Exclusively sixteenth-century.

161
Hōjō Ujinao to Kōshitsu-in monjo 1–2   北条氏直と高室院文書
Compiled by Zama Mitsuji. *Kanazawa bunko kenkyū* 113–114 (1965/6,
1965/7): 1–5, 1–6.

Brief selection of documents (with an accompanying essay) relating to the career
of the great *sengoku daimyō* Hōjō Ujinao.

162
Sagami no kuni no komonjo   相模国の古文書
Compiled by Aida Nirō. *Rekishi chiri* 62.2 (1933): 59–63.

A handful of documents from two sixteenth-century collections relating to the
Later Hōjō. Fully annotated.

163
Sagamihara shishi 5   相模原市史
Compiled by Sagamihara shishi hensan iinkai. Sagamihara, 1965.

The documents relating to the region of present-day Sagamihara City. Treatment
is thin, but each document is followed by explanatory notes. Coverage centers
on the sixteenth century and the Tokugawa age. A well-produced, attractive
volume.

164
Fujisawa shishi 1, shiryō hen   藤沢市史，資料編
Compiled by Fujisawa shishi hensan iinkai. Fujisawa, 1970.

Source materials of various kinds relating to the area of Fujisawa near Kamakura.
The medieval section contains only documents from the 1580's and 1590's. A photograph of each record is included, along with an analysis. Other sections in the
volume deal with archaeology, stone and metal inscriptions from historic times,
and written records from Tokugawa times.

165
Atsugi shishi shiryōshū 6, chūsei monjo hen   厚木市史史料集，中世文書編
Compiled by Atsugi shishi hensan iinkai. Atsugi, 1974.

Presents some 104 documents relating to medieval Atsugi. A special feature of
this volume is the rendering into Japanese of some of the materials contained.
There are also extensive notes plus genealogies. Chronological arrangement. An-

other volume in this series (*Chūsei kinseki hen*) presents tombstone inscriptions dating from medieval times.

Tōkai-Tōsan Region

KAI PROVINCE (YAMANASHI PREFECTURE)

• 166

Shimpen Kōshū komonjo　新編甲州古文書

Edited by Ogino Minahiko and Saitō Shunroku. 3 vols. Tōkyō, 1966.

A Tokugawa-period compilation of Kai Province documents dating mostly from the late Muromachi age; only a handful of Kamakura records. A chronological index is appended to Volume 3. Remains the standard series for Kai Province.

• 167

Kai Takeda shi monjo shū　甲斐武田氏文書集

Compiled by Takashima Rokuo (Chihōshi kenkyū kyōgikai). Tōkyō, 1965.

Documents relating to the Takeda *daimyō* house. Coverage begins in the 1330's. A comprehensive hardback edition was announced several years ago but has not yet appeared. An important collection.

168

Sengoku monjo shūei—Takeda shi hen　戦国文書聚影－武田氏篇

Compiled by Satō Hachirō et al. (Sengoku monjo kenkyūkai). Tōkyō, 1973.

Photographs of representative sixteenth-century documents of the Takeda *daimyō* house with transcriptions and notes. The photographs are of the highest quality, and the overall production is most effective.

SHINANO PROVINCE (NAGANO PREFECTURE)

• 169

Shinano shiryō　信濃史料

Compiled by Shinano shiryō kankōkai. 30 vols. Nagano, 1956–67.

The most exhaustive collection of source materials (not merely documents) on any single province. Treatment is chronological, with Volumes 3–5 covering the Kamakura age. Volumes 5–28 contain Muromachi records, and the final two volumes present materials that were missed earlier. A unique feature of this compilation is the rendering of all entries from Chinese into Japanese, which is given alongside the original. A monumental work of scholarship, indispensable for the study of medieval Shinano.

170

Oku Shinano komonjo　奥信濃古文書

Compiled by Shinano kyōikukai Shimo-takai bukai. 1937.

An assemblage of documents relating to Shinano Province. Very hard to use, with an all but impenetrable format. Coverage is Kamakura into Tokugawa. Not recommended.

171

Suwa komonjo shū　諏訪古文書集

Compiled by Suwa shiryō sōsho kankōkai (*Suwa shiryō sōsho* 15–16). 2 vols. Nagano, 1931.

The documents relating to a well-known shrine and its landholdings. Arrangement is by separate collections, but a chronological listing of all documents is appended to the second volume. Coverage is principally Muromachi, with special concentration on the sixteenth century and the Suwa *daimyō* house. But the majority of the Kamakura documents included are Bakufu-related and therefore also of great interest. The transcriptions contain some errors. A rare series.

172
Moriya monjo 守矢文書
Compiled by Shinano shiryō kankōkai. *Shimpen Shinano shiryō sōsho 7*: 3–55. Nagano, 1972.

Documents from the collection of the Moriya family, which held an important position within the Suwa Shrine hierarchy. Coverage is mid-Kamakura to Tokugawa, and there is much of interest for the earlier period.

173
Shinano no kuni mikuriya shiryō to sono kōsatsu 信濃国御厨史料とその考察
Compiled by Ichishi Shigeki. Nagano, 1936.

Source materials and commentary relating to the estate holdings of Ise Shrine in Shinano. Coverage is from late Heian times to the end of the sixteenth century, and some valuable documents are contained. This is a rare book.

174
Minamisaku gun no komonjo—kinseki bun 南佐久郡の古文書－金石文
Compiled by Minamisaku kyōikukai. Usuda (Nagano), 1938.

A handsomely produced volume containing documents and stone engravings from late medieval and Tokugawa times. The documents all date from the sixteenth century, and each is accompanied by notes and a photograph of the original.

175
Sanada monjo shū 眞田文書集
Compiled by Fujisawa Naoshi. Ueda (Nagano), 1930.

Documents relating to the Sanada *daimyō* house of Shinano. The 152 records all date from the late sixteenth and early seventeenth centuries, when the Sanada were a major force. Brief headnotes and various photographs are included.

• 176
Ichikawa monjo 市川文書
Compiled by Shinano shiryō kankōkai (*Shimpen shinano shiryō sōsho 3*: 1–60). Nagano, 1971.

One of the most interesting of all medieval document collections. Details the rise of a warrior family from the end of the Heian age into the Muromachi. The shift of patronage to the Kamakura Bakufu is vividly described, as is the Ichikawa effort to win greater control locally. Highly recommended. Also appeared as a separate pamphlet with no publishing details given.

177
Ikushima Tarujima jinja monjo 生島足島神社文書
Compiled by Shinano shiryō kankōkai. *Shimpen Shinano shiryō sōsho 1*: 347–412. Nagano, 1970.

Document collection exclusively from the years 1556–57. All of the 91 records appear to be pledges (*kishōmon*) by warriors to perform certain tasks on behalf of shrine interests.

178
Rengejō-in monjo 蓮華定院文書
Compiled by Shinano shiryō kankōkai. *Shimpen Shinano shiryō sōsho* 1: 423–58. Nagano, 1970.

Collection of Kōyasan-related documents from the fifteenth century to the end of Tokugawa. Many of these came to be housed in the Shinano region; hence their inclusion in this volume.

IZU PROVINCE (SHIZUOKA PREFECTURE)

• 179
Shizuoka ken shiryō 静岡県史料
Compiled by Shizuoka ken. 5 vols. Shizuoka, 1932–41.

A massive compilation of documents relating to Izu (Vol. 1), Suruga (Vols. 1–3), and Tōtomi provinces (Vols. 4–5). Arrangement is by collection, keyed to the various districts within the three provinces. Coverage is overwhelmingly Muromachi, though a number of useful Kamakura records are included. An index of materials (again by collection) is appended to each volume. Handsomely produced, and indispensable for the areas treated. Recently reprinted.

180
Itō ke monjo shū 伊東家文書集
Compiled by Nerima kyōdoshi kenkyūkai. Tōkyō, 1957.

Contains 32 Muromachi documents relating to a warrior family of eastern Japan. Though originating in Izu Province, the Itō house was active in Suruga during the fourteenth century. A summarizing essay is appended. Published in a limited mimeographed edition of 120 copies.

SURUGA PROVINCE (SHIZUOKA PREFECTURE)

Shizuoka ken shiryō 1–3, *see* [179]

Itō ke monjo shū, *see* [180]

181
Sengen monjo san 浅間文書纂
Compiled by Fuji Ōmiya Sengen jinja shamusho. Ōmiya (Shizuoka), 1931.

The documents of a shrine in Suruga Province. Coverage is from the 1330's into the Tokugawa with a good selection of *daimyō* records. Recently reprinted.

182
Shimizu shishi shiryō, chūsei hen 清水市史資料, 中世篇
Compiled by Shimizu shishi hensan iinkai. Tōkyō, 1972.

The medieval documents relating to a portion of Suruga Province. Contains only a handful of Kamakura records, with the great majority of materials dating from the sixteenth century. Arrangement is by the location of individual document collections, but a chronological index is appended. Also included are lists of terms, personal names, and place names—a valuable feature.

183
Gotemba shishi 1, kodai-chūsei-kinsei shiryō
御殿場市史, 古代 – 中世 – 近世史料

Compiled by Fukuda Ikuo (Gotemba shishi hensan iinkai). Gotemba, 1974.

Nearly 900 pages of sources relating to the Gotemba region at the foot of Mt. Fuji. Concentration is naturally on the later centuries, but considerable space is devoted to the medieval age, especially the *sengoku* period. Many photographs of original documents are included, and there are ample notes. Arrangement is chronological.

184
Sengoku daimyō Imagawa shi no kenkyū to komonjo
戦国大名今川氏の研究と古文書
Compiled by Kowada Tetsuo (Suruga komonjo kai). Shizuoka, 1974.

A pamphlet containing sixteenth-century documents relating to the Imagawa *daimyō* house. A total of 23 records, each with a photograph of the original and a rendering of the transcription into Japanese. An essay introduces these materials.

TŌTOMI PROVINCE (SHIZUOKA PREFECTURE)

Shizuoka ken shiryō 4–5, *see* [179]

• 185
Tōtomi no kuni goshinryō ki   遠江国御神領記
Zoku gunsho ruijū, 33.1: 503–39. Tōkyō, 1958.

A highly interesting assemblage of land records dating mostly from the Kamakura period. Testamentary and land-sale documents seem to predominate. Most of the records deal with tribute estates of Ise Shrine in Tōtomi. Unfortunately, the arrangement of materials is haphazard, and there are no notes. About 100 documents in total.

186
Hamamatsu shishi, shiryō hen 2   浜松市史，史料編
Compiled by Hamamatsu shiyakusho. Hamamatsu, 1959.

A scattering of documents drawn directly from the *Shizuoka ken shiryō* [179]. Of limited value. Six additional records appear in *Nihon rekishi* 300 (1973): 194–98.

MINO PROVINCE (GIFU PREFECTURE)

• 187
Gifu kenshi, kodai-chūsei shiryō   岐阜県史，古代－中世史料
Compiled by Gifu ken. 4 vols. Gifu, 1969–72.

An outstanding collection of materials, beautifully produced. Volume 1 contains over 1,000 pages of medieval documents drawn from the collections of Gifu warrior houses and religious institutions. Volume 2 contains other types of historical materials, plus an addendum with documents not included in Volume 1. Volume 3 contains the documents (arranged chronologically) of two Mino estates, Ōi and Akanabe, both Tōdaiji proprietorships established during Heian times. There are more than 1,000 documents bearing on Ōi, and nearly 500 relating to Akanabe. An ideal source for studying the estate system. Volume 4 contains documents stored in other prefectures that relate in some way to the Gifu region. Virtually every part of Japan is represented. Each volume contains brief descriptions of the collections presented (where housed, number of materials, etc.). There are no dates appended to individual documents, no index of place or personal names, and no overall chronological index; but this hardly diminishes from the importance of the work. Taken as a whole, the Gifu series is one of the finest of all prefectural efforts.

188
Mino no kuni shiryō　美濃国史料
Compiled by Abe Einosuke and Katano Nukushi (Mino shiryō kankōkai).
2 vols. Gifu, 1934–37.

Handsome volumes containing a variety of source materials (documents, monument inscriptions, etc.) relating to (or drawn from) Gunjō District (Volume 1) and Inaba District and Gifu City (Volume 2). An index of personal names, place names, temples, shrines, etc., is appended to each volume, along with numerous photographs. The coverage is 90 percent Muromachi. A portion of Volume 1 relating to Chōryūji Temple was published separately in 1933.

189
Saitō Dōzan monjo no kenkyū　斉藤道三文書之研究
Compiled by Matsuda Ryō. Gifu, 1974.

An interesting volume containing documents and other sources relating to a famous *sengoku daimyō* who became the father-in-law of Oda Nobunaga. A chronological arrangement (1494–1556) and copious annotations assist the user. There is much valuable background material on the Mino region during the *sengoku* age.

190
Ōgaki shishi 2　大垣市史
Compiled by Ōgaki shiyakusho. Ōgaki, 1931.

Contains nearly 300 documents relating to Ōi Estate in the region of Ōgaki City. A detailed chronology is appended along with a full index of names and terms. Should be used in conjunction with Volume 3 of [187].

191
Kōhon Ena gun shiryō　稿本恵那郡史料
Compiled by Yokoyama Sumio. 1972

An assemblage of 306 documents relating principally to Ena District in Mino Province. The materials are drawn from various collections and are arranged chronologically. Coverage is from the 1330's to early Tokugawa times. Useful notes are included, and citations are given when documents have appeared in other volumes. A special feature is an index of temple, shrine, and personal names.

192
Yōrō chōshi, shiryō hen 1　養老町史，史料編
Compiled by Yōrō chō. Yōrō, 1974.

Contains 34 pages of documents relating to a small portion of medieval Mino Province. Coverage begins in the 1330's and is chronological. The bulk of the volume presents Tokugawa sources.

193
Nambokuchō nairanki no ichi sojō　南北朝内乱期の一訴状
Compiled by Tanuma Mutsumi. *Gekkan rekishi* 34 (1971): 1–5.

A series of documents submitted by a lawsuit plaintiff of 1339. The documents go back to early Kamakura times and relate to Funagi Estate in Mino Province. An interesting sequence.

194
Mino Ryūshōji monjo ni tsuite　美濃立政寺文書について
Compiled by Suma Chikai. *Shigaku zasshi* 78.6 (1969): 56–77.

Brief collection of documents (mostly Muromachi) belonging to a local temple in Mino. The majority of these records deal with the transfer of land rights, whether by commendation, sale, or testament. The materials are carefully analyzed in an accompanying essay.

OWARI PROVINCE (AICHI PREFECTURE)

• 195
Aichi kenshi (bekkan)　愛知県史，別巻
Compiled by Aichi ken. Tōkyō, 1939.

A compendium of documents and other sources relating to Owari and Mikawa provinces. Arrangement is by subject: the emergence of *shōen*, the development of Buddhism, the condition of commerce and industry, etc. The format is unwieldy, but there are numerous important records. Coverage is from earliest times through the Tokugawa. Brief headnotes are included, but there is no index or adequate table of contents.

• 196
Ichinomiya shishi, shiryō hen 5–6　一宮市史，資料編
Compiled by Iyanaga Teizō (Ichinomiya shishi hensanshitsu). Ichinomiya, 1963–70.

In the absence of an up-to-date history of Aichi Prefecture, this series is the best source available, at least for Owari. Contains many fascinating documents hitherto unpublished. Of special note are the materials dealing with land sale during late Kamakura times. Volume 5 presents the records of Myōkōji Temple; Volume 6 contains documents housed in Ichinomiya City, relevant documents located elsewhere in Aichi Prefecture, and relevant documents housed outside Aichi. An important work.

197
Sanage jinja monjo　猿投神社文書
Compiled by Ōta Masahiro and Murata Masashi (*Aichi ken shiryō sōkan*). Nagoya, 1968.

The materials of a shrine in Owari Province. Limited coverage of the Kamakura period. Most sources date from Muromachi times, and one section of the book contains documents in original script only, without transcriptions. Also included are nondocumentary sources such as chronicles and gravestone inscriptions.

198
Atsuta jingū shiryō, chōshū zasshi shō　熱田神宮史料，張州雑志抄
Compiled by Atsuta jingū gūchō. Nagoya, 1969.

Contains a portion of the traditional texts of Atsuta Shrine. However, the materials have not been transcribed, but are merely reproduced from originals without notes of any kind. The arrangement is also confusing, though much of interest can be found. Numerous Kamakura and Muromachi documents are scattered throughout. There is a detailed table of contents.

199
Tajima shi monjo 田島氏文書
Compiled by Ozaki Hisaya. Nagoya, 1937.

Materials relating to an official family of Atsuta Shrine. Coverage is Kamakura into Tokugawa. Unfortunately, there are numerous errors, and the arrangement of documents is difficult to follow. Introductory essay and photograph section.

200
Seto shinai shozai shiryō 瀬戸市内所在史料
Compiled by Ōta Masahiro and Murata Masashi (*Aichi ken shiryō sōkan*). Nagoya, 1969.

Pamphlet containing a handful of medieval documents housed in temples and shrines in Seto City. Thin coverage and therefore of limited use.

201
Inuyama-Komaki shinai shozai shiryō 犬山－小枚市内所在史料
Compiled by Ōta Masahiro and Murata Masashi (*Aichi ken shiryō sōkan*). Nagoya, 1973.

Pamphlet containing records and gravestone inscriptions from two Owari area cities. Coverage mostly Muromachi; of limited use.

202
Tsushima shinai shozai shiryō 津島市内所在史料
Compiled by Ōta Masahiro and Murata Masashi (*Aichi ken shiryō sōkan*). Nagoya, 1971.

Same format as [201] but decidedly more interesting. A variety of documents are included, most notably a handful of Oda Nobunaga decrees.

203
Owari no kuni izon Oda Nobunaga shiryō shashin shū
尾張国遺存織田信長史料写真集
Compiled by Wakayama Zenzaburō. Nagoya, 1931.

A selection of documents written by or relating to Oda Nobunaga. These materials are in the ideal format: photograph, transcription, and analysis.

204
Owari no kuni izon Toyotomi Hideyoshi shiryō shashin shū
尾張国遺存豊臣秀吉史料写真集
Compiled by Wakayama Zenzaburō. Nagoya, 1934.

Same as [203] but with Hideyoshi as the subject.

205
Miyoshi Sakai ke—Komaki Ezaki ke monjo shō
三好酒井家－小枚江崎家文書抄
Compiled by Nagoya shi Hōsei nikō kenshōkan. Nagoya, 1974.

The sixteenth- and seventeenth-century documents of two local warrior houses, featuring relations with Oda Nobunaga and his family. Some 60 records; no notes.

206
Owari no kuni Horio-Nagaoka ryōshō no sakai sōron monjo—shoryō bu shozō "Sangun yōryaku shō" shihai
尾張国堀尾－長岡両庄の堺相論文書－書陵部所蔵「参軍要略抄」紙背

Compiled by Iikura Harutake. *Komonjo kenkyū* 3 (1970): 106–17.

A collection of 27 Kamakura-period documents dealing with a boundary dispute between two *shōen* in Owari. Interesting materials.

MIKAWA PROVINCE (AICHI PREFECTURE)

Aichi kenshi (bekkan), *see* [194]

Miyoshi Sakai ke—Komaki Ezaki ke monjo shō, *see* [205]

207
Toyohashi shishi 5　豊橋市史
Compiled by Toyohashi shishi hensan iinkai. Toyohashi, 1974.

The history of medieval Toyohashi through documents and other sources. The first section of the book is devoted to chronicles and diaries, but Part II contains 179 documents. Coverage of these records is from the 1330's into the sixteenth century. Numerous photographs of original documents are included. A third section contains tombstone inscriptions.

208
Toyoda shinai shozai shiryō　豊田市内所在史料
Compiled by Ōta Masahiro and Murata Masachi (*Aichi ken shiryō sōkan*). Nagoya, 1972.

Pamphlet containing documents and gravestone inscriptions located in Toyoda City. Coverage almost exclusively Muromachi.

HIDA PROVINCE (GIFU PREFECTURE)

Gifu kenshi, kodai-chūsei shiryō 1, 2, 4, *see* [187]

IGA PROVINCE (MIE PREFECTURE)

209
Sangoku chishi　三国地志
Dai Nihon chishi taikei 32–33. 2 vols. Tōkyō, 1970.

A seventeenth-century gazetteer for the provinces of Iga, Ise, and Shima. Contains a number of early and medieval documents (some originals of which have subsequently been lost). For Iga Province, the Tōdaiji records are outstanding.

• 210
Iga no kuni Kuroda-no-shō shiryō 1　伊賀国黒田荘史料
Compiled by Takeuchi Rizō (*Shōen shiryō sōsho*). Tōkyō, 1975.

Presents the Nara and Heian period documents of one of the most widely studied of all *shōen*, Kuroda of Iga, a Tōdaiji proprietorship. Some 252 documents are contained, with coverage to 1145. Indispensable for the study of the developing medieval estate system. A second volume is expected soon.

ISE PROVINCE (MIE PREFECTURE)

Kaburaya Ise hōki, *see* [110]

Sangoku chishi, *see* [209]

211
Kōtai jingū kenkyū ika komonjo 皇太神宮建久已下古文書
Compiled by Nishigaki Seiji. 3 vols. Tōkyō, 1971.

Three small pamphlets containing documents relating to Ise Shrine. Coverage is principally early Kamakura, with many records dating from the 1190's. Most materials deal with internal shrine affairs, but there are references to Ise's numerous landholdings. No notes, but a brief essay is appended to Volume 3.

SHIMA PROVINCE (MIE PREFECTURE)

Sangoku chishi, *see* [209]

212
Kunisaki Kambe monjo 国崎神戸文書
Compiled by Kōgakukan daigaku komonjo kenkyūkai. *Kōgakukan ronsō* 5.3 (1972): 59–64.

Brief collection of documents (mostly Kamakura), largely dealing with violations of fishing rights on shrine lands in Shima Province. Unusual materials.

Hokuriku Region

ECHIGO PROVINCE (NIIGATA PREFECTURE)

Uesugi ke monjo, *see* [77]

• 213
Essa shiryō 越佐史料
Compiled by Takahashi Yoshihiko. 7 vols. Niigata, 1925–31.

Historical materials relating to Echigo and Sado provinces, arranged chronologically. Entries of importance are introduced by a sentence or two. Volumes 1 and 2 cover up to the mid-fifteenth century, and Volumes 3–6 continue to 1584. Volume 7 is a chronological index. Despite its age, this series is of considerable value, with numerous documents of great interest. Recently reprinted.

• 214
Echigo monjo hōkanshū—Yahiko monjo 越後文書宝翰集－彌彦文書
Compiled by Satō Shin'ichi and Miya Eiji (Niigata ken kyōiku iinkai, *Niigata ken bunkazai chōsa hōkoku sho* 2). Niigata, 1954.

Part One is a valuable compendium of 18 document collections relating to Echigo Province. Land administration and warrior encroachments are the main subjects here, with coverage from the thirteenth to the sixteenth centuries. There are useful essays describing the major collections. Part Two (compiled by Miya Eiji) presents the documents of Yahiko Shrine, along with essays, genealogies, charts, tables, and photographs. The documents here, too, though few in number, are of considerable interest, covering the Kamakura to Tokugawa periods. Part Two of this book (and apparently Part One as well) was also published separately. An important work.

• 215
Okuyama-no-shō shiryōshū 奥山荘史料集
Compiled by Inoue Toshio (Niigata ken kyōiku iinkai, *Niigata ken bunkazai chōsa hōkoku sho* 10). Niigata, 1965.

An interesting compendium of more than 500 documents relating to a *shōen* in Echigo Province. Okuyama Estate received a *jitō* in 1192, and before long the appointee's family clashed with the absentee *shōen* holder. There were also inheritance disputes within the *jitō* house.

216
Irobe shiryōshū 色部史料集
Compiled by Inoue Toshio (Niigata shigakkai). Niigata, 1968.

Documents relating to a warrior family and its home area in Echigo Province. Contains Kamakura testamentary records and a variety of *jitō*-related material. A useful background essay is appended, along with an index and a chronological listing of all documents. A special feature is the occasional rendering of documents from Chinese into Japanese.

217
Uesugi ke gohanmotsu 上杉家御判物
Compiled by Chōkyūzan Honseiji. Sanjō (Niigata), 1974.

Pamphlet containing 27 documents relating to the great Uesugi *daimyō* house. Covers the fifteenth and sixteenth centuries. Most of the records were issued by the Uesugi, who were *shugo* of Echigo at this time, or by the Nagao, who were their deputies (*shugodai*). There are no notes; but photographs accompany each transcription, and there is a brief introductory essay. *See also* [77], [81], and [218].

218
Hokuetsu chūsei monjo 北越中世文書
Compiled by Satō Shin'ichi et al. Tōkyō, 1975.

Contains some 230-odd documents relating to the rise of the Uesugi *daimyō* house. Coverage is overwhelmingly sixteenth-century, with only a dozen documents dating from Kamakura times. Special features include a photograph of each record (though the quality is poor), useful notes, and essays describing the several document collections represented.

219
Hirako monjo 平子文書
Compiled by Ishii Kōtarō. *Kyōdo Yokohama* 20: 1–32 (1960).

A collection of 52 documents relating to a warrior house of Echigo. This family began as Kamakura *jitō* and developed interests as well in Suō Province far to the west. Coverage is from late Kamakura times into the sixteenth century, with most records dating from the later period. Numerous *daimyō* documents from the Uesugi house are included. Chronological arrangement with a genealogical chart appended.

SADO PROVINCE (NIIGATA PREFECTURE)

Essa shiryō, *see* [213]

220
Sado kokushi 佐渡国誌
Compiled by Niigata ken Sado gun'yakusho. Tōkyō, 1973.

Contains a sizable number of medieval documents, arranged as a gazetteer. The breakdown is by topic, however, rather than by geographical division. Thus there are separate groupings for materials on Bakufu administration, local officials, and so on.

221
Sado Honma ibun Sakurai ke monjo　佐渡本間遺文桜井家文書
Compiled by Shimode Sekiyo. Kanazawa, 1966.

Contains a variety of different source types, with much on the Tokugawa period. There are also documents dating from earlier times. A few Kamakura-period records, for example, show *jitō* appointments and the Bakufu's execution of justice. Photographs of documents are scattered throughout.

ETCHŪ PROVINCE (TOYAMA PREFECTURE)

• 222
Toyama kenshi, shiryō hen 2, chūsei　富山県史，　史料編，　中世
Compiled by Toyama ken. Toyama, 1975.

The historical sources (not merely documents) of medieval Etchū Province, arranged chronologically. Newly published and indispensable for the area treated. Almost 1,400 pages, covering the years 1185–1582. An index of source collections is appended, and there are useful headnotes. An earlier volume in the series, the *shiryō hen 1, kodai* (1970) presents historical materials to 1185.

223
Etchū shiryō　越中史料
Compiled by Toyama ken. 4 vols. Toyama, 1909.

Long the standard compendium of sources relating to Etchū Province, this series is now superseded by [222]. Spotty coverage, with many errors. The brief Kamakura section is in Volume 1. Modeled after the *Dai Nihon shiryō* [4] and recently reprinted.

224
Etchū kobunshō　越中古文抄
Compiled by Tobimi Takeshige. Takaoka, 1956.

A massive volume of documents and other source excerpts relating to Etchū Province. Coverage is thin, however, for the Heian and Kamakura periods, and the book is not generally well regarded. Arrangement is chronological. Predominantly Tokugawa treatment.

225
Etchū Tateyama komonjo　越中立山古文書
Compiled by Kigura Toyonobu. Toyama, 1962.

Contains a handful of Muromachi documents, but coverage is mostly Tokugawa. Photographs of some records are included, and there is an accompanying essay.

226
Yao Monmyōji komonjo　八尾聞名寺古文書
Compiled by Kigura Toyonobu. Toyama, 1940.

Pamphlet containing the records of a local temple in Etchū. Coverage is the sixteenth century and beyond.

227
Habu gokoku Hachimangū monjo　埴生護国八幡宮文書
Compiled by Kigura Toyonobu. Toyama, 1938.

Mostly Tokugawa, but presents a few sixteenth-century documents. There are also two records allegedly written by Kiso Yoshinaka in 1183, but these are obvious forgeries. Other document collections transcribed by Professor Kigura appear in the journal *Etchū shidan*, especially issues 1, 3, 6, 14–16, 20–24, 26, 28, 33, 35.

KAGA PROVINCE (ISHIKAWA PREFECTURE)

• 228

Zōtei Kano komonjo　増訂加能古文書
Compiled by Heki Ken (Kanazawa bunka kyōkai). Addendum compiled by Matsumoto Mitsumasa. Tōkyō, 1972.

> A reprint of the original *Kano komonjo* (Kanazawa, 1944), plus an appendix containing 503 additional records. Long the standard compendium of old documents relating to Kaga and Noto provinces. Arrangement is chronological (from 731 to 1600), and there is an index of personal and place names. Well produced and indispensable for the areas treated.

229

Ishikawa kenshi 1　石川県史
Compiled by Heki Ken. Kanazawa, 1927.

> Contains a special section for documents relating to Kaga and Noto provinces. Although all these materials appear in [228], this work can still be recommended as a valuable history of the region based on key sources. Recently reprinted.

230

Ishikawa ken meibun shūsei, chūsei kinsekibun hen
石川県銘文集成，　中世金石文編
Compiled by Sakurai Jin'ichi. Kanazawa, 1971.

> Wood, metal, and stone inscriptions dating from Kamakura and Muromachi times. There are numerous photographs and notes. A well-produced volume.

231

Togashi shi to Kaga Ikkō ikki shiryō　富樫氏と加賀一向一揆史料
Compiled by Tate Zan'ō. Tōkyō, 1973.

> A curious mélange of essays and source materials relating to the late medieval *Ikkō ikki* movement and the Togashi *daimyō*. Somewhat difficult to use because of a confused format and the absence of any chronological index; nevertheless, presents much that is new.

NOTO PROVINCE (ISHIKAWA PREFECTURE)

Zōtei Kano komonjo, *see* [228]

Ishikawa kenshi, *see* [229]

Ishikawa ken meibun shūsei, chūsei kinsekibun hen, *see* [230]

232

Shiga chōshi, shiryō hen　志賀町史，　資料編
Compiled by Shiga chōshi hensan iinkai. Shiga, 1974.

> A massive volume of archeological data and historical sources relating to a small region in Noto Province. Includes some 140 pages of medieval documents arranged by collection. There is also a Tokugawa section.

233
Tomiku chōshi, shiryō hen　富来町史，資料編
Compiled by Tomiku chōshi hensan iinkai. Tomiku, 1974.

Same format as the preceding entry, but containing only 35 pages of medieval records, arranged by collection.

234
Haguhi shishi, chūsei—shaji hen　羽咋市史，中世－社寺編
Compiled by Haguhi shishi hensan iinkai. Haguhi, 1975.

A volume describing the temples and shrines of medieval Haguhi. Included are a handful of document collections with records that begin from late Kamakura times. A chronology of the region is appended, and there are photographs of many documents.

235
Keta jinja bunken shū　気多神社文献集
Compiled by Ishikawa ken toshokan kyōkai. Kanazawa, 1940.

The documents of a local shrine in Noto Province, covering the sixteenth and seventeenth centuries. There are no notes. Recently reprinted.

236
Noto Agishi Honseiji monjo　能登阿岸本誓寺文書
Compiled by Kitanishi Hiroshi. Ōsaka, 1971.

The documents of a temple in Noto Province. Coverage is mostly Tokugawa, but there are a number of interesting Muromachi land records. Arrangement is chronological, and there are valuable place and name indexes.

ECHIZEN PROVINCE (FUKUI PREFECTURE)

• 237
Echizen Wakasa komonjo sen　越前若狭古文書選
Compiled by Makino Shinnosuke. Tōkyō, 1933.

A massive collection of documents relating to the two westernmost provinces of Hokuriku. Many materials deal with commercial affairs, especially coastal shipping, though the total range of the volume is much greater. Organized by district and individual collection, with a chronological index. Only 5 percent of the documents date from Kamakura times. A valuable work; recently reprinted.

238
Obama-Tsuruga-Mikuni minato shiryō　小浜－敦賀－三国湊史料
Compiled by Fukui kenritsu toshokan. Fukui, 1959.

Historical materials of all kinds from Echizen and Wakasa provinces. Of interest because many of these sources deal with coastal shipping, fishing, the internal movement of goods, etc. Coverage is Kamakura into Edo, with most materials dating from the later centuries. A minimal number of medieval documents. Descriptive essays are included.

239
Tsuruga gun komonjo　敦賀郡古文書
Compiled by Yamamoto Gen. Ōtsu, 1943.

Documents relating to Tsuruga District in Echizen Province. Coverage begins with the late Kamakura age, but most records date from the sixteenth century.

Arrangement is by collection, with a chronological index appended. Occasional notes.

240
Niu gunshi 丹生郡誌
Compiled by Niu gunshi henshū iinkai. 1960.

Presents materials from the various document collections relating to Niu District. The Hōunji, Ochi, and Ōtani collections are the most important, with the last two containing a scattering of records from Kamakura times. About 240 pages of documents in all.

241
Okamoto sonshi, shiryō hen 岡本村史, 史料編
Compiled by Obata Jun. Okamoto, 1956.

A handful of sixteenth-century documents dealing mostly with shrine affairs in a small sector of Echizen Province. Coverage is predominantly Tokugawa.

• 242
Saifukuji monjo 西福寺文書
Compiled by Tamayama Jōgen (Zoku gunsho ruijū kanseikai, *Shiryō sanshū—komonjo hen*). Tōkyō, 1973.

The 286 medieval documents of a temple in Echizen Province. Coverage is exclusively Muromachi (with one late Kamakura record). Many of the documents are commendation and confirmation records, showing that the influence of local religious institutions had not been totally displaced by that of warriors. Chronological arrangement, with excellent headnotes. A portion of the Saifukuji collection also appears in [237] and [239].

243
Hōunji monjo
Compiled by Yamada Shūho. Fukui, 1913. 法雲寺文書

Collection of some 40 sixteenth-century documents relating in part to the Asakura *daimyō* house. No notes.

244
Heisenji monjo 平泉寺文書
Compiled by Ōno gun Hiraizumi mura. 2 vols. 1924.

Mostly Tokugawa; however, Volume 1 contains 18 records dating from the sixteenth century. A section of photographs is in the front.

245
Ochi jinja monjo 越知神社文書
Compiled by Yamada Shūho. Ōgaki, 1920.

Interesting collection of shrine documents in a handsome old volume. Coverage is Kamakura into Tokugawa, with much of value on the earlier centuries. There is a brief photograph section in the front.

246
Hokkoku shōen shiryō 北国荘園史料
Compiled by Inoue Toshio (Fukui kenritsu toshokan). Fukui, 1965.

Materials relating to two *shōen* in Echizen Province. The only concession to the reader is a very thorough index of names and terms; there are no notes, introductory essay, or chronology. Very hard to use.

• 247
Ushigahara-no-shō kankei monjo　牛原荘関係文書
Compiled by Committee for the Publication of Dr. K. Asakawa's works.
Land and Society in Medieval Japan (Japanese section: 1–43). Tōkyō, 1965.

An assemblage of 73 documents depicting the history of Ushigahara Estate in Echizen Province. Coverage is from 1132 to 1468, with translations for the period before 1185 (English section: 37–68). A fascinating portrait emerges from these materials. Ushigahara was a holding of the Daigoji in Kyōto.

248
Echizen no kuni Kawaguchi–Tsuboe-no-shō shiryō
越前国河口－坪江庄史料
Compiled by Inoue Toshio (*Niigata daigaku hōkei ronshū*). 1958–60.

Four or more pamphlets containing documents detailing the history of a double estate in Echizen. Especially useful for the relationship of this region with the *shugo daimyō*.

249
Shōen monjo nitsū　荘園文書二通
Compiled by Taga Munehaya. *Nihon rekishi* 209 (1965): 65–66.

Presents two early Kamakura documents transcribed here for the first time. The first (1217) deals with a *shōen* in Echizen; the second (1221) treats a *shōen* in Aki.

WAKASA PROVINCE (FUKUI PREFECTURE)

Echizen Wakasa komonjo sen, *see* [237]

Obama-Tsuruga-Mikuni minato shiryō, *see* [238]

250
Fukui kenshi 1　福井県史
Compiled by Fukui ken. Fukui, 1920.

A lengthy field register dating from 1265 is appended to this general history of early and medieval Wakasa and Echizen. Included are voluminous data on the estates of Wakasa Province in the mid-Kamakura period. Recently reprinted.

251
Fukui ken Mikata gunshi　福井県三方郡誌
Compiled by Fukui ken Mikata gunshi kyōikukai. Tōkyō, 1911.

Contains a special section of 50 pages or so of medieval documents relating to the Mikata area. The rest of the volume is a gazetteer.

• 252
Wakasa gyoson shiryō　若狭漁村史料
Compiled by Fukui kenritsu toshokan. Fukui, 1963.

A fascinating collection of documents (Kamakura through early Edo) treating local industry and fishing in Wakasa Province. A sequel to [238]. Arrangement is by collection, but a chronological index is appended.

• 253
Obama shishi, shaji monjo hen 小浜市史，社寺文書編
Compiled by Obama shishi hensan iinkai. Obama, 1976.

A major assemblage of documents long awaited by scholars. More than 900 pages of medieval and early modern records, arranged by collection. No chronological index and almost no notes; but many of these documents appear here for the first time. The Myōtsūji collection, containing a number of Kamakura records, is outstanding.

Kinki Region

ŌMI PROVINCE (SHIGA PREFECTURE)

• 254
Shiga kenshi 5 滋賀県史
Compiled by Shiga ken. Ōtsu, 1928.

An excellent compendium of medieval records dealing with Ōmi Province, arranged by document collection. A major drawback is that no effort was made to present the different collections in their entirety; thus only representative documents were chosen. Still, an important contribution, since the medieval records of Ōmi are virtually without peer for intrinsic interest and variety; both courtier and warrior societies emerge vividly. The entire six-volume *Shiga kenshi* was recently reprinted. Volume 2 is a general history of early and medieval times.

• 255
Ōmi Sakata gunshi 1 近江坂田郡志
Compiled by Sakata gun'yakusho. Nagahama, 1913.

A generally neglected compendium of documents relating to a district in Ōmi Province. The coverage is from Nara to Tokugawa and includes 21 interesting Kamakura records. Documents are arranged chronologically, using large type and an appealing format. There are no notes. Recently reprinted and most worthwhile.

256
Ōmi Echi gunshi 1 近江愛知郡志
Compiled by Shiga ken Echi gun kyōikukai. Kyōto, 1929.

A large number of documents are incorporated in the text of this district history. The coverage is from earliest times to mid-Muromachi (Volume 2 treats the sixteenth century), and there is a special section on *shōen*, divided by proprietor. Numerous photographs of documents.

257
Ōmi Kurumoto gunshi 1 近江栗太郡志
Compiled by Shiga ken Kurumoto gun'yakusho. Ōgaki, 1926.

The same format and features as [256], for a neighboring district in Ōmi.

• 258
Higashiasai gunshi 4 東浅井郡志
Compiled by Higashiasai kyōikukai. Higashiasai gun, 1927.

A valuable compendium of documents relating to a *shōen*-rich section of Ōmi. The arrangement of materials is haphazard and unwieldy, but some fascinating records are contained. The Chikubujima collection is especially noteworthy for its data on the Sasaki *shugo* house. Overall, only a small percentage of the materials date from Kamakura times. Recently reprinted.

259
Minakuchi chōshi 2 水口町志
Compiled by Minakuchi chōshi hensan iinkai. Minakuchi, 1959.

Documents from a village area in Ōmi. Coverage is into Tokugawa times, but there are many interesting records from the early medieval period. Numerous documents relate to the successive Bakufu regimes and their vassals. Arrangement is by collection, with no notes, index, or table of contents. The Yamanaka collection is outstanding.

260
Shiga ken Hachiman chōshi, shiryō hen 滋賀県八幡町史, 史料編
Compiled by Fukuo Takeichirō. Ōsaka, 1970.

Contains a small selection of medieval documents dealing with one area of Ōmi. The Kamakura records (covering only a few pages) are mostly appointment edicts to local shrine headships. Arrangement of materials is chronological, from earliest times through the Meiji Restoration. Predominantly Tokugawa.

• 261
Sugaura monjo 菅浦文書
Compiled by Harada Toshimaru (Shiga daigaku keizaigakubu shiryōkan).
2 vols. Tōkyō, 1960–67.

Extremely important for the light it sheds on society at the lower levels. There is much material, for example, on the nature of village organization and the peasant class. The arrangement of documents is entirely random, but a chronological index is appended. There are no notes. A sampling of the Sugaura records appears in several other works (e.g. [254] and [258]).

• 262
Taga jinja monjo 多賀神社文書
Compiled by Nakamura Naokatsu. 2 vols. Taga, 1940.

The documents of an important shrine in Ōmi. Arrangement is roughly chronological, with more than half the materials from the sixteenth century. But the earlier documents are of great interest: many of them were issued by the Kamakura and Muromachi regimes, or by the Sasaki *shugo* house. The format of these volumes is exemplary. One volume contains photographs of documents, and the other presents transcriptions and analysis. Japanese-style binding makes this one of the most visually attractive of all document series.

• 263
Katsuragawa Myōō-in-shiryō 葛川明王院史料
Compiled by Murayama Shūichi. Tōkyō, 1964.

A massive collection of land documents relating to the *shōen* of a well-known Ōmi temple. A remarkable feature of the several hundred Kamakura records is the total absence of any reference to the Bakufu or its men: evidently, these estates were free from the burden of Kamakura-appointed *jitō*. No notes are included, and the summarizing essay is thin and unsatisfactory. A chronological index of documents is appended. There is very heavy treatment of the early decades of the fourteenth century, but almost no indication that major inroads were being made by warriors. A remarkable collection.

264

Asai shi sandai monjo shū 浅井氏三代文書集
Compiled by Kowada Tetsuo. Nagahama, 1972.

The story of the sixteenth-century Asai *daimyō* house through documents. Arrangement is chronological, but there are no notes. A chronology is appended. See also [258].

265

Sengoku monjo shūei—Asai shi hen 戦国文書聚影－浅井氏篇
Compiled by Nakamura Rin'ichi and Kowada Tetsuo (Sengoku monjo kenkyūkai). Tōkyō, 1973.

Photographs of representative documents of the Asai *daimyō* house, along with transcriptions and notes. The photographs are excellent, and the overall production is attractive. Exclusively sixteenth-century.

• 266

Imabori Hie jinja monjo 1–7 今堀日吉神社文書
Compiled by Mishina Akihide. *Bunka shigaku* 15–19, 21, 24 (1960/9, 1960/11, 1963/1, 1964/3, 1965/3, 1967/4, 1968/11).

A total of 413 documents belonging to the important Hie Shrine in Ōmi. Coverage is predominantly Muromachi, with many fascinating records bearing on Hie land administration. Unfortunately, materials are not arranged chronologically, and there are no notes. An expanded, one-volume assemblage of these documents has been announced for 1976.

267

Ōshima jinja–Okutsujima jinja monjo 大嶋神社－奥津島神社文書
Compiled by Shiga daigaku keizaigakubu shiryōkan. *Kenkyū kiyō* 1–9 (1968–75).

The documents of a pair of shrines in Ōmi. Coverage begins in mid-Kamakura times and includes a number of cultivators' agreements with higher authority. Important for data on *shōen* administration. There are no notes or research aids. A total of 223 documents, with treatment to the beginning of the seventeenth century.

268

Ōhara kannonji monjo 大原観音寺文書 ,
Compiled by Shiga ken kyōiku iinkai. Ōtsu, 1975.

An interesting assemblage of documents from several local collections with coverage dating from Kamakura times. The documents appear in handwritten rather than printed form, however, although reproduction is clear. Useful background data are presented.

YAMASHIRO PROVINCE (KYŌTO PREFECTURE)

• 269

Tōji hyakugō monjo 東寺百合文書
Compiled by Tōkyō daigaku shiryō hensanjo (*Dai Nihon komonjo, iewake* 10). 6 vols. to date. Tōkyō, 1925– .

The Tōji collection of medieval documents is Japan's largest, containing over 20 thousand old records. The six volumes in this series are only a beginning, but they include some of the medieval period's most important documents. Noteworthy are the records bearing on Tara and Ōyama estates, two of the Tōji's most prominent *shōen* (for Ōyama, see also [384]). For other Tōji documents, see the next four entries.

• 270
Kyōōgokokuji monjo　教王護国寺文書
Compiled by Akamatsu Toshihide. 10 vols. Kyōto, 1960–72.

Documents of the Tōji not included in the *Dai Nihon komonjo* assemblage of that temple's records [269]. Arrangement is chronological, and Volume 1 is devoted to the Kamakura and early Nambokuchō ages; the remaining volumes treat Muromachi times. The documents tend to be lengthy registers relating to taxation. No notes.

• 271
Zuroku Tōji hyakugō monjo　図録東寺百合文書
Compiled by Kyōto furitsu sōgō shiryōkan. Kyōto, 1970.

A magnificent portfolio volume containing 172 documents from the Tōji collection, complete with photographs, transcriptions, and notes. Coverage is Nara through Muromachi, with materials chosen largely for their content. The photographs are exemplary, and the overall production makes this the finest volume of its kind. Recently reprinted by a commercial publisher in Tōkyō (Yoshikawa kōbunkan).

• 272
Zoku zuroku Tōji hyakugō monjo　続図録東寺百合文書
Compiled by Kyōto furitsu sōgō shiryōkan. Kyōto, 1974.

Over 200 more Tōji documents in the same magnificent format as the preceding entry. A beautiful volume. Similarly reprinted.

273
Tōhōki　東寳記
Zokuzoku gunsho ruijū 12: 1–164 (*shūkyō bu*). Tōkyō, 1908.

A chronicle of the Tōji Temple compiled in the fourteenth century. Numerous documents from the Heian and Kamakura periods are included.

• 274
Daitokuji monjo　大徳寺文書
Compiled by Tōkyō daigaku shiryō hensanjo (*Dai Nihon komonjo, iewake* 17). 10 vols. to date. Tōkyō, 1943– .

The documents of Kyōto's Daitokuji Temple. Mostly land-administration records dating from Muromachi times. Organization (as with all *Dai Nihon komonjo* volumes) is haphazard, but there is a table of contents listing all documents, along with useful headnotes for each record.

275
Daitokuji komonjo　大徳寺古文書
Compiled by Fujii Sadabumi. *Ueno toshokan kiyō* 2 (1955): 69–93.

A total of 81 documents from the much larger Daitokuji collection. Coverage is from the mid-fifteenth century, and land-sale records predominate. There is much on the decline of the estate system.

• 276
Daigoji monjo　醍醐寺文書
Compiled by Tōkyō daigaku shiryō hensanjo (*Dai Nihon komonjo, iewake* 19).
7 vols. to date. Tōkyō, 1955– .

The documents of a major Kyōto temple. Contains many valuable materials on
shōen development and proprietor-warrior disputes over control of land. Coverage
begins in the Heian period, and there is much of interest on the Kamakura
Bakufu and its men. These volumes only begin the process of transcription for
one of Japan's largest medieval document collections.

277
Daigo zōjiki　醍醐雑事記
Edited by Nakajima Toshiji. 1931.

A chronicle of the Daigoji compiled in 1186. It contains the Heian-period documents and other sources of that institution, arranged chronologically. It was this
work that Professor Asakawa used in the preparation of his translations relating
to Ushigahara Estate in Echizen [247]. Recently reprinted.

• 278
Daigoji shin yōroku　醍醐寺新要録
Edited by Akamatsu Toshihide. 3 vols. Kyōto, 1951–53.

An early Tokugawa compilation incorporating historical materials up to the beginning of that age. The opening sections overlap with [277], but there is much
of value here on Kamakura and Muromachi times. Many of the documents in
Daigoji monjo [276] derive from this work.

• 279
Tōfukuji monjo　東福寺文書
Compiled by Tōkyō daigaku shiryō hensanjo (*Dai Nihon komonjo, iewake* 20).
5 vols. to date. Tōkyō, 1956– .

The documents of an important Zen temple in Kyōto. Materials relate to temple
organization and estate holdings. Coverage is overwhelmingly Muromachi.

• 280
Kōzanji komonjo　高山寺古文書
Compiled by Kōzanji tenseki monjo sōgō chōsadan (*Kōzanji shiryō sōsho* 4).
Tōkyō, 1975.

The documents of a major Kyōto temple in a large, handsomely produced volume.
Coverage is from late Heian times into the sixteenth century, and many of these
materials are published here for the first time. Arrangement is mostly chronological, and an essay is appended. A work of major importance.

281
Kōzanji ibunshō　高山寺遺文抄
Compiled by Horiike Shumpō and Tanaka Minoru. Kyōto, 1957.

A selection of 124 documents from the same temple as in [280]. No table of contents, notes, or index, and hence difficult to use. Now superseded by [280].

• 282
Nanzenji monjo　南禅寺文書
Compiled by Sakurai Kageo and Fujii Manabu. 2 vols. Kyōto, 1972–74.

The documents of a major temple founded in the mid-Kamakura period. Volume 1 covers 1258–1466, and Volume 2 continues into Tokugawa times. Arrangement is chronological, with excellent headnotes. Contains numerous Ashikaga Bakufu documents, and there is much data on the rise of *shugo*. An important work.

•283

Jingoji monjo 神護寺文書

Compiled by Tai Keigo. *Shirin* 25.1, 25.2, 25.3, 25.4, 26.1, 26.2, 26.3 (1940–41).

One of the most interesting of all document collections for late Heian and Kamakura times. There are numerous Bakufu records, including several edicts by Minamoto Yoritomo. The collection is especially rich for the transitional first third of the Kamakura period. A total of 274 records, with coverage into the Muromachi age. (Published also as a separate pamphlet, no date.)

•284

Ninnaji monjo shūi 仁和寺文書拾遺

Compiled by Tanaka Minoru. *Shigaku zasshi* 68.9 (1959): 74–86.

A handful of recently discovered temple records relating to lands held at the highest level by the imperial house. A document of 1184 helps to explain both the Bakufu's penetration of the Hokuriku region and the emergence of *jitō* as a political force (see Document 7 in Part I). Coverage is to the 1330's, and virtually all the records are of great interest. Such widely separated areas as Etchū, Tamba, and Hizen provinces are dealt with.

285

Ninnaji monjo shō 仁和寺文書抄

Compiled by Morikawa Yukio. Nara, 1959.

Pamphlet containing essentially the same documents as [284], minus all notes and commentary. An unusually rich collection.

286

Kaijūzanji monjo 海住山寺文書

Compiled by Sawaki Sadaaki. *Shigaku zasshi* 70.2 (1961): 59–72.

Collection of 14 documents (mostly Kamakura) belonging to a branch temple of the Kōfukuji, and dealing with internal temple affairs. There is an accompanying essay.

287

Chōfukuji monjo 長福寺文書

Compiled by Meiji daigaku keiji hakubutsukan iinkai. *Meiji daigaku keiji hakubutsukan nempō* 2 (1959).

Presents 7 documents from the collection of Chōfukuji Temple. Coverage begins in late Kamakura times.

288

Chōrakuji shozō "Konkōji monjo" 長楽寺所蔵「金光寺文書」

Compiled by Kikuchi Yūjirō and Ōhashi Toshio. *Nihon bukkyōshi* 4 (1958): 65–76.

Selected sixteenth- and seventeenth-century documents of the Konkōji temple, mostly the private letters of priests of that institution.

• 289
Iwashimizu monjo 石清水文書
Compiled by Tōkyō daigaku shiryō hensanjo (*Dai Nihon komonjo, iewake* 4).
6 vols. Tōkyō, 1909–15.

One of the famous document collections, with materials dating from the Heian period on. Iwashimizu Shrine was a holder of *shōen* in many parts of the country, and the documents reflect this. The records are of all types, including Bakufu and imperial decrees, as well as records of the shrine and its local land managers. The organization of materials is haphazard, however, and there is no chronological index.

• 290
Iwashimizu Hachimangū shi 石清水八幡宮史
Compiled by Iwashimizu Hachimangū shamusho. 9 vols. Kyōto, 1932–39.

Nine massive volumes containing source materials of all kinds relating to Iwashimizu Shrine. Each volume is arranged differently and purports to deal with a separate subject (e.g. ceremonials or land administration). Obviously there is much overlap, though the final volume presents a chronological index of all materials. Volumes 5–6, dealing with landholdings, contain the most documents, and there are some records not included in the much better-known *DNK* series [289]. Coverage is from Heian times into the Tokugawa. A valuable compilation.

• 291
Yasaka jinja monjo 八坂神社文書
Compiled by Hirono Saburō (Yasaka jinja shamusho). 2 vols. Kyōto, 1939–40.

The documents of Kyōto's Gion (Yasaka) Shrine. Coverage is overwhelmingly Muromachi, but there are a number of interesting Kamakura-period records. Arrangement is by subject and is therefore very confusing. Volume 1 purports to contain documents relating to shrine organization (broken down into various subcategories); Volume 2 presents materials dealing with shrine estates (subdivided by provinces and smaller administrative units). There is a considerable overlap, and no master index is provided. A chronological list of records is appended to Volume 2.

292
Yasaka jinja kiroku 八坂神社記録
Compiled by Hirono Saburō (Yasaka jinja shamusho). 2 vols. Kyōto, 1972.

Because paper was a luxury item in medieval times, several hundred Yasaka Shrine documents have survived on the reverse side of the well-known Yasaka Chronicle. Coverage is mostly Muromachi, but there are some materials from the late Kamakura age. Content tends to focus on internal matters, though a number of land-related records are also included.

293
Inari jinja shiryō 5–9 稲荷神社史料
Compiled by Kojima Shōsaku (Inari jinja shamusho). Tōkyō, 1936–41.

Five massive volumes containing Inari-related source materials. A relatively small number of documents, however, and the content is mostly Tokugawa and later. Of limited use to the medievalist.

294
Hagura monjo 羽倉文書
Compiled by Hagura Takanao. Tōkyō, 1934.

Brief volume containing a handful of sixteenth-century documents from the collection of an official family of the Inari Shrine. There are no notes, but a chronology is included.

295
Kamo chūshin zakki　賀茂注進雑記
Compiled by Kamowake Ikazuchi jinja. Kyōto, 1940.

A chronicle containing a selection of documents from the important Kamo Shrine of Kyōto. Coverage is from late Heian times, with much on the Kamakura age and the problems of controlling far-flung estates. No notes, but a mostly chronological arrangement. Recently reprinted. Published under the same title in *Zokuzoku gunsho ruijū* 1, *jingi bu*.

296
Torii Ōji monjo　鳥居大路文書
Compiled by Kinoshita Masao and Naniwada Tōru. *Yamato bunka kenkyū* 12.4 (1967): 1–15.

Important collection of 12 documents belonging to an official family of the Kamo Shrine in Kyōto. Each document is accompanied by a photograph, and coverage is late Heian into Muromachi. The content of these materials, relating mostly to land problems, is especially interesting. Half the total is Kamakura.

297
Kami Kamo shake (Iwasa ke—Umetsuji ke) monjo ni tsuite
上賀茂社家（岩佐家－梅辻家）文書について
Compiled by Shimosaka Mamoru. *Nihon shi kenkyū* 109 (1970): 56–63.

Selected documents from the collections of two official families of a well-known shrine in Kyōto. Materials are exclusively from the sixteenth century. There is an accompanying essay.

• 298
Ruijū fusenshō　類聚符宣抄
Compiled by Kunaishō toshoryō. Tōkyō, 1930.

A famous collection of Nara and Heian documents (covering 737–1093), with emphasis on "public orders" from the different ministries of state. Arrangement is by subject matter and is often a bit arbitrary, but there is a chronological index appended. Published under the same title in *Shintei zōho kokushi taikei* 27, Tōkyō, 1974.

• 299
Mibu shinsha komonjo　壬生新写古文書
Compiled by Kunaishō toshoryō. Tōkyō, 1930.

A famous collection of documents relating to estates held by the imperial house. Coverage is evenly distributed from the late Heian through the Muromachi ages. Particularly interesting are two Bakufu judicial decrees of 1207 and 1216 concerning *jitō* encroachments in Wakasa Province (see Pt. I, Documents 92–93). A chronological index of materials is appended. Published as a two-volume set with [298]. Appears also as *Zoku sajōshō*, in *Shintei zōho kokushi taikei* 27, Tōkyō, 1974.

• 300
Ruijū sandai kyaku　類聚三代格
Shintei zōho kokushi taikei 25–26. 2 vols. Tōkyō, 1974.

Contains a large assemblage of imperial state council edicts (*dajōkanpu*) issued between 701 and 907. Arrangement is by subject matter, but there is a chronological index at the end. A compilation of major importance.

• 301
Betsujū fusenshō　別聚符宣抄
Shintei zōho kokushi taikei 27. Tōkyō, 1974.

A selection of ministerial decrees dating from the tenth century. Although there is some duplication here of documents appearing in the *Ruijū fusenshō* [298], there is also much that is new. A basic source for the mid-Heian period.

• 302
Kujō ke monjo　九条家文書
Compiled by Kunaichō shoryōbu. 6 vols. to date. Tōkyō, 1971– .

One of the few published collections of documents relating to a central noble family. The Kujō were a major branch of the Fujiwara. Arrangement is principally by the *shōen* to which documents refer. Each volume contains a brief introductory essay, but there are no notes or index. Volume 3 is of special interest because of its large Kamakura content, principally land-sale and testamentary records. Volume 6 contains a number of Bakufu settlement edicts hitherto unknown.

• 303
Koga ke monjo　久我家文書
Compiled by Kokugakuin daigaku toshokan. *Kokugakuin zasshi*; serialized monthly beginning May 1957.

A fascinating collection of Kamakura and Muromachi records relating to the lands held by a noble house in Kyōto. There are numerous decrees issued by the successive Bakufu regimes. A hard cover edition was discussed several years ago, but it has not appeared. Highly recommended.

304
Koga ke monjo tekiei　久我家文書摘英
Compiled by Kokushi gakkai. Tōkyō, 1935.

Photographs of a small portion of the Koga document collection. No transcriptions or notes.

305
Tachiiri Munetsugu monjo—Kawabata Dōki monjo
立入宗継文書－川端道喜文書
Compiled by Nishida Naojirō and Shibata Minoru (Kokumin seishin bunka kenkyūjo). Tōkyō, 1937.

The documents relating to two important sixteenth-century figures. The condition of Kyōto and the imperial family during this period emerges vividly. Background information is provided.

306
Kammon nikki shihai monjo　看聞日記紙背文書
Compiled by Takahashi Ryūzō (Kunaichō shoryōbu). Tōkyō, 1965.

Presents private letters contained in the diary of a fifteenth-century court figure. Coverage is 1416–48, but there are gaps for several years. The letters provide data on the economic condition of the court and the political tensions within Kyōto. The volume suffers from an absence of notes.

307
Fujinami ke monjo　藤波家文書
Compiled by Meiji daigaku keiji hakubutsukan iinkai. *Meiji daigaku keiji hakubutsukan nempō* 1 (1957).

Brief assemblage of fifteenth- and sixteenth-century records from the collection of a central noble house. Declining revenues from the provinces are a major topic of treatment.

308
Kanjizai-in monjo　観自在院文書
Compiled by Iikura Harutake. *Komonjo kenkyū* 2 (1969): 111–15.

Transcriptions of eleven documents dated 1185 to 1187 and concerning Kizu Estate in Yamashiro Province. Useful for a study of this critical period.

309
Negishi ke kyūzō monjo　根岸家旧蔵文書
Compiled by Fujii Sadabumi. *Ueno toshokan kiyō* (1957): 52–65.

Collection of 29 documents relating mostly to Yamashiro and Ōmi provinces. Coverage is exclusively Heian, an unusual feature. There is much of interest on the formation of *shōen*.

310
Manase Dōsan monjo ni tsuite　曲直瀬道三文書について
Compiled by Takahashi Masahiko. *Shigaku* 36.2 (1963): 227–42.

The sixteenth-century records of a famous Kyōto physician.

311
Kyōto daigaku bungaku bu kokushi kenkyūshitsu shozō monjo
京都大学文学部国史研究室所蔵文書
Compiled by Atsuta Isao. *Komonjo kenkyū* 2 (1969): 116–27.

Description of the document collections held by Kyōto University, with photographs of several individual records.

YAMATO PROVINCE (NARA PREFECTURE)

•312
Yamato komonjo shūei　大和古文書聚英
Compiled by Nagashima Fukutarō (Nara ken toshokan kyōkai). Nara, 1943.

An important sampling of documents relating to (and housed in) Yamato Province. Though only a handful of Kasuga Shrine and Tōdai Temple records are included, there are numerous materials from less prominent collections. Documents from the Saidaiji are especially noteworthy. A chronological index of records is appended. Coverage is fairly even from the fourteenth through the sixteenth century.

•313
Kasuga jinja monjo　春日神社文書
Compiled by Kasuga jinja shamusho. 3 vols. Nara, 1928–42.

A famous document collection in three handsomely produced volumes. The labeling of documents is somewhat uneven, however, and there are numerous errors. Volumes 1 and 2 (the shrine documents proper) contain a chronological index of documents and other tables; and Volume 3 (the materials of shrine-related official houses) offers brief but helpful headnotes. Kasuga Shrine was one of the great medieval estate holders, and these documents tell us much about society and economy over five centuries. Volume 2 is quite rare.

314
Danzan jinja monjo 談山神社文書
Compiled by Danzan jinja kansho hōsankai. Kyōto, 1929.

A large collection of late medieval and Tokugawa records in a beautifully bound old volume. The documents are arranged haphazardly, however, and the volume is little used today.

• 315
Tōdaiji monjo 東大寺文書
Compiled by Tōkyō daigaku shiryō hensanjo (*Dai Nihon komonjo, iewake* 18). 10 vols. to date. Tōkyō, 1944– .

One of the most important compendia of Japanese land documents. Tōdaiji possessed estates in many parts of the country, and was more assiduous than most proprietors in administering its domains. The collection is noteworthy for its unusually high concentration of Heian records and is unsurpassed for the study of early *shōen*. Volume 4 contains facsimiles of original maps and land surveys. There are hundreds of valuable Kamakura documents in this series.

• 316
Tōdaiji monjo 東大寺文書
Compiled by Nakamura Naokatsu. Ōsaka, 1945.

Intended as the first volume in a Tōdaiji series, but apparently cut short by the war; nevertheless, a volume of major importance. The majority of the documents date from Kamakura times, and all aspects of land administration are treated. A table of contents lists all documents, but there are no notes.

• 317
Tōdaiji zoku yōroku 東大寺続要録
Zokuzoku gunsho ruijū 11: 195–348 (*shūkyō bu*). Tōkyō, 1908.

A famous chronicle of the Tōdaiji compiled toward the end of the thirteenth century. Contains many important documents from the Kamakura period including a number of Bakufu-related records. Invaluable for the study of Tōdaiji estates during the early medieval age. But there are no notes and the arrangement of materials is haphazard. The *Tōdaiji yōroku* proper (in *ibid.*) is an earlier work containing mostly chronicle-type materials rather than documents.

318
Tōdaiji ibun 東大寺遺文
Compiled by Horiike Shumpō. 8 vols. Nara, 1951–53.

Pamphlets containing records that appear in a longer Tōdaiji-related narrative. Many of the documents are private letters, some undated. Those that have dates are largely from Kamakura times. No notes, but an introductory essay is included.

319
Shunjōbō Chōgen shiryō shūsei　俊乗房重源史料集成
Compiled by Kobayashi Takeshi. Tōkyō, 1965.

Source materials relating to a well-known land administrator of the Tōdaiji during early Kamakura times. Comprehensive, but unwieldy because of a crammed format and a total absence of notes; still, the only volume of its kind. Chōgen had especially close involvement with Bizen and Suō provinces in the Chūgoku region.

• 320
Tōshōdaiji shiryō 1　唐招提寺史料
Compiled by Nara kokuritsu bunkazai kenkyūjo. Tōkyō, 1971.

An important assemblage of document collections relating to the Tōshōdaiji of Nara. Documents range over the entire expanse from Heian through Muromachi, dealing primarily with Tōshōdaiji holdings in the provinces of central Japan and Chūbu. Northern Kyūshū is also treated. No chronological index or notes, though a brief explanatory essay is appended. Most of these materials have never before been printed. Other volumes to follow.

321
Gangōji hennen shiryō　元興寺編年史料
Compiled by Iwashiro Takatoshi. 3 vols. Tōkyō, 1963–65.

The historical materials relating to Gangōji Temple in Nara. Volume 2 covers the Kamakura and Muromachi ages, with sources arranged chronologically. Contains mostly chronicle and diary excerpts, with very few documents. No notes, no table of contents, and no index. Of limited value and interest.

322
Yamato Kōriyama shishi, shiryō hen　大和郡山市史，史料編
Compiled by Yanagizawa bunko semmon iinkai. Kyōto, 1966.

The documents of a district in Yamato Province. Contains a number of inheritance and land-sale records from Kamakura times, along with materials describing a famous *shōen* division (*shitaji chūbun*) in Bizen Province. The Gakuanji document collection is featured.

323
Gojō shishi 1　五条市史
Compiled by Gojō shishi chōsa iinkai. Nara, 1958.

Contains 45 pages of temple materials dating principally from post-Kamakura times. Thin coverage.

324
Tenri shishi, shiryō hen　天理市史，史料編
Compiled by Tenri shishi hensan iinkai. Tenri, 1958.

Contains a scattering of fifteenth- and sixteenth-century documents, mostly from well-known collections like the Tōji. Arrangement of materials is by individual place name, but there is no chronological index. Overwhelmingly Tokugawa. No notes.

325
Kashihara shishi, shiryōshū　橿原市史，史料集
Compiled by Kashihara shishi hensan iinkai. Kashihara, 1962.

Overwhelmingly Tokugawa, but contains a handful of records dating back to Kamakura times. Unfortunately, the arrangement is by district within the Kashihara region, and there is no chronological index: thus documents are difficult to locate. No notes and only minimally useful.

326
Yamato Shimoichi shi, shiryō hen 大和下市史, 史料編
Compiled by Shimoichi chōshi henshū iinkai. 1974.

A slender volume containing several document collections, each arranged chronologically. No notes, but rather numerous photographs. Coverage is from the fourteenth century.

327
Yamato no kuni Wakatsuki-no-shō shiryō 1 大和国若槻庄史料
Compiled by Watanabe Sumio and Kita Yoshiyuki. Tōkyō, 1973.

Materials relating to a domain in central Japan. Coverage begins in the tenth century, before the area became a *shōen*. However, lengthy gaps reduce the utility of this volume. When and how the estate was incorporated, or who the successive proprietors were, is not clear. Coverage is overwhelmingly Muromachi, and most of the materials are lengthy tax registers. Brief notes to the documents are appended, along with an explanatory essay. A separate insert contains maps and facsimiles of registers. Two additional volumes treat the Tokugawa age.

328
Hayashi Rokurō shi shozō "Kōfukuji kankei monjo" ni tsuite
林陸朗氏所蔵「興福寺関係文書」について
Compiled by Yuyama Ken'ichi. *Kokushigaku* 80 (1970): 65–68.

Introduces several new documents relating to estate holdings of the Kōfukuji of Nara. These materials all date from late Kamakura times and are of special interest.

329
Tōshōdaiji reidō shaka nyoraizō nōnyū monjo
唐招提寺礼堂釈迦如来像納入文書
Compiled by Kobayashi Takeshi. *Yamato bunka kenkyū* 2–3 (1954): 57–65.

Presents about a dozen documents discovered inside a Buddhist image from the Tōshōdaiji. These materials all date from the year 1258 and deal with religious matters.

KII PROVINCE (MIE PREFECTURE)

Kii zoku fudoki, *see* [331]

Kii no kuni kinsekibun shūsei, *see* [332]

KII PROVINCE (WAKAYAMA PREFECTURE)

• 330
Wakayama kenshi, chūsei shiryō 1 和歌山県史, 中世史料
Compiled by Wakayama kenshi hensan iinkai. Wakayama, 1975.

A magnificent volume containing a portion of the vast documentary holdings of Wakayama Prefecture. Coverage is from late Heian times into the sixteenth century and arrangement is by individual collection. A large number of these materials are printed here for the first time. There are no notes to individual documents but an essay discussing each of the collections is appended. An assemblage of the first importance, with other volumes to follow.

331
Kii zoku fudoki　紀伊続風土記
Compiled by Niita Kōko (Wakayama ken shinshiki torishimarisho). 5 vols. 1910.

An Edo-period compilation containing numerous Kii Province documents. Very unwieldy to use, since there is no index, and since many of the documents themselves are buried in a text using several print sizes. In Volume 3, however, there is a 350-page section containing only documents, many of great interest. Coverage is from Heian times on, and arrangement is by district, township, and *shōen*. Recently reprinted.

332
Kii no kuni kinsekibun shūsei　紀伊国金石文集成
Compiled by Tatsumi Saburō. 1974.

A handsome new book containing the gravestone inscriptions of Kii Province. There is much from the medieval age.

• 333
Kōyasan monjo　高野山文書
Compiled by Kōyasan shi hensanjo. 7 vols. Kyōto, 1936–41.

A famous collection of land documents relating to one of medieval Japan's greatest estate holders, the monastic complex at Kōyasan. Contains many fascinating records, though there are numerous errors in transcription and (especially) labeling. Twelve volumes were originally planned, but the project was interrupted by the war and never resumed. Most of the documents are not included in the much better known *Dai Nihon komonjo* Kōyasan series [334]. No notes or index, and the arrangement of documents follows no usable pattern. The seven volumes published are numbered 2, 5, 6, 7, 9, 10, and 11. Recently reprinted.

• 334
Kōyasan monjo　高野山文書
Compiled by Tōkyō daigaku shiryō hensanjo (*Dai Nihon komonjo, iewake* 1). 8 vols. Tōkyō, 1904–7.

For an examination of medieval land administration and proprietary disputes with warriors this collection is without peer. As a consequence, it is probably the most exhaustively researched of all pre-1600 document compilations. An indispensable work, highlighted by the records of several of Kōyasan's most famous estates. The only drawback (as with all *Dai Nihon komonjo* volumes) is the bizarre arrangement of documents: ordering is haphazard, and there is no chronological or place-name index. To locate documents use the separately published chronological index *Kōyasan monjo hennen mokuroku* (Wakayama, 1963), compiled by Wada Akio.

335
Kōyasan Shōchi-in monjo shūi　高野山正智院文書拾遺
Compiled by Wada Akio. *Shigaku zasshi* 70.7 (1961): 70–85.

A selection of Kamakura and Muromachi records not included in the two great Kōyasan collections [333, 334].

Rengejō-in monjo, *see* [178]

·336
Kumano Nachi taisha monjo (Mera monjo)　熊野郡智大社文書（米良文書）
Compiled by Nagashima Fukutarō and Oda Motohiko (Zoku Gunsho ruijū
kanseikai, *Shiryō sanshū—komonjo hen*). 3 vols. to date. Tōkyō, 1971– .

Presents a portion of the vast document resources held by Nachi taisha, one of
the three major Kumano shrines. Coverage is almost exclusively Muromachi.
Testamentary and land-sale documents abound. A table of contents lists all
materials included, and there are brief headnotes. But there is no explanatory
essay.

337
Kumano Hayatama taisha komonjo kokiroku　熊野速玉大社古文書古記録
Compiled by Takigawa Masajirō et al. Ōsaka, 1971.

The documents and other sources from one of the three major shrines in the
Kumano complex. Unfortunately, there are few medieval records—only a single
example from Kamakura times and 35 from the Muromachi age. Coverage in the
document section is mostly Tokugawa; a long diary-essay-chronicle section then
follows. There are useful headnotes for the documents, and arrangement is chronological.

·338
Kii no kuni Ategawa-no-shō shiryō 1　紀伊国阿氐河荘史料
Compiled by Nakamura Ken (*Shōen shiryō sōsho*). Tōkyō, 1976.

The documents relating to one of the most interesting of all medieval *shōen*. The
major theme here is the pressure applied by a resident *jitō* against both the
estate proprietor and the cultivators of the land. Contains the famous peasants'
appeal against the *jitō*'s cutting off of noses and ears as a way of intimidating
the local population. Announced for publication early in 1976, with a second
volume to follow.

·339
Kii no kuni Wasa-no-shō Kangiji monjo　紀伊国和佐庄観喜寺文書
Compiled by Sonoda Kōyū (Kansai daigaku tōzai gakujutsu kenkyūjo).
Ōsaka, 1968.

A very useful collection of temple documents relating to an estate in Kii Province. The chronological arrangement permits easy access. A highlight is a territorial division in the 1320's between the proprietor and a Kamakura vassal. Contains much fascinating detail. Highly recommended.

340
Nade-no-shō—Niuya mura yōsui sōron no shin shiryō
名手庄－丹生屋村用水相論の新史料
Compiled by Ōishi Naomasa. *Gekkan rekishi* 27 (1970): 1–4.

A brief collection of documents relating to a Kamakura-period water rights dispute.

341
Kii Suda ke monjo　紀伊隅田家文書
Chūsei shi kenkyū 2: 61–71 (1968), 3–4: 71–80 (1970).

A collection of 20 late Kamakura documents dealing with land administration in a Kii Province *shōen*. Several essays in the same periodical issue (2: 1–52) analyze the materials presented.

342
Kishū Kata no shiryō—Nihon gyoson shiryō　紀州加太の史料－日本漁村史料
Compiled by Uno Shūhei. Tōkyō, 1955.

A large volume of diverse source materials relating generally to the fishing industry in Kii Province. One section contains the Mukai family records, which date back to mid-Kamakura times. These are the only medieval documents in the volume, but they shed considerable light on local conditions in Kii. No Bakufu records are included.

343
Kashiwabara kuyū monjo　柏原区有文書
Compiled by Ōsaka rekishi gakkai. Ōsaka, n.d.

Pamphlet containing the documents of a village area in Kii. Materials begin in the mid-Kamakura age and carry up to the end of Muromachi times. Numerous land-sale, transfer, and commendation records are included. No notes, but interesting.

344
"Myōken jinja monjo" "Ōga jinja monjo" shōkai
「妙見神社文書」「相賀神社文書」紹介
Chūsei shi kenkyū 1 (1967): 48–57.

Five Muromachi-period documents from the collections of two shrines in Kii Province. These records are transcribed here for the first time. No notes.

KAWACHI PROVINCE (ŌSAKA PREFECTURE)

· 345
Kanshinji monjo　観心寺文書
Compiled by Tōkyō daigaku shiryō hensanjo (*Dai Nihon komonjo, iewake* 6).
Tōkyō, 1917.

The documents of Kanshinji Temple. An important collection of land records with emphasis on the fourteenth and fifteenth century. There is much data on relations with the Southern Court and with *daimyō* such as the Hatakeyama.

· 346
Kongōji monjo　金剛寺文書
Compiled by Tōkyō daigaku shiryō hensanjo (*Dai Nihon komonjo, iewake* 7).
Tōkyō, 1920.

The documents of an important temple in Kawachi. Contains a good cross section of materials from the Kamakura period: land administration records, imperial decrees, Bakufu edicts, etc. Coverage is Heian to Tokugawa, with an even distribution between Kamakura and Muromachi.

347
Kongōji koki　金剛寺古記
Compiled by Ōsaka fu shiseki meishō tennen kinenbutsu chōsakai. Ōsaka, 1935.

Fine old volume containing more than 200 documents, mostly from the late

Kamakura period. These are primarily records dealing with internal temple affairs. Unfortunately, the arrangement is haphazard, and there are no notes; but an excellent photograph section is included, as well as an introductory essay.

348
Yaō shishi, shiryō hen 八尾市史，史料編
Compiled by Yaō shishi hensan iinkai. Yaō, 1960.

Sources relating to the Yaō district in Kawachi Province. The format is confusing and the print small, but scattered throughout are records of considerable interest. Some 15 or 20 items date from the Kamakura age, with several times that number from Muromachi times. Tokugawa sources predominate. No chronological index or notes.

349
Moriguchi shishi, shiryō hen 1 守口市史，史料編
Compiled by Moriguchi shishi hensan iinkai. Moriguchi, 1962.

Overwhelmingly Tokugawa, but contains a brief selection of medieval documents. Many of these are thirteenth-century land-sale records from the Katsuodera collection [362, 363]. Some interesting materials from the 1330's and 1340's are also included.

350
Hirakata shishi 6, shiryō hen 1 枚方市史，史料編
Compiled by Hirakata shishi hensan iinkai. Hirakata, 1969.

Source materials on the Hirakata area, from earliest times through the Tokugawa. The medieval section is arranged by type of material: "general," i.e. well-known chronicles or document collections; local document collections; and local chronicles or diaries. There are no notes or indexes, but the volume is carefully done.

351
Kawachinagano shishi 4, shiryō hen 1 河内長野市史，史料編
Compiled by Kawachinagano shishi hensan iinkai. Kawachinagano, 1973.

The early and medieval records of a city in the southeastern part of Ōsaka Prefecture. Introduces a small number of new documents from the Kanshinji collection while also presenting some 600 records that appeared earlier in the *Dai Nihon komonjo* Kanshinji volume [345]. In the present work the materials are arranged chronologically. A useful collection.

352
Tondabayashi shishi 4, shiryō hen 1 富田林市史，史料編
Compiled by Tondabayashi shishi hensan iinkai. Tondabayashi, 1972.

The history of the Tondabayashi area through documents and other sources. Coverage is from earliest times into the Tokugawa period. Handsomely produced with extensive notes and photographs.

IZUMI PROVINCE (ŌSAKA PREFECTURE)

353
Izumi Kumedadera monjo 和泉久米田寺文書
Compiled by Ōsaka-fu kyōiku iinkai. Ōsaka, 1959.

A small but highly interesting collection of documents from an Izumi temple. Unlike most source books, which crowd several documents together, this volume includes only one per page, each with a photograph. However, there are no notes or index, and the editors have not inserted standard transcription punctuation (commas, periods, etc.). Particularly noteworthy is a lengthy judicial edict of the Kamakura Bakufu dating from 1248.

· 354
Senshū Kumedadera monjo　泉州久米田寺文書
Compiled by Toda Yoshimi. *Kishiwada shishi shiryō* 1. Kishiwada, 1973.

Same as [353], but in a revised format that includes some 95 documents from the Kanazawa bunko collection that relate to Kumeda Temple. A critical essay is appended. A valuable work.

355
Izumi Matsuodera monjo　和泉松尾寺文書
Compiled by Uozumi Sōgorō (Ōsaka-fu kyōiku iinkai). Ōsaka, 1957.

Same format as [353]. A small, handsomely produced volume containing the materials of another Izumi temple. Includes Kamakura-period contracts concerning dues and labor services agreed to by peasants.

· 356
Sakai shishi 4, shiryō hen 1　堺市史, 資料編
Compiled by Sakai shiyakusho. Ōsaka, 1930.

Documents relating to the great medieval city of Sakai. Coverage is focused on the late Muromachi period—the age of Sakai's greatest influence—but there are also materials from Kamakura times. An attractive volume, though marred by a confusing arrangement of records. There is no chronological index.

357
Kaizuka shishi 3, shiryō hen　貝塚市史, 史料編
Compiled by Rinji Kaizuka shishi henshūbu. Ōsaka, 1958.

Contains a number of interesting documents from a region near Ōsaka City. The records from early Kamakura times describe an area untouched by Bakufu power. Only after the Jōkyū War (1221) does this condition change. Coverage is from earliest times through the Tokugawa, with only some 60 pages on the medieval period (mostly the sixteenth century).

· 358
Izumi shishi 1, hompen-shiryō hen　和泉市史, 本編－史料編
Compiled by Izumi shishi hensan iinkai. Ōsaka, 1965.

One of the best of the city histories from central Japan. Source materials (arranged chronologically) treat from earliest times to the mid-sixteenth century, and there are a huge number of Heian and Kamakura entries. No notes, but the first half of the volume is a general history of the Izumi City region. Highly recommended.

· 359
Izumi no kuni jōri sei kankei shiryōshū　和泉国条里制関係史料集
Compiled by Ōkoshi Katsuaki. Kishiwada, 1954.

An interesting assemblage of land documents in a little-known work. Coverage ranges from Nara times to the end of the Muromachi age, but the period of greatest concentration is 1200–1400. The nature of landholding and administration in Izumi Province is the main subject here; and although most of these records have been published elsewhere, the book is nevertheless of great value. A table of contents lists all documents, arranged by collection. No notes. Pri-

vately printed and very rare. The Preface refers to a similar volume devoted to
Kawachi Province.

• 360
Nambokuchō to Izumi 南北朝と和泉
Compiled by Aizawa Masahiko. Ōsaka, 1939.

Misleading title for a little-known volume containing many fascinating documents from the thirteenth to fifteenth centuries. Though the book is essentially
a history of Izumi during this period, it is the document sections that stand out,
especially the Tannowa collection. The changing character of local land officer-
ships is prominent in these documents.

SETTSU PROVINCE (ŌSAKA PREFECTURE)

361
Minase jingū monjo 水無瀬神宮文書
Compiled by Ōsaka-fu shiseki meishō tennen kinenbutsu chōsakai. Ōsaka,
1939.

The documents belonging to a shrine that was built to commemorate three emperors of the thirteenth century—Go-Toba, Tsuchimikado, and Juntoku. The volume itself appeared on the 700th anniversary of Go-Toba's death. The most important records date from the fourteenth century, with more than 200 documents
in all.

362
Katsuodera monjo 勝尾寺文書
Compiled by Ōsaka-fu shiseki meishō tennen kinenbutsu chōsakai. Ōsaka,
1931.

The documents of a major landholding temple in central Japan. Voluminous
Kamakura-period materials, which are remarkable for the absence of any reference to the Bakufu: Katsuodera and its estates were evidently free from interference by eastern warriors. A better organized and somewhat more comprehensive assemblage of these records appears in [363]. Still, a handsome and
highly useful volume. Photographs of some documents are included.

• 363
Minoo shishi, shiryō hen 1–2 箕面市史, 史料編
Compiled by Minoo shishi hensan iinkai. Minoo, 1968–73.

The Katsuodera documents in a new and error-free format. Volume 1 treats the
Kamakura and Volume 2 covers the Muromachi. Together they constitute a major contribution to scholarship. The documents should be used with Volume 1 of
the full series, which is a general history of the Minoo area and Katsuo Temple.
Volume 3 in the *shiryō hen* treats Tokugawa times.

• 364
Settsu no kuni shiryōshū ei—Kasuga sharyō Tarumi Nishimaki kankei monjo
摂津国史料集英－春日社領垂水西牧関係文書
Compiled by Ōsaka shigaku kenkyūkai. Ōsaka, 1957.

An important volume of documents and other sources relating to a *shōen* held
by Kasuga Shrine. Coverage is from the end of the Heian era to the sixteenth
century, and most entries have notes. There are numerous photographs of original records.

• 365

Takatsuki shishi 3, shiryō hen 1　高槻市史，史料編
Compiled by Takatsuki shishi hensan iinkai. Takatsuki, 1973.

A history of the Takatsuki area through documents and other sources. Coverage is from earliest times to the end of the sixteenth century, using a chronological arrangement. An unusually rich selection of documents, with much of great interest. The inroads of *shugo* and *jitō* under the Kamakura and Muromachi regimes are amply described.

366

Toyonaka shishi, shiryō hen 1　豊中市史，史料編
Compiled by Toyonaka shishi hensan iinkai. Toyonaka, 1960.

Documents relating to or housed in the Toyonaka area. The handful of Kamakura records are all of great interest, with extensive data on *shugo* and *jitō*. Beautifully produced with helpful notes; materials are arranged chronologically. A number of records are drawn from the Tōji and Katsuodera collections.

367

Ikeda shishi, shiryō hen 1　池田市史，史料編
Compiled by Ikeda shishi hensan iinkai. Ikeda, 1967.

A beautifully produced volume replete with photographs of archeological remains, iconography, etc. The document section, though only 29 pages, contains a number of interesting items, mostly from temple and shrine collections. Photographs of many documents are included, and arrangement is chronological. There is a separate chronicle and diary section. Ikeda City is on the site of what was once Ikeda-no-shō.

SETTSU PROVINCE (HYŌGO PREFECTURE)

• 368

Saihan Kōbe shishi, shiryō hen 1　再版神戸市史，資料編
Compiled by Kōbe shiyakusho. Kōbe, 1937.

A generally neglected volume containing some excellent medieval documents, many dealing with commercial matters. Materials are arranged chronologically, with coverage beginning in the late Kamakura period. Tōdaiji documents are best represented. The final section covers Tokugawa times. Recently reprinted.

369

Nishinomiya shishi 4, shiryō hen 1　西宮市史，資料編
Compiled by Mutō Makoto and Arisaka Takamichi. Nishinomiya, 1962.

Contains many interesting materials on this region of Settsu Province. Arrangement is by period, with a very useful subsection on *shōen*. Especially prominent are land-sale and commendation documents from the Daitokuji collection. Coverage is into Tokugawa.

370

Ashiya shishi, shiryō hen　芦屋市史，史料編
Compiled by Uozumi Sōgorō. 2 vols. Ashiya, 1955–57.

Volume 1 contains materials relating to the Ashiya area, arranged chronologically from Nara through Edo times. Coverage is overwhelmingly Tokugawa, and there are very few medieval documents. Page 1 of Volume 2 includes a single Muromachi record; the remainder deals with early modern times.

371
Itami shishi 4, shiryō hen 1 伊丹市史，史料篇
Compiled by Itami shishi hensan iinkai. Itami, 1968.

Historical materials relating to the Itami region of Settsu Province. Coverage is
from earliest times through the Tokugawa age, but there is much of interest on
the medieval period. Each entry is annotated, and sources of all types are included. Arrangement is chronological. See also [372].

• 372
Itami chūsei shiryō 伊丹中世史料
Compiled by Kuroda Toshio. *Itami shiryō sōsho* 2. Itami, 1974.

A beautifully produced volume containing about 300 documents and other source
excerpts chronicling the history of the Itami City region. Coverage is from the
Heian through *sengoku* periods. Special features include detailed genealogical
information and a section for related literary sources. A partial update of [371],
although this work does not supersede the *Itami shishi*.

373
Miki chōyū komonjo 三木町有古文書
Compiled by Nagashima Fukutarō. Miki, 1952.

Contains a handful of Settsu area documents from the 1580's. Coverage is overwhelmingly Tokugawa.

374
Kyū Amagi monjo to Toga-no-shō 旧天城文書と都賀荘
Compiled by Imai Rintarō (Kōbe shi kyōiku iinkai). Kōbe, 1960.

Pamphlet containing 19 documents dating from the fifteenth and sixteenth centuries. Good headnotes, photographs, and an essay.

• 375
Manganji monjo 満願寺文書
Compiled by Nakagawa Keishi (*Kita Settsu kyōdo shigaku sōsho*). 1952.

Pamphlet containing some 91 documents from the collection of Manganji Temple.
Coverage is mid-Heian to Tokugawa, with about 40 percent Kamakura. The balance between civil and military interests, and between the "public" and "private"
land sectors, emerges from these materials. There is much data on Tada Estate in
Settsu. A rare book.

376
Settsu no kuni Yabe gun Osada jinja monjo 摂津国八部郡長田神社文書
Compiled by Morimoto Masatoshi and Mogi Kazushige. *Hisutoria* 51 (1968):
52–59.

Introduces some 15 documents belonging to a shrine in Settsu. Coverage is early
Kamakura to the end of the sixteenth century, with land-commendation documents predominating. No notes.

377
Shitenōji shozō "Nyoihōju Mishūhō nikki"—"dō" shihai "Togashi shi kankei"
monjo ni tsuite
四天王寺所蔵「如意宝珠御修法日記」—「同」紙背「富樫氏関係」文書について
Compiled by Sugihashi Takao. *Shirin* 53.3 (1970): 115–31.

A collection of highly interesting late Kamakura and Nambokuchō documents featuring directives of the successive Bakufu regimes. Each document (relating to lands in numerous provinces) is separately analyzed. The materials themselves appear on the reverse side of a late Heian or early Kamakura Buddhist diary. The Shitenōji temple is in the Settsu region of Hyōgo Prefecture.

TANGO PROVINCE (KYŌTO PREFECTURE)

378
Tango no chūsei monjo　丹後の中世文書
Compiled by Nakajima Toshio. *Maizuru chihōshi kenkyū* 11–13 (1970–71).

Includes documents relating to Shiraku Estate, a holding of Nara's Saidaiji Temple. Coverage is late Kamakura into the sixteenth century, with much on local taxation and the inheritance or sale of land rights. Provides an intimate portrait of village conditions and local tensions. The *Maizuru shishi, shiryō hen,* published in 1973, reportedly contains these same medieval records.

379
Tango no kuni densūchō　丹後国田数帳
Shinkō zōho shiseki shūran 12: 144–46 (*buke bu*). Kyōto, 1967.

A field register of 1459 listing proprietors and tax information for estate holdings in Tango Province. Important for the study of *shōen* in this region on the eve of the Ōnin War (1467–77).

TAMBA PROVINCE (KYŌTO PREFECTURE)

380
Tosa monjo kaisetsu　土佐文書解説
Compiled by Kimura Tokue. Tōkyō, 1935.

A small volume entirely unknown to most scholars. Contains the records of a warrior house named Tosa. The earliest document is a Kamakura investiture decree of 1204, followed by records tracing the family's development into the Tokugawa. Arrangement of materials is chronological, often with analyses of individual records. Documents relate principally to Tamba Province, and there are many photographs.

381
Kajika chūsei shiryō　何鹿中世史料
Compiled by Ayabe shidankai. Kyōto, 1951.

A pamphlet containing three temple document collections from Tamba. Coverage is mostly Muromachi, with interesting records issued by the Ashikaga Bakufu. There are a few land-commendation documents from the Kamakura period. A chronological index is appended.

382
Tamba no kuni Yamakuni-no-shō shiryō　丹波国山国荘史料
Compiled by Noda Tadao. Kyōto, 1958.

The history of a Tamba *shōen* through documents. A scattering of records from the late Kamakura age, but overwhelmingly Muromachi and beyond. Yamakuni Estate was an imperial house holding. A background essay is provided.

383
Tamba no kuni Kuroda mura shiryō　丹波国黒田村史料
Compiled by Noda Tadao. Kyōto, 1966.

A large compendium dealing with the Kuroda area of Yamakuni Estate [382].
Contains only a handful of medieval records, and coverage is mostly Tokugawa.
Only occasional notes, no chronological index, and no descriptive essay. Difficult
to use.

TAMBA PROVINCE (HYŌGO PREFECTURE)

· 384
Ōyama sonshi, shiryō hen　大山村史, 史料篇
Compiled by Miyagawa Mitsuru. Hyōgo, 1964.

The documents relating to one of the best known of all medieval estates—the
Tōji proprietorship of Ōyama in Tamba. Coverage begins in the ninth century
and carries up into Tokugawa times. An extremely useful work, permitting study
of a *shōen* over many centuries. There is a companion volume that tells the story
of this domain as gleaned from the documents.

385
Tamba no kuni Ōyama-no-shō no shin shiryō　丹波国大山庄の新史料
Compiled by Kurokawa Naonori. *Hyōgo ken no rekishi* 3 (1970).

Reportedly contains Ōyama-related documents missed in [384].

386
Nigitadera monjo　和田寺文書
Compiled by Kuroda Toshio. *Hyōgo shigaku* 24 (1960): 33–45.

Some 58 documents from the collection of a local temple in Tamba. Coverage
begins in 1318 and carries into the Tokugawa, but most of the materials are
Muromachi. There is much of interest here on village organization and on the
activities of the Hosokawa *daimyō*.

387
Ōimo monjo ni tsuite　大芋文書について
Compiled by Ishida Yoshito. *Hyōgo ken no rekishi* 4 (1970): 52–56.

Introduces a handful of Muromachi records from Ōimo Shrine in Tamba. Materials are individually analyzed.

TAJIMA PROVINCE (HYŌGO PREFECTURE)

388
Tajima no kuni Ōokadera monjo　但馬国大岡寺文書
Compiled by Ishida Yoshito. *Hyōgo shigaku* 38–39 (1964).

Brief collection of documents held by a local temple in Tajima. Interesting Muromachi age records.

389
Tajima no kuni ōtabumi　但馬国太田文
Zokuzoku gunsho ruijū 16: 217–41 (*zatsu bu*). Tōkyō, 1910.

A field register of 1285 listing estates in Tajima Province, their proprietors, and their *jitō*. Very detailed and of basic importance for a study of this province during the Kamakura period.

HARIMA PROVINCE (HYŌGO PREFECTURE)

· 390

Himeji shishi, shiryō hen 1　姫路市史，史料編
Compiled by Himeji shishi henshū iinkai. Himeji, 1974.

A volume of truly major importance containing documents relating to the history-rich area of Himeji City. Documents are arranged by collection, with an excellent table of contents listing individual records. Almost 900 pages of documents, covering from late Heian times to the end of the medieval age, with many records printed here for the first time. The Hiromine Shrine collection is outstanding.

391

Shinshū Katō gunshi　新修加東郡誌
Compiled by Katō gunshi hensan iinkai. 1974.

A massive volume containing a 400-page section for sources. These are materials dealing with Katō District (*gun*). There is much of interest on the medieval period, with the Kiyomizu collection outstanding.

392

Harima Taizanji monjo　播磨太山寺文書
Compiled by Uchiyama Jōshin. Hyōgo, 1935.

A pamphlet presenting 80 documents from a local temple of Harima. These records are highly interesting, with much detail on *shugo* and *jitō*. Coverage is from the 1220's into Tokugawa times. Chronological arrangement, with a brief introductory essay. In 1957 a pamphlet, *Taizanji monjo*, was published by the Hyōgo shigakkai. Presumably it contains the same materials.

393

Amazaki Daikakuji monjo　尼崎大覚寺文書
Compiled by Hyōgo shigakkai. Kōbe, 1955.

Pamphlet containing some 52 local temple records. Coverage is from the end of the Kamakura age to the 1580's. An interesting collection, with many land-sale and land-commendation records from the fourteenth and fifteenth centuries.

394

Harima no kuni Ikaruga-no-shō shiryō　播磨国鵤荘史料
Compiled by Abe Takeshi and Ōta Junzō. Tōkyō, 1970.

Documents and other sources relating to an estate in Harima Province. Curiously unsatisfying. The organization of materials is difficult to follow, and there are no accompanying notes. A summarizing essay at the end of the volume is the best place to begin. Very little from Kamakura times.

395

Harima no kuni Kanzaki gun Naitō ke monjo　播磨国神崎郡内藤家文書
Compiled by Naitō Asashichi and Mogi Kazushige. *Hisutoria* 62 (1973): 73–76.

Introduces eight Muromachi documents relating to the activities of a Harima warrior house. Brief introduction, but no notes.

396
Harima no kuni Akashi gun Shōkaiji monjo　播磨国明石郡性海寺文書
Compiled by Totoki Shūzen and Mogi Kazushige. *Hisutoria* 53 (1969):
42–56.

Introduces some 33 documents belonging to a local temple in Harima. Coverage
is early Kamakura to the end of the sixteenth century. Land records of various
types are included, and the collection is an unusually rich one. Harima governor's
decrees are featured.

AWAJI PROVINCE (HYŌGO PREFECTURE)

• 397
Awaji no kuni ōtabumi　淡路国太田文
Zoku gunsho ruijū 33.1: 472–76. Tōkyō, 1958.

A field register of 1223 listing estate holdings, their proprietors, their *jitō*, and
other data. Of special interest for the light it sheds on personnel changes resulting from the Jōkyū War of two years earlier. A document of major importance.

Chūgoku Region

GENERAL

• 398
Mōri ke monjo　毛利家文書
Compiled by Tōkyō daigaku shiryō hensanjo (*Dai Nihon komonjo, iewake* 8).
4 vols. Tōkyō, 1920–24.

Documents of one of the greatest *daimyō* families of western Honshū. Coverage
begins in Kamakura times, when the Bakufu appointed the Mōri to a land mana-
gership. The family's rise can be traced into the Tokugawa period.

• 399
Kikkawa ke monjo　吉川家文書
Compiled by Tōkyō daigaku shiryō hensanjo (*Dai Nihon komonjo, iewake* 9).
3 vols. Tōkyō, 1925–32.

A valuable collection of warrior materials relating to western Honshū (Aki,
Iwami, Suō, and other provinces). Coverage is overwhelmingly Muromachi,
though there are some Kamakura records. The Kikkawa's rise began in 1200
with an investiture by the Bakufu. At the end of Volume 2 is a chronological
index for the first two volumes. Volume 3 treats the sixteenth and seventeenth
centuries exclusively.

BIZEN PROVINCE (OKAYAMA PREFECTURE)

Shunjōbō Chōgen shiryō shūsei, *see* [319]

• 400
Okayama ken komonjo shū　岡山県古文書集
Compiled by Fujii Shun and Mizuno Kyōichirō. 3 vols. Okayama, 1953–56.

The major compendium of documents for medieval Bizen, Mimasaka, and Bitchū
provinces. Coverage is Kamakura to Edo. Especially notable are the Anyōji collection of Bizen, which contains land-commendation documents of the tradi-

tional type from as late as the fourteenth century; the Kinzanji collection showing the imperial governor's influence in Bizen during Kamakura times; and the Kibitsu Shrine documents of Bitchū, the area's largest medieval collection. All collections presented are described in an introductory essay. But no notes are included, and there is no overall chronological index.

401
Kibi kokanshū 黄薇古簡集
Compiled by Saitō Kazuoki (*Okayama ken chihōshi shiryō sōsho* 8).
Okayama, 1971.

A Tokugawa compilation of early documents from the region centering on Bizen Province. Difficult to use, lacking index and notes; also, the documents are arranged haphazardly, and many are undated. Very limited treatment of the Kamakura period. The materials in this volume relate to provinces in many parts of Japan; they merely resided in Bizen at the time of compilation.

402
Kibitsuhiko jinja shiryō monjo hen 吉備津彦神社史料文書編
Compiled by Kibitsuhiko jinja shamusho. Okayama, 1936.

The documents of the main provincial shrine (*ichinomiya*) in Bizen, along with records of related interest from other collections. Muromachi and Tokugawa coverage, with the majority of the materials dating from the later period. For the medieval age, this volume is superseded by [403], which contains more reliable transcriptions.

•403
Kibitsuhiko jinja monjo 吉備津彦神社文書
Compiled by Fujii Shun. Okayama, 1955.

Contains the full complement of Kibitsuhiko documents, arranged chronologically. Coverage is into the Tokugawa age. A rare book with only 100 copies printed. A pamphlet adding several new documents appeared in 1957 (*Kibitsuhiko jinja monjo, zoku hen*).

404
Saidaiji monjo 西大寺文書
Compiled by Kondō Isamu. Okayama, 1947.

The Muromachi-period records of a temple in Bizen. Some 27 pages of documents, followed by a long explanatory essay.

MIMASAKA PROVINCE (OKAYAMA PREFECTURE)

Okayama ken komonjo shū, *see* [400]

BITCHŪ PROVINCE (OKAYAMA PREFECTURE)

Okayama ken komonjo shū, *see* [400]

•405
Bitchū no kuni Niimi-no-shō shiryō 備中国新見荘史料
Compiled by Setonaikai sōgō kenkyūjo. Okayama, 1952.

Superb collection of materials dealing with Niimi Estate in Bitchū Province, a Tōji proprietorship. Chronological arrangement allows the Niimi story to unfold gradually. Coverage begins in 1221 but is most detailed for the Muromachi period, since Niimi was essentially a post-Kamakura *shōen*. There are no notes, but numerous secondary works derive from these documents.

406
Bitchū no kuni Niimi-no-shō shiryō 備中国新見荘史料
Compiled by Kokugakuin daigaku. 3 vols. Tōkyō, n.d.

Contains a somewhat larger selection of Niimi-related sources than [405] and corrects some errors in that edition. Chronological arrangement but no notes. Soft-cover series missing from most libraries.

407
Ihara shiryō 3 井原史料
Compiled by Kishi Kajirō. Ihara, 1972.

Contains the documents and other materials relating to the Ise warrior house, from whose stock, according to some, the progenitor of the later Hōjō was descended; see [154]. Records date from the fifteenth century into Meiji, but there is a good selection from late medieval times. A valuable feature is the inclusion of careful notes. Several *shugo* records of the fifteenth century are of special interest.

408
Sanshōji monjo ni mieru Bitchū no kuni Kosaka-no-shō
三聖寺文書に見える備中国小坂庄
Fujii Shun. *Okayama daigaku hōbungakubu gakujutsu kiyō* 19 (1964): 38–46.

Essay presenting mostly Kamakura-period documents relating to Kosaka Estate in Bitchū Province.

INABA PROVINCE (TOTTORI PREFECTURE)

• 409
Tottori kenshi 2, chūsei 鳥取県史, 中世
Compiled by Tottori ken. Tottori, 1973.

A comprehensive history of Inaba and Hōki provinces, containing a special section for source records. Some 173 of these relate to Inaba, and 160 to Hōki. Arranged by collection with coverage from 1187 to 1600. A valuable work, though it would be surprising if the 333 documents presented here were exhaustive for the medieval age.

HŌKI PROVINCE (TOTTORI PREFECTURE)

Tottori kenshi 2, chūsei, see [409]

BINGO PROVINCE (HIROSHIMA PREFECTURE)

Yamanouchi Sudō ke monjo, see [79] and [80]

Takasu monjo, see [56]

• 410
Hiroshima kenshi, kodai-chūsei shiryō hen 1 広島県史, 古代 – 中世資料篇
Compiled by Hiroshima ken. Hiroshima, 1974.

The first volume in what will become the major source series for Bingo and Aki provinces. Contains chronicle, essay, and diary excerpts, with coverage from earliest times to 1600. Copies of documents found in narrative texts are included, but there are no document originals; these will appear in additional volumes. Chronological arrangement, but no notes. Useful introductory essay and source-name index. Volume 2, containing a portion of the massive Itsukushima Shrine collection of Aki Province, has just appeared (1976).

411
Innoshima Murakami ke monjo 因島村上家文書
Compiled by Innoshima shi kyōiku iinkai. Innoshima, 1965.

Pamphlet containing the documents of a warrior house of Bingo Province. A total of 51 records, from Kamakura to early Tokugawa. The Murakami were estate managers (*kumon*) during Kamakura times. A brief essay is appended. See also *Nihon engyō taikei, shiryō hen, kodai-chūsei* 1 [447].

AKI PROVINCE (HIROSHIMA PREFECTURE)

Hiroshima kenshi, *see* [410]

Kumagai ke monjo, *see* [133]

Kumagai ke monjo—Miura ke monjo—Hiraga ke monjo, *see* [78]

412
Geihan tsūshi 芸藩通志
Compiled by Rai Gyōhyō (Hiroshima toshokan). 5 vols. Hiroshima, 1908.

An early nineteenth-century compilation containing a variety of traditional sources with some documents. Of particular interest are the Itsukushima Shrine documents of the late Heian and early Kamakura ages (Volume 1, pp. 239ff). Our knowledge of the Taira family's usage of the *jitō* title derives from this collection. (Unfortunately, the full collection is not here; for the Heian portion, see *Heian ibun* [2], and also [413].) The volumes contain occasional notes; but there is no index, and arrangement is haphazard. Recently reprinted.

•413
Itsukushima jinja kankei monjo no denzon seiri jōkyō to mishōkai shiryō
厳島神社関係文書の伝存整理状況と未紹介史料
Compiled by Matsuoka Hisato (*Hiroshima daigaku bungakubu kiyō, bekkan* 2). Hiroshima, 1974.

An extremely important volume, containing many hitherto unpublished documents from the Itsukushima Shrine collection. The first part of the book consists of essays. Coverage is late Heian to the end of the Muromachi, with much on Kamakura times. See also [410, 412].

414
Asano ke monjo 浅野家文書
Compiled by Tōkyō daigaku shiryō hensanjo (*Dai Nihon komonjo, iewake* 2). Tōkyō, 1906.

Materials relating to the Asano house of Aki Province. Of little value to the medievalist, since coverage begins in the 1570's.

• 415
Kobayagawa ke monjo　小早川家文書
Compiled by Tōkyō daigaku shiryō hensanjo (*Dai Nihon komonjo, iewake* 11).
2 vols. Tōkyō, 1927.

Documents relating to the Kobayagawa warrior house of Aki. Extremely important for the Kamakura period, since the Kobayagawa were a *jitō* family in constant trouble with absentee estate owners. Coverage is Kamakura to early Tokugawa, with the majority of the documents dating from the sixteenth century.
Here was a Kantō family that established itself in western Japan and survived
into early modern times.

416
Gakuonji monjo ni tsuite　楽音寺文書について
Compiled by Kawai Masaharu (*Hiroshima ken bunkazai chōsa hōkoku* 2).
Hiroshima, 1962.

Pamphlet containing the 54 documents of the Gakuonji collection. Coverage begins in mid-Kamakura times, and the arrangement of records is chronological.
There is much of interest on land administration by a local temple. An essay is
appended.

417
Hiroshima daigaku bungakubu shozō Inokuma monjo ni tsuite
広島大学文学部所蔵猪熊文書について
Compiled by Fukuo Takeichirō (*Fukuo sensei kinenroku*). Hiroshima, 1972.

A selection of documents from several collections held by Hiroshima University.
Some 33 records are included, each with a lengthy analysis. Coverage is from
1221 to the end of the Muromachi age, but this is only a sampling of larger
holdings.

418
Fudōin monjo　不動院文書
Compiled by Iwama Takeo. *Shigaku kenkyū* 1.3 (1930): 436–44.

Brief collection of sixteenth- and early seventeenth-century documents from a
local temple in Aki. These are mostly private letters (*shojō*).

IZUMO PROVINCE (SHIMANE PREFECTURE)

• 419
Shinshū Shimane kenshi, shiryō hen 1　新修島根県史，史料篇
Compiled by Shimane ken. Hirata, 1966.

The major assemblage of documents for three western Honshū provinces (Izumo,
Iwami, and Oki). Coverage is from earliest times through the sixteenth century,
organized by collection. A chronological index is appended, along with an index
of terms, personal names, and place names. A companion volume, *Shinshū Shimane kenshi, tsūshi hen* 1, is a history of the region based on these sources. See
also [420].

• 420
Shimane kenshi 5–7　島根県史
Compiled by Shimane ken gakumubu Shimane kenshi hensangakari. Tōkyō,
1927.

Magnificent old volumes that integrate into their texts a huge number of medieval documents. The records themselves appear in a more modern format in [419], but the older work is still of value. The chronological index in [419] gives page references to the original series.

421
Gakuenji monjo no kenkyū　鰐淵寺文書の研究
Compiled by Sone Kenzō (Gakuenji monjo kankōkai). Hirata, 1963.

The medieval documents of a temple in Izumo Province. The first section of the book presents a detailed study of Gakuenji, its lands, and its political connections; the second section presents the documents. Unfortunately, the volume is marred by numerous errors in transcription. The same materials appear more accurately in [419]. Still, the format of this volume—historical text followed by sources—makes it a useful work. An index is appended.

• 422
Izumo Kokuzō ke monjo　出雲国造家文書
Compiled by Murata Masashi. Ōsaka, 1968.

Documents relating to a major family in Izumo Province. Materials date from the beginning of the Kamakura age and detail the Bakufu's involvement in Izumo, especially through its *shugo* appointee. Other documents show the imperial governorship working as a parallel force. Useful notes are appended. Coverage is into Tokugawa times.

423
Izumo Ou rokusha monjo　出雲意宇六社文書
Compiled by Shimane ken bunkazai aigo kyōkai. Matsue, 1974.

Massive volume containing materials of the six traditional shrines of Ou District in Izumo. Coverage is Kamakura to Meiji, with the later centuries predominating. Arrangement is chronological by individual collection, and there are brief headnotes. Very little on Kamakura.

IWAMI PROVINCE (SHIMANE PREFECTURE)

Shinshū Shimane kenshi, shiryō hen 1, *see* [419]

Shimane kenshi 5–7, *see* [420]

424
Iwami Kuri monjo no kenkyū　石見久利文書の研究
Compiled by Kinugasa Yasuki (*Ritsumeikan daigaku jimbun kagaku kenkyūjo kiyō* 16). Kyōto, 1967.

A small but richly annotated document collection relating to the Kuri warrior family of Iwami Province. Half a dozen late Heian records survive, but none for Kamakura; most of the materials date from the Muromachi age. Relevant documents from other collections are also presented.

425
Iwami Uchida ke monjo ni tsuite　石見内田家文書について
Compiled by Kunimori Susumu. *Yamaguchi ken monjokan kenkyū kiyō* 1 (1972): 89–109.

Collection of 94 documents relating to a warrior family in Iwami. About one-quarter date from Kamakura times, and many of these refer to the Bakufu and its men. No notes, but a brief introductory essay. Interesting collection.

OKI PROVINCE (SHIMANE PREFECTURE)

Shinshū Shimane kenshi, shiryō hen 1, *see* [419]

Shimane kenshi 5–7, *see* [420]

SUŌ PROVINCE (YAMAGUCHI PREFECTURE)

Kumagai ke monjo—Miura ke monjo—Hiraga ke monjo, *see* [78]

Shunjōbō Chōgen shiryō shūsei, *see* [319]

• 426
Hagi han batsu etsuroku 萩藩閥閲録
Compiled by Yamaguchi ken monjokan. 5 vols. Yamaguchi, 1967–71.

> An Edo compilation relating to Suō and Nagato provinces at the western end of Honshū. A massive compendium of documents, mostly from the sixteenth century. Unfortunately, the arrangement of materials follows no useful pattern, and there are no notes or chronological index. The patient researcher, however, can find much of interest. A scattering of documents date from Kamakura times.

427
Bōchō fūdo chūshin an 防長風土注進案
Compiled by Yamaguchi ken monjokan. 23 vols. Yamaguchi, 1961–65.

> An early nineteenth-century compilation containing a vast quantity of traditional sources. A few medieval documents, but overwhelmingly Tokugawa. There are no notes, index, or guides to the location of materials. Of minimal value.

428
Suō kokufu no kenkyū 周防国府の研究
Misaka Keiji. Tōkyō, 1933.

> A monograph containing an unusual number of medieval documents; the absence or inaccessibility elsewhere of many of these records warrants the inclusion of this title here. There is no document index, but the chapter headings and sub-sections serve as a guide. Coverage is Heian through Meiji.

429
Tokuyama shishi shiryō 徳山市史史料
Compiled by Tokuyama shishi hensan iinkai. Tokuyama, 1964.

> Materials relating to the region of modern Tokuyama City. Most of the documents are from the Iwashimizu Shrine collection [289, 290] and concern *shōen* held by that institution. The records are interesting, but they are drawn largely from a central (not a local) collection.

430
Bōchō komonjo (Hikamisan Kōryūji monjo) 防長古文書（氷上山興隆寺文書）
Compiled by Bōchō shidankai. 5 vols. Yamaguchi, 1930–32.

> Highly interesting collection of documents bearing largely on the rise of the Ōuchi *daimyō* house. Arrangement of these pamphlets is chronological, with only

one document dating from Kamakura times. There are no notes. Volume 5 presents documents missed earlier. A very scarce series. An apparent reprint of these materials was published in 1962 by the Hōfu shiryō hozonkai.

431
Ōuchi shi bushō Sugi shi monjo ni tsuite 大内氏武将杉氏文書について
Compiled by Tamura Tetsuo. *Yamaguchi ken chihōshi kenkyū* 16 (1966): 28–35.

The Muromachi-period documents of a retainer house of the Ōuchi *daimyō*. A total of 45 records, with introductory essay.

432
Jōshi ke monjo 上司家文書
Compiled by Kokushi gakkai. *Kokushigaku* 29 (1936): 42–67.

Collection of 41 documents relating to an estate administrator house in service to the Tōdaiji. This family was sent to Suō Province to represent Tōdaiji interests there. A number of Suō governor's decrees are included, and the materials, which begin in the early Kamakura period, are unusually interesting. A sequel (*Kokushigaku* 30 [1937], pp. 68–84) continues the coverage from Muromachi to Meiji.

NAGATO PROVINCE (YAMAGUCHI PREFECTURE)

Hagi han batsu etsuroku, *see* [426]

Bōchō fūdo chūshin an, *see* [427]

433
Nagato Chōfu shiryō 長門長府史料
Compiled by Chōfu shi hensankai. Tōkyō, 1909.

Contains numerous documents relating to Nagato Province. The materials, however, are incorporated in a traditional text that has thoroughly outmoded chapter breakdowns. Difficult to use.

· 434
Nagato no kuni ichinomiya—Sumiyoshi jinja shiryō 1 長門国一宮住吉神社史料
Compiled by Sumiyoshi jinja shamusho. Shimonoseki, 1975.

An important volume containing a number of document collections (whole or partial) relating to Nagato's major official shrine. Coverage is Kamakura into Tokugawa, arranged by collection. Nicely produced.

435
Ichiki ke monjo 櫟木家文書
Compiled by Sumiyoshi jinja shamusho. Shimonoseki, 1975.

The documents of the official "carpenter-blacksmith" family of the Nagato provincial headquarters. Coverage is mostly Tokugawa, but there are some 52 medieval records, beginning from the thirteenth century. Chronological arrangement and an attractive format, though there are few notes and no accompanying essay.

436
Nagato no kuni Shōgakuzan Shōbōji monjo 長門国松嶽山正法寺文書
Compiled by Bōchō shidankai. Yamaguchi, 1931.

Collection of 66 documents, of which about one-third date from Kamakura times. A variety of Bakufu-related records are included. The Muromachi materials concern the Ōuchi *daimyō* house. Interesting collection.

• 437
Nagato no kuni Iminomiya jinja monjo　長門国忌宮神社文書
Compiled by Bōchō shidankai. Yamaguchi, 1932.

Collection of 185 documents, of which 23 date from Kamakura times. More than half of these records are Bakufu decrees, and a majority of the fourteenth- and fifteenth-century documents concern the Ōuchi. An important collection, but published in an extremely scarce series.

438
Tawara ke monjo ni tsuite　田原家文書について
Compiled by Kunimori Susumu. *Yamaguchi ken chihōshi kenkyū* 23 (1970): 37–42.

Introduces a handful of documents from the collection of a one-time governor's family that settled in Nagato and became powerful there. Materials begin at the end of the Kamakura age and range to the sixteenth century. A descriptive essay and genealogy are included.

Shikoku Region

SANUKI PROVINCE (KAGAWA PREFECTURE)

I have encountered no document publications here, and no plans have been announced for a major prefectural history.

AWA PROVINCE (TOKUSHIMA PREFECTURE)

439
Awa no kuni chōko zasshō　阿波国徴古雑抄
Compiled by Kosugi Un'son. Tōkyō, 1913.

More than 1,000 pages of source materials (medieval and early modern) relating to Awa Province in Shikoku. Roughly 400 pages of documents. Organization is by collection, but there is no chronological index. A minimal number of Kamakura-period documents. Despite its age and various transcription errors, this remains the standard compendium for Awa. Recently reprinted.

• 440
Awa no kuni shōen shiryōshū　阿波国荘園史料集
Compiled by Okino Shun'ichi. Tokushima, 1972.

Deserves to become the basic source book for medieval Awa, though as yet largely unknown. Contains documents and other materials relating to the *shōen* of that province. Arrangement is by individual estate, making this an easy volume to use. Coverage is Heian through Muromachi. A truly important work.

441
Tokushima ken shiryō 1　徳島県史料
Compiled by Tokushima kenshi hensan iinkai. Tokushima, 1964.

A narrow selection of old records arranged chronologically. Unsatisfactory owing to thinness of coverage. One of the weakest prefectural histories.

IYO PROVINCE (EHIME PREFECTURE)

• 442

Ehime ken hennen shi 1–7　愛媛県編年史
Compiled by Ehime kenshi hensan iinkai. Matsuyama, 1963–71.

An outstanding history of Iyo Province through source materials. Volume 1 treats to 1067, and Volume 2 covers late Heian through Kamakura times. Volumes 3–7 deal with Iyo during the Muromachi age. A drawback of this series is the absence of both a document index and an essay describing the collections presented; but brief notes direct the user to the next document in a sequence. Highly recommended, despite occasional transcription and punctuation errors. Additional volumes continue into Tokugawa times.

443

Kutsuna ke monjo　忽那家文書
Compiled by Kageura Tsutomu (*Iyo shiryō shūsei* 1). Matsuyama, 1964.

The documents relating to a native warrior house of Iyo. The Kutsuna became *jitō* of their homeland estate and were soon plunged into a series of disputes with the *shōen* owner. There is a long introductory essay. Should be used with the Kutsuna-related Chōryūji documents appended to Volume 2 in this series [444]. See Part I, Docs. 100–106.

444

Zennōji monjo　善応寺文書
Compiled by Kageura Tsutomu (*Iyo shiryō shūsei* 2). Matsuyama, 1965.

The documents of a temple in Iyo Province. Although coverage begins in the late Kamakura age, all but a few records date from Muromachi times. A long introductory essay describes the temple and its history. Also presented is the Chōryūji collection, which is of much greater interest to the Kamakura researcher. Arranged chronologically.

• 445

Kōno ke monjo　河野家文書
Compiled by Kageura Tsutomu (*Iyo shiryō shūsei* 3). Matsuyama, 1967.

Documents of the Kōno house, which emerged from the Gempei War as Iyo Province's major warrior family. As vassals of Kamakura they survived a difficult relationship with the Bakufu, including a massive dispossession of their holdings in 1221. The family prospered in Muromachi times, but, like so many others, it was finally destroyed in the 1580's. The first half of the book is a historical essay on the Kōno. Highly recommended.

446

Kannenji monjo　観念寺文書
Compiled by Kageura Tsutomu (*Iyo shiryō shūsei* 4). Matsuyama, 1968.

The documents of a temple in Iyo Province. Coverage is almost exclusively Muromachi. A long introductory essay places the documents in perspective. A fifth volume in this series was announced but never published.

• 447

Nihon engyō taikei, shiryō hen, kodai-chūsei 1
日本塩業大系，史料編，古代－中世
Compiled by Nihon engyō taikei henshū iinkai. Tōkyō, 1970.

A volume of major importance, presenting the documents relating to Yugeshima Estate in Iyo Province and the Innoshima region of Bingo Province. The volume is part of a new series dealing with the salt industry in Japanese history. The materials themselves, however, relate to land and local power in the two areas concerned. The Yugeshima collection, by far the more important, contains over 300 documents tracing the history of this estate from late Heian times to the middle of the fifteenth century. An unusually rich selection of Kamakura records can be found. The Innoshima materials update those contained in [411]. A valuable essay is appended.

448
Nakajima chōshi shiryōshū　中島町誌史料集
Compiled by Kageura Tsutomu. Nakajima, 1975.

A massive volume containing records bearing on a small but important region of Iyo Province. Most of the sources date from Tokugawa times, but there is a useful section containing medieval documents (about 55 pages). Highlighted is the Kutsuna collection [443].

TOSA PROVINCE (KŌCHI PREFECTURE)

449
Tosa tokanshū. 3 vols.　土佐と簡集
Compiled by Yokogawa Suekichi. Kōchi, 1966.

A Tokugawa-period compilation of Tosa-related source materials. Volume 1 contains documents from the late Heian period to the mid-sixteenth century; Volume 2 covers the latter half of that century; and Volume 3 deals with the early Tokugawa. There are a number of interesting Kamakura records, but the absence of notes or a document list makes this volume difficult to use. The documents, moreover, are transcribed without punctuation and without standard titles (e.g. Kantō gechijō).

450
Kōsokabe shiryō　香宗我部史料
Compiled by Maeda Kazuo. Kōchi, 1964.

A mimeographed assemblage of source materials bearing on one of the important native warrior houses of Tosa. Like the much better-known Chōsokabe, the Kōsokabe were originally a subject family of the pre-Taika Soga clan. Contains many valuable documents, with coverage beginning in the 1180's. The Kōsokabe head was granted a Kamakura *jitō shiki* in 1193, and the fortunes of the family can be traced into the sixteenth century. Poor printing and the absence of indexes or other aids, however, make this a difficult work to use.

451
Sengoku monjo shūei—Chōsokabe shi hen　戦国文書聚影－長宗我部氏篇
Compiled by Yamamoto Takeshi (Sengoku monjo kenkyūkai). Tōkyō, 1974.

Photographs and transcriptions of representative documents relating to the great sixteenth-century Chōsokabe *daimyō*. Excellent notes, and the photographs are superb.

452
Aki monjo　安芸文書
Compiled by Kinsei sonraku kenkyūkai (*Kinsei sonraku jiji shiryō* 2). 1956.

Mimeographed collection of documents relating to a Tosa warrior house. The paper and printing are of very low quality, and there are no notes, index, or accompanying essay. Contains records beginning in Kamakura times, but extremely difficult to use.

Kyūshū Region

GENERAL

Kamakura Bakufu saikyojō shū 2, *see* [9]

•453
Kyūshū shiryō sōsho 九州史料叢書
Compiled by Kyūshū shiryō kankōkai. Fukuoka, 1955–66.

A major series of document volumes dealing with Kyūshū history. Unfortunately, the user must contend with mimeographed (as opposed to regularly printed) characters, and the extreme scarcity of the books involved. Editions range between 100 and 300 copies. Nevertheless, a crucial series. Individual volumes dealing with the medieval age appear separately [474, 519, 520, 525, 546, 569].

•454
Kyūshū shōen shiryō sōsho 九州荘園史料叢書
Takeuchi Rizō, gen. ed. 18 vols. Tōkyō, 1962–70.

A series presenting the documents relating to various *shōen* in Kyūshū. Invaluable for the study of different patterns of estate development. Each volume is self-contained, with the focus on one or more *shōen* in a limited geographical region. Individual titles are listed below [475, 484, 485, 488, 497, 504, 510, 511, 512, 516, 518, 527, 538, 539, 540, 559, 581, 582]. Unfortunately, the limitations mentioned in [453] also apply here.

•455
Chinzei tandai shiryōshū 鎮西探題史料集
Compiled by Kawazoe Shōji. 2 vols. Fukuoka, 1965.

The indispensable source book for Kyūshū during late Kamakura times (1293–1333). The collection contains virtually all known documents (a total of 1,075) relating to the Bakufu's special deputyship for Kyūshū, the Chinzei *tandai*. Arrangement is chronological. Unfortunately, there are no notes or index, though each document is labeled by type and collection name. A rare work.

•456
Chūkai Genkō bōrui hennen shiryō—ikoku keigo ban'yaku shiryō no kenkyū
注解元寇防塁編年史料－異国警固番役史料の研究
Compiled by Kawazoe Shōji (Fukuoka shi kyōiku iinkai). Fukuoka, 1971.

A documentary history of the defense effort against the Mongol Invasions (1274 and 1281) and its aftermath. Copious notes and a rendering of the materials from Chinese into Japanese make this a highly useful book. See also [482].

457
Genkō shiryōshū 元寇史料集
Compiled by Kokumin seishin bunka kenkyūjo. 2 vols. Tōkyō, 1935.

A compendium of materials relating to the Mongol Invasions. Long standard but now considered incomplete and unreliable, though no single work has taken its place. The invasions are better studied through volumes such as [456] and [459], which are completely authoritative.

458
Fukuteki hen　伏敵篇
Compiled by Yamada An'ei. Tōkyō, 1891.

A large collection of materials bearing on Japanese foreign relations during the period 1260–1443. Coverage is most detailed for the Mongol Invasion period, though more modern works are recommended. Still, this remains an important volume.

•459
Dazaifu—Dazaifu Tenmangū shiryō　太宰府－太宰府天満宮史料
Compiled by Takeuchi Rizō. 9 vols. to date. Dazaifu, 1964– .

A major series documenting the history of the Dazaifu, the imperial headquarters for Kyūshū. Indispensable for a study of early relations with Korea and China, and for the nature of imperial power in western Japan. All types of materials are included, and many entries are prefaced by a brief summary. Volumes 1–6 cover the period before 1156, and Volumes 7–9 carry events to 1316. The last three books are a major source on the Kamakura Bakufu's involvement (through the Dazaifu) in Kyūshū. There are also extensive data on the Mongol Invasions. This hard-cover series will eventually supersede the next three entries [460–62].

460
Dazaifu shiryō, jōsei hen　太宰府史料，上世編
Compiled by Takeuchi Rizō (Kyūshū bunka sōgō kenkyūjo). 10 vols. Fukuoka, 1954–57.

Contains Dazaifu-related sources dating from the seventh century to 1185. Superseded by [459].

•461
Dazaifu—Dazaifu Tenmangū shiryō, chūsei hen
太宰府－太宰府天満宮史料，中世編
Compiled by Takeuchi Rizō (Kyūshū bunka sōgō kenkyūjo). 8 vols. Fukuoka, 1957–58.

Dazaifu-related sources dating from 1185 to 1392. Volumes 5–8 treat the period after 1316, and Volume 8 includes materials missed earlier.

•462
Dazaifu—Dazaifu Tenmangū—Hakata shiryō, zoku chūsei hen
太宰府－太宰府天満宮－博多史料，続中世編
Compiled by Takeuchi Rizō (Kyūshū bunka sōgō kenkyūjo). 8 vols. Fukuoka, 1958–60.

Sources relating to the Dazaifu and to foreign trade conducted through the adjacent port town of Hakata. Coverage is 1395–1600. A work of major importance.

463
Seisei shōgun no miya　征西將軍宮
Compiled by Fujita Akira. 1915.

A handsome old volume containing 170 pages of documents relating to Kyūshū during Nambokuchō times. Most of the volume consists of essays dealing with a variety of subjects, from the activities of different warrior houses to the role of the Dazaifu. The connecting thread is the story of Kanenaga Shinnō, son of the emperor Go-Daigo, who was Southern Court military commander for western Japan (*seisei shōgun no miya*). Recently reprinted.

464
Dazai kannaishi 太宰管内志
Compiled by Itō Tsunetari. 3 vols. Ōsaka, 1934.

An early 19th-century compilation containing materials on all the provinces of Kyūshū. The documents, however, are buried within a gazetteer text, and individual records are difficult to locate. Rarely used today.

• 465
Imagawa Ryōshun kankei hennen shiryō 今川了後関係編年史料
Compiled by Kawazoe Shōji. 2 vols. Fukuoka, 1960–61.

Imagawa was an important figure in Kyūshū during the late fourteenth century. A highly useful work that documents the character and extent of Muromachi Bakufu influence in that region. Chronological arrangement of materials, but no notes. A rare work.

• 466
Kyūshū chihō chūsei hennen monjo mokuroku (Kamakura-Nambokuchō jidai hen)
九州地方中世編年文書目録（鎌倉 - 南北朝時代編）
Compiled by Seno Seiichirō. 2 vols. Tōkyō, 1974.

An indispensable listing of all Kyūshū-related documents from the Kamakura and Nambokuchō periods, along with the volumes in which they can be found. Basic for any research on this part of Japan during the early medieval age. Unfortunately, there are no comparable works for other regions.

467
Kyūshū chihō chūsei hennen monjo mokuroku (Kamakura jidai hen)
九州地方中世編年文書目録（鎌倉時代編）
Compiled by Seno Seiichirō. Fukuoka, 1966.

An earlier version of Volume 1 of [466]. Now entirely superseded.

CHIKUZEN PROVINCE (FUKUOKA PREFECTURE)

Chūkai Genkō bōrui hennen shiryō, *see* [456]

468
Fukuoka kenshi shiryō 福岡県史資料
Compiled by Itō Bishirō. 12 vols. Fukuoka, 1932–40.

The source materials (documents, essays, chronicles, etc.) of Chikuzen, Chikugo, and Buzen provinces. Of special note are Volumes 7–10, which contain lengthy document sections dealing with the Gempei and Kamakura periods. Nearly all of the other volumes have a scattering of old records arranged by collection. For the most part, however, this series is unwieldy and unsatisfactory, and most of its nondocumentary materials are of little value to the historian. There is no index of documents, and the total offerings are incomplete.

469
Kyūshū no sekitō—Fukuoka ken 九州の石塔－福岡県
Compiled by Tadakuma Toyoaki. Fukuoka, 1974.

Stone inscriptions in Fukuoka, dating from Heian to Tokugawa. A beautifully produced volume, replete with photographs and notes and containing detailed introductory essays.

• 470
Kaho chihōshi, kodai-chūsei hen　嘉穂地方史，古代－中世篇
Kawazoe Shōji. Tōkyō, 1968.

The study of a district in Chikuzen through documents and other source excerpts. Coverage is from earliest times through the end of the sixteenth century. The notes are unusually thorough. A model effort.

• 471
Munakata gunshi 2　宗像郡誌
Compiled by Itō Bishirō. 1932.

The documents of Munakata Shrine in Chikuzen Province's Munakata District. An extremely important collection, with coverage beginning in the late Heian period. Munakata was closely connected with the Taira, and after them with the Minamoto. Chronological arrangement, but no notes. Volumes 1 and 3 also have a scattering of documentary materials. Recently reprinted.

472
Hakozaki gū shiryō　筥崎宮史料
Compiled by Murata Masashi. Fukuoka, 1970.

Sources relating to Hakozaki Shrine in modern Fukuoka City. Most of the documents presented derive from the Iwashimizu collection in Kyōto [289, 290]. The Hakozaki materials, especially those on the early medieval period, are too few to constitute a major collection. No notes and no chronological index. Coverage is through the Meiji era.

473
Fukuoka shi Hakozaki Hachimangū shozō "On'aburaza monjo utsushi," "Hakozaki jingū monjo," "Ishidōrō meibun"
福岡市筥崎八幡宮所蔵「御油座文書写」「筥崎神宮文書」「石燈籠銘文」
Compiled by Kawazoe Shōji. *Kyūshū shigaku* 7 (1958): 40–50.

Documents from the first collection (Aburaza) predominate here (36 records), and these date mostly from Muromachi times. They are transcribed here for the first time. No notes.

474
Asō monjo　麻生文書
Compiled by Shinjō Tsunezō (*Kyūshū shiryō sōsho* 17). Fukuoka, 1966.

Important document collection for Chikuzen Province during the Muromachi period. Only four documents relate to the Asō house during Kamakura times. Materials arranged chronologically, with 60 percent or more dating from the sixteenth century. The Asō were originally deputy *jitō* over three land units in Chikuzen.

475
Chikuzen no kuni Ito-no-shō shiryō　筑前国怡土荘史料
Compiled by Shinjō Tsunezō and Masaki Kisaburō (*Kyūshū shōen shiryō sōsho* 4). Tōkyō, 1963.

The documents of a Chikuzen *shōen* held in proprietorship by the Hōkongō-in temple of Kyōto. Coverage begins in the late Heian era, and there are numerous records from Kamakura times. The Bakufu had extensive dealings with this estate, and the documents reflect this. Coverage continues into the sixteenth century.

476
Kyū Kama–Honami ryōgun kankei hennen shiryō
旧嘉麻ー穂波両郡関係編年史料
Compiled by Kawazoe Shōji. Fukuoka, 1960.

Pamphlet containing documents and other source excerpts relating to two districts in Chikuzen. Arrangement is chronological, from Heian through Muromachi. There are no notes.

477
Usui-no-shō no kenkyū, shiryō hen 1　碓井荘の研究，史料篇
Compiled by Kawazoe Shōji. Fukuoka, 1959.

Pamphlet containing the Heian-period records of a *shōen* in Chikuzen; 40 documents in all, arranged chronologically. No notes.

478
Chikuzen no kuni Kayuda-no-shō shiryō　筑前国粥田荘史料
Compiled by Masaki Kisaburō. Fukuoka, 1961.

Pamphlet containing the Kamakura and Muromachi documents of a *shōen* in Chikuzen. There are many Bakufu-related records, since this estate received a *jitō* early on. No notes.

479
Shikanoumi jinja shozō monjo　志賀海神社所蔵文書
Shikan 70 (1964): 67–81.

The documents held by a shrine in Chikuzen. Coverage is from the fifteenth century to the end of the Tokugawa. There are notes and an accompanying essay.

480
Ihara ke monjo　井原家文書
Compiled by Moriyama Tsuneo. *Kyūshū shigaku* 17 (1961): 53–59.

Brief collection of fifteenth- and sixteenth-century documents transcribed here for the first time. Documents issued by the Ōuchi *daimyō* house predominate.

481
Aoki monjo　青木文書
Compiled by Fukuoka shi kyōiku iinkai. *Shimoyama mon iseki.* Fukuoka, 1973.

Collection of 31 documents relating to the Aoki warrior house of Chikuzen. Coverage is the fifteenth and sixteenth centuries. A brief introduction is included.

482
Shiseki Genkō bōrui kankei hennen shiryō　史跡元寇防塁関係編年史料
Compiled by Fukuoka shi kyōiku iinkai. Fukuoka, 1967.

A pamphlet containing a selection of documents relating to the anti-Mongol defense effort centered in Chikuzen. Much more modest than *Chūkai Genkō bōrui hennen shiryō* [456], which takes a wide-angle view of this resistance.

CHIKUGO PROVINCE (FUKUOKA PREFECTURE)

Fukuoka kenshi shiryō, *see* [468]

Kyūshū no sekitō—Fukuoka ken, *see* [469]

483
Chikugo kokushi 1–2　筑後国史
Compiled by Yano Kazusada. Kurume, 1926.

Traditional-style volumes containing a large number of source materials, including documents. In Volume 2, which deals with warrior families in Chikugo, there are a few records not to be found elsewhere. Volume 1, which treats historical incidents and personages, is somewhat weaker on documents. Unfortunately, there are no notes or research aids. Recently reprinted.

484
Chikugo no kuni Mizuta-no-shō–Hirokawa-no-shō shiryō
筑後国水田荘－広川荘史料
Compiled by Katayama Naoyoshi and Era Hiroshi (*Kyūshū shōen shiryō sōsho* 10). Tōkyō, 1965.

The documents of two *shōen* in Chikugo. Materials on Mizuta are almost exclusively from the Muromachi age and include a number of edicts by Imagawa Ryōshun, Kyūshū deputy for the Ashikaga (see [465]). The handful of records on Hirokawa are too meager to trace the rise of this estate.

• 485
Chikugo no kuni Mizuma-no-shō shiryō　筑後国三潴荘史料
Compiled by Seno Seiichirō (*Kyūshū shōen shiryō sōsho* 14). Tōkyō, 1966.

The documents of a *shōen* incorporated in the twelfth century. Various records survive to show that this estate was parceled out on the *jitō* level to deserving Bakufu vassals after the Mongol Invasions. This was followed by a territorial division of the *shōen* near the end of the Kamakura period. Vividly documents the erosion of central proprietary control over a distant domain.

486
Miike shi kankei hennen shiryō　三池氏関係編年史料
Compiled by Ōki Michinobu (*Kyū Miike gun kyōdo shiryō, chūsei hen*). N.d.

Documents relating to the Miike house of northern Kyūshū, arranged chronologically. Coverage is from the 1270's to the end of the sixteenth century. The materials are from a variety of collections and tell a most interesting story. This family held a *jitō shiki* during Kamakura times. See [487, 488].

487
Nakamura shi shozō Miike monjo ni tsuite　中村氏所蔵三池文書について
Compiled by Asoshina Yasuo. *Kumamoto shigaku* 29 (1965): 42–51.

Presentation of 18 new documents relating to the Miike warrior house of northern Kyūshū. Coverage is late Kamakura to 1600. Photographs of several records are included, and there is an accompanying essay.

488
Chikugo no kuni Miike-no-shō shiryō　筑後国三池荘史料
Compiled by Kawazoe Shōji (*Kyūshū shōen shiryō sōsho* 13). Tōkyō, 1966.

The documents relating to a Chikugo estate probably established in the twelfth century. The proprietary title was subsequently transferred to several different central holders. A secure local lordship [486, 487] began to emerge during late Kamakura times.

489
Shōen sonraku no ikō—Chikugo Setaka shimo-no-shō no baai
庄園村落の遺構－筑後瀬高下庄の場合
Kagamiyama Takeshi. *Shien* 81 (1960): 1–65.

A major essay introducing the Takao document collection. Should be used with [490].

• 490
Chikugo Takao monjo 筑後鷹尾文書
Compiled by Kumamoto chūsei shi kenkyūkai. Kumamoto, 1974.

The documents of a local shrine and its chief family of officers. Coverage is principally Kamakura, and there is much data here on internal shrine affairs and local land administration. Typically, however, most estates seem to have been held at the highest level by figures in Kyōto. An explanatory essay is appended, and there are useful headnotes. A volume long awaited by Japanese scholars. The documents are vivid in their descriptions, and the volume is finely produced.

491
Nanchō kankei Gojō ke monjo no kenkyū 南朝関係五条家文書の研究
Compiled by Murata Masashi. *Kokushikan daigaku jimbungaku kiyō* 1 (1969).

Essay presenting the documents of a central noble family that went to Kyūshū during the 1330's in service to the court. They remained and became a considerable power locally, fighting on the side of the Southern Court during the Nambokuchō wars. Each of the 47 documents is individually analyzed.

• 492
Gojō ke monjo 五条家文書
Compiled by Murata Masashi and Kurokawa Takaaki (Zoku Gunsho ruijū kanseikai, *Shiryō sanshū—komonjo hen*). Tōkyō, 1975.

The full collection of Gojō house documents, arranged chronologically. A total of 364 records, with genealogical data, an index of personal names, and a descriptive essay. Coverage is the fourteenth through sixteenth centuries. An important work.

493
"Kōra ki" shihai monjo 「高良記」紙背文書
Compiled by Kumamoto chūsei shi kenkyūkai. *Gekkan rekishi* 3 (1968): 9–12.

A collection of 12 Kamakura and Nambokuchō documents copied on the reverse side of the Kōra Chronicle of Kōra Shrine in Chikugo. Mostly land sale and testamentary records, though one Kamakura Bakufu communique to a *shugo* deputy is included. See also [494].

494
Kōra Tamatare gū shimpisho—dō shihai 高良玉垂宮神秘書－同紙背
Kawazoe Shōji et al. Fukuoka, 1972.

Massive volume containing the Kōra Chronicle, essays by several scholars, and a brief section for documents. The 12 documents [see 493] date from the thirteenth and fourteenth centuries. Published by Kōra Shrine.

495
Tachibana monjo 立花文書
Compiled by Tachibana Kanji. Fukuoka, 1914.

A collection of late Muromachi documents relating to northern Kyūshū. The Tachibana were a fourteenth-century offshoot of the house of Ōtomo and eventually became *daimyō* in their own right.

496
Monchūjo ke monjo　問註所家文書
Compiled by Asano Yōkichi. *Chikugo* 8.3 (1935).

Contains a large number of sixteenth-century documents relating to a local family of Chikugo. This house was in contact with many of the great *daimyō* of the period.

BUZEN PROVINCE (FUKUOKA PREFECTURE)

Fukuoka kenshi shiryō, *see* [468]

Kyūshū no sekitō—Fukuoka ken, *see* [469]

• 497
Buzen no kuni shōen shiryō　豊前国荘園史料
Compiled by Iida Hisao (*Kyūshū shōen shiryō sōsho* 18). Tōkyō, 1970.

Documents bearing on a variety of *shōen* in Buzen Province. Contains numerous Kamakura records, highlighted by materials on Kamata Estate, which received a Bakufu-appointed *jitō*.

498
Utsunomiya monjo　宇都宮文書
Compiled by Odachi Koretaka. Tōkyō, 1915.

The documents of a Kantō family that settled in Kyūshū. Only three or four records survive from Kamakura times; the rest date from the Muromachi age. Extensive headnotes make this a useful book. A rare work.

499
Kiyosue monjo　清末文書
Compiled by Miki Toshiaki and Kuwahada Kō. *Hōnichi shigaku* 132 (1960).

Collection of 81 fifteenth- and sixteenth-century documents relating to lands held by Usa Shrine. The Kiyosue were *myōshu* who became estate managers for Usa Shrine. Chronological arrangement.

500
Tagawa chihō shōen shiryō shūsei　田川地方荘園史料集成
Compiled by Era Hiroshi. *Kyōdo Tagawa* 25 (1966).

Brief compendium of documents relating to *shōen* in the Tagawa region of Buzen.

501
Monji shi shiryō　門司氏史料
Compiled by Yoshinaga Utarō. *Moji kyōdo sōsho* 1 (1954).

Contains the late Kamakura and Muromachi documents of a warrior house of Buzen Province. An unusually interesting collection, especially for the fourteenth century.

502
Ōzumi kei Monji shi monjo　大積系門司氏文書
Compiled by Kudō Keiichi. *Nihon rekishi* 280 (1971): 87–91.

Presents five new documents relating to a branch of the Monji warrior house. Coverage is 1333–1560. Photographs of all five records are included, and there is an accompanying essay.

BUZEN PROVINCE (ŌITA PREFECTURE)

Buzen no kuni shōen shiryō, *see* [497]

Zōho teisei hennen Ōtomo shiryō, *see* [505]

Hennen Ōtomo shiryō, *see* [506]

Ōtomo shiryō, *see* [508]

• 503
Ōita ken shiryō　大分県史料
Compiled by Ōita ken shiryō kankōkai. 28 vols to date. Ōita, 1960– .
One of the major document series for Kyūshū. Volumes 1–7 contain the records of the Usa Hachiman Shrine, which had a close and important relationship with the Kamakura Bakufu. Volumes 8–13 contain warrior documents from the Buzen-Bungo area; and Volumes 24–26 are records missed in 1–13. Volumes 14–23 cover the Tokugawa period, and Volumes 27–28 deal with the Christian movement. One flaw is the absence of a comprehensive index of materials: the arrangement of documents is not always clear. Nevertheless, an indispensable series.

504
Buzen no kuni Itōzu-no-shō–Tsubusa-no-shō shiryō
豊前国到津荘－津布佐荘史料
Compiled by Nakano Hatayoshi (*Kyūshū shōen shiryō sōsho* 8). Tōkyō, 1964.
Documents for Itōzu begin in the Mongol War period and show the Bakufu "commending" the *jitō shiki* to Usa Shrine, which largely controlled the estate anyway. Coverage is most extensive for the sixteenth century. Tsubusa Estate was an Usa Shrine land during late Heian times, but became a Mirokuji holding during the 1180's. The patron's right (*honke shiki*) was then commended to Iwashimizu Shrine in Kyōto. Coverage continues into the sixteenth century.

BUNGO PROVINCE (ŌITA PREFECTURE)

Ōita ken shiryō, *see* [503]

• 505
Zōho teisei hennen Ōtomo shiryō　増補訂正編年大友史料
Compiled by Takita Manabu. 33 vols. Ōita, 1962–71.
A true monument of historical scholarship: the collected documents relating to the great Kyūshū house of Ōtomo. The product of a lifetime of research. Supersedes [506] and [507], and indeed, transcends the Ōtomo themselves. The most comprehensive source book on northern Kyūshū, covering a period of 450 years. Unfortunately, a limited edition of 100 makes this work extremely rare.

• 506
Hennen Ōtomo shiryō　編年大友史料
Compiled by Takita Manabu. 2 vols. Kyōto, 1942–46.

Superb collection of materials relating to the Ōtomo warrior house of Bungo Province. Volume 1 covers to 1312, and Volume 2 to 1351. Copious notes make this series a starting point for any study of this great family. Although superseded by [505] in terms of breadth, the present work is better focused and more readily available. Highly recommended.

507
Ōtomo shiryō 大友史料
Compiled by Takita Manabu. 2 vols. Ōita, 1937–38.

Documents of the Ōtomo house during the sixteenth century. Chronological arrangement beginning with 1537. Occasional notes. See [505].

508
Sengoku monjo shūei—Ōtomo shi hen 戦国文書聚影－大友氏篇
Compiled by Watanabe Sumio and Akutagawa Tatsuo (Sengoku monjo kenkyūkai). Tōkyō, 1973.

Photographs of representative sixteenth-century documents of the Ōtomo house, along with transcriptions and notes. The photographs are superb, and the overall production is most effective.

• 509
Bungo no kuni Ōno-no-shō no kenkyū 豊後国大野荘の研究
Compiled by Kyūshū shōen sōgō kenkyūkai. Ōita, 1965.

The first half of this book contains essays on different aspects of Ōno Estate history. Part 2 presents all the Ōno-related documents, arranged chronologically. Many of these records deal with the Ōtomo, who became the region's dominant family. An exemplary format, combining text and documents.

510
Bungo no kuni Ōno-no-shō shiryō 豊後国大野荘史料
Compiled by Watanabe Sumio (*Kyūshū shōen shiryō sōsho* 1). Tōkyō, 1962.

Mostly the same materials (minus the essays) as [509], but contains useful headnotes and a map of the Ōno region. Historically one of the richest *shōen*.

511
Bungo no kuni Anami-no-shō shiryō 豊後国阿南荘史料
Compiled by Watanabe Sumio (*Kyūshū shōen shiryō sōsho* 12). Tōkyō, 1966.

The documents of a Bungo Province area that became a *shōen* in the 1230's. Of special interest because of the survival of materials from the twelfth century: the transition from the "public" to the "private" sector can be traced. Later documents carry the history of Anami to the end of the Muromachi era.

512
Bungo no kuni Kaku-no-shō–Wasada-no-shō shiryō
豊後国賀来荘－植田荘史料
Compiled by Watanabe Sumio (*Kyūshū shōen shiryō sōsho* 16). Tōkyō, 1967.

The documents of two *shōen* established during the final decades of the Heian period. In the case of Kaku Estate, we see the process of acquiring an exemption from the provincial office, as well as early attempts at administration by Yusahara Shrine. Later, Kaku-no-shō was subjected to a *jitō's* lawlessness, with control finally coming to rest with the Ōtomo house. Documentation extends to the sixteenth century, with about 20 records from Kamakura times. Wasada Estate became a retired emperor's holding after the Hōgen Incident (1156), but documentation is sparse until the early fourteenth century. Wasada also fell under Ōtomo sway.

513
Hagiwara monjo 萩原文書
Compiled by Ono Seiichi. Ōita, 1930.

Most of this volume is a history of the Hagiwara warrior house, but there is also a document section with extensive notes. These materials date from the sixteenth and seventeenth centuries. A house genealogy and chronology are included.

514
Bungo no kuni zudenchō 豊後国図田帳
Zoku gunsho ruijū 33.1: 477–88. Tōkyō, 1958.

A field register of 1285 containing voluminous data on the estates of Bungo Province. Tax information and the names of proprietors and *jitō* are given.

HIZEN PROVINCE (SAGA PREFECTURE)

•515
Saga ken shiryō shūsei 佐賀県史料集成
Compiled by Saga kenshi hensan iinkai. 16 vols. to date. Saga, 1955– .

A major compendium of documents, and an indispensable series for the history of Kyūshū. Perhaps the most interesting collections are those of Takeo Shrine in Volume 2, the Ryūzōji *daimyō* house in Volume 3, and the Fukabori warrior house in Volume 4. But each of the first seven volumes plus Volume 15 contains much of value on the medieval age; Volumes 8–14 and 16 are mostly Tokugawa. Arrangement is by collection, with an unusually large share of Bakufu-related materials, both Kamakura and Muromachi.

516
Hizen no kuni Kanzaki-no-shō shiryō 肥前国神崎荘史料
Compiled by Seno Seiichirō (*Kyūshū shōen shiryō sōsho* 2). Tōkyō, 1963.

One of the most interesting volumes in this series, with records dating back to pre-Kamakura times. During the twelfth century Kanzaki was a trade center under Taira management. Later it became the appointment site for a Kamakura *jitō*. In the years after the Mongol wars Kanzaki was parceled out by the Bakufu as rewards for its men. Coverage continues into the sixteenth century.

•517
Hizen no kuni Kanzaki-no-shō shiryō 肥前国神崎荘史料
Compiled by Seno Seiichirō (*Shōen shiryō sōsho*). Tōkyō, 1975.

A revised and expanded version of [516] in a new hardcover edition. Carefully organized and handsomely produced. A descriptive essay is appended. A volume of major importance.

518
Hizen no kuni Nagashima-no-shō shiryō 肥前国長嶋荘史料
Compiled by Seno Seiichirō (*Kyūshū shōen shiryō sōsho* 11). Tōkyō, 1965.

The documents of a Hizen Province *shōen* during Kamakura and Muromachi times. Held as a proprietorship by an imperial chapel, Nagashima became the second largest *shōen* in Hizen. Interesting for examining both the inroads made by a Kamakura *jitō* and the rising influence of an important local shrine.

519
Ogashima monjo—Ōkawa monjo—Madarashima monjo
小鹿島文書－大川文書－斑島文書
Compiled by Seno Seiichirō (*Kyūshū shiryō sōsho* 11). Fukuoka, 1960.

Contains three important document collections: (1) the records of a Kamakura vassal house that moved from eastern Japan to Kyūshū; (2) those of a Bakufu houseman family native to Kyūshū; (3) the records of a vassal house that was part of the Matsuura (or Matsura) warrior league. A valuable work.

520
Matsuura tō shoke monjo   松浦党諸家文書
Compiled by Seno Seiichirō (*Kyūshū shiryō sōsho* 7). Fukuoka, 1958.

A compendium of documents bearing on the famous Matsuura warrior league (*tō*) centered in Hizen Province. The individual members of this group became Kamakura vassals. Arranged by collection, with brief headnotes. Interesting materials.

521
Hirado Matsuura ke shiryō   平戸松浦家資料
Compiled by Kyōto daigaku bungakubu kokushi kenkyūshitsu. Kyōto, 1951.

A slim volume containing a number of extremely important documents relating to warrior organization in Hizen Province. Coverage is Kamakura and Muromachi. Includes much data on the medieval inheritance system and the proliferation of branches within the Matsuura warrior league. A genealogical chart is appended.

522
Matsuura tō no "Ariura monjo" ni tsuite   松浦党の「有浦文書」について
Compiled by Fukuda Ikuo. *Nihon rekishi* 240 (1968): 14–27.

Collection of 19 documents relating to a member family of the Matsuura warrior league. Coverage is the Nambokuchō era, and there is an accompanying essay. These materials shed light on the Matsuura group's relations with the Muromachi Bakufu.

523
Honkōji monjo   本光寺文書
Compiled by Moriyama Tsuneo. *Kyūshū shigaku* 19 (1961): 44–66.

Brief collection of sixteenth-century temple documents.

524
Tsukushi monjo   筑紫文書
Compiled by Fujii Sadabumi. *Ueno toshokan kiyō* 2 (1955): 55–68.

Collection of 29 sixteenth-century documents relating to a warrior family of Hizen. A number of records bearing Toyotomi Hideyoshi's seal are included.

HIZEN PROVINCE (NAGASAKI PREFECTURE)

Ogashima monjo—Ōkawa monjo—Madarashima monjo, *see* [519]

Matsuura tō shoke monjo, *see* [520]

Hirado Matsuura ke shiryō, *see* [521]

• 525
Aokata monjo 青方文書
Compiled by Seno Seiichirō (*Kyūshū shiryō sōsho* 5). 2 vols. Fukuoka, 1957–59.

Extremely rich collection relating to a native warrior family in Hizen Province. Volume 1 contains 202 Kamakura-period documents, with valuable data on local warrior relations, the Kamakura inheritance system, trade with China, and Bakufu interests in Hizen. Volume 2 is devoted to Muromachi records. Materials arranged chronologically, with brief headnotes.

• 526
Aokata monjo 1 青方文書
Compiled by Seno Seiichirō (Zoku Gunsho ruijū kanseikai, *Shiryō sanshū—komonjo hen*). Tōkyō, 1975.

A revised and expanded version of Volume 1 of [525]. Contains 234 documents with coverage to 1333. Handsomely produced. A second volume is expected soon.

527
Hizen no kuni Sonogi-no-shō–Isahaya-no-shō shiryō
肥前国彼杵荘－伊佐早荘史料
Compiled by Seno Seiichirō (*Kyūshū shōen shiryō sōsho* 7). Tōkyō, 1964.

Documentation for Sonogi begins in the mid-Kamakura age. By the end of the century proprietorship had shifted to the Tōfukuji in Kyōto. In the meantime, the eastern Fukabori family were appointed as *jitō*, encountering many difficulties from entrenched local interests. Isahaya had a vaguely similar history: revolving proprietorships and *jitō* difficulties with local officers during the thirteenth century.

528
Shimabara Tajima ke monjo 島原田島家文書
Compiled by Adachi Akitarō. *Rekishi chiri.* 57.1,3 (1931): 64–74, 76–86.

Collection of 27 warrior-house records from the sixteenth century. Contains documents under the seal of such *daimyō* as Oda, Takeda, and Imagawa. Fully annotated.

TSUSHIMA PROVINCE (NAGASAKI PREFECTURE)

• 529
Nagasaki kenshi, shiryō hen 1 長崎県史, 史料編
Compiled by Nagasaki kenshi hensan iinkai. Tōkyō, 1963.

The documents of Tsushima Island between Kyūshū and Korea. The rise of the Sō family from *jitō* to *daimyō* status can be traced. Coverage is from the late Kamakura age. There are no notes, but a chronological listing of documents is included.

530
Tsushima komonjo tenjikai kaisetsu furoku 対馬古文書展示会解説附録
Compiled by Kokushikan daigaku bungakubu kokushigaku kenkyūshitsu. 1967.

Pamphlet containing documents relating to the Sō *daimyō* house of Tsushima.

Several of these records date from late Kamakura times, when the Sō were still deputy *jitō*.

IKI PROVINCE (NAGASAKI PREFECTURE)

No known document publications for this small island province.

HIGO PROVINCE (KUMAMOTO PREFECTURE)

• 531
Kumamoto ken shiryō, chūsei hen　熊本県史料，中世篇
Compiled by Kumamoto kenshi hensankai. 5 vols. Kumamoto, 1961–67.

Five massive volumes containing several thousand documents relating to (or housed in) Higo Province. Arrangement is by collection, keyed to individual districts. At the beginning of each volume there is a brief description of the various document collections represented, though no comprehensive chronological index is included. Although the coverage is principally Muromachi, there are numerous Kamakura-period documents of note. Another indispensable series for the study of Kyūshū.

532
Kumamoto ken shiryō, chūsei hen hoi 1–3　熊本県史料，中世篇補遺
Compiled by Hanaoka Okiteru. *Kumamoto shigaku* 40–42 (1972–73): 46–62, 29–41, 36–54.

Parts 1 and 2 contain a collection of sixteenth-century and early seventeenth-century documents not included in [531]. The subject is the Yoshimura warrior house of Higo. Part 3 presents documents of the Shōdai family left out of Volume 1 of the Kumamoto series. For the Shōdai, see also [544].

533
Higo kokushi　肥後国誌
Compiled by Gotō Zezan. 2 vols. 1916–17.

Contains source materials for Higo Province, including numerous medieval documents. Arrangement is by district (*gun*), but the materials are incorporated in a traditional text. Recently reprinted. See [534].

534
Higo kokushi hoi—sakuin　肥後国誌補遺－索引
Compiled by Matsumoto Jusaburō. Kumamoto, 1972.

A supplement to the *Higo kokushi* [533] that adds many new documents and includes invaluable indexes to the main work. The series has now been rendered usable.

• 535
Sagara ke monjo　相良家文書
Compiled by Tōkyō daigaku shiryō hensanjo (*Dai Nihon komonjo, iewake* 5). 2 vols. Tōkyō, 1917–18.

The documents of an eastern warrior family that settled under Bakufu sponsorship in Higo Province. A highly interesting collection, with much detail on the interplay between contending local interests. Coverage is into Tokugawa times.

· 536

Aso monjo 阿蘇文書

Compiled by Tōkyō daigaku shiryō hensanjo (*Dai Nihon komonjo, iewake* 13).
3 vols. Tōkyō, 1932–34.

Excellent collection of documents relating to Aso Shrine in Higo. Coverage is from
the late Heian period on. During Kamakura times the Bakufu's leading house, the
Hōjō, exercised a major influence over this shrine. Especially important for the
Nambokuchō era. Materials range over all subjects, but most deal with land administration. Useful headnotes, but no comprehensive index of documents.

537

Aso monjo 阿蘇文書

Compiled by Kumamoto ken kyōiku iinkai. 3 vols. Kumamoto, 1973.

The same collection as [536], in two massive volumes. In this set, however, reproductions of originals rather than printed transcriptions are presented. Arrangement is chronological. The third volume provides supporting data, tables, and
an introductory essay.

· 538

Higo no kuni Kanokogi–Hitoyoshi-no-shō shiryō
肥後国鹿子木－人吉荘史料

Compiled by Sugimoto Hisao (*Kyūshū shōen shiryō sōsho* 3). Tōkyō, 1963.

The study of two Kyūshū *shōen* through documents. Kanokogi (near modern
Kumamoto City) is a classic "commended" *shōen* and therefore has been much
studied by scholars (e.g. Nakada Kaoru and Nagahara Keiji). Many of the documents are drawn from the Ōtomo-related Takuma collection. The Hitoyoshi records contain much of interest on warrior inheritance and the organization of agriculture. An important volume.

539

Higo no kuni Kamikura–Moritomi–Yatsushiro-no-shō shiryō
肥後国神蔵－守富－八代荘史料

Compiled by Sugimoto Hisao (*Kyūshū shōen shiryō sōsho* 9). Tōkyō, 1964.

The documents of three estates in Higo. Yatsushiro was a *shōen* whose managerial privilege had been seized from the Taira by the Minamoto. The same was
true for Moritomi, which soon fell under a Hōjō-controlled *jitō* post. Kamikura,
which has the largest number of Kamakura-period records, was likewise subjected to a *jitō* investiture. The growth of warrior power is vividly described in
the documents for this last *shōen*.

540

Higo no kuni hokubu shōen shiryō 肥後国北部荘園史料

Compiled by Sugimoto Hisao (*Kyūshū shōen shiryō sōsho* 17). Tōkyō, 1968.

Documents relating to various domains in the northern part of Higo Province.
Arrangement is by district (*gun*), with the heaviest concentration of records in
the fourteenth century. Eight *shōen* are represented.

541

Amakusa gun shiryō 2 天草郡史料

Compiled by Amakusa gun kyōikukai. Amakusa, 1914.

Contains a scattering of Higo-related medieval documents not available elsewhere. However, only a few pages of this massive volume are devoted to documentary sources. Recently reprinted.

542
Kyōdo ni kansuru komonjo no kenkyū (Higo Kōfukuji monjo)
郷土に関する古文書の研究（肥後廣福寺文書）
Compiled by Kumamoto ken Tamana chūgakkō. Kumamoto, 1934.

Pamphlet containing several document collections from Higo Province. The Kōfukuji local temple records are featured, and there is much of interest. Chronological
arrangement by collection, with coverage from the thirteenth century on.

543
Kikuchi monjo 菊池文書
Compiled by Hanaoka Okiteru. *Kumamoto shigaku* 28 (1964): 43–59.

Contains 36 documents relating to the Kikuchi warrior house during Muromachi
times. There are two Kamakura-period records, but both are clearly forgeries.

544
Shōdai monjo hoi 小代文書補遺
Compiled by Asoshina Yasuo. *Kumamoto shigaku* 27 (1964): 43–51.

Brief collection of documents relating to an eastern warrior house that moved to
Kyūshū during the later Kamakura period. The 17 documents included all date
from the Muromachi age.

545
Daijiji no Kangan Giin monjo 大慈寺の寒厳義尹文書
Compiled by Shimoda Kyokusui. *Kumamoto ken bunkazai chōsa hōkoku* 3
(1962).

Contains the documents relating to a well-known thirteenth-century priest of the
Sōtō sect who left Kyōto to take up residence in distant Higo. These materials
are presented here for the first time and are carefully analyzed.

SATSUMA PROVINCE (KAGOSHIMA PREFECTURE)

•546
Sappan kyūki zatsuroku, zempen 薩藩旧記雑録，前編
Compiled by Takeuchi Rizō (*Kyūshū shiryō sōsho* 1). 10 vols. Fukuoka,
1955–66.

The outstanding document collection for southern Kyūshū in the early medieval
age. Coverage is 1041–1372 and includes some 2,200 old records, arranged chronologically. The series itself, which is a nineteenth-century compilation, continues
into Tokugawa times, but publication of the remaining medieval sections has
ceased for the time being. Nevertheless, indispensable for a study of the great
Shimazu family, who rose from *jitō* to *daimyō* during the twelfth to fourteenth
centuries. Extremely scarce, owing to a very small edition. There is talk of a
reprint.

•547
Shimazu ke monjo 島津家文書
Compiled by Tōkyō daigaku shiryō hensanjo (*Dai Nihon komonjo, iewake* 16).
3 vols. to date. Tōkyō, 1942– .

The documents of the Shimazu *daimyō* house of southern Kyūshū. Coverage begins with the emergence of the family in the 1180's, when the first scion, a warrior of uncertain lineage from the Kantō, was made *jitō* of Japan's largest *shōen*, Shimazu. Unlike entry [546], which concentrates on a region, the present work tells the story of a family. Since the Shimazu during Kamakura times had dealings in many parts of Japan, documents from a number of provinces are included. Only later was the house limited to southern Kyūshū. Coverage is through the sixteenth century. A fascinating collection.

• 548
The Documents of Iriki 入来文書
Compiled by Asakawa Kan'ichi (Committee for the Publication of Dr. K. Asakawa's Works). Tōkyō, 1955 reprint.

Asakawa's classic study of southern Kyūshū through documents. However, the materials contained constitute less than 5 percent of the documentary total for that part of Japan. The Japanese sections have been published separately as *Iriki monjo* (Tōkyō, 1967).

549
Iriki-in Yamaguchi shi ni tsuite—Yamaguchi monjo no shōkai
入来院山口氏について－山口文書の紹介
Compiled by Gomi Yoshio. *Kadai shigaku* 11 (1963): 1–14.

A handful of late Kamakura documents relating to Iriki District in Satsuma. These materials are not contained in Asakawa's *Documents of Iriki* [548].

• 550
Kagoshima shishi 3 鹿児島市史
Compiled by Kagoshima shishi hensan iinkai. Kagoshima, 1971.

The historical materials relating to Satsuma's Kagoshima District. Coverage is from earliest times to the twentieth century. Appended are descriptions of the document collections, a historical chronology, a comprehensive bibliography, and an index. A handsomely produced volume.

551
Satsuma no kuni Nitta jinja monjo 薩摩国新田神社文書
Compiled by Kagoshima kenritsu toshokan (*Kagoshima ken shiryōshū* 3). Kagoshima, 1960.

A highly interesting collection of documents relating to a local shrine's land holdings in southern Kyūshū. Coverage is mostly Kamakura, with numerous documents issued by the Bakufu. Valuable headnotes are included. See [552, 553].

552
Satsuma no kuni Nitta jinja monjo hoi 薩摩国新田神社文書補遺
Compiled by Kagoshima kenritsu toshokan. Kagoshima, 1964.

A supplement to [551] that adds a few more documents.

• 553
Satsuma no kuni Nitta jinja monjo 薩摩国新田神社文書
Compiled by Kawauchi kyōdoshi hensan iinkai (*Kawauchi shi shiryōshū* 1,5). 2 vols. Kawauchi, 1972–73.

A revised and expanded edition of [551–52]. Volume 1 contains the Nitta Shrine documents proper, and Volume 2 related documents found in other collections.

An index of all materials is appended. A total of 308 records, along with full genealogical data. An important series.

554
Satsuma no kuni Yamada monjo　薩摩国山田文書
Compiled by Kagoshima kenritsu toshokan (*Kagoshima ken shiryōshū* 5).
Kagoshima, 1964.

The documents of a branch line of the Shimazu family. The Yamada became vassals and *jitō* in their own right. Many of these documents were printed earlier in [546], but appear here arranged chronologically. A genealogical chart is appended; and there is an insert to correct errata, including seven documents missed in the main volume.

555
Satsuma no kuni Ata gun shiryō　薩摩国阿多郡史料
Compiled by Kagoshima kenritsu toshokan (*Kagoshima ken shiryōshū* 7).
Kagoshima, 1967.

The documents relating to a district in Satsuma. Many of these records can be found elsewhere (e.g. [546]), but they are presented here in a single volume. Even distribution between Kamakura and Muromachi. A fifteenth-century diary, the *Yamada shōei nikki*, is also included.

556
Chūsei Yamato-in–Izumi gun kankei monjo shū
中世山門院－和泉郡関係文書集
Compiled by Gomi Yoshio. Kagoshima, 1967.

The documents relating to two administrative units within Satsuma Province. A brief introductory essay places the materials in perspective. The records themselves are drawn largely from [546].

557
Ishūin monjo　伊集院文書
Compiled by Gomi Yoshio (*Kagoshima ken shiryō shūi* 2). Kagoshima, 1965.

Pamphlet containing a handful of sixteenth-century records relating to a branch of the Shimazu house.

· 558
Satsuma no kuni Isaku-no-shō shiryō　薩摩国伊作荘史料
Compiled by Kōriyama Yoshimitsu (*Kyūshū shōen shiryō sōsho* 5).
Tōkyō, 1963.

The documents of an interior *shōen* within massive Shimazu Estate. A three-sided struggle for control of Isaku developed in the thirteenth century between a native officer house, a Kamakura *jitō* who was an easterner, and the Fujiwara proprietor. Documentation begins in the 1180's, and two-thirds of the materials date from Kamakura times. An important volume.

559
Satsuma no kuni Ketō-in ichibu jitō Madarame shi ni tsuite—Madarame monjo no shōkai o chūshin ni
薩摩国祁答院－分地頭斑目氏について－斑目文書の紹介を中心に
Compiled by Gomi Yoshio. *Kagoshima daigaku bungakka ronshū* 4 (1968):
41–69.

The Madarame collection and related documents, with commentary and a genealogical chart. The Madarame are believed to have come originally from Dewa Province in the north; a Kamakura *jitō* appointment moved them to the other end of Japan. There is much of interest on the final decades of the Kamakura age.

560
Madarame monjo 斑目文書
Compiled by Era Hiroshi. *Kyūshū shigaku* 16 (1962): 51–54.

Initial transcription of the Madarame collection. Superseded by [559].

561
Kuwahata monjo 桑幡文書
Compiled by Gomi Yoshio. *Kagoshima ken bunkazai chōsa hōkoku sho* 11 (1963): 9–16.

A collection of ten documents (late Heian to Nambokuchō) relating to southern Kyūshū. There is an accompanying essay.

562
Kawada ke monjo 川田家文書
Compiled by Gomi Yoshio. *Kadai shigaku* 15: 1–7 (1966).

The documents relating to a warrior family of southern Kyūshū. Most of these date from the fourteenth century. A brief introduction describes the Kawada background.

563
Satsuma no kuni goke'nin Hajima shi narabi ni Nobutoki shi ni tsuite—
Hajima monjo to Nobutoki monjo no shōkai
薩摩国御家人羽島氏並びに延時氏について－羽島文書と延時文書の紹介
Compiled by Gomi Yoshio. *Kagoshima daigaku hōbungakubu kiyō* 2 (1966).

Essay containing the documents relating to two Kamakura vassal families in Satsuma. More than 80 records, mostly from the thirteenth century.

564
Satsuma no kuni goke'nin Ushikuso–Shinohara shi ni tsuite
薩摩国御家人牛屎－篠原氏について
Compiled by Gomi Yoshio. *Kagoshima daigaku hōbungakubu kiyō* 3 (1967).

Essay containing some 53 documents dating from late Heian to mid-Muromachi times. The materials relate to two vassal families of the Kamakura Bakufu.

565
Satsuma no kuni Koshikijima jitō Ogawa shi no shiryō
薩摩国甑島地頭小川氏の史料
Compiled by Gomi Yoshio. *Kadai shigaku* 10 (1962): 37–43.

Essay introducing several Kamakura-period documents relating to a Satsuma *jitō* house.

566
Ibusuki shi shizoku Harada shi ni tsuite 指宿氏支族原田氏について
Compiled by Gomi Yoshio. *Kadai shigaku* 13 (1964).

Essay containing some 30 Kamakura-period documents bearing on two related local families. Interesting materials.

567
Kagoshima chūsei shi kenkyū kaihō　鹿児島中世史研究会報
Edited by Gomi Yoshio. Kagoshima, quarterly from 1966.

Journal dealing with southern Kyūshū history during the Kamakura and Muromachi ages. Virtually every issue introduces a handful of new documents, many of considerable interest.

ŌSUMI PROVINCE (KAGOSHIMA PREFECTURE)

Sappan kyūki zatsuroku, zempen, *see* [546]

Shimazu ke monjo, *see* [547]

• 568
Nejime monjo　禰寝文書
Compiled by Kawazoe Shōji (*Kyūshū shiryō sōsho* 14). 3 vols. Fukuoka, 1955–58.

One of the largest and most important document collections for a warrior house in Kyūshū. Intimate detail on relations with estate owners, the provincial office, neighboring magnates, retainers and peasants, and the Nejime's own extended family. Documents are arranged chronologically, with Volume 1 covering the Kamakura period and Volumes 2–3 the Muromachi. A rare work, with a very small printing.

569
Kamakura jidai no Kimotsuki gun to Kimotsuki shi—kankei shiryō no shōkai
鎌倉時代の肝付郡と肝付氏－関係史料の紹介
Compiled by Gomi Yoshio. *Kōyama chōshi*, 1968.

An important collection of 52 Shimazu Estate documents, most hitherto unpublished. An accompanying essay places these records in perspective. Various Bakufu-issued documents are included, adding to the collection's worth.

570
Ōsumi goke'nin Hishikari–Sogi shi ni tsuite—Sogi monjo no shōkai o chūshin ni
大隅御家人菱刈－曽木氏について－曽木文書の紹介を中心に
Compiled by Gomi Yoshio (*Kagoshima daigaku bunri-gakubu shigakka hōkoku* 13). Kagoshima, 1964.

Thirty-five documents relating to a pair of Kamakura vassal houses in southern Kyūshū. An essay and genealogical charts are included.

571
Kajiki Honda monjo　加治木本田文書
Compiled by Gomi Yoshio (*Kagoshima ken shiryō shūi* 1). Kagoshima, 1964.

Brief pamphlet containing records (Muromachi) of a local warrior house.

572
Iso shōko shūseikan monjo 1　磯尚古集成館文書
Compiled by Gomi Yoshio (*Kagoshima ken shiryō shūi* 3). Kagoshima, 1966.

Pamphlet containing about 100 Shimazu-related documents ranging from early Kamakura to the end of the sixteenth century.

573
Iso shōko shūseikan monjo 2—Kajiki Shimazu ke monjo—Kirishima jingū monjo
磯尚古集成館文書－加治木島津家文書－霧島神宮文書
Compiled by Gomi Yoshio (*Kagoshima ken shiryō shūi* 8). Kagoshima, 1966.
Pamphlet containing three collections of Shimazu-related documents from the sixteenth century.

574
Shibushi Daijiji monjo—Nagashima Kamachi monjo
志布志大慈寺文書－長島竈千文書
Compiled by Gomi Yoshio (*Kagoshima ken shiryō shūi* 10). Kagoshima, 1968.
Pamphlet containing two document collections relating to southern Kyūshū. Mostly Muromachi coverage, but includes a few testamentary records from the late Kamakura period.

575
Arima ke monjo 有馬家文書
Compiled by Gomi Yoshio. *Kadai shigaku* 12 (1963): 1–12.
Newly transcribed late Kamakura documents from Ōsumi Province. Materials are mostly testamentary records and bills of sale, though there are also important documents relating to the Bakufu. A collection of unusual interest.

576
Shijime ke monjo 志々目家文書
Compiled by Gomi Yoshio. *Kadai shigaku* 14 (1965): 1–24.
Introduces the documents of a local administrator's family within a small sector of Shimazu Estate. There is much of value on local conditions in the early fourteenth century.

577
Tanegashima monjo 1 種子島文書
Compiled by Gomi Yoshio (*Kagoshima ken bunkazai hōkoku* 21). 1974.
Pamphlet containing the documents of a *daimyō* house of southern Kyūshū. Originally deputies of a branch of the Kamakura Hōjō, the Tanegashima later expanded their influence and became notables of considerable power. Documentation begins in the fourteenth century and continues to the seventeenth. A genealogical chart is appended.

578
Shimazu-no-shō Ōsumi-gata Kanoya-in shōkō 島津庄大隅方鹿屋院小考
Compiled by Gomi Yoshio. *Kagoshima daigaku hōbungakubu kiyō* 1 (1965).
Essay containing about 40 documents relating to a single district within Shimazu Estate. Coverage begins in the 1190's, and about half the document total dates from Kamakura times. The history of the dominant local family in that area is traced through these records.

HYŪGA PROVINCE (MIYAZAKI PREFECTURE)

Sappan kyūki zatsuroku, zempen, *see* [546]

Shimazu ke monjo, *see* [547]

579
Hyūga komonjo shūsei 日向古文書集成
Compiled by Miyazaki ken. Miyazaki, 1938.

A massive assemblage of documents relating to Hyūga Province. Arrangement is
by document collection, but there is an excellent chronological index. Most of the
materials presented also appear in more recent source books, but the work remains
standard. There are numerous records bearing on the Hyūga portion of Shimazu
Estate. Recently reprinted.

580
Hyūga no kuni shōen shiryō   日向国荘園史料
Compiled by Hidaka Jikichi (*Kyūshū shōen shiryō sōsho* 6). Tōkyō, 1963.

The documents of more than a dozen *shōen* within Hyūga Province. More than
half of these were proprietary holdings of Usa Shrine, but they experienced different histories. Interesting volume.

581
Hyūga no kuni shōen shiryōshū 2   日向国荘園史料集
Compiled by Hidaka Jikichi (*Kyūshū shōen shiryō sōsho* 15). Tōkyō, 1967.

Documents relating to various additional *shōen* in Hyūga Province. A continu-
ation of [581].

582
Takahashi monjo   高橋文書
Compiled by Yanagi Kōkichi. Miyazaki, 1972.

Pamphlet containing a handful of late sixteenth-century documents relating to
the Takahashi house of Hyūga. Most of the records are early Tokugawa. There
is an introductory essay.

583
Nobe monjo   野辺文書
Compiled by Gomi Yoshio (*Kagoshima ken shiryō shūi* 6). Kagoshima, 1966.

A pamphlet containing documents relating to a warrior family of Hyūga Province.
All but two of the records date from Muromachi times. A genealogical chart and
brief introduction are included.

584
Kamakura Nambokuchō no Hyūga no kuni Masaki-in—kankei shiryō no shōkai
鎌倉南北朝の日向国真幸院－関係史料の紹介
Compiled by Gomi Yoshio. Miyazaki, 1964.

Pamphlet containing 38 documents relating to an administrative unit within
Hyūga Province. Coverage is exclusively fourteenth-century. There is an accompanying essay.

TITLE INDEX

In seeking titles the user should be aware of the standard terms for "annotated," "revised," or "expanded" editions: *chūkai, kaitei shimpen, shimpen, zōho teisei,* and *zōtei.* These occasionally appear as integral parts of titles. It should also be noted that entries for two different compilations sometimes bear the same title (e.g. *Aokata monjo*).

Madarame monjo [560]
Maizuru shishi, shiryō hen [378]
Manase Dōsan monjo ni tsuite [310]
Manganji monjo [375]
Masaki komonjo (Nitta Iwamatsu monjo) [84]
Matsugi monjo ni mieru Heian matsu-Nambokuchō ki no monjo ni tsuite [42]
Matsumoto monjo no kenkyū [54]
Matsuura tō no "Ariura monjo" ni tsuite [522]
Matsuura tō shoke monjo [520]
Meguro ku shi, shiryō hen [126]
Mibu shinsha komonjo [299]
Miike shi kankei hennen shiryō [486]
Miki chōyu komonjo [373]
Minakuchi chōshi [259]
Minamisaku gun no komonjo—kinseki bun [174]
Minase jingū monjo [361]
Mino no kuni Chōryūji shiryō [189]
Mino no kuni shiryō [188]
Minoo shishi, shiryō hen [363]
Mino Ryūshōji monjo ni tsuite [194]
Mito shishi [102]
Miyagi ken Nenoshiroishi sonshi [61]
Miyagi kenshi [57]
Miyoshi Sakai ke—Komaki Ezaki ke monjo shō [205]
Mogi Chikugo kezō monjo—jūnisho no kuchi Boshin sensō kankei monjo [91]
Monchūjo ke monjo [496]
Monji shi shiryō [501]
Moriguchi shishi, shiryō hen [349]
Mōri ke monjo [398]
Morioka Hamada ke monjo [53]
Morioka Nambu ke kankei monjo sonota [52]
Moriya monjo [172]
Munakata gunshi [471]
Muromachi ke gonaisho an [27]
Musashi shiryō meikishū [121]
"Myōken jinja monjo" "Oga jinja monjo" shōkai [344]

Nade-no-shō—Niuya mura yōsui sōron no shin shiryō [340]

Nagasaki kenshi, shiryō hen [529]
Nagato Chōfu shiryō [433]
Nagato no kuni ichinomiya—Sumiyoshi jinja shiryō [434]
Nagato no kuni Iminomiya jinja monjo [437]
Nagato no kuni Shōgakuzan Shōbōji monjo [436]
Nakajima chōshi shiryōshū [448]
Nakamura shi shozō Miike monjo ni tsuite [487]
Nakamura Naokatsu hakushi shūshū komonjo [19]
Nakayama Hokekyōji shiryō [115]
Nambokuchō nairanki no ichi sojō [193]
Nambokuchō to Izumi [360]
Nambu ke monjo [48]
Nanchō kankei Gojō ke monjo no kenkyū [491]
Nanzan junkaroku tsuika [28]
Nanzenji monjo [282]
Nara ibun [1]
Negishi ke kyūzō monjo [309]
Nejime monjo [568]
Nichiren shū shiryōshū, chūsei hen [116]
Nichiren shū shūgaku zensho, shiden kyūki bu [34]
Nigitadera monjo [386]
Nihon bukkyō keizai shi ronkō [35]
Nihon chūsei komonjo no kenkyū [25]
Nihon engyō taikei, shiryō hen, kodai-chūsei [447]
Nihon komonjogaku [22]
Nihon no komonjo [21]
Ninnaji monjo shō [285]
Ninnaji monjo shūi [284]
Nishinomiya shishi, shiryō hen [369]
Nitta Yoshisada kō kompon shiryō [83]
Niu gunshi [240]
Nobe monjo [583]
Noto Agishi Honseiji monjo [236]

Obama shishi, shoji monjo hen [253]
Obama-Tsuruga-Mikuni minato shiryō [238]
Ōba mikuriya monjo [153]

Sengoku daimyō Imagawa shi no
  kenkyū to komonjo [184]
Sengoku monjo shūei—Asai shi hen
  [265]
Sengoku monjo shūei—Chōsokabe
  shi hen [451]
Sengoku monjo shūei—Date shi hen
  [46]
Sengoku monjo shūei—Go-Hōjō shi
  hen [160]
Sengoku monjo shūei—Ōtomo shi
  hen [508]
Sengoku monjo shūei—Takeda shi
  hen [168]
Senshū Kumedadera monjo [354]
Setagaya ku shiryō [127]
Seto shinai shozai shiryō [200]
Settsu no kuni shiryōshū ei—Kasuga
  sharyō Tarumi Nishimaki kankei
  monjo [364]
Settsu no kuni Yabe gun Osada
  jinja monjo [376]
Shibushi Daijiji monjo—Nagashima
  Kamachi monjo [574]
Shichō bokuhō [16]
Shiga chōshi, shiryō hen [232]
Shiga ken Hachiman chōshi, shiryō
  hen [260]
Shiga kenshi [254]
Shijime ke monjo [576]
Shikanoumi jinja shozō monjo [479]
Shimabara Tajima ke monjo [528]
Shimane kenshi [420]
Shimazu ke monjo [547]
Shimazu-no-shō Ōsumi-gata
  Kanoya-in shōkō [578]
Shimizu shishi shiryō, chūsei hen
  [182]
Shimpen Aizu fudoki [67]
Shimpen Bushū komonjo [119]
Shimpen Hitachi kokushi [93]
Shimpen Kōshū komonjo [166]
Shimpen Musashi no kuni fudoki
  kō [120]
Shimpen Sagami no kuni fudoki
  kō [148]
Shimpen Sōshū komonjo [147]
Shinano no kuni mikuriya shiryō
  to sono kōsatsu [173]

Shinano shiryō [169]
Shinkan eiga [37]
Shinshū Katō gunshi [391]
Shinshū shimane kenshi, shiryō
  hen [419]
Shiroishi shishi, shiryō hen [62]
Shiryō sōran [5]
Shiseki Genkō bōrui kankei hennen
  shiryō [482]
Shitenōji shozō "Nyoihōju
  mishūhō nikki"—"dō" shihai
  "Togashi shi kankei" monjo ni
  tsuite [377]
Shizuoka ken shiryō [179]
Shōdai monjo hoi [544]
Shōen monjo nitsū [249]
Shōen shiryō [10]
Shōen shi shiryō [11, 12]
Shōen sonraku no ikō—Chikugo
  Setaka shimo-no-shō no baai
  [489]
Shoshin shōmon—Yamanouchi ke
  shōmon nukigaki [80]
Shoshū komonjo—Sōshū monjo
  shō [82]
Shōsōin monjo [7]
Shunjōbō Chōgen shiryō shūsei [319]
Sōdōshū komonjo [33]
Sōma shishi, shiryō hen [74]
Sorimachi monjo [41]
Sōsha jinja monjo [96]
Sōshū Tamanawa jōshu—Tamanawa
  Hōjō shi monjo shū [159]
Sōunji monjo [154]
Sugaura monjo [261]
Suō kokufu no kenkyū [428]
Suwa komonjo shū [171]

Tachibana monjo [495]
Tachiiri Munetsugu monjo—
  Kawabata Dōki monjo [305]
Taga jinja monjo [262]
Tagawa chihō shōen shiryō shūsei
  [500]
Tajima no kuni Ōokadera monjo
  [388]
Tajima no kuni ōtabumi [389]
Tajima shi monjo [199]
Takahashi monjo [582]

COMPILERS AND PUBLISHERS
OF DOCUMENTS

As noted in the Bibliography Introduction, identifying the actual compiler or publisher of a document series is often a complicated matter. The following listing is an eclectic one, including publishers, journals, learned societies, sponsoring organizations, and titles of document series, as well as individual compilers. Bracketed numbers refer to the Bibliography titles assembled or issued by a compiler.

Abe Einosuke [188] 阿部栄之助
Abe Takeshi [394] 阿部 猛
Adachi Akitarō [528] 足立鍬太郎
Aichi ken [195] 愛知県
Aichi ken shiryō sōkan [197,200–202, 208] 愛知県史料叢刊
Aida Nirō [21,95,147,162] 相田二郎
Aizawa Masahiko [360] 相澤正彦
Akamatsu Toshihide [270,278] 赤松俊秀
Akita kenshi hensan iinkai [65] 秋田県史編纂委員会
Akutagawa Tatsuo [508] 芥川竜男
Amakusa gun kyōikukai [541] 天草郡教育会
Amino Yoshihiko [42] 網野善彦

Aomori kenshi hensan iinkai [47] 青森県史編纂委員会
Arisaka Takamichi [369] 有坂隆道
Asano Yōkichi [496] 浅野ようきち
Ashida Ijin [36] 蘆田伊人
Asoshina Yasuo [487,544] 阿蘇品保夫
Atsugi shishi hensan iinkai [165] 厚木市史編纂委員会
Atsuta Isao [311] 熱田 公
Atsuta jingū gūchō [198] 熱田神宮宮庁
Ayabe shidankai [381] 綾部史談会

Bōchō shidankai [430,436–37] 防長史談会

Hagiwara Tatsuo [119]
萩原龍夫

Haguhi shishi hensan iinkai [234]
羽咋市史編纂委員会

Hagura Takanao [294] 羽倉敬尚

Hakone no bunkazai [154]
箱根の文化財

Hamamatsu shiyakusho [186]
浜松市役所

Hanaoka Okiteru [532,543]
花岡興輝

Harada Toshimaru [261] 原田敏丸

Hashimura Hiroshi [87] 橋村　博

Heki Ken [228–29] 日置　謙

Hennenshi hensangakari [16]
編年史編纂掛

Hidaka Jikichi [580–81] 日高次吉

Higashiasai kyōikukai [258]
東浅井教育会

Himeji shishi henshū iinkai [390]
姫路市史編集委員会

Hirakata shishi hensan iinkai [350]
枚方市史編纂委員会

Hirono Saburō [291–92]
広野三郎

Hiroshima daigaku bungakubu kiyō
[413] 広島大学文学部紀要

Hiroshima ken [410] 広島県

*Hiroshima ken bunkazai chōsa
hōkoku* [416] 広島県文化
財調査報告

Hiroshima toshokan [412]
広島図書館

Hisutoria [376,395–96] ヒストリア

Hōnichi shigaku [499]　豊日史学

Horiike Shumpō [281,318]
堀池春峰

Hoshino Hisashi [13] 星野　恒

Hosokawa Kameichi [35] 細川亀市

Hyōgo ken no rekishi [336,387]
兵庫県の歴史

Hyōgo shigakkai [392–93]
兵庫史学会

Hyōgo shigaku [386,388]　兵庫史学

Ibaragi ken komonjo shūsei [96–97]
茨城県古文書集成

Ibaragi kenshi hensan chūsei shi bukai
[92] 茨城県史編纂中世史部会

Ichikawa shishi hensan iinkai [114]
市川市史編纂委員会

Ichinomiya shishi hensanshitsu [196]
一宮市史編纂室

Ichishi Shigeki [173]　一志茂樹

Iida Hisao [497] 飯田久雄

Iikura Harutake [206,308]　飯倉晴武

Ikeda shishi hensan iinkai [367]
池田市史編纂委員会

Ikeuchi Yoshisuke [8] 池内義資

Imai Rintarō [374] 今井林太郎

Inamura Tangen [121] 稲村担元

Inari jinja shamusho [293]
稲荷神社社務所

Innoshima shi kyōiku iinkai [411]
因島市教育委員会

Inoue Toshio [215–16,246,248]
井上鋭夫

Ishida Yoshito [387–88] 石田善人

Ishii Kōtarō [219]　石井光太郎

Ishikawa ken toshokan kyōkai [235]
石川県図書館協会

Ishino Ei [156] 石野　瑛

Ishioka shi kyōiku iinkai [99]
石岡市教育委員会

Ishioka shishi hensan shiryō [99]
石岡市史編纂資料

Itami shiryō sōsho [372]
伊丹資料叢書

Itami shishi hensan iinkai [371]
伊丹市史編纂委員会

Itō Bishirō [468,471] 伊東尾四郎

Itō Tasaburō [102] 伊東多三郎

Itō Tsunetari [464] 伊藤常足

Iwahashi Koyata hakushi kōju
kinenkai [129] 岩橋小彌太
博士公寿記念会

Kinsei sonraku jiji shiryō [452]
近世村落自治史料

Kinsei sonraku kenkyūkai [452]
近世村落研究会

Kinugasa Yasuki [424] 衣笠安喜

Kishi Kajirō [407] 岸　加四郎

Kishiwada shishi shiryō [354]
岸和田市史史料

Kitagami shi [55] 北上市

Kitanishi Hiroshi [236] 北西　弘

Kita Settsu kyōdo shigaku sōsho [375]
北摂津郷土史学叢書

Kita Yoshiyuki [327] 喜多芳之

Kobayashi Seiji [46] 小林清治

Kobayashi Takeshi [319,329]
小林　剛

Kōbe shi kyōiku iinkai [374]
神戸市教育委員会

Kōbe shiyakusho [368] 神戸市役所

Kōgakukan daigaku komonjo
kenkyūkai [212] 皇学館
大学古文書研究会

Kōgakukan ronsō [212] 皇学館論叢

Koiwa Sueji [54] 小岩末治

Kojima Shōsaku [95,293] 小島鉦作

Koki kinenkai [19] 古稀記念会

Kokugakuin daigaku [406]
国学院大学

Kokugakuin daigaku toshokan [303]
国学院大学図書館

Kokugakuin zasshi [303]
国学院雑誌

Kokumin seishin bunka kenkyūjo [20,
305,457] 国民精神文化研究所

Kokushi gakkai [304,432] 国史学会

Kokushigaku [104,328,432]
国史学

Kokushikan daigaku bungakubu
kokushigaku kenkyūshitsu [530]
国士館大学文学部国史学研究室

*Kokushikan daigaku jimbungaku
kiyō* [491] 国士館大学人文学紀要

Kokushi kenkyūjo [71] 国史研究所

Komonjo kenkyū [43,206,308,311]
古文書研究

Kondō Isamu [404] 近藤　勇

Kōriyama shi [70] 郡山市

Kōriyama Yoshimitsu [558] 郡山良光

Kosugi Un'son [439] 小杉温邨

Kowada Tetsuo [184,264–65]
小和田哲男

Kōyama chōshi [569] 高山町誌

Kōyasan shi hensanjo [333]
高野山史編纂所

Kōzanji shiryō sōsho [280]
高山寺資料叢書

Kōzanji tenseki monjo sōgō
chōsadan [280] 高山寺
典籍文書綜合調査団

Kudō Keiichi [502] 工藤敬一

Kumamoto chūsei shi kenkyūkai [490,
493] 熊本中世史研究会

*Kumamoto ken bunkazai chōsa
hōkoku* [545,561] 熊本県
文化財調査報告

Kumamoto ken kyōiku iinkai [537]
熊本県教育委員会

Kumamoto kenshi hensankai [531]
熊本県史編纂会

Kumamoto ken Tamana chūgakkō
[542] 熊本県玉名中学校

Kumamoto shigaku [487,532,543–44]
熊本史学

Kunaichō shoryōbu [302,306]
宮内庁書陵部

Kunaishō toshoryō [298–99]
宮内省図書寮

Kunimi chō [75] 国見町

Kunimori Susumu [425,438]
国守　進

Kuroda Toshio [372,386] 黒田俊雄

Kuroita Katsumi [14] 黒板勝美

Kurokawa Naonori [385] 黒川直則

Kurokawa Takaaki [492] 黒川高明

Kusogami Noboru [40] 久曽神　昇

Kuwahada Kō [499] 桑波田　興

Murayama Shūichi [263] 村山修一

Nagasaki kenshi hensan iinkai [529]
長崎県史編纂委員会

Nagashima Fukutarō [39,312,336,
373] 永島福太郎

*Nagoya daigaku bungakubu kenkyū
ronshū* [42] 名古屋大学文学部
研究論集

Nagoya shi Hōsei nikō kenshōkan
[205] 名古屋市豊清二公顕彰館

Naitō Asashichi [395] 内藤浅七

Nakagawa Keishi [375] 中川啓史

Nakajima Toshiji [277] 中島俊司

Nakajima Toshio [378] 中島利雄

Nakamura Ken [338] 中村　研

Nakamura Naokatsu [22,262,316]
中村直勝

Nakamura Rin'ichi [265] 中村林一

Nakano Hatayoshi [504] 中野幡能

Nakao Gyō [115–16] 中尾　堯

Nakayama Nobuna [93] 中山信名

Naniwada Tōru [296] 難波田　徹

Nara ken toshokan kyōkai [312]
奈良県図書館協会

Nara kokuritsu bunkazai kenkyūjo
[320] 奈良国立文化財研究所

Nenoshiroishi sonshi hensan iinkai
[61] 根白石村史編纂委員会

Nerima kyōdoshi kenkyūkai [81,
123–25,180] 練馬郷土史研究会

Nihon bukkyōshi [288] 日本仏教史

*Nihon bunka kenkyūjo kenkyū
hōkoku* [73] 日本文化研究所
研究報告

Nihon engyō taikei henshū iinkai
[447] 日本塩業大系編集委員会

Nihon rekishi [186,249,502,522]
日本歴史

Nihon shi kenkyū [297] 日本史研究

Nihon shiseki ronshū [129]
日本史蹟論集

Niigata daigaku hōkei ronshū [248]
新潟大学法経論集

*Niigata ken bunkazai chōsa hōkoku
sho* [214–15] 新潟県文化財調査
報告書

Niigata ken kyōiku iinkai [214–15]
新潟県教育委員会

Niigata ken Sado gun'yakusho [220]
新潟県佐渡郡役所

Niigata shigakkai [216] 新潟史学会

Niita Kōko [331] 仁井田好古

Nishida Naojirō [305] 西田直二郎

Nishigaki Seiji [113,153,211]
西垣晴次

Nishioka Toranosuke [11–12]
西岡虎之助

Niu gunshi henshū iinkai [240]
丹生郡誌編集委員会

Noda Tadao [382–83] 野田只夫

Nōdomi Jōten [139] 納富常天

Nuki Tatsuto [146] 貫　達人

Obama shishi hensan iinkai [253]
小浜市史編纂委員会

Obata Jun [241] 小葉田　淳

Odachi Koretaka [498] 尾立維孝

Oda Motohiko [336] 小田基彦

Ōdate shishi hensan iinkai [91]
大館市史編さん委員会

Odawara shi kyōiku iinkai [155]
小田原市教育委員会

Ōgaki shiyakusho [190] 大垣市役所

Ogino Minahiko [25,166]
荻野三七彦

Ōhashi Toshio [288] 大橋俊雄

Ōishi Naomasa [46,64,340]
大石直正

Ōita ken shiryō kankōkai [503]
大分県史料刊行会

*Okayama daigaku hōbungakubu
gakujutsu kiyō* [408] 岡山大学
法文学部学術紀要

Okayama ken chihōshi shiryō sōsho
[401] 岡山県地方史資料叢書

Ōki Michinobu [486] 大城美知信

Okino Shun'ichi [440] 沖野舜一

Shigaku kenkyū [418]　史学研究
Shigaku zasshi [194,284,286,335]
　史学雑誌
Shikan [479]　史観
Shimane ken [419]　島根県
Shimane ken bunkazai aigo kyōkai
　[423]　島根県文化財愛護協会
Shimane ken gakumubu Shimane
　kenshi hensangakari [420]　島根県
　学務部島根県史編纂掛
Shimizu Masatake [10]　清水正健
Shimizu shishi hensan iinkai [182]
　清水市史編纂委員会
Shimoda Kyokusui [545]　下田曲水
Shimode Sekiyo [221]　下出積世
Shimoichi chōshi henshū iinkai [326]
　下市町史編集委員会
Shimosaka Mamoru [297]　下坂　守
Shimoyama Haruhisa [157–58]
　下山治久
Shimoyama mon iseki [481]
　下山門遺跡
Shimpen Shinano shiryō sōsho [172,
　176–78]　新編信濃史料叢書
Shinano kyōikukai shimo-takai bukai
　[170]　信濃教育会下高井部会
Shinano shiryō kankōkai [169,172,
　176–78]　信濃史料刊行会
Shinjō Tsunezō [474–75]
　新城常三
Shinkō zōho shiseki shūran [27,28,
　379]　新校増補史跡集覧
Shintei zōho Kokushi taikei [149,
　300–301]　新訂増補国史大系
Shirin [283,377]　史林
Shiroishi shishi hensan iinkai [62]
　白石市史編纂委員会
Shiryō sanshū—komonjo hen [242,
　336,492,526]　史料纂集－古文書篇
Shizuoka ken [179]　静岡県
Shōbara shi bunkazai hogo iinkai [80]
　庄原市文化財保護委員会
Shōen shiryō sōsho [210,338,517]
　荘園史料叢書

Sōma shishi hensankai [74]
　相馬市史編纂会
Sone Kenzō [421]　曽根研三
Sonoda Kōyū [339]　薗田香融
Sugihashi Takao [377]　杉橋隆夫
Sugimoto Hisao [538–40]　杉本尚雄
Sugiyama Hiroshi [119,129,160]
　杉山　博
Suma Chikai [194]　須磨干穎
Sumiyoshi jinja shamusho [434–35]
　住吉神社社務所
Suruga komonjo kai [184]
　駿河古文書会
Suwa shiryō sōsho [171]
　諏訪史料叢書
Suwa shiryō sōsho kankōkai [171]
　諏訪史料叢書刊行会

Tachibana Kanji [495]　立花寛治
Tadakuma Toyoaki [469]　多田隈豊秋
Taga Munehaya [249]　多賀宗隼
Tai Keigo [283]　田中啓吾
Takahashi Masahiko [41,310]
　高橋正彦
Takahashi Ryūzō [306]　高橋隆三
Takahashi Tomio [69]　高橋富雄
Takahashi Yoshihiko [213]　高橋義彦
Takashima Rokuo [167]　高島緑雄
Takatsuki shishi hensan iinkai [365]
　高槻市史編纂委員会
Takayanagi Mitsutoshi [145]
　高柳光寿
Takeuchi Rizō [1–3,10,210,454,459–
　62,546]　竹内理三
Takigawa Masajirō [15,337]
　滝川政次郎
Takita Manabu [505–7]　田北　学
Tamura Tetsuo [432]　田村哲夫
Tanaka Kitami [53]　田中喜多美
Tanaka Minoru [43,281,284]
　田中　稔
Tanuma Mutsumi [193]　田沼　睦
Tashiro Osamu [73]　田代　脩

Tatebayashi shishi hensan iinkai [86] 館林市誌編纂委員会

Tate Zan'ō [231] 館　残翁

Tatsumi Saburō [332] 巽　三郎

Teikoku gakushi-in [37] 帝国学士院

Tenri shishi hensan iinkai [324] 天理市史編纂委員会

Tobimi Takeshige [224] 飛見丈繁

Tochigi kenshi hensan iinkai [89] 栃木県史編纂委員会

Toda Yoshimi [354] 戸田芳実

Tōhoku bunka kenkyūshitsu kiyō [64, 76] 東北文化研究室紀要

Tōhoku daigaku Tōhoku bunka kenkyūkai [44] 東北大学 東北文化研究会

Tokushima kenshi hensan iinkai [441] 徳島県史編纂委員会

Tokuyama shishi hensan iinkai [429] 徳山市史編纂委員会

Tōkyō daigaku shiryō hensanjo [4–7, 45,77–79,269,274,276,279,289, 315,334,345–46,398–99,414–15, 535–36,547] 東京大学史料 編纂所

Tōkyō gakugeidai fuzoku kō [113] 東京学芸大付属高

Tōkyō teikoku daigaku shiryō hensanjo [17] 東京帝国 大学史料編纂所

Tōkyō to Chiyoda kushi hensan iinkai [122] 東京都千代田区 史編纂委員会

Tōkyō toritsu daigaku gakujutsu kenkyūkai [126] 東京都立 大学学術研究会

Tomiku chōshi hensan iinkai [233] 富来町史編纂委員会

Tondabayashi shishi hensan iinkai [352] 富田林市史編纂委員会

Totoki Shūzen [396] 十時秀全

Tottori ken [409] 鳥取県

Toyama ken [222–23] 富山県

Toyoda Takeshi [73] 豊田　武

Toyohashi shishi hensan iinkai [207] 豊橋市史編纂委員会

Toyonaka shishi hensan iinkai [366] 豊中市史編纂委員会

Tsurugaoka Hachimangū shamusho [150] 鶴岡八幡宮社務所

Uchiyama Jōshin [392] 内山定眞

Ueno toshokan kiyō [275,309,524] 上野図書館紀要

Uno Shūhei [342] 宇野脩平

Uozumi Sōgorō [355,370] 魚澄惣五郎

Wada Akio [334–35] 和田昭夫

Wakayama kenshi hensan iinkai [330] 和歌山県史編纂委員会

Wakayama ken shinshiki torishimarisho [331] 和歌山県神職取締所

Wakayama Zenzaburō [203–4] 若山善三郎

Waseda daigaku [12] 早稲田大学

Washio Yoritaka [48] 鷲尾順敬

Watanabe Sumio [327,508,510–12] 渡辺澄夫

Yamada An'ei [458] 山田安栄

Yamada Shūho [243,245] 山田秋甫

Yamaguchi ken chihōshi kenkyū [432,438] 山口県地方史研究

Yamaguchi ken monjokan [426–27] 山口県文書館

Yamaguchi ken monjokan kenkyū kiyō [425] 山口県文書館 研究紀要

Yamamoto Takeshi [451] 山本　大

Yamamoto Gen [239] 山本　元

Yamato bunka kenkyū [296,329] 大和文化研究

Yanagi Kōkichi [582] 柳　宏吉

Yanagizawa bunko semmon iinkai [322] 柳沢文庫専門委員会

Yano Kazusada [483] 矢野一貞

Yao shishi hensan iinkai [348]
八尾市史編纂委員会

Yasaka jinja shamusho [291–92]
八坂神社社務所

Yokogawa Suekichi [449] 横川末吉

Yokohama shiritsu daigaku ronsō
[141] 横浜市立大学論叢

Yokoi Akio [30] 横井金男

Yokoyama Sumio [191] 横山住雄

Yōrō chō [192] 養老町

Yoshinaga Utarō [501] 吉永卯太郎

Yoshino chō shiseki chōsakai [48]
吉野朝史跡調査会

Yuyama Ken'ichi [328]
湯山賢一

Zama Mitsuji [161] 座間美都治

Zoku gunsho ruijū [103,185,397,514]
続群書類従

Zoku gunsho ruijū kanseikai [242,
336,492,526] 続群書類従完成会

Zokuzoku gunsho ruijū [26,273,295,
317,389] 続々群書類従

GENERAL INDEX

GENERAL INDEX

The index presented here is a general information guide to the translations, the two part introductions (Documents and Bibliography), and the Document Originals section. The Bibliography proper has its own indexes for titles and compilers and is therefore not included here. Several features of the present listing should be noted. (1) All personal names are listed by both given name and surname. In the case of the former, the surname follows in parentheses. In the case of the latter, a brief identification of the individual (e.g. *jitō* of X Estate) appears within parentheses. (2) Virtually all place names are identified by some larger unit in which they were located. Estates, for example, are invariably followed in parentheses by a province name. Similarly, all provinces are broken down into component units, including religious institutions. The reader should take care to distinguish temple and shrine holdings, which might be scattered among several provinces, from the locations of the institutions themselves. Full lists of temples and shrines and their locations appear under the headings Buddhism and Shinto. (3) Information contained in the signature area of documents, unless specially annotated, has not been indexed.